WHAT WE CANNOT KNOW

From consciousness to the cosmos,
the cutting edge of science explained

MARCUS DU SAUTOY

4th Estate • London

HarperCollins
PUBLISHERS *Since 1817*

4th Estate
An imprint of HarperCollinsPublishers
1 London Bridge Street
London SE1 9GF
www.4thEstate.co.uk

First published in Great Britain by 4th Estate in 2016
This 4th Estate paperback edition 2017

Copyright © Marcus du Sautoy 2016

1

The right of Marcus du Sautoy to be identified as the
author of this work has been asserted by him in accordance
with the Copyright, Designs and Patents Act 1988

A catalogue record for this book is available from the British Library

ISBN 978-0-00-757659-3

Typeset in Minion and Novecento sans wide

Printed and bound in Great Britain by Clays Ltd, St Ives plc

To my parents,
who started me on my journey
to the edges of knowledge

CONTENTS

EDGE ZERO:
THE KNOWN UNKNOWNS

Everyone by nature desires to know.

Aristotle, *Metaphysics*

Science is king.

Every week, headlines announce new breakthroughs in our understanding of the universe, new technologies that will transform our environment, new medical advances that will extend our lives. Science is giving us unprecedented insights into some of the big questions that have challenged humanity ever since we've been able to formulate those questions. Where did we come from? What is the ultimate destiny of the universe? What are the building blocks of the physical world? How does a collection of cells become conscious?

In the last ten years alone we've landed a spaceship on a comet, made robots that can create their own language, used stem cells to repair the pancreas of diabetic patients, discovered how to use the power of thought alone to manipulate a robotic arm, sequenced the DNA of a 50,000-year-old cave girl. Science magazines are bursting with the latest breakthroughs emerging from the world's laboratories. We know so much. The advances of science are extremely intoxicating.

Science has given us our best weapon in our fight against fate. Instead of giving in to the ravages of disease and natural disaster, science has created vaccines to combat deadly viruses like polio and even ebola. Faced with an escalating world population, it is scientific advances that provide the best hope of feeding the 9.6 billion people who are projected to be alive in 2050. It is science that is warning us about the deadly impact we are having on our environment and giving us the chance to do something about it before it is too late. An asteroid might have wiped out the dinosaurs, but the science that humans have developed is our best shield against any future direct hits. In the human race's constant battle with death, science is its best ally.

Science is king not only when it comes to our fight for survival but also in improving our quality of life. We are able to communicate with friends and family across vast distances. We have unparalleled access to the database of knowledge we have accumulated over generations of investigation. We have created virtual worlds that we can escape to in our leisure time. We can recreate in our living rooms the great performances of Mozart, Miles and Metallica at the press of a button.

That desire to know is programmed into the human psyche. Those early humans with a thirst for knowledge are those who have survived, adapted, transformed their environment. Those not driven by that craving were left behind. Evolution has favoured the mind that wants to know the secrets of how the universe works. The adrenaline rush that accompanies the discovery of new knowledge is nature's way of telling us that the desire to know is as important as the drive to reproduce. As Aristotle articulated in the opening line of his book *Metaphysics*, understanding how the world works is a basic human need.

As a schoolkid, science very quickly drew me into its outstretched arms. I fell in love with its extraordinary power to tell us so much about the universe. The fantastic stories that my science teachers told seemed even more fanciful than the fiction I'd been reading at home. As it worked its spell on me I consumed every outlet of science I could get my hands on.

I persuaded my parents to buy me a subscription to *New Scientist*. I devoured *Scientific American* in our local library. I hogged the television each week to watch episodes of my favourite science programmes: *Horizon* and *Tomorrow's World*. I was captivated by Jacob Bronowski's *Ascent of Man*, Carl Sagan's *Cosmos*, Jonathan Miller's *Body in Question*. Every Christmas the Royal Institution Christmas Lectures provided a good dollop of science alongside our family turkey. My stocking was stuffed with books by Gamow and Feynman. It was a heady time, with new breakthroughs being announced each week.

Alongside reading these stories of the discovery of things we know, I began to get more fired up by the untold tales. What we knew lay in the past but what we didn't yet know was the future, my future. I became obsessed with the puzzle books of mathematician Martin Gardner that my maths teacher gave me. The excitement of wrestling with a conundrum and the sudden release of euphoria as I cracked each puzzle got me addicted to the drug of discovery. Those puzzles were my training ground for the greater challenge of tackling questions that didn't have an answer in the back of the book. It was the unanswered questions, the mathematical mysteries and scientific puzzles that no one had cracked that would become the fuel for my life as a scientist.

WHAT WE KNOW

If I look back to the Seventies when I was at school and compare the things that we knew then to what we know now, it is quite extraordinary how much more we have understood about the universe even in the half century that I've been alive. Technology has extended our senses so we can see things that were beyond the conception of the scientists who excited me as a kid.

The new range of telescopes that look out at the night sky have discovered planets like the Earth that could be home to intelligent life. They have revealed the amazing fact that three-quarters of the way into the lifetime of our universe the expansion of the universe started to accelerate. I remember reading as a kid that we were in for a big crunch, but now it seems that we have a completely different future waiting for us.

The particle colliders like the Large Hadron Collider at CERN (the European Organization for Nuclear Research in Switzerland) have allowed us to penetrate the inner workings of matter itself, revealing new particles – like the top quark discovered in 1994 and the Higgs boson discovered in 2012 – that were bits of speculative mathematics when I was reading my *New Scientist* at school.

And since the early Nineties the fMRI scanner has allowed us to look inside the brain and discover things that in the Seventies were frankly not even considered part of the remit of scientists. The brain was the preserve of philosophers and theologians, but today the technology can reveal when you are thinking about Jennifer Aniston or predict what you are going to do next even before you know.

Biology has seen an explosion of breakthroughs. In 2003 it was announced that scientists had mapped one whole human DNA sequence consisting of 3 billion letters of genetic code. In 2011 the complete neuronal network of the *C. elegans* worm was published, providing a complete picture of how the 302 neurons in the worm are connected.

Chemists too have been breaking new territory. A totally new form of carbon was discovered in 1985, which binds together like a football, and chemists surprised us again in 2003 by creating the first examples of graphene, showing how carbon can form a honeycomb lattice one atom thick.

And in my lifetime the subject to which I would eventually dedicate myself, mathematics, has seen some of the great enigmas finally resolved: Fermat's Last Theorem and the Poincaré conjecture, two challenges that had outfoxed generations of mathematicians. New mathematical tools and insights have opened up hidden pathways to navigate the mathematical universe.

Keeping up with all these new advances, let alone making your own contribution, is a challenge in its own right.

THE KNOW-IT-ALL PROFESSORSHIP

A few years ago I got a new job title to add to my role as a professor of mathematics at the University of Oxford. It often makes me laugh: the Simonyi Professor for the Public Understanding of Science. There seems to be a belief that with such a title I should know it all. People ring me up expecting that I know the answers to every question of science. Shortly after I'd taken on the job, the Nobel Prize for medicine was announced. A journalist called, hoping for an explanation of the breakthrough that was being rewarded: the discovery of telomeres.

Biology has never been my strong point, but I was sitting in front of my computer screen and so I'm embarrassed to admit I got the Wikipedia page up on telomeres and, after a quick scan, proceeded to explain authoritatively that they are the bit of genetic code at the end of our chromosomes that controls ageing among other things. The technology we have at our fingertips has increased that sense that we have the potential to know anything. Just tap my question into a search engine and the device seems to predict, even before I've finished typing, what it is I want to know and provides a list of places to find the answer.

But understanding is different from a list of facts. Is it possible for any scientist to know it all? To know how to solve non-linear partial differential equations? To know how SU(3) governs the connection between fundamental particles? To know how cosmological inflation gives rise to the state of the universe? To know how to solve Einstein's equations of general relativity or Schrödinger's wave equation? To know how neurons and synapses trigger thought? Newton, Leibniz and Galileo were perhaps the last scientists to know all that was known.

I must admit that the arrogance of youth infused me with the belief that I could understand anything that was known. If someone's human brain out there has found a way to navigate a path to new knowledge, then if the proof works in their brain it should work in mine. With enough time, I thought, I could crack the mysteries of mathematics and the universe, or at least master the current lie of the land. But increasingly I am beginning to question that belief, to worry that some things will forever remain beyond my reach. Often my brain struggles to navigate the science we currently know. Time is running out to know it all.

My own mathematical research is already pushing the limits of what my human brain feels capable of understanding. I have been working for over ten years on a conjecture that remains stubbornly resistant to my attempts to crack it. But my new role as the Professor for the Public Understanding of Science has pushed me outside the comfort zone of mathematics into the messy concepts of neuroscience, the slippery ideas of philosophy, the unfounded theories of physics. It has required a different way of thinking that is alien to my mathematical mode of thought, which deals in certainties, proofs and precision. My attempts to understand everything that is currently regarded as scientific knowledge has severely tested the limits of my own ability to understand.

The process of attaining knowledge necessarily relies on our standing on the shoulders of giants, as Newton famously declared about his own breakthroughs. And so my own journey to the edges of knowledge has involved reading how others have articulated the current state of knowledge, listening to lectures and seminars by those immersed in the field I'm trying to understand, talking to those pushing the boundaries, questioning contradictory stories, consulting the evidence and data recorded in the scientific journals that support a theory, even at times looking up an idea on Wikipedia. Although we teach students to question any information that pops up from a Google search, research has revealed that Wikipedia's accounts of topics at the less controversial end of the scientific spectrum, like the theory of general relativity, are regarded as on a par with accounts in the scientific literature. Choose a more contested issue, like climate change, and the content might depend on what day you look.

This raises the question of how much can you trust any of these stories. Just because the scientific community accepts a story as the current best fit, this doesn't mean it is true. Time and again, history reveals the opposite to be the case, and this must always act as a warning that current scientific knowledge is provisional. Mathematics perhaps has a slightly different quality, as I will discuss in the final two chapters. Mathematical proof provides the chance to establish a more permanent state of knowledge. But it's worth noting that even when I am creating new mathematics, I will often quote results by fellow mathematicians whose proofs I won't have checked myself. To do so would mean running in order to keep still.

And for any scientist the real challenge is not to stay within the secure garden of the known but to venture out into the wilds of the unknown. That is the challenge at the heart of this book.

WHAT WE DON'T KNOW

Despite all the breakthroughs made in science over the last centuries, there are still lots of deep mysteries waiting out there for us to solve. Things we don't know. The knowledge of what we are ignorant of seems to expand faster than our catalogue of breakthroughs. The known unknowns outstrip the known knowns. And it is those unknowns that drive science. A scientist is more interested in the things he or she can't understand than in telling all the stories we already know how to narrate. Science is a living, breathing subject because of all those questions we can't answer.

For example, the stuff that makes up the physical universe we interact with seems to account for only 4.9% of the total matter content of our universe. So what is the other 95.1% of so-called dark matter and dark energy made up of? If our universe's expansion is accelerating, where is all the energy coming from that is fuelling that acceleration?

Is our universe infinite? Are there infinitely many other infinite universes parallel to our own? If there are, do they have different laws of physics? Were there other universes before our own universe emerged from the Big Bang? Did time exist before the Big Bang? Does time exist at all or does it emerge as a consequence of more fundamental concepts?

Why is there a layer of fundamental particles with another two almost identical copies of this layer but with increasing mass, the so-called three generations of fundamental particles? Are there yet more particles out there for us to discover? Are fundamental particles actually tiny strings vibrating in 11-dimensional space?

How can we unify Einstein's theory of general relativity, the physics of the very large, with quantum physics, the physics of the very small? This is the search for something called quantum gravity, an absolute necessity if we are ever going to understand the Big Bang, when the universe was compressed into the realm of the quantum.

And what of the understanding of our human body, something so complex that it makes quantum physics look like a high-school exercise. We are still trying to get to grips with the complex interaction between gene expression and our environment. Can we find a cure for cancer? Is it possible to beat ageing? Could there be someone alive today who will live to be a 1000 years old?

And what about where humans came from? Evolution is a process of random mutations, so would a different roll of the evolutionary dice still produce organisms with eyes? If we rewound evolution and pressed 'play', would we get intelligent life, or are we the result of a lucky roll of the dice? Is there intelligent life elsewhere in our universe? And what of the technology we are creating? Can a computer ever attain consciousness? Will I eventually be able to download my consciousness so that I can survive the death of my body?

Mathematics too is far from finished. Despite popular belief, Fermat's Last Theorem was not the last theorem. Mathematical unknowns abound. Are there any patterns in prime numbers or are they outwardly random? Will we be able to solve the mathematical equations for turbulence? Will we ever understand how to factorize large numbers efficiently?

Despite so much that is still unknown, scientists are optimistic that these questions won't remain unanswered forever. The last few decades give us reason to believe that we are in a golden age of science. The rate of discoveries in science appears to grow exponentially. In 2014 the science journal *Nature* reported that the number of scientific papers published has been doubling every nine years since the end of the Second World War. Computers too are developing at an exponential rate. Moore's law is the observation that computer processing power seems to double every two years. Engineer Ray Kurzweil believes that the same applies to technological progress: that the rate of change of technology over the next 100 years will be comparable to what we've experienced in the last 20,000 years.

And yet can scientific discoveries maintain this exponential growth? Kurzweil talks about the Singularity, a moment when the intelligence of our technology will exceed our human intelligence. Is scientific progress destined for its own singularity? A moment when we know it all. Surely at some point we might actually discover the underlying equations that explain how the universe works. We will discover the final list of particles that make up the building blocks of the physical universe and how they interact with each other. Some scientists believe that the current rate of scientific progress will lead to a moment when we might discover a theory of everything. They even give it a name: ToE.

As Hawking declared in *A Brief History of Time*: 'I believe there are grounds for cautious optimism that we may be near the end of the search for the ultimate laws of nature', concluding dramatically with the provocative statement that then 'we would know the mind of God'.

Is such a thing possible? To know everything? Would we want to know everything? Science would ossify. Scientists have a strangely schizophrenic relationship with the unknown. On the one hand, it is what we don't know that intrigues and fascinates us, and yet the mark of success as a scientist is resolution and knowledge, to make the unknown known.

Could there be some quests that will never be resolved? Are there limits to what we can discover about our physical universe? Are some regions of the future beyond the predictive powers of science and mathematics? Is time before the Big Bang a no-go area? Are there ideas so complex that they are beyond the conception of our finite human brains? Can brains even investigate themselves, or does the analysis enter an infinite loop from which it is impossible to rescue itself? Are there mathematical conjectures that can never be proved true?

WHAT WE'LL NEVER KNOW

What if there are questions of science that can never be resolved? It seems defeatist, even dangerous, to admit there may be any such questions. While the unknown is the driving force for doing science, the unknowable would be science's nemesis. As a fully signed-up member of the scientific community, I hope that we can ultimately answer the big open questions. So it seems important to know if the expedition I've joined will hit boundaries beyond which we cannot proceed. Questions that won't ever get closure.

That is the challenge I've set myself in this book. I want to know if there are things that by their very nature we will never know. Are there things that will always be beyond the limits of knowledge? Despite the marauding pace of scientific advances, are there things that will remain beyond the reach of even the greatest scientists? Will there remain mysteries that will resist our attempts to lift the veils that currently mask our view of the universe?

It is, of course, very risky at any point in history to try to articulate Things We Cannot Know. How can you know what new insights are suddenly going to pull the unknown into the knowable? This is partly why it is useful to look at the history of how we know the things we do, because it reveals how often we've been at points where we think we have hit the frontier, only to find some way across.

Take the statement made by French philosopher Auguste Comte in 1835 about the stars: 'We shall never be able to study, by any method, their chemical composition or their mineralogical structure.' An absolutely fair statement given that this knowledge seemed to depend on our visiting the star. What Comte hadn't factored in was the possibility that the star could visit us, or at least that photons of light emitted by the star could reveal its chemical make-up.

A few decades after Comte's prophecy, scientists had determined the chemical composition of our own star, the Sun, by analysing the spectrum of light emitted. As the nineteenth-century British astronomer Warren de la Rue declared: 'If we were to go to the Sun, and to bring some portions of it and analyse them in our laboratories, we could not examine them more accurately than we can by this new mode of spectrum analysis.'

Scientists went on to determine the chemical composition of stars we are unlikely ever to visit. As science in the nineteenth century continued to give us an ever greater understanding of the mysteries of the universe, there began to emerge a feeling that we might eventually have a complete picture.

In 1900 Lord Kelvin, regarded by many as one of the greatest scientists of his age, believed that moment had come when he declared to the meeting of the British Association of Science: 'There is nothing new to be discovered in physics now. All that remains is more and more precise measurement.' American physicist Albert Abraham Michelson concurred. He too thought that the future of science would simply consist of adding a few decimal places to the results already obtained. 'The more important fundamental laws and facts of physical science have all been discovered . . . our future discoveries must be looked for in the sixth place of decimals.'

Five years later Einstein announced his extraordinary new conception of time and space, followed shortly after by the revelations of quantum physics. Kelvin and Michelson couldn't have been more wrong about how much new physics there was still to discover.

What I want to try to explore is whether there are problems that we can prove will remain beyond knowledge despite any new insights. Perhaps there are none. As a scientist that is my hope. One of the dangers when faced with currently unanswerable problems is to give in too early to their unknowability. But if there are unanswerables, what status do they have? Can you choose from the possible answers and it won't really matter which one you opt for?

Talk of known unknowns is not reserved to the world of science. The US politician Donald Rumsfeld strayed into the philosophy of knowledge with the famous declaration:

> There are known knowns; there are things that we know that we know. We also know there are known unknowns; that is to say, we know there are some things we do not know. But there are also unknown unknowns, the ones we don't know we don't know.

Rumsfeld received a lot of stick for this cryptic response to a question fired at him during a briefing at the Department of Defense about the lack of evidence connecting the government of Iraq with weapons of mass destruction. Journalists and bloggers had a field day, culminating in Rumsfeld being given the Foot in Mouth award by the Plain English Campaign. And yet if one unpicks the statement, Rumsfeld very concisely summed up different types of knowledge. He perhaps missed one interesting category: The unknown knowns. The things that you know yet dare not admit to knowing. As the philosopher Slavoj Zizek argues, these are possibly the most dangerous, especially when held by those with political power. This is the domain of delusion. Repressed thoughts. The Freudian unconscious.

I would love to tell you about the unknown unknowns, but then they'd be known! Nassim Taleb, author of *The Black Swan*, believes that it is the emergence of these that are responsible for the biggest changes in society. For Kelvin it was relativity and quantum physics that turned out to be the unknown unknown that he was unable to conceive of. So in this book I can at best try to articulate the known unknowns and ask whether any will remain forever unknown. Are there questions that by their very nature will always be unanswerable, regardless of progress in knowledge?

I have called these unknowns 'Edges'. They represent the horizon beyond which we cannot see. My journey to the Edges of knowledge to articulate the known unknowns will pass through the known knowns that demonstrate how we have travelled beyond what we previously thought were the limits of knowledge. This journey will also test my own ability to know, because it's becoming increasingly challenging as a scientist to know even the knowns.

As much as this book is about what we cannot know, it is also important to understand what we do know and how we know it. My journey to the limits of knowledge will take me through the terrain that scientists have already mapped, to the very limits of today's cutting-edge breakthroughs. On the way I will stop to consider those moments when scientists thought they had hit a wall beyond which progress was no longer possible, only for the next generation to find a way, and this will give us an important perspective on those problems that we might think are unknowable today. By the end of our journey I hope this book will provide a comprehensive survey not just of what we cannot know but also of the things we do know.

To help me through those areas of science that are outside my comfort zone, I have enlisted the help of experts to guide me as I reach each science's Edge and to test whether it is my own limitations, or limitations inherent in the questions I am tackling, that make them unknowable.

What happens then if we encounter a question that cannot be answered? How does one cope with not knowing? Dare I admit to myself that some things will forever remain beyond my reach? How do we as a species cope with not knowing? That is a challenge that has elicited some interesting responses from humans across the millennia, not least the creation of an idea called God.

TRANSCENDENCE

There is another reason why I have been driven to investigate the unknowable, which is also related to my new job. The previous incumbent of the chair for the Public Understanding of Science was a certain Richard Dawkins. When I took over the position from Dawkins I braced myself for the onslaught of questions that I would get, not about science, but about religion. The publication of *The God Delusion* and his feisty debates with creationists resulted in Dawkins spending a lot of the later years of his tenure debating questions of religion and God.

So it was inevitable that when I took up the chair people would be interested in my stance on religion. My initial reaction was to put some distance between myself and the debate about God. My job was to promote scientific progress, and to engage the public in the breakthroughs happening around them. I was keen to move the debate back to questions of science rather than religion.

As a strategy to deflect the God questions I actually admitted that I was in fact a religious man. Before journalists got too excited, I went on to explain that my religion is the Arsenal. My temple is the Emirates (it used to be Highbury Stadium) in north London, and each Saturday I worship my idols and sing songs to them. And at the beginning of each season I reaffirm my faith that this will be the year we finally win some silverware. In an urban environment like London, football has taken over the role that religion played in society of binding a community together, providing rituals that they can share.

For me, the science that I began to learn as a teenager did a pretty good job of pushing out any vaguely religious thoughts I had had as a kid. I sang in my local church choir, which exposed me to the ideas that Christianity had to offer for understanding the universe. School education in the Seventies in the UK was infused with mildly religious overtones: renditions of 'All Things Bright and Beautiful' and the Lord's Prayer in assemblies. Religion was dished up as something too simplistic to survive the sophisticated and powerful stories that I would learn in the science labs at my secondary school. Religion was quickly pushed out. Science . . . and football . . . were much more attractive.

Inevitably the questions about my stance on religion would not be fobbed off with such a flippant answer. I remember that during one radio interview on a Sunday morning on BBC Northern Ireland I was gradually sucked into considering the question of the existence of God. I guess I should have seen the warning signs. On a Sunday morning in Northern Ireland, God isn't far from the minds of many listeners.

As a mathematician I am often faced with the challenge of proving the existence of new structures or coming up with arguments to show why such structures cannot exist. The power of the mathematical language to produce logical arguments has led a number of philosophers throughout the ages to resort to mathematics as a way of proving the existence of God. But I always have a problem with such an approach. If you are going to prove existence or otherwise in mathematics, you need a very clear definition of what it is that you are trying to prove exists.

So after some badgering by the interviewer about my stance on the existence of God, I pushed him to try to define what God meant for him so that I could engage my mathematical mind. 'It is something which transcends human understanding.' At first I thought: what a cop-out. You have just defined it as something which by its very nature I can't get a handle on. But I became intrigued by this as a definition. Perhaps it wasn't such a cop-out after all.

What if you *define* God as the things we cannot know. The gods in many ancient cultures were always a placeholder for the things we couldn't explain or couldn't understand. Our ancestors found volcanic eruptions or eclipses so mysterious that they became acts of gods. As science has explained such phenomena, these gods have retreated.

This definition has some things in common with a God commonly called the 'God of the gaps'. This phrase was generally used as a derogatory term by religious thinkers who could see that this God was shrinking in the face of the onslaught of scientific knowledge, and a call went out to reject this kind of God. The phrase 'God of the gaps' was coined by the Oxford mathematician and Methodist church leader Charles Coulson, when he declared: 'There is no "God of the gaps" to take over at those strategic places where science fails.'

But the phrase is also associated with a fallacious argument for the existence of God, one that Richard Dawkins spends some time shooting down in *The God Delusion*: if there are things that we can't explain or know, there must be a God at work filling the gap. But I am more interested not in the existence of a God to fill the gap, but in equating God with the abstract idea of the things we cannot know. Not in the things we currently don't know, but the things that by their nature we can never know. The things that will always remain transcendent.

Religion is more complex than the simple stereotype often offered up by modern society. For many ancient cultures in India, China and the Middle East, religion was not about worshipping a Supernatural Intelligence but precisely the attempt to appreciate the limits of our understanding and language. As the theologian Herbert McCabe declared: 'To assert the existence of God is to claim that there is an unanswered question about the universe.' Science has pushed hard at those limits. So is there anything left? Will there be anything that will always be beyond the limit. Does McCabe's God exist?

This is the quest at the heart of this book. Can we identify questions or physical phenomena that will always remain beyond knowledge? If we can identify things that will remain in the gaps of knowledge, then what sort of God is this? What potency would such a concept have? Could the things we cannot know act in the world and affect our futures? Are they worthy of worship?

But first we need to know if in fact there is anything that will remain unanswered about the universe. Is there really anything we cannot know?

FIRST EDGE: THE CASINO DICE

1

The unpredictable and the predetermined
unfold together to make everything the way it
is. It's how nature creates itself, on every scale,
the snowflake and the snowstorm. It makes
me so happy. To be at the beginning again,
knowing almost nothing.

Tom Stoppard, *Arcadia*

There is a single red dice sitting on my desk next to me. I got the dice
on a trip to Las Vegas. I fell in love with it when I saw it on the craps
table. It was so perfectly engineered. Such precise edges coming to a
point at the corners of the cube. The faces so smooth you couldn't feel
what number the face was representing. The pips are carved out of the
dice and then filled with paint that has the same density as the plastic
used to make the dice. This ensures that the face representing the 6
isn't a touch lighter than the face on the opposite side with a single pip.
The feeling of the dice in the hand is incredibly satisfying. It is a thing
of beauty.

And yet I hate it.

It's got three pips pointing up at me at the moment. But if I pick
it up and let it fall from my hand I have no way of knowing how it is
going to land. It is the ultimate symbol of the unknowable. The future
of the dice seems knowable only when it becomes the past.

I have always been extremely unsettled by things that I cannot
know. Things that I cannot work out. I don't mind not knowing something provided there is some way ultimately to calculate what's going
on. With enough time. Is this dice truly so unknowable? Or with
enough information can I actually deduce its next move? Surely it's

just a matter of applying the right laws of physics and solving the appropriate mathematical equations. Surely this is something I can know.

My subject, mathematics, was invented to give people a glimpse of what's out there coming towards us. To look into the future. To become masters of fate, not its servants. I believe that the universe runs according to laws. Understand those laws and I can know the universe. Spotting patterns has given the human species a very powerful way to take control. If there's a pattern then I have some chance to predict the future and know the unknowable. The pattern of the Sun means I can rely on it rising in the sky tomorrow or the Moon taking 28 sunrises before it becomes full again. It is how mathematics developed. Mathematics is the science of patterns. Being able to spot patterns is a powerful tool in the evolutionary fight for survival. The caves in Lascaux show how counting 13 quarters of the Moon from the first winter rising of the Pleiades will bring you to a time in the year when the horses are pregnant and easy to hunt. Being able to predict the future is the key to survival.

But there are some things which appear to have no pattern or that have patterns that are so complex or hidden that they are beyond human knowledge. The individual roll of the dice is not like the rising of the Sun. There seems to be no way to know which of the six faces will be pointing upwards once the cube finally comes to rest. It is why the dice has been used since antiquity as a way to decide disputes, to play games, to wager money.

Is that beautiful red cube with its white dots truly unknowable? I'm certainly not the first to have a complex relationship with the dynamics of this cube.

KNOWING THE WILL OF THE GODS

On a recent trip to Israel I took my children to an archaeological dig at Beit Guvrin. It was such a popular settlement in ancient times that the site consists of layer upon layer of cities built on top of each other. There is so much stuff in the ground that the archaeologists are happy to enlist amateurs like me and my kids to help excavate the site even if a few pots get broken along the way. Sure enough, we pulled out lots of bits of pottery. But we also kept unearthing a large number of animal bones. We thought they were the remains of dinner, but our guide explained that in fact they were the earliest form of dice.

Archaeological digs of settlements dating back to Neolithic times have revealed a disproportionately high density of heel bones of sheep or other animals among the shattered pottery and flints that are usually found in sites that humans once inhabited. These bones are in fact ancestors of my casino dice. When thrown, the bones naturally land on one of four sides. Often there are letters or numbers carved into the bones. Rather than gambling, these early dice are thought to have been used for divination. And this connection between the outcome of the roll of a dice and the will of the gods is one that has persisted for centuries. Knowledge of how the dice would land was believed to be something that transcended human understanding. Its outcome was in the lap of the gods.

Increasingly these dice assumed a more prosaic place as part of our world of leisure. The first cube-shaped dice like the one on my desk were found around Harappa in what is now northeast Pakistan, where one of the first urban civilizations evolved, dating back to the third millennium BC. At the same time, you find four-faced pyramid dice appearing in a game that was discovered in the city of Ur, in ancient Mesopotamia.

The Romans and Greeks were addicts of games of dice, as were the soldiers of the medieval era who returned from the Crusades with a new game called hazard, deriving from the Arabic word for a dice: *al-zahr*. It was an early version of craps, the game that was being played in the casino in Vegas where I picked up my dice.

If I could predict the fall of the dice, all the games that depend on them would never have caught on. The excitement of backgammon or hazard or craps comes from not knowing how the dice are going to land. So perhaps gamers won't thank me as I try to predict the roll of my dice.

For centuries no one even thought that such a feat was possible.

The ancient Greeks, who were among the first to develop mathematics as a tool to navigate their environment, certainly didn't have any clue how to tackle such a dynamic problem. Their mathematics was a static, rigid world of geometry, not one that could cope with the dice tumbling across the floor. They could produce formulas to describe the geometric contours of the cube, but once the dice started moving they were lost.

What about doing experiments to get a feel for the outcomes? The anti-empiricist attitude of the ancient Greeks meant they had no motivation to analyse the data and try to make a science of predicting how the dice would land. After all, the way the dice had just landed was going to have no bearing on the next throw. It was random and for the ancient Greeks that meant it was unknowable.

Aristotle believed that events in the world could essentially be classified into three categories: 'certain events' that happen by necessity following the laws of nature; 'probable events' that happen in most cases but can have a few exceptions; and finally 'unknowable events' that happened by pure chance. Aristotle put my dice firmly in the last category.

As Christian theology made its impact on philosophy, matters worsened. Since the throw of the dice was in the hands of God, it was not something that humans could aspire to know. As St Augustine had it: 'We say that those causes that are said to be by chance are not non-existent but are hidden, and we attribute them to the will of the true God.'

There was no chance. No free will. The unknowable was known by God, who determined the outcome of the dice. Any attempt to try to predict the roll was the work of a heretic, someone who dared to think they could know the mind of God. King Louis XI of France even went as far as prohibiting the manufacture of dice, believing that games of chance were ungodly. But the dice like the one I have on my desk eventually began to yield their secrets. It took till the sixteenth century before dice were wrestled out of the hands of God and their fate put in the hands, and minds, of humans.

FINDING THE NUMBERS IN THE DICE

I've put another two dice next to my beautiful Las Vegas dice. So here's a question: if I throw all three dice, is it better to bet on a score of 9 or a score of 10 coming up? Prior to the sixteenth century there were no tools available to answer such a question. And yet anyone who had played for long enough would know that if I was throwing only two dice then it would be wise to bet on 9 rather than 10. After all, experience would tell you before too long that on average you get 9 a third more often than you get 10. But with three dice it is harder to get a feel for which way to bet, because 9 and 10 seem to occur equally often. But is that really true?

It was in Italy at the beginning of the sixteenth century that an inveterate gambler by the name of Girolamo Cardano first realized that there are patterns that can be exploited in the throw of a dice. They weren't patterns that could be used on an individual throw. Rather, they emerged over the long run, patterns that a gambler like Cardano, who spent many hours throwing dice, could use to his advantage. So addicted was he to the pursuit of predicting the unknowable that on one occasion he even sold his wife's possessions to raise the funds for the table stakes.

Cardano had the clever idea of counting how many different futures the dice could have. If I throw two dice, there are 36 different futures. They are depicted in the following diagram.

Only in three of them is the total 10, while four give you a score of 9. So Cardano reasoned that, in the case of two dice being thrown, it makes sense to bet on 9 rather than 10. It did not help in any individual game, but in the long run it meant that Cardano, if he stuck to his maths, would come out on top. Unfortunately, while a disciplined mathematician, he wasn't very disciplined when it came to his gambling. He managed to lose all the inheritance from his father and would get into knife fights with his opponents when the dice went against him.

He was nevertheless determined to get one prophecy correct. He had apparently predicted the date of his death: 21 September 1576. To make sure he got this bet right he took matters into his own hands. He committed suicide when the date finally struck. As much as I crave knowledge, I think this is going a little far. Indeed, the idea of knowing the date of your death is something that most would prefer to opt out of. But Cardano was determined to win, even when he was dicing with Death.

Before taking his life, he wrote what many regard as the first book that made inroads into predicting the behaviour of the dice as it rolls across the table. Although written around 1564, *Liber de Ludo Aleae* didn't see the light of day until it was eventually published in 1663.

It was in fact the great Italian physicist Galileo Galilei who applied the same analysis that Cardano had described to decide whether to bet on a score of 9 or 10 when three dice are thrown. He reasoned that there are $6 \times 6 \times 6 = 216$ different futures the dice could take. Of these, 25 gave you a 9 while 27 gave you a 10. Not a big difference, and one that would be difficult to pick up from empirical data, but large enough that betting on 10 should give you an edge in the long run.

AN INTERRUPTED GAME

The mathematical mastery of the dice shifted from Italy to France in the mid-seventeenth century when two big hitters, Blaise Pascal and Pierre de Fermat, started applying their minds to predicting the future of these tumbling cubes. Pascal had become interested in trying to understand the roll of the dice after meeting one of the great gamblers of the day, Chevalier de Méré. De Méré had challenged Pascal with a number of interesting scenarios. One was the problem Galileo had cracked. But the others included whether it was advisable to bet that at least one 6 will appear if a dice is thrown four times, and also the now famous problem of 'points'.

Pascal entered into a lively correspondence with the great mathematician and lawyer Pierre de Fermat in which they tried to sort out the problems set by de Méré. With the throw of four dice, one could consider the $6 \times 6 \times 6 \times 6 = 1296$ different outcomes and count how many include a 6, but that becomes pretty cumbersome.

Instead, Pascal reasoned that there is a 5/6 chance that you won't see a 6 with one throw. Since each throw is independent, that means there is a $5/6 \times 5/6 \times 5/6 \times 5/6 = 625/1296 = 48.2\%$ chance that you won't get a 6 in four throws. Which means there is a 51.8% chance that you will see a 6. Just above an evens chance, so worth betting on.

The problem of 'points' was even more challenging. Suppose two players – let's call them Fermat and Pascal – are rolling a dice. Fermat scores a point if the dice lands on 4 or higher; Pascal scores a point otherwise. Each, therefore, has a 50:50 chance of winning a point on any roll of the dice. They've wagered £64, which will go to the first to score 3 points. The game is interrupted, however, and can't be continued, when Fermat is on 2 points and Pascal is on 1 point. How should they divide the £64?

Traditional attempts to solve the problem focused on what had happened in the past. Maybe, having won twice as many rounds as Pascal, Fermat should get twice the winnings. This makes no sense if, say, Fermat had won only one round before the game was interrupted. Pascal would get nothing but still has a chance of winning. Niccolò Fontana Tartaglia, a contemporary of Cardano, believed after much thought that it had no solution: 'The resolution of the question is judicial rather than mathematical, so that in whatever way the division is made there will be cause for litigation.'

Others weren't so defeated. Attention turned not to the past, but to what could happen in the future. In contrast to the other problems, they are not trying to predict the roll of the dice but instead need to imagine all the different future scenarios and to divide the spoils according to which version of the future favours which player.

It is easy to get fooled here. There seem to be three scenarios.

Fermat wins the next round and pockets £64. Pascal wins the next round, resulting in a final round which either Pascal wins or Fermat wins. Fermat wins in two out of these three scenarios so perhaps he should get two-thirds of the winnings. It was the trap that de Méré fell into. Pascal argues that this isn't correct. 'The Chevalier de Méré is very talented but he is not a mathematician; this is, as you know, a great fault.' A great fault, indeed!

Pascal, in contrast, was great on the mathematical front and argued that the spoils should be divided differently. There is a 50:50 chance that Fermat wins in one round, in which case he gets £64. But if Pascal wins the next round then they are equally likely to win the final round, so could divide the spoils £32 each. In either case Fermat is guaranteed £32. So the other £32 should be split equally, giving Fermat £48 in total.

Fermat, writing from his home near Toulouse, concurred with Pascal's analysis: 'You can now see that the truth is the same in Toulouse as in Paris.'

PASCAL'S WAGER

Pascal and Fermat's analysis of the game of points could be applied to much more complex scenarios. Pascal discovered that the secret to deciding the division of the spoils is hidden inside something now known as Pascal's triangle.

$$
\begin{array}{ccccccccccc}
 & & & & & 1 & & & & & \\
 & & & & 1 & & 1 & & & & \\
 & & & 1 & & 2 & & 1 & & & \\
 & & 1 & & 3 & & 3 & & 1 & & \\
 & 1 & & 4 & & 6 & & 4 & & 1 & \\
1 & & 5 & & 10 & & 10 & & 5 & & 1
\end{array}
$$

The triangle is constructed in such a way that each number is the sum of the two numbers immediately above it. The numbers you get are key to dividing the spoils in any interrupted game of points. For example, if

Fermat needs 2 points for a win while Pascal needs 4, then you consult the 2 + 4 = 6th row of the triangle and add the first four numbers together and the last two. This is the proportion in which you should divide the spoils. In this case it's a 1 + 5 + 10 + 10 = 26 to 1 + 5 = 6 division. So Fermat gets 26/32 × 64 = £52 and Pascal gets 6/32 × 64 = £12. In general, a game where Fermat needs n points to Pascal's m points can be decided by consulting the $(n + m)$th row of Pascal's triangle.

There is evidence that the French were beaten by several millennia to the discovery that this triangle is connected to the outcome of games of chance. The Chinese were inveterate users of dice and other random methods like the *I Ching* to try to predict the future. The text of the *I Ching* dates back some 3000 years and contains precisely the same table that Pascal produced to analyse the outcomes of tossing coins to determine the random selection of a hexagram that would then be analysed for its meaning. But today the triangle is attributed to Pascal rather than the Chinese.

Pascal wasn't interested only in dice. He famously applied his new mathematics of probability to one of the great unknowns: the existence of God.

'God is, or He is not.' But to which side shall we incline? Reason can decide nothing here. There is an infinite chaos which separated us. A game is being played at the extremity of this infinite distance where heads or tails will turn up . . . Which will you choose then? Let us see. Since you must choose, let us see which interests you least. You have two things to lose, the true and the good; and two things to stake, your reason and your will, your knowledge and your happiness; and your nature has two things to shun, error and misery. Your reason is no more shocked in choosing one rather than the other, since you must of necessity choose . . . But your happiness? Let us weigh the gain and the loss in wagering that God is . . . If you gain, you gain all; if you lose, you lose nothing. Wager, then, without hesitation that He is.

Called Pascal's wager, he argued that the payout would be much greater if one opted for a belief in God. You lose little if you are wrong and win eternal life if correct. On the other hand, wager against the existence of God and losing results in eternal damnation, while winning gains you nothing beyond the knowledge that there is no God. The argument falls to pieces if the probability of God existing is actually 0, and even if it isn't, perhaps the cost of belief might be too high when set against the probability of God's existence.

The probabilistic techniques developed by mathematicians like Fermat and Pascal to deal with uncertainty were incredibly powerful. Phenomena that were regarded as beyond knowledge, the expression of the gods, were beginning to be within reach of the minds of men. Today these probabilistic methods are our best weapon in trying to navigate everything from the behaviour of particles in a gas to the ups and downs of the stock market. Indeed, the very nature of matter itself seems to be at the mercy of the mathematics of probability, as we shall discover in the Third Edge, when we apply quantum physics to predict what fundamental particles are going to do when we observe them. But for someone on the search for certainty, these probabilistic methods represent a frustrating compromise.

I certainly appreciate the great intellectual breakthrough that Fermat, Pascal and others made, but it doesn't help me to know how many pips are going to be showing when I throw my dice. As much as I've studied the mathematics of probability, it has always left me with a feeling of dissatisfaction. The one thing any course on probability drums into you is that it doesn't matter how many times in a row you get a 6: this has no influence on what the dice is going to do on the next throw.

So is there some way of knowing how my dice is going to land? Or is that knowledge always going to be out of reach? Not according to the revelations of a scientist across the waters in England.

THE MATHEMATICS OF NATURE

Isaac Newton is my all-time hero in my fight against the unknowable. The idea that I could possibly know everything about the universe has its origins in Newton's revolutionary work *Philosophiae Naturalis Principia Mathematica*. First published in 1687, the book is dedicated to developing a new mathematical language that promised the tools to unlock how the universe behaves. It was a dramatically new model of how to do science. The work 'spread the light of mathematics on a science which up to then had remained in the darkness of conjectures and hypotheses', declared the French physicist Alexis Clairaut in 1747.

It is also an attempt to unify, to create a theory that describes the celestial and the earthly, the big and the small. Kepler had come up with laws that described the motions of the planets, laws he'd developed empirically by looking at data and trying to fit equations to create the past. Galileo had described the trajectory of a ball flying through the air. It was Newton's genius to understand that these were examples of a single phenomenon: gravity.

Born on Christmas Day in 1643 in the Lincolnshire town of Woolsthorpe, Newton was always trying to tame the physical world. He made clocks and sundials, constructed miniature mills powered by mice, sketched countless plans for buildings and ships, and drew elaborate illustrations of animals. The family cat apparently disappeared one day, carried away by a hot-air balloon that Newton had made. His school reports, however, did not anticipate a great future, describing him as 'inattentive and idle'.

Idleness is not necessarily such a bad trait in a mathematician. It can be a powerful incentive to look for some clever shortcut to solve a problem rather than relying on hard graft. But it's not generally a quality that teachers appreciate.

Indeed, Newton was doing so badly at school that his mother decided the whole thing was a waste of time and that he'd be better off learning how to manage the family farm in Woolsthorpe. Unfortunately, Newton was equally hopeless at managing the family estate, so he was sent back to school. Although probably apocryphal, it is said that Newton's sudden academic transformation coincided with a blow to the head that he received from the school bully. Whether true or not, Newton's academic transformation saw him suddenly excelling at school, culminating in a move to study at the University of Cambridge.

When bubonic plague swept through England in 1665, Cambridge University was closed as a precaution. Newton retreated to the house in Woolsthorpe. Isolation is often an important ingredient in coming up with new ideas. Newton hid himself away in his room and thought.

> Truth is the offspring of silence and meditation. I keep the subject constantly before me and wait 'til the first dawnings open slowly, by little and little, into a full and clear light.

In the isolation of Lincolnshire, Newton created a new language that could capture the problem of a world in flux: the calculus. This mathematical tool would be key to our knowing how the universe would behave ahead of time. It is this language that gives me any hope of gleaning how my casino dice might land.

MATHEMATICAL SNAPSHOTS

The calculus tries to make sense of what at first sight looks like a meaningless sum: zero divided by zero. As I let my dice fall from my hand, it is such a sum that I must calculate if I want to try to understand the instantaneous speed of my dice as it falls through the air.

The speed of the dice is constantly increasing as gravity pulls it to the ground. So how can I calculate what the speed is at any given instance of time? For example, how fast is the dice falling after one second? Speed is distance travelled divided by time elapsed. So I could record the distance it drops in the next second and that would give me an average speed over that period. But I want the precise speed. I could record the distance travelled over a shorter period of time, say half a second or a quarter of a second. The smaller the interval of time, the more accurately I will be calculating the speed. Ultimately, to get the precise speed I want to take an interval of time that is infinitesimally small. But then I am faced with calculating 0 divided by 0.

Calculus: making sense of zero divided by zero

Suppose that a car starts from a stationary position. When the stopwatch starts, the driver slams his foot on the accelerator. Suppose that we record that after t seconds the driver has covered t x t metres. How fast is the car going after 10 seconds? We get an approximation of the speed by looking at how far the car has travelled in the period from 10 to 11 seconds. The average speed during this second is (11 x 11 − 10 x 10)/1 = 21 metres per second.

But if we look at a smaller window of time, say the average speed over 0.5 seconds, we get:

(10.5 x 10.5 − 10 x 10)/0.5 = 20.5 metres per second.

Slightly slower, of course, because the car is accelerating, so on average it is going faster in the second half second from 10 seconds to 11 seconds. But now we take an even smaller snapshot. What about halving the window of time again:

(10.25 x 10.25 − 10 x 10)/0.25 = 20.25 metres per second.

Hopefully the mathematician in you has spotted the pattern. If I take a window of time which is x seconds, the average speed over this time will be $20 + x$ metres per second. The speed as I take smaller and smaller windows of time is getting closer and closer to 20 metres per second. So, although to calculate the speed at 10 seconds looks like I have to figure out the calculation 0/0, the calculus makes sense of what this should mean.

Newton's calculus made sense of this calculation. He understood how to calculate what the speed was tending towards as I make the time interval smaller and smaller. It was a revolutionary new language that managed to capture a changing dynamic world. The geometry of the ancient Greeks was perfect for a static, frozen picture of the world. Newton's mathematical breakthrough was the language that could describe a moving world. Mathematics had gone from describing a still life to capturing a moving image. It was the scientific equivalent of how the dynamic art of the Baroque burst forth during this period from the static art of the Renaissance.

Newton looked back at this time as one of the most productive of his life, calling it his *annus mirabilis*. 'I was in the prime of my age for invention and minded Mathematicks and Philosophy more than at any time since.'

Everything around us is in a state of flux, so it was no wonder that this mathematics would be so influential. But for Newton the calculus was a personal tool that helped him reach the scientific conclusions that he documents in the *Principia*, the great treatise published in 1687 that describes his ideas on gravity and the laws of motion.

Writing in the third person, he explains that his calculus was key to the scientific discoveries contained inside: 'By the help of this new Analysis Mr Newton found out most of the propositions in the *Principia*.' But no account of the 'new analysis' is published. Instead, he privately circulated the ideas among friends, but they were not ideas that he felt any urge to publish for others to appreciate.

Fortunately this language is now widely available and it is one that I spent years learning as a mathematical apprentice. But in order to attempt to know my dice I am going to need to mix Newton's mathematical breakthrough with his great contribution to physics: the famous laws of motion with which he opens his *Principia*.

THE RULES OF THE GAME

Newton explains in the *Principia* three simple laws from which so much of the dynamics of the universe evolve.

Newton's First Law of Motion: *A body will continue in a state of rest or uniform motion in a straight line unless it is compelled to change that state by forces acting on it.*

This was not so obvious to the likes of Aristotle. If you roll a ball along a flat surface it comes to rest. It looks like you need a force to keep it moving. There is, however, a hidden force that is changing the speed: friction. If I throw my dice in outer space away from any gravitational fields then the dice will indeed just carry on flying in a straight line at constant speed.

In order to change an object's speed or direction you needed a force. Newton's second law explained how that force would change the motion, and it entailed the new tool he'd developed to articulate change. The calculus has already allowed me to articulate what speed my dice is going at as it accelerates down towards the table. The rate of change of that speed is got by applying calculus again. The second law of Newton says that there is a direct relationship between the force being applied and the rate of change of the speed.

Newton's Second Law of Motion: *The rate of change of motion, or acceleration, is proportional to the force that is acting on it and inversely proportional to its mass.*

To understand the motion of bodies like my cascading dice I need to understand the possible forces acting on them. Newton's universal law of gravitation identified one of the principal forces that had an effect on, say, his apple falling or the planets moving through the solar system. The law states that the force acting on a body of mass m_1 by another body of mass m_2 which is a distance of r away is equal to

$$\frac{G \times m_1 \times m_2}{r^2}$$

where G is an empirical physical constant that controls how strong gravity is in our universe.

With these laws I can now describe the trajectory of a ball flying through the air, or a planet through the solar system, or my dice falling from my hand. But the next problem occurs when the dice hits the table. What happens then? Newton has a third law which provides a clue:

Newton's Third Law of Motion: *When one body exerts a force on a second body, the second body simultaneously exerts a force equal in magnitude and opposite in direction to that of the first body.*

Newton himself used these laws to deduce an extraordinary string of results about the solar system. As he wrote: 'I now demonstrate the system of the World.' To apply his ideas to the trajectory of the planets he began by reducing each planet to a point located at the centre of mass and assumed that all the planet's mass was concentrated at this point. Then by applying his laws of motion and his new mathematics he successfully deduced Kepler's laws of planetary motion.

He was also able to calculate the relative masses for the large planets, the Earth and the Sun. He explained a number of the curious irregularities in the motion of the Moon due to the pull of the Sun. He also deduced that the Earth isn't a perfect sphere but should be squashed between the poles due to the Earth's rotation causing a centrifugal force. The French thought the opposite would happen: that the Earth should be pointy in the direction of the poles. An expedition set out in 1733 which proved Newton – and the power of mathematics – correct.

NEWTON'S THEORY OF EVERYTHING

It was an extraordinary feat. The three laws were the seeds from which all motion of particles in the universe could potentially be deduced. It deserved to be called a Theory of Everything. I say 'seeds' because it required other scientists to grow these seeds and apply them to more complex settings than Newton's solar system made up of point particles of mass. For example, in their original form the laws are not suited to describing the motion of less rigid bodies or bodies that deform. It was the great eighteenth-century Swiss mathematician Leonhard Euler who would provide equations that generalized Newton's laws. Euler's equations could be applied more generally to something like a vibrating string or a swinging pendulum.

More and more equations appeared that controlled various natural phenomena. Euler produced equations for non-viscous fluids. At the beginning of the nineteenth century French mathematician Joseph Fourier found equations to describe heat flow. Fellow compatriots Pierre-Simon Laplace and Siméon-Denis Poisson took Newton's equations to produce more generalized equations for gravitation, which were then seen to control other phenomena like hydrodynamics and electrostatics. The behaviours of viscous fluids were described by the Navier–Stokes equations, and electromagnetism by Maxwell's equations.

With the discovery of the calculus and the laws of motion, it seemed that Newton had turned the universe into a deterministic clockwork machine controlled by mathematical equations. Scientists believed they had indeed discovered the Theory of Everything. In his *Philosophical Essay on Probabilities* published in 1812, the mathematician Pierre-Simon Laplace summed up most scientists' belief in the extraordinary power of mathematics to tell you everything about the physical universe.

> We may regard the present state of the universe as the effect of its past and the cause of its future. An intellect which at a certain moment would know all forces that set nature in motion, and all positions of all items of which nature is composed, if this intellect were also vast enough to submit these data to analysis, it would embrace in a single formula the movements of the greatest bodies of the universe and those of the tiniest atom; for such an intellect nothing would be uncertain and the future just like the past would be present before its eyes.

This view that, in theory, the universe was knowable, both past and present, became dominant among scientists in the centuries following Newton's great opus. It seemed as if any idea of God acting in the world had been completely removed. A God might be responsible for getting things up and running, but from that point on the equations of mathematics and physics took over.

So what of my lowly dice? Surely with the laws of motion at hand I can simply combine the geometry of the cube with the initial direction of motion and the subsequent interactions with the table to predict the outcome? I've written out the equations on my notepad and they look pretty daunting.

Newton too contemplated the problem of trying to predict the dice. Newton's interest was prompted by a letter he received from Samuel Pepys. Pepys wanted Newton's advice on which option he should back in a wager he was about to make with a friend:

(1) Throwing six dice and getting at least one 6
(2) Throwing twelve dice and getting at least two 6s
(3) Throwing eighteen dice and getting at least three 6s

Pepys was about to stake £10, the equivalent of £1000 in today's money, and he was quite keen to get some good advice. Pepys's intuition was that (3) was the more likely option, but Newton replied that the mathematics implied the opposite was true. He should put his money on the first option. However, it wasn't his laws of motion and the calculus to which Newton resorted to solve the problem but the ideas developed by Fermat and Pascal.

But even if Newton could have solved the equations I've written out to describe the trajectory of the dice, there turned out to be another problem that could scupper any chance of knowing the future of my dice. Although Pascal was talking about his wager with God, there is an interesting line in his analysis which throws a spanner in the works when it comes to knowing the future: 'Reason can decide nothing here. There is an infinite chaos which separated us.'

THE FATE OF THE SOLAR SYSTEM

If Newton is my hero, then French mathematician Henri Poincaré should be the villain in my drive to predict the future. And yet I can hardly blame him for uncovering one of the most devastating blows for anyone wanting to know what's going to happen next. He was hardly very thrilled himself with the discovery, given that it cost him rather a lot of money.

Born a hundred years after Laplace, Poincaré believed, like his compatriot, in a clockwork universe, a universe governed by mathematical laws and utterly predictable. 'If we know exactly the laws of nature and the situation of the universe at the initial moment, we can predict exactly the situation of the same universe at a succeeding moment.'

Understanding the world was Poincaré's prime motivation for doing mathematics. 'The mathematical facts worthy of being studied are those which, by their analogy with other facts, are capable of leading us to the knowledge of a physical law.'

Although Newton's laws of motion had spawned an array of mathematical equations to describe the evolution of the physical world, most of them were still extremely complicated to solve. Take the equations for a gas. Think of the gas as made up of molecules crashing around like tiny billiard balls, and theoretically the future behaviour of the gas was bound up in Newton's laws of motion. But the sheer number of balls meant that any exact solution was well beyond reach. Statistical or probabilistic methods were still by far the best tool to understand the behaviour of billions of molecules.

There was one situation where the number of billiard balls was reasonably small and a solution seemed tractable. The solar system. Poincaré became obsessed with the question of predicting what lay in store for our planets as they danced their way into the future.

Because the gravitational pull of a planet on another planet at some distance from the first planet is the same as if all the mass of the planet is concentrated at its centre of gravity, to determine the ultimate fate of the solar system one can consider planets as if they are just points in space, as Newton had done. This means that the evolution of the solar system can be described by three coordinates for each planet that locate the centre of mass in space together with three additional numbers recording the speed in each of the three dimensions of space. The forces acting on the planets are given by the gravitational forces exerted by each of the other planets. With all this information one just needs to apply Newton's second law to map out the course of the planets into the distant future.

The only trouble is that the maths is still extremely tricky to work out. Newton had solved the behaviour of two planets (or a planet and a sun). They would follow elliptical paths, with their common focal point being the common centre of gravity. This would repeat itself periodically to the end of time. But Newton was stumped when he introduced a third planet. Trying to calculate the behaviour of a solar system consisting, say, of the Sun, the Earth and the Moon seemed simple enough, but already you are facing an equation in 18 variables: 9 for position and 9 for the speed of each planet. Newton conceded that 'to consider simultaneously all these causes of motion and to define these motions by exact laws admitting of easy calculation exceeds, if I am not mistaken, the force of any human mind'.

The problem got a boost when King Oscar II of Norway and Sweden decided to mark his sixtieth birthday by offering a prize for solving a problem in mathematics. There are not many monarchs around the world who would choose maths problems as their way to celebrate their birthdays, but Oscar had always enjoyed the subject ever since he had excelled at it when he was a student at Uppsala University.

> His majesty Oscar II, wishing to give a fresh proof of his interest in the advancement of mathematical science has resolved to award a prize on January 21, 1889, to an important discovery in the field of higher mathematical analysis. The prize will consist of a gold medal of the eighteenth size bearing his majesty's image and having a value of a thousand francs, together with the sum of two thousand five hundred crowns.

Three eminent mathematicians convened to choose a number of suitable mathematical challenges and to judge the entries. One of the questions they posed was to establish mathematically whether the solar system was stable. Would it continue turning like clockwork, or, at some point in the future, might the Earth spiral off into space and disappear from our solar system?

To answer the question required solving the equations that had stumped Newton. Poincaré believed that he had the skills to win the prize. One of the common tricks used by mathematicians is to attempt a simplified version of the problem first to see if that is tractable. So Poincaré started with the problem of three bodies. This was still far too difficult, so he decided to simplify the problem further. Instead of the Sun, Earth and Moon, why not try to understand two planets and a speck of dust? The two planets won't be affected by the dust particle, so he could assume, thanks to Newton's solution, that they just repeated ellipses round each other. The speck of dust, on the other hand, would experience the gravitational force of the two planets. Poincaré set about trying to describe the path traced by the speck of dust. Some understanding of this trajectory would form an interesting contribution to the problem.

Although he couldn't crack the problem completely, the paper he submitted was more than good enough to secure King Oscar's prize. He'd managed to prove the existence of an interesting class of paths that would repeat themselves, so-called periodic paths. Periodic orbits were by their nature stable because they would repeat themselves over and over, like the ellipses that two planets would be guaranteed to execute.

The French authorities were very excited that the award had gone to one of their own. The nineteenth century had seen Germany steal a march on French mathematics, so the French academicians excitedly heralded Poincaré's win as proof of a resurgence of French mathematics. Gaston Darboux, the permanent secretary of the French Academy of Sciences, declared:

> From that moment on the name of Henri Poincaré became known to the public, who then became accustomed to regarding our colleague no longer as a mathematician of particular promise but as a great scholar of whom France has the right to be proud.

A SMALL MISTAKE WITH BIG IMPLICATIONS

Preparations began to publish Poincaré's solution in a special edition of the Royal Swedish Academy of Science's journal *Acta Mathematica*. Then came the moment every mathematician dreads. Every mathematician's worst nightmare. Poincaré thought his work was safe. He'd checked every step in the proof. Just before publication, one of the editors of the journal raised a question over one of the steps in his mathematical argument.

Poincaré had assumed that a small change in the positions of the planets, a little rounding up or down here or there, was acceptable as it would result in only a small change in their predicted orbits. It seemed a fair assumption. But there was no justification given for why this would be so. And in a mathematical proof, every step, every assumption, must be backed up by rigorous mathematical logic.

The editor wrote to Poincaré for some clarification on this gap in the proof. But as Poincaré tried to justify this step, he realized he'd made a serious mistake. He wrote to Gösta Mittag-Leffler, the head of the prize committee, hoping to limit the damage to his reputation:

The consequences of this error are more serious than I first thought. I will not conceal from you the distress this discovery has caused me . . . I do not know if you will still think that the results which remain deserve the great reward you have given them. (In any case, I can do no more than to confess my confusion to a friend as loyal as you.) I will write to you at length when I can see things more clearly.

Mittag-Leffler decided he needed to inform the other judges:

Poincaré's memoir is of such a rare depth and power of invention, it will certainly open up a new scientific era from the point of view of analysis and its consequences for astronomy. But greatly extended explanations will be necessary and at the moment I am asking the distinguished author to enlighten me on several important points.

As Poincaré struggled away he soon saw that he was simply mistaken. Even a small change in the initial conditions could result in wildly different orbits. He couldn't make the approximation that he'd proposed. His assumption was wrong.

Poincaré telegraphed Mittag-Leffler to break the bad news and tried to stop the paper from being printed. Embarrassed, he wrote:

It may happen that small differences in the initial conditions produce very great ones in the final phenomena. A small error in the former will produce an enormous error in the latter. Prediction becomes impossible.

Mittag-Leffler was 'extremely perplexed' to hear the news.

It is not that I doubt that your memoir will be in any case regarded as a work of genius by the majority of geometers and that it will be the departure point for all future efforts in celestial mechanics. Don't therefore think that I regret the prize . . . But here is the worst of it. Your letter arrived too late and the memoir has already been distributed.

Mittag-Leffler's reputation was on the line for not having picked up the error before they'd publicly awarded Poincaré the prize. This was not the way to celebrate his monarch's birthday! 'Please don't say a word of this lamentable story to anyone. I'll give you all the details tomorrow.'

The next few weeks were spent trying to retrieve the printed copies without raising suspicion. Mittag-Leffler suggested that Poincaré should pay for the printing of the original version. Poincaré, who was mortified, agreed, even though the bill came to over 3500 crowns, 1000 crowns more than the prize he'd originally won.

In an attempt to rectify the situation, Poincaré set about trying to sort out his mistake, to understand where and why he had gone wrong. In 1890, Poincaré wrote a second, extended paper explaining his belief that very small changes could cause an apparently stable system suddenly to fly apart.

What Poincaré discovered, thanks to his error, led to one of the most important mathematical concepts of the last century: chaos. It was a discovery that places huge limits on what we humans can know. I may have written down all the equations for my dice, but what if my dice behaves like the planets in the solar system? According to Poincaré's discovery, if I make just one small error in recording the starting location of the dice, that error could expand into a large difference in the outcome of the dice by the time it comes to rest on the table. So is the future of my Vegas dice shrouded behind the mathematics of chaos?

The chaotic path mapped out by a single planet orbiting two suns.

2

If nature were not beautiful it would not be worth knowing, and if nature were not worth knowing, life would not be worth living.

Henri Poincaré

I wasted a lot of time at university playing billiards in our student common room. I could have pretended that it was all part of my research into angles and stuff, but the truth is that I was procrastinating. It was a good way of putting off having to cope with not being able to answer that week's set of problems. But in fact the billiard table hides a lot of interesting mathematics in its contours. Mathematics that is highly relevant to my desire to understand my dice.

If I shoot a ball round a billiard table and mark its path, then follow that by shooting another ball off in very nearly the same direction, the second ball will trace out a very similar path to the first ball. Poincaré had believed that the same principle applied to the solar system. Fire a planet off in a slightly different direction then the solar system will evolve in a very similar pattern. This is most people's intuition: if I make a small change in the initial conditions of the planet's trajectory it won't alter the course of the planet much. But the solar system seems to be playing a slightly more interesting game of billiards than the one I played as a student.

Rather surprisingly, if I change the shape of the billiard table this intuition turns out to be wrong. For example, fire balls round a billiard table shaped like a stadium with semicircular ends but straight sides and the paths can diverge dramatically even though they started in almost the same direction. This is the signature of chaos: sensitivity to very small changes in the initial conditions.

Two quickly diverging paths taken by a billiard ball round
a stadium-shaped billiard table.

So the challenge for me is to determine whether the fall of my dice is predictable, like a conventional game of billiards, or whether the dice is playing a game of chaotic billiards.

THE DEVIL IN THE DECIMALS

Despite Poincaré being credited as the father of chaos, it is striking that this sensitivity of many dynamical systems to small changes was not very well known for decades into the twentieth century. Indeed, it really took the rediscovery of the phenomenon by scientist Edward Lorenz, when he, like Poincaré, thought he'd made some mistake, before the ideas of chaos became more widely known.

While working as a meteorologist at MIT in 1963, Lorenz had been running equations for the change of temperature in a dynamic fluid on his computer when he decided he needed to rerun one of his models for longer. So he took some of the data that had been output earlier in the run and re-entered it, expecting to be able to restart the model from that point.

When he returned from coffee, he discovered to his dismay that the computer hadn't reproduced the previous data but had generated very quickly a wildly divergent prediction for the change in temperature. At first he couldn't understand what was happening. If you input the same numbers into an equation, you don't expect to get a different answer at the other end. It took him a while to realize what was going on: he hadn't input the same numbers. The computer printout of the data he'd used had only printed the numbers to three decimal places, while it had been calculating using the numbers to six decimal places.

Even though the numbers were actually different, they differed only in the fourth decimal place. You wouldn't expect it to make that big a difference, but Lorenz was struck by the impact such a small difference in the numbers had on the resulting data. Here are two graphs created using the same equation but where the data that is put into the equations differ very slightly. One graph uses the input data 0.506127. The second graph approximates this to 0.506. Although the graphs start out following similar paths, they very quickly behave completely differently.

The model that Lorenz was running was a simplification of models for the weather that analysed how the flow of air behaves when subjected to differences in temperature. His rediscovery of how small changes in the way you start a system can have such a big impact on the outcome would have huge implications for our attempts to use mathematical equations to make predictions into the future. As Lorenz wrote:

> Two states that were imperceptibly different could evolve to two considerably different states. Any error in the observation of the present state – and in a real system, this appears to be inevitable – may render an acceptable prediction of the state in the distant future impossible.

THE REVENGE OF THE GRASSHOPPER

When Lorenz explained his findings to a colleague, he received the reply: 'Edward, if your theory is correct, one flap of a seagull's wings could alter the course of history forever.'

The seagull would eventually be replaced by the now famous butterfly when Lorenz presented his findings in 1972 at the American Association for the Advancement of Science in a paper entitled: 'Does the Flap of a Butterfly's Wings in Brazil Set Off a Tornado in Texas?'

Curiously, both the seagull and the butterfly might have been pre-empted by the grasshopper. It seems that already in 1898 Professor W. S. Franklin had realized the devastating effect that the insect community could have on the weather. Writing in a book review, he believed:

An infinitesimal cause may produce a finite effect. Long-range detailed weather prediction is therefore impossible, and the only detailed prediction which is possible is the inference of the ultimate trend and character of a storm from observations of its early stages; and the accuracy of this prediction is subject to the condition that the flight of a grasshopper in Montana may turn a storm aside from Philadelphia to New York!

This is an extraordinary position to be in. The equations that science has discovered give me a completely deterministic description of the evolution of many dynamical systems like the weather. And yet in many cases I am denied access to the predictions that they might make because any measurement of the location or wind speed of a particle is inevitably going to be an approximation to the true conditions.

This is why the MET office, when it is making weather predictions, takes the data recorded by the weather stations dotted across the country and then, instead of running the equations on this data, the meteorologists do several thousand runs, varying the data over a range of values. The predictions stay close for a while, but by about five days into the future the results have often diverged so wildly that one set of data predicts a heat wave to hit the UK while a few changes in the decimal places of the data result in rain drenching the country.

Starting from nearly the same conditions, forecast A predicts strong wind and rain over the British Isles in 4 days' time, while forecast B predicts incoming high pressure from the Atlantic.

The great Scottish scientist James Clerk Maxwell articulated the important difference between a system being deterministic yet unknowable in his book *Matter and Motion*, published in 1877: 'There is a maxim which is often quoted, that "The same causes will always produce the same effects."' This is certainly true of a mathematical equation describing a dynamical system. Feed the same numbers into the equation and you won't get any surprises. But Maxwell continues: 'There is another maxim which must not be confounded with this, which asserts that "Like causes produce like effects." This is only true when small variations in the initial circumstances produce only small variations in the final state of the system.' It is this maxim that the discovery of chaos theory in the twentieth century revealed as false.

This sensitivity to small changes in initial conditions has the potential to sabotage my attempts to use the equations I've written down to predict the outcome of my dice. I've got the equations, but can I really be sure that I've accurately recorded the angle at which the cube leaves my hand, the speed at which it is spinning, the distance to the table?

Of course, everything isn't completely hopeless. There are times when small changes don't alter the course of the equations dramatically, like the paths in the classical billiard table. What is important is to know when you cannot know. A beautiful example of knowing the point when you can't know what is going to happen next was discovered by mathematician Robert May when he analysed the equations for population growth.

KNOWING WHEN YOU CAN'T KNOW

Born in Australia in 1938, May had originally trained as a physicist working on superconductivity. But his academic work took a dramatic turn when he was exposed in the late 1960s to the newly formed movement in social responsibility in science. His attention shifted from the behaviour of collections of electrons to the more pressing questions of the behaviour of population dynamics in animals. Biology at the time was not a natural environment for the mathematically minded, but following May's work that would all change. It was this fusion of the hardcore mathematical training he'd received as a physicist combined with a new sensibility to biological issues that led to his great breakthrough.

In a paper in *Nature* called 'Simple Mathematical Models with Very Complicated Dynamics', published in 1976, May explored the dynamics of a mathematical equation describing population growth from one season to the next. He revealed how even a quite innocent equation can produce extraordinarily complex behaviour in the numbers. His equation for population dynamics wasn't some complicated differential equation but a simple discrete feedback equation that anyone with a calculator can explore.

Feedback equation for population dynamics

Suppose I consider an animal population whose numbers can vary between 0 and some hypothetical maximum value that I will call N. Given some fraction Y (lying between 0 and 1) of that maximum, the equation determines what in the next season is the revised fraction of the population that survives after reproduction and competition for food. Let's suppose that each season the reproduction rate is given by a number r. So that if the fraction of the maximum population that survived to the end of the season was Y, the next generation swells to $r \times Y \times N$.

But not all of these new animals will survive. The equation determines that the fraction that will not survive is also given by Y. So out of the $r \times Y \times N$ animals that start the season, $Y \times (r \times Y \times N)$ die. So the total left at the end of the season is $(r \times Y \times N) - (r \times Y^2 \times N) = [r \times Y \times (1 - Y)] \times N$, which means that the fraction of the maximum population that exists in the current season is $r \times Y \times (1 - Y)$.

Essentially the model assumes that at the end of each season the surviving population gets multiplied by a constant factor, called r, the reproduction rate, to produce the number of animals at the beginning of the next season. But there aren't enough resources for them all to survive. The equation then calculates how many of these animals will make it till the end of the season. The resulting number of animals that survive then gets multiplied by the factor r again for the next generation. The fascinating property of this equation is that its behaviour really depends only on the choice of r, the reproduction rate. Some choices of r lead to extremely predictable behaviours. I can know exactly how the numbers will evolve. But there is a threshold beyond which I lose control. Knowledge is no longer within reach because the addition of one extra animal into the mix can result in dramatically different population dynamics.

For example, May discovered that if r lies between 1 and 3 then the population eventually stabilizes. In this case it doesn't matter what the initial conditions are, the numbers will gradually tend to a fixed value depending on r. It's like playing billiards on a table where there is a sinkhole in the middle. However I shoot the ball off, it eventually finds its way to the bottom of the sinkhole.

For r above 3, I still see a region of predictable behaviour but of a slightly different character. With r between 3 and $1 + \sqrt{6}$ (which is approximately 3.44949), the population dynamics eventually ping-pong between two values that depend on r. As r passes $1 + \sqrt{6}$, we see the population dynamics changing character again. For r between $1 + \sqrt{6}$ and 3.54409 (or more precisely the solution of a polynomial equation of degree 12), there are 4 values that the population periodically cycles through. As r gets bigger, I get 8 values, then 16, and so on. As r climbs, the number of different values doubles each time until I hit a threshold moment when the character of the dynamics flips from being periodic to chaotic.

When May first explored this equation, he admitted that he frankly hadn't a clue what was going on beyond this point – he had a black-board outside his office in Sydney on which he offered a prize of 10 Australian dollars to anyone who could explain the behaviour. As he wrote on the blackboard: 'It looks like a mess.'

It was on a visit to Maryland that he got his answer and where the term 'chaos' was actually coined. In the seminar he gave, he explained the region in which the period doubles but admitted he'd hit a point beyond which he didn't know what the hell was happening. In the audience was a mathematician who did know. Jim Yorke had never seen the doubling behaviour but he knew exactly what was going on in this higher region. And it was what he called chaos.

Beyond $r = 3.56995$ (or more precisely the limit point of the solutions of a system of equations of increasing degree), the behaviour becomes very sensitive to what the initial population looks like. Change the initial number of animals by a minute amount and a totally different result can ensue.

Two populations with *r* = 4 that start off with a difference of just one animal in a thousand. Although they start behaving similarly, by year 15 they are demonstrating very different behaviours.

But as I turn up the dial on *r*, there can still be pockets of regular behaviour, as Jim Yorke had discovered. For example, take *r* = 3.627 and the population becomes periodic again, bouncing around between 6 different values. Keep dialling *r* up and the 6 changes to 12 which becomes 24, doubling each time until chaos strikes again.

Bob May recognized just what a warning shot such a simple system was to anyone who thought they knew it all: 'Not only in research, but in the everyday world of politics and economics, we would be better off if more people realized that simple systems do not necessarily possess simple dynamic properties.'

THE POLITICS OF CHAOS

Bob May is currently practising what he preaches. Or perhaps I should say Lord May of Oxford, as I was corrected by a man in a top hat who greeted me at the door to the peers' entrance of the House of Lords. May has in recent years combined his scientific endeavours with energetic political activism. He now sits as a cross-party member of the House of Lords, which is where I popped in for lunch to find out how he was doing in his mission to alert politicians to the impact of chaotic systems on society.

Ushered through the peers' entrance to the Lords by the man in the top hat and policemen with machine guns, I found May waiting for me on the other side of metal detectors and X-ray machines. May has no truck with all these formal titles and in his earthy Australian manner still insists on being called Bob. 'I'm afraid I messed up and already ate lunch but I'll come and eat cake while you get some lunch.' As I ate fish he consumed an enormous piece of House of Lords chocolate cake. At 79, May is as energetic and engaged as ever and was rushing off after his second lunch to a select committee discussing the impact of a new rail link between London and the northwest of England.

Before joining the Lords, May was chief scientific adviser both to John Major's Conservative government and then subsequently to Tony Blair's Labour government. I wondered how tricky a balancing act such a political position is for a man who generally is not scared to tell it like it is.

'At the interview I was told that there would be occasions where I would be called upon to defend the decisions of a minister and how would I feel about that? I said that I would never under any circumstances deny a fact. On the other hand, I'm fairly good at the kind of debating competition where you're given a topic and according to a flip of a coin you've got to argue for either side of the debate. So I said I'd be happy explaining why the minister's choice was arrived at. I simply wouldn't agree to endorse it if it wasn't right.'

A typical mathematical response. Set up the minister's axioms and then demonstrate the proof that led to the conclusion. A judgement-free approach. That's not to say that May isn't opinionated and prepared to give his own views on the subject at hand.

I was curious how governments deal with the problems that chaos theory creates for anyone trying to make policy decisions. How do politicians cope with the challenges of predicting or manipulating the future, given that we can have only partial knowledge of the systems being analysed?

'I think that's rather a flattering account of what goes on here. With some notable exceptions it's mostly a bunch of very egotistical people, very ambitious people, who are primarily interested in their own careers.'

What about May personally? What impact did the discoveries he'd made have on his view of science's role in society?

'It was weird. It was the end of the Newtonian dream. When I was a graduate student it was thought that with better and better computer power we would get better and better weather predictions because we knew the equations and we could make more realistic models of the Earth.'

But May is cautious not to let the climate change deniers use chaos theory as a way to undermine the debate.

'Not believing in climate change because you can't trust weather reports is a bit like saying that because you can't tell when the next wave is going to break on Bondi beach you don't believe in tides.'

May likes to quote a passage from Tom Stoppard's play *Arcadia* to illustrate the strange tension that exists between the power of science to know some things with extraordinary accuracy and chaos theory, which denies us knowledge of many parts of the natural world. One of the protagonists, Valentine, declares:

> We're better at predicting events at the edge of the galaxy or inside the nucleus of an atom than whether it'll rain on auntie's garden party three Sundays from now.

May jokes that his most-cited works are not the high-profile academic papers he's published in prestigious scientific journals like *Nature*, but the programme notes he wrote for Stoppard's play when it was first staged at the National Theatre in London. 'It makes a mockery of all these citation indexes as a way of measuring the impact of scientific research.'

THE HUMAN EQUATION

So what are the big open questions of science that May would like to know the answer to? Consciousness? An infinite universe?

'I think I'd look at it in a less grand way, so I'd look at it more in terms of the things I am working on at the moment. Largely by accident I've been drawn into questions about banking.'

That was a surprise. The question of creating a stable banking system seemed very parochial, but May has recently been applying his models of the spread of infectious diseases and the dynamics of ecological food webs to understanding the banking crisis of 2008. Working with Andrew Haldane at the Bank of England, he has been considering the financial network as if it were an ecosystem. Their research has revealed how financial instruments intended to optimize returns to individual institutions with seemingly minimal risk can nonetheless cause instability in the system as a whole.

May believes that the problem isn't necessarily the mechanics of the market itself. It's the way small things in the market are amplified and perverted by the way humans interact with them. For him the most worrying thing about the banking mess is getting a better handle on this contagious spreading of worry.

'The challenge is: how do you put human behaviour into the model? I don't think human psychology is mathematizable. Here we are throwing dice with our future. But if you're trying to predict the throw of the dice then you want to know the circumstance of who owns the dice.'

That was something I hadn't taken into account in my attempts to predict the outcome of my casino dice. Perhaps I need to factor in who sold me my dice in the first place.

'I think many of the major problems facing society are outside the realm of science and mathematics. It's the behavioural sciences that are the ones we are going to have to depend on to save us.'

Looking round the canteen at the House of Lords, you could see the sheer range and complexity of human behaviour at work. It makes the challenge of mathematizing even the interactions in this tiny microcosm of the human population nigh impossible. As the French historian Fernand Braudel explained in a lecture on history he gave to his fellow inmates in a German prison camp near Lübeck during the Second World War: 'An incredible number of dice, always rolling, dominate and determine each individual existence.' Although each individual dice is unpredictable, there are still patterns that emerge in the long-range behaviour of many throws of the dice. In Braudel's view this is what makes the study of history possible. 'History is indeed "a poor little conjectural science" when it selects individuals as its objects . . . but much more rational in its procedure and results when it examines groups and repetitions.'

But May believes that understanding the history and origins of the collection of dice that make up the whole human race is not as straightforward as Braudel makes out. For example, it's not at all clear that we can unpick how we got to this point in our evolutionary journey.

'I'll tell you one of the questions that I think is a particularly interesting one: trying to understand our evolutionary trajectory as humans on our planet. Is the trajectory we seem to be on what happens on all or most planets, or is it the result of earlier fluctuations in the chaos which took us on this trajectory rather than another. Will we ever know enough to be able to ask whether the disaster we seem to be heading for is inevitable or whether there are lots of other planets where people are more like Mr Spock, less emotional, less colourful, but much more detached and analytical.'

Until we discover other inhabited planets and can study their trajectories, it's difficult to assess whether evolution inevitably leads to mismanaged ecosystems based on just one dataset called Earth.

'The question of whether where we're heading is something that happens to all inhabited planets or whether there are other planets where it doesn't happen is something I think we'll never know.'

And with that May polished off the last few crumbs of his chocolate cake and plunged back into the chaos of the select committees and petty politics of Westminster.

May's last point relates to the challenge that chaos theory poses for knowing something about the past as much as the future. At least with the future we can wait and see what the outcome of chaotic equations produces. But trying to work backwards and understand what state our planet was in to produce the present is equally if not more challenging. The past even more than the future is probably something we can never truly know.

LIFE: A CHANCE THROW OF THE DICE?

May's pioneering research explored the dynamics of a population as it went from season to season. But what determines which animals survive and which die before reproducing? According to Darwin, this is simply down to a lucky roll of the evolutionary dice.

The model of the evolution of life on Earth is based on the idea that once you have organisms with DNA, then the offspring of these organisms share the DNA of their parent organisms. But parts of the genetic code in the DNA can undergo random mutations. These are essentially down to the chance throw of the evolutionary dice. But there is a second important strand to Darwin's proposal, which is the idea of natural selection.

Some of those random changes will give the offspring an increased chance of survival, while other changes will result in a disadvantage. The point of evolution by natural selection is that it is more likely that the advantageous change will survive long enough to reproduce.

Suppose, for example, that I start with a population of giraffes that have short necks. The environment of the giraffes changes such that there is more food in the trees, so that any giraffe born with a longer neck is going to have a better chance of survival. Let's suppose that I throw my Vegas dice to determine the chance of a mutation for each giraffe born in the next generation following this environmental change. A roll of a 1, 2, 3, 4 or 5 condemns the giraffe to a neck of the same size or shorter, while a throw of a 6 corresponds to a chance mutation which causes a longer neck. The lucky longer-necked giraffes get the food and the shorter-necked giraffes don't survive to reproduce. So it is just the longer-necked giraffes that get the chance to pass on their DNA.

In the next generation the same thing happens. Roll a 1, 2, 3, 4 or 5 on the dice and the giraffe doesn't grow any taller than its parents. But another 6 grows the giraffe a bit more. The taller giraffes survive again. The environment favours the giraffes that have thrown a 6. Each generation ends up a bit taller than the last generation until there comes a point where it is no longer an advantage to grow any further.

It's the combination of chance and natural selection that results in us seeing more giraffes with ancestors that all threw 6s. In retrospect it looks like amazing chance that you see so many 6s in a row. But the point is that you don't see any of the other rolls of the dice because they don't survive. What looks like a rigged game is just the result of the combination of chance and natural selection. There is no design or fixing at work. The run of consecutive 6s isn't a lucky streak but is actually the only thing we would expect to see from such a model.

It's a beautifully simple model, but, given the complexity of the changes in the environment and the range of mutations that can occur, this simple model can produce extraordinary complexity, which is borne out by the sheer variety of species that exist on Earth. One of the reasons I never really fell in love with biology is that there seemed to be no way to explain why we got cats and zebras out of this evolutionary model and not some other strange selection of animals. It all seemed so arbitrary. So random. But is that really fair?

There is an interesting debate going on in evolutionary biology about how much chance there is in the outcomes we are seeing. If we rewound the story of life on Earth to some point in the past and threw the dice again, would we see very similar animals appearing or could we get something completely different? It is the question that May raised at the end of our lunch.

It does appear that some parts of evolution seem inevitable. It is striking that throughout evolutionary history the eye evolved independently 50 to 100 times. This is strong evidence for the fact that the different rolls of the dice that have occurred across different species seem to have produced species with eyes regardless of what is going on around them. Lots of other examples illustrate how some features, if they are advantageous, seem to rise to the top of the evolutionary swamp. This is illustrated every time you see the same feature appearing more than once in different parts of the animal kingdom. Echolocation, for example, is used by dolphins and bats, but they evolved this trait independently at very different points on the evolutionary tree.

But it isn't clear how far these outcomes are guaranteed by the model. If there is life on another planet, will it look anything like the life that has evolved here on Earth? This is one of the big open questions in evolutionary biology. As difficult as it may be to answer, I don't believe it qualifies as something we can never know. It may remain something we will never know, but there is nothing by its nature that makes it unanswerable.

WHERE DID WE COME FROM?

Are there other great unsolved questions of evolutionary biology that might be contenders for things we can never know? For example, why, 542 million years ago, at the beginning of the Cambrian period, was there an explosion of diversity of life on Earth? Before this moment life consisted of single cells that collected into colonies. But over the next 25 million years, a relatively short period on the scale of evolution, there is a rapid diversification of multicellular life that ends up resembling the diversity that we see today. An explanation for this exceptionally fast pace of evolution is still missing. This is in part due to lack of data from that period. Can we ever recover that data, or could this always remain a mystery?

Chaos theory is usually a limiting factor in what we can know about the future. But it can also imply limits on what we can know about the past. We see the results, but deducing the cause means running the equations backwards. Without complete data the same principle applies backwards as forwards. We might find ourselves at two very divergent starting points which can explain very similar outcomes. But we'll never know which of those origins was ours.

One of the big mysteries in evolutionary biology is how life got going in the first place. The game of life may favour runs of 6s on the roll of the evolutionary dice, but how did the game itself evolve? Estimates have been made for the chances of everything lining up to produce molecules that replicate themselves. In some models of the origins of life it is equivalent to nature having to throw 36 dice and get them all to land on 6. For some this is proof of needing a designer to rig the game. But this is to misunderstand the huge timescale that we are working on.

Miracles do happen . . . given enough time. Indeed, it would be more striking if we didn't get these strange anomalies happening. The point is that the anamolies often stick out. They get noticed, while the less exciting rolls of the dice get ignored.

The lottery is a perfect test bed for the occurrence of miracles in a random process. On 6 September 2009 the following six numbers were the winning numbers in the Bulgarian state lottery:

4, 15, 23, 24, 35, 42

Four days later the same six numbers came up again. Incredible, you might think. The government in Bulgaria certainly thought so and ordered an immediate investigation into the possibility of corruption. But what the Bulgarian government failed to take into account is that each week, across the planet, different lotteries are being run. They have been running for decades. If you do the mathematics, it would be more surprising not to see such a seemingly anomalous result.

The same principle applies to the conditions for producing self-replicating molecules in the primeval soup that made up the Earth before life emerged. Mix together plenty of hydrogen, water, carbon dioxide and some other organic gases and subject them to lightning strikes and electromagnetic radiation and already experiments in the lab show the emergence of organic material found only in living things. No one has managed to spontaneously generate anything as extraordinary as DNA in the lab. The chances of that are very small.

But that's the point, because given the billion billion or so possible planets available in the universe on which to try out this experiment, together with the billion or so years to let the experiment run, it would be more striking if that outside chance of creating something like DNA didn't happen. Keep rolling 36 dice on a billion billion different planets for a billion years and you'd probably get one roll with all 36 dice showing 6. Once you have a self-replicating molecule it has the means to propagate itself, so you only need to get lucky once to kick off evolution.

Our problem as humans, when it comes to appreciating the chance of a miracle such as life occurring, is that we have not evolved minds able to navigate very large numbers. Probability is therefore something we have little intuition for.

THE FRACTAL TREE OF LIFE

But it's not only the mathematics of probability that is at work in evolution. The evolutionary tree itself has an interesting quality that is similar to the shapes that appear in chaos theory, a quality known as fractal.

The fractal evolutionary tree.

The evolutionary tree is a picture of the evolution of life on Earth. Making your way through the tree corresponds to a movement through time. Each time the tree branches, this represents the evolution of a new species. If a branch terminates, this means the extinction of that species. The nature of the tree is such that the overall shape seems to be repeated on smaller and smaller scales. This is the characteristic feature of a shape mathematicians call a fractal. If you zoom in on a small part of the tree it looks remarkably like the large-scale structure of the tree. This self-similarity means that it is very difficult to tell at what scale we are looking at the tree. This is the classic characteristic of a fractal.

Fractals are generally the geometric signature of a chaotic system, so it is suggestive of chaotic dynamics at work in evolution: the small changes in the genetic code that can result in huge changes in the outcome of evolution. This model isn't necessarily a challenge to the idea of convergence, as there can still be points in chaotic systems towards which the model tends to evolve. Such points are called attractors. But it certainly questions whether if you reran evolution it would look anything like what we've got on Earth today. The evolutionary biologist Stephen Jay Gould has contended that if you were to rerun the tape of life that you would get very different results. This is what you would expect from a chaotic system. Just as with the weather, very small changes in the initial conditions can result in a dramatically different outcome.

Gould also introduced the idea of punctuated equilibria, which captures the fact that species seem to remain stable for long periods and then undergo what appears to be quite rapid evolutionary change. This has also been shown to be a feature of chaotic systems. The implications of chaos at work in evolution are that many of the questions of evolutionary biology could well fall under the umbrella of things we cannot know because of their connections to the mathematics of chaos.

For example, will we ever know whether humans were destined to evolve from the current model of evolution? An analysis of DNA in different animals has given us exceptional insights into the way animals have evolved in the past. The fossil record, although incomplete in places, has also given us a way to know our origins. But given the time scales involved in evolution it is impossible to experiment and rerun the tape of life evolving on Earth and see if something different could have happened. As soon as we find life on other planets (if we do), this will give us new sample sets to analyse. But until then all is not lost. Just as the MET office doesn't have to run real weather to make predictions, computer models can illustrate different possible outcomes of the mechanism of evolution, speeding up time. But the model will only be as good as the hypotheses we have made on the model. If we've got the model wrong, it won't tell us what is really happening in nature.

It's such computer models that are at the heart of trying to answer the question Poincaré first tackled when he discovered chaos: will there even be a stable Earth orbiting the Sun for evolution to continue playing its game of dice? How safe is our planet from the vagaries of chaos? Is our solar system stable and periodic, or do I have to worry about a grasshopper disrupting our orbit around the Sun?

A BUTTERFLY CALLED MERCURY

Poincaré wasn't able to answer the King of Sweden's question about the solar system: whether it would remain in a stable equilibrium or might fly apart in a catastrophic exhibition of chaotic motion. His discovery that some dynamical systems can be sensitive to small changes in data opened up the possibility that we may never know the precise fate of the solar system much in advance of any potentially devastating scenario unfolding.

It is possible that, like population dynamics with a low reproductive rate, the solar system is in a safe predictable region of activity. Unfortunately, the evidence suggests that we can't console ourselves with this comforting mathematical hope. Recent computer modelling has provided new insights which reveal that the solar system is indeed within a region dominated by the mathematics of chaos.

I can measure how big an effect a small change will have on the outcome using something called the Lyapunov exponent. For example, in the case of billiards played on differently shaped tables, I can give a measure of how catastrophic a small change will be on the evolution of a ball's trajectory. If the Lyapunov exponent of a system is positive, it means that if I make a small change in the initial conditions then the distance between the paths diverges exponentially. This can be used as a definition of chaos.

With this measure several groups of scientists have confirmed that our solar system is indeed chaotic. They have calculated that the distance between two initially close orbital solutions increases by a factor of ten every 10 million years. This is certainly on a different timescale to our inability to predict the weather. Nevertheless, it means that I can have no definite knowledge of what will happen to the solar system over the next 5 billion years.

If you're wondering in despair whether we can know anything about the future, then take heart in the fact that mathematics isn't completely hopeless at making predictions. There is an event that the equations guarantee will occur if we make it to 5 billion years from now, but it's not good news: the mathematics implies that at this point the Sun will run out of fuel and evolve into a red giant engulfing planet Earth and the other planets in our solar system in the process. But until this solar blowout engulfs the solar system, I am faced with trying to solve chaotic equations if I want to know which planets will still be around to see that red giant.

This means that, like the predictions of the weather, if I want to know what is going to happen, I am reduced to running simulations in which I vary the precise locations and speeds of the planets. The forecast is in some cases rather frightening. In 2009 French astronomers Jacques Laskar and Mickael Gastineau ran several thousand models of the future evolution of our solar system. And their experiments have identified a potential butterfly: Mercury.

The simulations start by feeding in the records we have of the positions and velocities of the planets to date. But it is difficult to know these with 100% accuracy. So each time they run the simulation they make small changes to the data. Because of the effects of chaos theory, just a small change could result in a large deviation in the outcomes.

For example, astronomers know the dimensions of the ellipse of Mercury's orbit to an accuracy of several metres. Laskar and Gastineau ran 2501 simulations where they varied these dimensions over a range of less than a centimetre. Even this small perturbation resulted in startlingly different outcomes for our solar system.

You might expect that if the solar system was going to be ripped apart it would have to be one of the big planets like Jupiter or Saturn that would be the culprit. But the orbits of the gas giants are extremely stable. It's the rocky terrestrial planets that are the troublemakers. In 1% of simulations that they ran, it was tiny Mercury that posed the biggest risk. The models show that Mercury's orbit could start to extend due to a certain resonance with Jupiter, with the possibility that Mercury could collide with its closest neighbour, Venus. In one simulation, a close miss was enough to throw Venus out of kilter, with the result that Venus collides with Earth. Even close encounters with the other planets would be enough to cause such tidal disruption that the effect would be disastrous for life on our planet.

This isn't simply a case of abstract mathematical speculation. Evidence of such collisions has been observed in the planets orbiting the binary star Upsilon Andromedae. Their current strange orbits can be explained only by the ejection of an unlucky planet sometime in the star's past. But before we head for the hills, the simulations reveal that it will take several billion years before Mercury might start to misbehave.

INFINITE COMPLEXITY

What of my chances to predict the throw of the dice that sits next to me? Laplace would have said that, provided I can know the dimensions of the dice, the distribution of the atoms, the speed at which it is launched, its relationship to its surrounding environment, theoretically the calculation of its resting point is possible.

The discoveries of Poincaré and those who followed have revealed that just a few decimal places could be the difference between the dice landing on a 6 or a 2. The dice is designed to have only six different outcomes, yet the input data ranges over a potentially continuous spectrum of values. So there are clearly going to be points where a very small change will flip the dice from landing on a 6 to a 2. But what is the nature of those transitions?

Computer models can produce very good visual representations that give me a handle on the sensitivity of various systems to the starting conditions. Next to my Vegas dice I've got a classic desktop toy that I can play with for hours. It consists of a metal pendulum that is attracted to three magnets, coloured white, black and grey. Analysis of the dynamics of this toy has led to a picture that captures the ultimate outcome of the pendulum as it starts over each point in the square base of the toy. Colour a point white if starting the pendulum at this point results in it ending at the white magnet. Similarly, colour the point grey or black if the ultimate destination is grey or black. This is the picture you get:

As in the case of population dynamics, there are regions which are entirely predictable. Start close to a magnet and the pendulum will just be attracted to that magnet. But towards the edges of the picture I find myself in far less predictable terrain. Indeed, the picture is now an example of a fractal.

There are regions where there isn't a simple transition from black to white. If I keep zooming in, the picture never becomes just a region filled with one colour. There is complexity at all scales.

A one-dimensional example of such a picture can be cooked up as follows. Draw a line of unit length and begin by colouring one half black and the other white. Then take half the line from the point 0.25 to 0.75 and flip it over. Now take the half in between that and flip it over again. If we keep doing this to infinity then the predicted behaviour around the point at 0.5 is extremely sensitive to small changes. There is no region containing the point 0.5 which has a single colour.

There is a more elaborate version of this picture. Start again with a line of unit length. Now rub out the middle third of the line. You are left with two black lines with a white space in between. Now rub out the middle third of each of the two black lines. Now we have a black line of length 1/9, a white line of length 1/9, a black line of length 1/9, then the white line of length 1/3 that was rubbed out on the first round, and then a repeat of black–white–black.

You may have guessed what I am going to do next. Each time rub out the middle third of all the black lines that you see. Do this to infinity. The resulting picture is called the Cantor set, after the German mathematician Georg Cantor, whom we will encounter in the last Edge, when I explore what we can know about infinity. Suppose this Cantor set was actually controlling the outcome of the pendulum in my desktop toy. If I move the pendulum along this line, I find that this picture predicts some very complicated behaviour in some regions.

A rather strange calculation shows that the total length of the line that has been rubbed out is 1. But there are still black points left inside: 1/4 is a point that is never rubbed out, as is 3/10. These black points, however, are not isolated. Take any region round a black point and you will always have infinitely many black and white points inside the region.

What do the dynamics of my dice look like? Are they fractal and hence beyond my knowledge? My initial guess was that the dice would be chaotic. However, recent research has turned up a surprise.

KNOWING MY DICE

A Polish research team has recently analysed the throw of a dice mathematically, and by combining this with the use of high-speed cameras they have revealed that my dice may not be as chaotic and unpredictable as I first feared. The research group consists of father-and-son team Tomasz and Marcin Kapitaniak together with Jaroslaw Strzalko and Juliusz Grabski, and they are based in Lódź. In their paper in the journal *Chaos,* published in 2012, the team draw similar pictures to those for the magnetic pendulum, but the starting positions are more involved than just two coordinates because they have to give a description of the angle at which the cube is launched and also the speed. The dice will be predictable if for most points in this picture when I alter the starting conditions a little the dice ends up falling on the same side. I can think of the picture being coloured by six colours corresponding to the six sides of the dice. The picture is fractal if however much I zoom in on the shape I still see regions containing at least two colours. The dice is predictable if I don't see this fractal quality.

The model the Polish team considered assumes the dice is perfectly balanced like the dice I brought back from Vegas. Air resistance, it turns out, can be ignored as it has very little influence on the dice as it tumbles through the air. When the dice hits the table a certain proportion of the dice's energy is dissipated, so that after sufficiently many bounces the dice has lost all kinetic energy and comes to rest.

Friction on the table is also key, as the dice is likely to slide in the first few bounces but won't slide in later bounces. However, the model explored by the Polish team assumed a frictionless surface as the dynamics get too complicated to handle when friction is present. So imagine throwing the dice onto an ice rink.

I'd already written down equations based on Newton's laws of motion for the dynamics of the dice as it flies through the air. In the hands of the Polish team they turn out not to be too complicated. It is the equations for the change in dynamics after the impact with the table that are pretty frightening, taking up ten lines of the paper they wrote.

They discovered that if the amount of energy dissipated on impact with the table is quite high, the picture of the outcome of the dice does not have a fractal quality. This means that if one can settle the initial conditions with appropriate accuracy, the outcome of the throw of my dice is predictable and repeatable. This predictability implies that, more often than not, the dice will land on the face that was lowest when the dice is launched. A dice that is fair when static may actually be biased when one adds in its dynamics.

But as the table becomes more rigid, resulting in less energy being dissipated and hence the dice bouncing more, I start to see a fractal quality emerging.

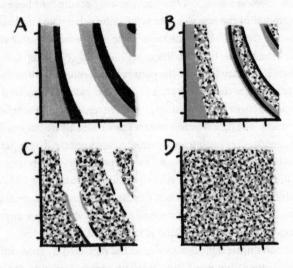

Moving from (a) to (d), the table dissipates less energy, resulting in a more fractal quality for the outcome of the dice.

This picture looks at varying two parameters: the height from which the dice is launched and variations in the angular velocity around one of the axes. The less energy that is dissipated on impact with the table, the more chaotic its resulting behaviour and the more it seems that the outcome of my dice recedes back into the hands of the gods.

DOES GOD PLAY DICE?

What of the challenge to define God as the things we cannot know? Chaos theory asserts that I cannot know the future of certain systems of equations because they are too sensitive to small inaccuracies. In the past gods weren't supernatural intelligences living outside the system but were the rivers, the wind, the fire, the lava – things that could not be predicted or controlled. Things where chaos lay. Twentieth-century mathematics has revealed that these ancient gods are still with us. There are natural phenomena that will never be tamed and known. Chaos theory implies that our futures are often beyond knowledge because of their dependence on the fine-tuning of how things are set up in the present. Because we can never have complete knowledge of the present, chaos theory denies us access to the future. At least until that future becomes the present.

That's not to say that all futures are unknowable. Very often we are in regions which aren't chaotic and small fluctuations have little effect on outcomes. This is why mathematics has been so powerful in helping us to predict and plan. Here we have knowledge of the future. But at other times we cannot have such control, and yet this unknown future will certainly impact on our lives at some point.

Some religious commentators who know their science and who try to articulate a scientific explanation for how a supernatural intelligence could act in the world have intriguingly tried to use the gap that chaos provides as a space for this intelligence to affect the future.

One of these religious scientists is the quantum physicist John Polkinghorne. Based at the University of Cambridge, Polkinghorne is a rare mind who combines both the rigours of a scientific education with years of training to be a Christian priest. I will be meeting Polkinghorne in person in the Third Edge when I explore the unknowability inherent in his own scientific field of quantum physics. But he has also been interested in the gap in knowledge that the mathematics of chaos theory provides as an opportunity for his God to influence the future course of humanity.

Polkinghorne has proposed that it is via the indeterminacies implicit in chaos theory that a supernatural intelligence can still act without violating the laws of physics. Chaos theory says that we can never know the set-up precisely enough to be able to run deterministic equations, and hence there is room in Polkinghorne's view for divine intervention, to tweak things to remain consistent with our partial knowledge but still influence outcomes.

Polkinghorne is careful to stress that to use infinitesimal data to effect change requires a complete holistic top-down intervention. This is not a God in the detail but by necessity an all-knowing God. Given that chaos theory means that even the location of an electron on the other side of the universe could influence the whole system, we need to have complete, holistic knowledge of the whole system – the whole universe – to be able to steer things. We cannot successfully isolate a part of the universe and hope to make predictions based on that part. So it would require knowledge of the whole to act via this chink in that which is unknown to us.

Chaos theory is deterministic, so this isn't an attempt to use the randomness of something like quantum physics as a way to have influence. Polkinghorne's take on how to square the circle of determinism and influence the system is to use the gap between epistemology and ontology, between what we know and what is true. Since we cannot know a complete description of the state of the universe at this moment in time, this implies that from our perspective there is no determinacy. There are many different scenarios that coincide with our impartial description of what we currently know about how the universe is set up. Polkinghorne's contention is that at any point in time this gives a God the chance to intervene and shift the system between any of these scenarios without us being aware of the shift. But, as we have seen, chaos theory means that these small shifts can still have hugely different outcomes. Polkinghorne is careful to assert that you allow shifts between systems where there is change only in information, not energy. The rule here is not to violate any rules of physics. As Polkinghorne says: 'The succession of the seasons and the alternations of day and night will not be set aside.'

Even if you think this is rather fanciful (which I certainly do), a similar principle is probably key to our own feeling of agency in the world. The question of free will is related ultimately to questions of a reductionist philosophy. Free will describes the inability to make any meaningful reduction in most cases to an atomistic view of the world. So it makes sense to create a narrative in which we have free will because that is what it looks like on the level of human involvement in the universe. If things were so obviously deterministic, with little variation to small undetectable changes, we wouldn't think that we had free will.

It is striking that Newton, the person who led us to believe in a clockwork deterministic universe, also felt that there was room in the equations for God's intervention. He wrote of his belief that God would sometimes have to reset the universe when things looked like they were going off course. He got into a big fight with his German mathematical rival Gottfried Leibniz, who couldn't see why God wouldn't have set it up perfectly from the outset:

> Sir Isaac Newton and his followers have also a very odd opinion concerning the work of God. According to their doctrine, God Almighty wants to wind up his watch from time to time: otherwise it would cease to move. He had not, it seems, sufficient foresight to make it a perpetual motion.

ON THE EDGE OF CHAOS

Newton and his mathematics gave me a feeling that I could know the future, that I could shortcut the wait for it to become the present. The number of times I have heard Laplace's quote about ultimately being able to know everything thanks to the equations of motion is testament to a general feeling among scientists that the universe is theoretically knowable.

The mathematics of the twentieth century revealed that theory doesn't necessarily translate into practice. Even if Laplace is correct in his statement that complete knowledge of the current state of the universe together with the equations of mathematics should lead to complete knowledge of the future, I will never have access to that complete knowledge. The shocking revelation of twentieth-century chaos theory is that even an approximation to that knowledge won't help. The divergent paths of the chaotic billiard table mean that since we can never know which path we are on, our future is not predictable.

Chaos theory implies that there are things we can never know. The mathematics in which I had placed so much faith to give me complete knowledge has revealed the opposite. But it is not entirely hopeless. Many times the equations are not sensitive to small changes and hence give me access to predictions about the future. After all, this is how we landed a spaceship on a passing comet. Not only that: as Bob May's work illustrates, the mathematics can even help me to know when I can't know.

But a discovery at the end of the twentieth century even questions Laplace's basic tenet of the theoretical predictability of the future. In the early 1990s a PhD student by the name of Zhihong Xia proved that there is a way to configure five planets such that when you let them go, the combined gravitational pull causes one of the planets to fly off and reach an infinite speed in a finite amount of time. No planets collide, but still the equations have built into them this catastrophic outcome for the residents of the unlucky planet. The equations are unable to make any prediction of what happens beyond this point in time.

Xia's discovery is a fundamental challenge to Laplace's view that Newton's equations imply that we can know the future if we have complete knowledge of the present, because there is no prediction even within Newton's equations for what happens next for that unlucky planet once it hits infinite speed. The theory hits a singularity at this point, beyond which prediction makes no sense. As we shall see in later Edges, considerations of relativity will limit the physical realization of this singularity since the unlucky planet will eventually hit the cosmic speed limit of the speed of light, at which point Newton's theory is revealed to be an approximation of reality. But it nevertheless reveals that equations aren't enough to know the future.

It is striking to listen to Laplace on his deathbed. As he sees his own singularity heading towards him with only a finite amount of time to go, he too admits: 'What we know is little, and what we are ignorant of is immense.' The twentieth century revealed that, even if we know a lot, our ignorance will remain immense.

But it turns out that it is isn't just the outward behaviour of planets and dice that is unknowable. Probing deep inside my casino dice reveals another challenge to Laplace's belief in a clockwork deterministic universe. When scientists started to look inside the dice to understand what it is made of, they discovered that knowing the position and the movement of the particles that make up the dice may not even be theoretically possible. As I shall discover in the next two Edges, there might indeed be a game of dice at work that controls the behaviour of the very particles that make up my red Las Vegas cube.

SECOND EDGE: THE CELLO

3

Everyone takes the limits of his own vision
for the limits of the world.

Arthur Schopenhauer

When I started at my comprehensive school, I remember my music teacher asking the class if there was anyone who wanted to learn a musical instrument. Three of us put up our hands. The teacher led us into the storeroom cupboard to see what instruments were available. The cupboard was bare except for three trumpets stacked up on top of each other.

'It looks like you're learning the trumpet.'

I don't regret the choice (even if there wasn't one). I had a great time playing in the local town band and larking around in the brass section of the county orchestra as we counted bars rest. But I used to look over with a little envy at the strings who seemed to be playing all the time, getting all the good tunes. A few years ago, during a radio interview, I was asked what new musical instrument I would choose to learn, given the opportunity, and which piece of music I would aspire to play.

'The cello. Bach's suites.'

The question has been nagging at the back of my mind since that interview: could I learn to play those beautiful cello suites? Perhaps it was too late to pick up such new skills, but I needed to know. So I bought a cello.

It sits behind me as I write about trying to predict the outcome of the dice. When I need a break from analysing the equations that control the fall of the red cube on my desk, I massacre one of the gigues from the first suite for cello. I can feel Bach turning in his grave but I am enjoying myself.

One of the fun things about the cello is the possibility of sliding your finger up the string to create a continuous glissando of notes. Not something I can do on my trumpet, which is an instrument of discrete notes corresponding to the different combinations of fingers I put down. It turns out that this tension between the continuous glissando of the cello and the discrete notes of the trumpet is relevant to my attempts to predict the behaviour of my dice.

ZOOMING IN

To predict how the dice might land I need to know what my cube is made from. Denser acetate in one corner of the shape will lead to one side of the dice being favoured over the others. So if I am going to attempt to apply Newton's laws to my dice as it tumbles through the air, I need to know how my dice is put together. Is it a continuous structure, or, if I look closely, is it made up of discrete pieces?

If I accept the limits of my own vision, as Schopenhauer's quote at the beginning of this Edge suggests I tend to, then I can't see anything other than the clear red acetate that makes up the dice. But with an optical microscope I can magnify the dice by a factor of 1500, which would scale my dice up to the size of a large building. Peering inside this huge dice still won't reveal much about the secrets of how it is built. Everything still looks pretty smooth and continuous.

In the twentieth century microscopes exploiting different bits of the electromagnetic spectrum have allowed scientists to create images which magnify things a further 1000 times. Now my dice will span from one side of London to the other. At this magnification the dice is looking grainier. The sense of the continuous structure is giving way to something more discrete. Current electron microscopes allow me to zoom in another 10 times closer, at which point I might start to see the carbon and oxygen atoms that I know are some of the ingredients of the acetate from which my dice is made.

The intriguing thing is that scientists had already formulated an atomic view of matter long before I could actually see these atoms under the modern microscopes in the labs across the road from the mathematics department. And it is a combination of a mathematical and theoretical perspective with a physical vision that is the best tool for knowing what my dice is made from.

But atoms like oxygen and carbon turned out not to be as atomic as the name suggests. Beyond the atomic structure revealed by current electron microscopes, I know that there is more internal structure. Atoms give way to electrons, protons and neutrons. Protons and neutrons in turn give way to quarks. In 2013 quantum microscopes even captured pictures of electrons orbiting the nucleus of a hydrogen atom. But is there a theoretical limit to how far I can dig down inside my dice?

What happens, for example, if I take my dice and keep dividing it in half? Just how far can I go? The mathematical side of me says: no problem. If I have a number I can keep dividing it by two:

$$1, \ \frac{1}{2}, \frac{1}{4}, \frac{1}{8}, \frac{1}{16}, \ldots$$

There is no point mathematically where I have to stop. Yet if I start trying to do the same thing with the physical dice sitting on my desk and cut it in half, then in half again, just how far can I keep going?

The tension between the continuous versus the discrete nature of matter, between what is possible mathematically versus the limits placed by physical reality, has been raging for millennia. Is the universe dancing to the sound of my trumpet or shimmying to the glissando of my cello?

THE MUSIC OF THE SPHERES

How did I personally come to know about these electrons and quarks that are believed to be the last layer of my dice? I've never seen them. If I actually ask myself how I know about them, the answer is that I've been told and read about them so many times that I've actually forgotten why or how I know. Or, come to think of it, was I ever told how we know? Is it a bit like the way I know Everest is the tallest mountain? I know that only because I've been told it enough times. So before I ask whether there is anything beyond this layer, I need to know how we got to these building blocks.

Reading through the history, I am surprised that it is only just over a hundred years ago that convincing evidence was provided for the fact that things like my dice are made of discrete building blocks called atoms and are not just continuous structures. Despite being such a relatively recent discovery, the hunch that this was the case goes back thousands of years. In India it was believed that matter was made from basic atoms corresponding to taste, smell, colour and touch. They divided atoms into ones that were infinitesimally small and took up no space, and others that were 'gross' and took up finite space – an extremely prescient theory, as you will see once I explain our current model of matter.

In the West it was the ancient Greeks who first proposed an atomistic philosophy of nature, advocating the reductionist view that physical reality could be reduced to fundamental units that made up all matter. These atoms could not be broken down into anything smaller, and their properties should not depend on some further complex inner structure. One of the seeds for this belief in a universe made from indivisible building blocks was the Pythagorean philosophy that number is at the heart of explaining the secrets of the universe.

The conviction in the power of whole numbers had its origins in a rather remarkable discovery attributed to Pythagoras: namely, that number is the basis of the musical harmony that both my cello and my trumpet exploit. The story has it that inspiration struck when he passed a blacksmith and heard the hammers banging out a combination of harmonious notes. (We can't be sure whether this and similar stories told about Pythagoras are true, or even whether he really existed and wasn't an invention of later generations used to promote new ideas.)

This story goes that he went home and experimented with the notes made by a stringed instrument. If I take the vibrating string on my cello then I can produce a continuous sequence of notes by gradually pushing my finger up towards the bridge of the cello, making a sound called a glissando (although the question of whether this is truly producing a continuous sequence of notes will be challenged in the next Edge). If I stop at the positions that produce notes that sound harmonious when combined with the open vibrating string, it turns out that the lengths of the strings are in a perfect whole-number ratio with each other.

For example, if I place my finger at the halfway point along the vibrating string I get a note which sounds almost like the note I started with. The interval is called the octave, and to the human ear the note sounds so similar to the note on the open string that in the musical notation that emerged we give these notes the same names. If I place my finger a third of the distance from the head of the cello, I get a note which sounds particularly harmonious when combined with the note of the open string. Known as the perfect fifth, what our brains are responding to is a subliminal recognition of this whole-number relationship between the wavelengths of the two notes.

Having found that whole numbers were at the heart of harmony, the Pythagoreans began to build a model of the universe that had these whole numbers as the fundamental building blocks of everything they saw or heard around them. Greek cosmology was dominated by the idea of a mathematical harmony in the skies. The orbits of the planets were believed to be in a perfect mathematical relationship to each other, giving rise to the idea of the music of the spheres.

More importantly for understanding the make-up of my dice, it was also believed that discrete numbers rather than a continuous glissando were the key to understanding what constituted matter. The Pythagoreans proposed the idea of fundamental atoms that, like numbers, could be added together to get new matter. The Greek philosopher and mathematician Plato developed the Pythagorean philosophy and makes these atoms into discrete pieces of geometry.

Plato believed the atoms were actually bits of mathematics: triangles and squares. These were the building blocks for the shapes that he believed were the key to the ingredients of Greek chemistry: the elements of fire, earth, air and water. Each element, Plato believed, had its own three-dimensional mathematical shape.

Fire was the shape of a triangular-based pyramid, or tetrahedron, made from 4 equilateral triangles. Earth was cube-shaped like my Vegas dice. Air was made from a shape called an octahedron, constructed from 8 equilateral triangles. It is a shape that looks like two square-based pyramids fused together along the square faces. Finally, water corresponded to the icosahedron, a shape made from 20 equilateral triangles. Plato believed that it was the geometrical interaction of these basic shapes that gave rise to the chemistry of the elements.

The atomistic view of matter was not universally held across the ancient world. After all, there was no evidence for these indivisible bits. You couldn't see them. Aristotle was one of those who did not believe in the idea of fundamental atoms. He thought that the elements were continuous in nature, that you could theoretically keep dividing my dice up into smaller and smaller pieces. He believed that fire, earth, air and water were elemental in the sense that they could not be divided into 'bodies different in form'. If you kept dividing, you would still get water or air. If you take a glass of water then to the human eye, it appears to be a continuous structure which can theoretically be infinitely divided. If I take a piece of rubber then I can stretch it in a smooth manner making it appear continuous in nature. The stage was set for the battle between the continuous and discrete models of matter. The glissando versus the discrete notes of the musical scale. The cello versus the trumpet.

Intriguingly, it was a discovery credited to the Pythagoreans that would threaten the atomistic view and which turned the tide for many years in favour of the belief that matter could be divided infinitely.

NUMBERS AT THE EDGE

From the atomistic point of view, if I draw two lines on the page then each line will be made from a certain number of these indivisible atoms and hence their lengths would be in a ratio of whole numbers corresponding to the number of atoms making up each line. But things didn't turn out to be so orderly. In fact, it was Pythagoras' own theorem about right-angled triangles that revealed that the world of geometry could give rise to lines whose relative lengths could not be captured by simple fractions.

The dimensions of my dice already have hidden in them a challenge to this atomistic view of nature. Take two of the edges of the cube at 90 degrees to each other. They have equal length. Now consider the diagonal line across the face of the cube that completes the triangle made up from the two edges of equal length. How long is this diagonal line relative to the shorter sides?

Pythagoras' theorem about right-angled triangles says that the square of the length of the diagonal is equal to the sum of the squares of the lengths of the two shorter sides. If I set the length of the sides of my dice as 1, then Pythagoras' theorem implies that the length of the diagonal across the face of my dice is a number which, when you square it, is equal to 2. So what is this number?

The Babylonians had been fascinated by the challenge of calculating this length. Dating back to the Old Babylonian period (1800–1600 BC), a tablet housed at Yale University has an estimate for the distance. Written using the sexagesimal system, or base 60, they got the length to be:

$$1 + \frac{24}{60} + \frac{51}{60^2} + \frac{10}{60^3} = \frac{30,547}{21,600}$$

which in decimal notation comes out at 1.41421296296 . . . , where the 296 repeats itself infinitely often. It is true of all fractions that when written as decimals they repeat themselves after some point. Indeed, any decimal expansion which does repeat itself can always be written as a fraction. The Babylonian calculation is quite a feat. It is correct to six decimal places. But when you square that fraction it just misses being 2. What the ancient Greeks discovered is that however hard the Babylonian scribes tried, they would always find that their fractions just missed squaring to 2.

It was one of Pythagoras' followers, Hippasus, who is credited with the discovery that the Babylonians were doomed to failure. He proved that the length of this diagonal across the side of my dice could never be expressed as a fraction.

Pythagoras' theorem about right-angled triangles implied that this long side had length the square root of 2 times the length of the short sides. But Hippasus could prove that there was no fraction whose square was exactly 2. The proof uses one of the classic tools in the mathematician's arsenal: proof by contradiction. Hippasus began by assuming there was a fraction whose square was 2. By some deft manipulation this always led to the contradictory statement that there was a number that was both odd and even. The only way to resolve this contradiction was to realize that the original assumption must have been false: there can be no fraction whose square is 2.

His fellow Pythagoreans were reputed to be dismayed by the revelation that their beautiful right-angled triangles could produce such inharmonic lengths. The sect took a vow of silence, but when Hippasus let the discovery out of the bag, the story goes that he was drowned at sea for revealing such disharmony in the physical world. But these new numbers, called irrational numbers because they are not ratios of whole numbers, were not so easily silenced.

Irrational lengths inside the cube.

I certainly have the feeling that this length exists. I can see it on a ruler held up against the long side of the triangle. It is the distance between two opposite corners of any side of my dice. Yet try to write down the number as an infinite decimal and I can never capture it. It begins 1.414213562 . . . and then continues to infinity never repeating itself.

IRRATIONAL EXUBERANCE

The discovery by the ancient Greeks that there were lengths that couldn't be expressed as simple ratios of whole numbers led the mathematicians of the time to create new mathematics, the mathematics of irrational numbers, in order to truly take the measure of the universe. Other basic lengths like π, the circumference of a circle of unit diameter, also turned out to be irrational and not captured by ratios of whole numbers. Although the ancient Greeks knew 2000 years ago about the irrationality of the square root of 2, it took till the eighteenth century for Swiss mathematician Johann Heinrich Lambert to prove that no fraction could capture π.

Despite my aversion to things we cannot know, reading about numbers that can't be captured using simple whole-number ratios or fractions was one of the defining moments that sparked my love affair with mathematics. The same year that my music teacher introduced me to the trumpet in the storeroom cupboard, my maths teacher introduced me to the proof of the irrationality of the square root of 2. The proof was contained in one of the books my maths teacher recommended to me to ignite the mathematical fire in me. It worked. I was amazed to find that you could prove with a finite logical argument that only the infinite could articulate what a length such as the diagonal across a square measured. If I couldn't write out this length, the next best thing was knowing why I couldn't know this number.

Since reading that proof as a schoolkid I have learnt about alternative ways to explore these irrational numbers – so perhaps these are numbers we can know. There are infinite expressions with patterns that make the number less mysterious. For example,

$$\sqrt{2} = 2 \times \left(1 - \frac{1}{3}\right) \times \left(1 + \frac{1}{5}\right) \times \left(1 - \frac{1}{7}\right) \times \left(1 + \frac{1}{9}\right) \times \cdots$$

or

$$\pi = 4 \times \left(1 - \frac{1}{3} + \frac{1}{5} - \frac{1}{7} + \frac{1}{9} - \cdots\right)$$

The discovery of these expressions pulls these irrational numbers into the known. A fraction is a number whose decimal expansion repeats itself from some point. Couldn't I regard these expressions as a pattern, not too dissimilar from the repeating pattern of the decimal expansion of the fraction? The repeating pattern of the fraction means that there are two numbers whose ratio captures the number, while in the case of √2 and π I am resigned to needing infinitely many numbers to pin down these lengths. The question of whether something has to be finite to be known will haunt me continually throughout my journey to the frontiers of the unknown.

Of course, for any practical application of these numbers, I could probably get away with an approximation which is a fraction. Most engineers are happy to use the estimate 22/7 for π that Archimedes got by approximating a circle with a 96-sided figure. In fact, I need only know 39 digits of π to be able to calculate the circumference of a circle the size of the observable universe to a precision comparable to the size of a hydrogen atom. There even exists a formula that can tell me what the millionth digit of π is without calculating all the intervening digits. Not something that I'm desperate to know. But this formula will only ever give me finite knowledge of a number that necessitates the infinite to fully embrace it.

The discovery of these numbers seemed to imply an infinite divisibility of space. Only by dividing space infinitely would I be able to measure the precise dimensions of my simple cube. The discovery meant that in the West Aristotle's continuous view of matter would remain dominant until the Renaissance.

THE HARMONY OF TINY SPHERES

With the insights of the science of Newton's generation and beyond, the tide would turn in favour of the view that the universe is indeed made from basic building blocks. Newton's contemporary, Robert Boyle, was perhaps the first to question the Aristotelian view of matter, which had dominated for nearly 2000 years. In his book *The Sceptical Chymist*, Boyle challenged the idea that matter was made up of the four elements of fire, earth, air and water. These might be good descriptions of the states of matter but not of the constituents.

Instead, he argued for a new list of chemical elements. Not only that, he made what at the time was rather a heretical statement. He believed that these elements would be minute bodies or atoms differing only in 'bulk, figure, texture and motion'. This was regarded as theologically dangerous: a materialistic godless view of the world in the eyes of the Church, which had always favoured the Aristotelian view. Some have declared Boyle the Galileo of the chemical revolution.

Although Newton would concur with Boyle's proposal for a material world made from indivisible units, the mathematical tools that Newton developed at the same time as Boyle's work relied heavily on time and space being infinitely divisible. The calculus that allowed one to take a snapshot of a universe in constant flux made sense only as a process in which space is divided up into ever smaller pieces and then interpreting what happens in the limit as the pieces become infinitesimally small.

The question of the infinite divisibility of time and space had fuelled philosophical argument since the ancient Greek thinker Zeno of Elea came up with paradoxes that seemed to arise from this cutting up of space. For example, Zeno proposed that an arrow can never hit its target because it must first cover half the distance to the target, then half the distance again, and then half again, requiring infinitely many moves if it is ever going to make it to the target. The success of Newton's calculus reignited the debate. There were still those who considered such infinite divisibility as almost heretical.

Bishop Berkeley dedicated a whole treatise called *The Analyst* to arguing that trying to make sense of dividing by zero was absurd, which the subtitle made clear: it was 'Addressed to an Infidel MATHEMATICIAN'.

While most infidel mathematicians quickly latched on to the power of the calculus, Newton's other breakthroughs supported a view that, although space and time could be infinitely divided, matter could not. His idea of a world made up of indivisible matter would in time become the prevalent theory of the universe. But at this point it was still very much a theory without a great deal of evidence.

His theory of forces acting on large objects like planets and apples had been so successful that Newton believed that if the ideas worked on the very large and the medium sized then why not on the very small.

Why should there be a change in the way the laws of motion dictate the behaviour of the universe as we zoom in on my dice? The success of his calculus when applied to the movement of the planets depended on regarding them as single points with the mass concentrated at a point corresponding to the centre of gravity of the body. Maybe all matter consisted of particles like tiny planets whose behaviour was determined by his laws of motion. In his *Principia* he stated his belief that by applying his ideas to these individual particles one could predict the behaviour of all material things.

Newton's theory of light also contributed to the growing feeling that an atomistic perspective was the best way to understand the world. Regarding light as a particle seemed the easiest way to describe the phenomena he documented in his book *Opticks*. The way that light reflected seemed to mimic the behaviour of a billiard ball as it bounced off the sides of the table. But from a scientific point of view there was no empirical evidence for this model of a universe made from indivisible particles.

Even with the microscopes that were emerging in the seventeenth century, you couldn't see anything to justify this atomistic model. Even if you could see discrete objects, it wouldn't prove anything about their indivisibility. But we can judge that the tide was turning by the fact that the atomistic view of matter made it into the popular culture of the time. Nicholas Brady's 'Ode to Saint Cecilia', set to music by Purcell in 1691, talks of seeds of matter:

> Soul of the World! Inspir'd by thee,
> The jarring Seeds of Matter did agree,
> Thou didst the scatter'd Atoms bind,
> Which, by thy Laws of true proportion join'd,
> Made up of various Parts one perfect Harmony.

The best evidence for an atomistic view of matter came a hundred years later from experiments that showed how matter combined to make new materials. And it was full of perfect harmony, as Brady had intimated.

ATOMIC ALGEBRA

It was the work of the English chemist John Dalton at the beginning of the nineteenth century that provided the first real experimental justification for thinking of matter as made of indivisible atoms. His discovery that compounds seemed to be made up of substances that were combined in fixed whole-number ratios was the breakthrough, and it led to the scientific consensus that these substances really did come in discrete packages.

For example: 'The elements of oxygen may combine with a certain portion of nitrous gas or with twice that portion, but with no intermediate quantity.' It certainly didn't constitute a proof that matter was discrete, and it was not strong enough to knock the belief of those who favoured a continuous model of matter. But it was highly suggestive. There had to be some explanation for the way these substances were combining.

The notation developed to express these reactions added to the atomistic view. The combination of nitrogen and oxygen could be expressed algebraically as $N + O$ or $N + 2O$. There was nothing in between. It seemed that all compounds came in proportions that were whole-number ratios. For example, aluminium sulphide was given algebraically as $2Al + 3S = Al_2S_3$, elements combining in a 2-to-3 ratio. Elements never combined in a non-whole-number relationship. It was like musical harmony at the heart of the chemical world. The music of tiny spheres.

The Russian scientist Dmitri Mendeleev is remembered for laying out this growing list of molecular ingredients in such a way that a pattern began to emerge, a pattern based on whole numbers and counting. It seemed that the Pythagorean belief in the power of number was making a comeback. Like several scientists before him, Mendeleev arranged them in increasing relative weight, but he realized that to get the patterns he could see emerging he needed to be flexible.

He'd written the known elements down on cards and was continually placing them on his desk in a game of chemical patience, trying to get them to yield their secrets. But nothing worked. It was driving him crazy. Eventually he collapsed in exhaustion and the secret emerged in a dream that, when he woke, gave him the pattern for laying out the cards. One of the important points that led to his successful arrangement was the realization that he needed to leave some gaps – that some of the cards from the pack were missing.

The key to his arrangement was something called the atomic number, which depended on the number of protons inside the nucleus rather than the combination of protons and neutrons that gave rise to the overall weight. But since no one had any clue yet about these smaller ingredients, Mendeleev was guessing somewhat at the underlying reason for his arrangement.

It was a bit like recognizing that a conventional pack of cards can be laid out in suits, but also that across those suits there are cards that are of equal value. A periodicity of eight seemed to underlie the elements, so that elements eight along seemed to share very similar properties. Eight on from lithium was sodium, followed after another eight by potassium. All soft shiny highly reactive metals. Similar patterns matched up gases with related properties.

This rule of eight had been picked up before Mendeleev's breakthrough and was called the law of octaves. It was compared to the musical octave: if I play the eight notes of a major scale on my cello, the top and bottom notes sound very similar and are given the same letter names. When this law of atomic octaves was proposed by its originator John Newlands, it was laughed out of the Royal Society. 'Next you'll be trying to tell us that the elements can be understood by putting them in alphabetical order', joked one Fellow. Mendeleev's arrangement confirmed to a certain extent the veracity of this law of octaves. It was this idea of repeating or periodic patterns that led to Mendeleev's arrangement being called the periodic table.

Mendeleev's genius was to realize that if sometimes the elements didn't quite match up, it perhaps indicated a missing element. The gaps in his table were probably his most insightful contribution. The fact that there was a hole in the 31st place of his table, for example, led Mendeleev to predict in 1871 the existence and properties of a new substance that would later be called gallium. Four years later French chemist Lecoq de Boisbaudran isolated the first samples of this new atom, predicted thanks to the mathematical patterns discovered by Mendeleev.

RECIPE FOR MAKING A DICE

Here then was a list of the atoms that were meant to make up all of matter. For example, my dice is made from putting together carbon atoms, oxygen atoms and hydrogen atoms into a structure called cellulose acetate. My own body is predominantly made up of combinations of these atoms but with a different structure. The cellulose acetate is a homogeneous structure free from bubbles, which makes it more likely to be fair. The more antique dice were made from a nitrate-based cellulose concocted by John Wesley Hyatt in 1868. His cocktail of nitric acid, sulphuric acid, cotton fibres and camphor produced an impressive substance with great tensile strength that resisted the effects of water, oils and even diluted acids.

Hyatt's brother named it celluloid and it became a highly cost-effective substitute for objects that had previously been carved out of ivory or horn. Billiard balls and removable collars, piano keys and even my dice were made from this synthetic plastic. The dice that were made from cellulose nitrate were the industry standard in the early twentieth century, but after several decades of use they would almost instantaneously crystallize and decompose, crumbling in on themselves and releasing nitric acid gas.

The real collectors' dice are those Vegas dice made from cellulose nitrate in the late Forties that avoided this crystallization. My dice won't suffer the same fate. Here is a picture of how the atoms are put together inside my dice.

The identification of these elements was not a proof of a discrete model of matter. There was no reason that this picture of the ingredients of my dice couldn't be a formula for the way a continuous structure combines. Although the chemists were tending towards an atomistic view of the universe, this was far from the case in the physics community. Those, like the German physicist Ludwig Boltzmann, who proposed atomic models of matter were laughed out of the lab.

Boltzmann believed that this atomic theory was a powerful way to interpret the concept of heat based on the idea that a gas was made up of tiny molecules bashing around like a huge game of micro-billiards. Heat was just the combined kinetic energy of these tiny moving balls. Using this model, combined with ideas of probability and statistics, he was successfully able to explain the large-scale behaviour of a gas. But most physicists were still committed to a continuous view of matter and were very dismissive of Boltzmann's ideas.

Boltzmann was so ridiculed that he was forced to retreat from his belief that this billiard-ball theory of matter represented a true picture of reality, and instead was obliged to refer to it as a heuristic model if he wanted to get his ideas in print. As Ernst Mach, his great nemesis in the debate about the reality of atoms, declared mockingly: 'Have you ever seen an atom?'

Boltzmann was plagued by fits of depression, and there is evidence that he was in fact bipolar. The rejection of his ideas by the scientific community is believed to have contributed to the depression that struck in 1906 and that led to him hanging himself during a holiday with his family near Trieste while his daughter and wife were out swimming.

It was a tragic end, not least because the most convincing evidence that he was right was just emerging. And it was one of the big names of physics who produced ideas that supported the atomistic view and were very hard to ignore. The work that Einstein and others did on Brownian motion would prove extremely difficult to explain for those who, like Mach, believed in a continuous view of the world.

POLLEN PING-PONG

Although conventional microscopes don't allow one to see individual atoms, they did allow scientists in the nineteenth century to see the effect that these atoms were having on their surroundings. It's called Brownian motion after Robert Brown, who in 1827 noticed the random behaviour of small particles of pollen floating on the surface of water. Since pollen was organic, Brown's first thought was that it might be exhibiting signs of life as it jumped around the surface. A similar random behaviour of coal dust floating on alcohol had also been observed by Dutch scientist Jan Ingenhousz in 1785. When Brown saw the pollen's behaviour replicated by inorganic matter, he was rather stumped as to what was causing the jittery motion.

It's striking that the idea that it might be invisible atoms bashing into the larger visible material had been suggested by the Roman poet Lucretius in his didactic poem *On the Nature of Things*:

> Observe what happens when sunbeams are admitted into a building and shed light on its shadowy places. You will see a multitude of tiny particles mingling in a multitude of ways . . . their dancing is an actual indication of underlying movements of matter that are hidden from our sight . . . It originates with the atoms which move of themselves. Then those small compound bodies that are least removed from the impetus of the atoms are set in motion by the impact of their invisible blows and in turn cannon against slightly larger bodies. So the movement mounts up from the atoms and gradually emerges to the level of our senses, so that those bodies are in motion that we see in sunbeams, moved by blows that remain invisible.

This was written in 60 BC, but it would take Einstein's mathematical analysis of the motion to confirm this atomic explanation of the random movement in Lucretius' sunbeams and Brown's pollen.

The goal is to provide some model that will produce the strange motion exhibited by the small pieces of pollen on the surface of the water. If you divide the surface into a grid, there seems to be an equal probability that the pollen will move left–right–up–down. It is similar to the motion of a drunken man who randomly makes steps according to the toss of a four-sided dice. The picture below shows the paths of various particles of pollen as plotted by the French physicist Jean Baptiste Perrin, who took up the challenge of explaining the pollen's motion in his book *Les Atomes*.

The proposal emerged at the beginning of the twentieth century that scientists were observing the pollen being buffeted by the motion of much smaller molecules of water.

It was Einstein's mathematical brilliance that allowed him to analyse this model in which a large object was subjected to the impact of much smaller objects that were moving randomly. He proved that the model predicted precisely the observed behaviour. Think of an ice rink with a large puck sitting in the middle of the rink and then introduce a whole system of tiny pucks that are set off in random directions at particular speeds. Every now and again the tiny pucks will hit the large puck, causing it to move in one direction. The skill was to assess how many small pucks you would need, and their relative size, in order to produce the observed behaviour of the larger puck.

Einstein's success in producing such a mathematical model that replicated the motion of the pollen was a devastating blow to anyone who believed that a liquid like water was a continuous substance. It was very hard for anyone who still believed in Aristotle's view of matter to come up with a comparably convincing explanation.

The calculations allowed one to estimate how small the molecules of water were in comparison with the pollen they were knocking around. Although it was convincing evidence that matter came in discrete pieces, it did not answer the question of whether you could still infinitely divide these pieces into ever smaller parts.

Indeed, the indivisible atoms turned out to be far from indivisible with the discovery of smaller constituents that made up atoms of carbon or oxygen. The next layer down revealed that an atom is made up of even tinier pucks called electrons, protons and neutrons, the first of which had already come to light some eight years before Einstein's theoretical breakthrough.

PULLING APART THE ATOM

The way science works is that you can hang on to your model of the universe until something pops up that doesn't fit: something new that you can't seem to explain with the current model. The realization that the atom might be made up of smaller bits emerged out of experiments that revealed something particle-like but much tinier than the atoms that made up the periodic table.

This tiny particle-like object materialized from the British physicist J. J. Thomson's experiments at the end of the nineteenth century to understand electricity. He had been investigating how electricity was conducted through a gas. Early experiments took a glass tube with two electrodes at either end, and by applying a high voltage between the electrodes an electric current was produced. The strange thing was that he seemed to be able to actually see the current because an arc of light appeared between the two electrodes.

Things became even stranger when he removed the gas completely from the tube and applied the voltage across a vacuum. The arc of light disappeared. But, bizarrely, the glass at the end of one tube was found to fluoresce. Stick a metal cross in the tube and a cross-shaped shadow appeared in the middle of the glowing fluorescent patch.

Electrons emitted from the cathode that hit the opposite wall
cause the glass to fluoresce.

The shadow always appeared opposite the negative electrode, otherwise known as the cathode. The best explanation was that the cathode was emitting some sort of ray that interacted with matter and made it glow – either the gas in the tube or, in the case of the vacuum, the glass of the tube itself.

These 'cathode rays' were something of a mystery. They were found to pass right through thin sheets of gold when they were placed in the way. Were they some sort of wave-like phenomenon like light? Others thought they were made up of negatively charged particles spat out by the negative electrode and then attracted to the positive electrode. But how could these particles pass through solid gold?

If they were negatively charged particles, then, Thomson believed, he should be able to change their path through the tube by applying a magnetic field. The German physicist Heinrich Hertz had already tried this and failed, but Hertz hadn't removed enough gas, which interfered with the experiment. With the gas removed, things worked just as Thomson had hoped. Apply a magnetic field to the rays and sure enough the shadow shifted. The rays were being bent by the magnet.

The real surprise came when Thomson made a mathematical calculation of what the mass of these charged particles must be. If you apply a force to a mass then, as Newton's laws of motion state, the amount you'll be able to move it will depend on the mass. So the amount of deflection that a magnetic field will cause will have encoded in it information about the mass of this proposed particle.

The calculation also depends on the charge on the particle, and once this was determined in a separate experiment Thomson could work out the mass. The answer was startling. It was nearly 2000 times smaller than the mass of a hydrogen atom, the smallest atom in the periodic table.

That these particles seemed to originate from the metal making up the electrode led to the hunch that these particles were actually smaller constituents of the atom. The atom wasn't indivisible after all. There were smaller bits. They were called electrons, the name originating from the Greek word for amber, the first substance to exhibit a charge.

The discovery that atoms are made up of even smaller constituents was a shock to many scientists' view of the world. After Thomson gave a lecture on his findings:

> I was told long afterwards by a distinguished physicist who had been present at my lecture that he thought I had been pulling their leg.

THE NEXT LAYER

Even when Thomson used a different metal, the masses of particles emitted by the metal didn't change. It seemed like every atom had these particles as constituents. The first thought was that a hydrogen atom, given that it is 2000 times heavier than this new electron, might be made up of 2000 or so of these electrons. But a helium atom was roughly four times the mass of a hydrogen atom. Why would the number of electrons jump from 2000 to 4000 with nothing in between? This whole-number ratio between masses of atoms in the periodic table had been one of the reasons for supposing they were truly atomic. So what could account for these discrete steps in mass? Furthermore, atoms were electrically neutral. So were there other particles that cancelled out the charge on the electron? Could you get atoms to emit positive particles to counter these negative electrons?

There was actually evidence in the experiments for a positive ray of particles running in the opposite direction. When a magnetic field was applied, they were much harder to deflect, implying that they were more massive than the electrons. The curious feature this time was that the masses of these particles seemed to vary according to the gas that was being used to fill the tubes. For hydrogen the mass was essentially the mass of the atom you started with. It seemed that the hydrogen atoms in the tube were having their electrons stripped off, leaving a large positive particle that was then attracted to the opposite electrode.

Thomson managed to achieve a similar effect with other gases: helium, nitrogen, oxygen. The masses were all whole-number multiples of the positive particle produced by the hydrogen atom. Atomic harmony yet again. As yet, there was no reason to believe that there weren't just many sorts of positive particles, just as there were many sorts of atoms. Thomson had suggested a model of the atom known as the plum pudding. The positively charged part of the atom, which was more massive than the negative electron, formed the pudding making up the bulk of the atom, while the electrons were the tiny fruit inside.

Then the age of the bombardment of the atom began which would eventually lead to the ultimate atom smasher: the Large Hadron Collider at CERN. The New Zealand-born British physicist Ernest Rutherford is generally credited with the discovery of the proton, the particle that was the building block for all these positive particles that Thomson had investigated.

Rutherford became fascinated by the new subject of radioactivity. Uranium atoms seemed to be spitting out particles that could be picked up by photographic plates. There appeared to be two types of radiation, and these became known as alpha particles and beta particles. The alpha particles were more easily detected. Rutherford found that using a magnetic field he could deflect these alpha rays in the same way that Thomson had deflected the negative particles. Calculations showed that they had the same mass as the stripped helium atoms. Their hunch that the alpha rays being emitted by the uranium were actually bits of helium atoms was confirmed when the alpha rays were combined with a shower of electrons, which resulted in a stable gas being formed. Chemical analysis soon confirmed that the gas was indeed helium.

TISSUE PAPER BALLISTICS

It was when Rutherford's student Hans Geiger placed a thin sheet of gold foil between a stream of alpha particles and the plate detecting the particles that the evidence once again contradicted the theoretical model of the atom. In the model of the atom which has positive charge distributed evenly like a pudding, positive alpha particles passing through the metal would be repelled by the positive charge in the atom. Given that the charge is distributed over the full extent of the atom, you wouldn't expect much deflection.

Alpha particles being deflected by the nuclei of atoms of gold.

Geiger found that, on the contrary, some of the alpha particles were deflected wildly, to the extent that some bounced back off the gold foil in the direction they'd been fired from. Rutherford was staggered: 'It was as if you fired a 15-inch shell at a piece of tissue paper and it came back and hit you.'

Again it was mathematical calculations that gave rise to a new model. By counting how many alpha particles were deflected, and by how much, they discovered that the data was consistent with the charge and mass being concentrated in a tiny centre of the atom, which became known as the nucleus. It still wasn't clear whether this nucleus was indivisible or not.

When Rutherford bombarded lighter atoms with alpha particles evidence emerged that the nucleus wasn't a single entity but made up of constituent particles. Tracing the paths of the alpha particles in a cloud chamber, he detected paths that were four times longer than they should be. It was as if another particle four times as light was being kicked out of the nucleus by the impact of the alpha particles. Different gases produced the same result. Indeed, Rutherford found that pure nitrogen was being converted into oxygen by the impact. Knock out one of these particles and the element changed.

Here was evidence for a building block from which all nuclei of atoms were built. It behaved just like the hydrogen atom with its electron stripped off. Rutherford had discovered the proton. The nuclei of atoms were built by taking multiples of this proton. The only trouble was that the charge on the atom didn't make sense. Helium had a nucleus that was four times as heavy as the hydrogen atom, yet the charge was only twice as big. Perhaps there were electrons in the nuclei attached to protons, cancelling out the charge. But the physics being developed to explain the behaviour of these particles precluded electrons and protons in such close proximity, so that couldn't be the answer.

This led Rutherford in the 1920s to guess that there might be a third constituent, which he called a neutron, with the same ball-park mass as the proton but no charge. Producing evidence for this particle proved very tricky. He used to discuss with his colleague James Chadwick crazy ways by which they might reveal the neutron. Experiments conducted in the 1930s in Germany and France eventually picked up particles being emitted when various nuclei were bombarded with alpha particles, and, unlike the proton, these particles did not seem to possess any charge. But the experimenters mistakenly believed it was some sort of electromagnetic radiation, like the high-frequency gamma rays that had been discovered by French physicist Paul Villard at the beginning of the century.

Chadwick, though, was convinced that these particles must be the neutrons he'd discussed with Rutherford. Further experiments revealed that they had mass just slightly bigger than the proton, and without charge this new particle was the missing ingredient that made sense of the numbers. With Chadwick's discovery it seemed as if the building blocks of matter had been revealed.

It was a very attractive model. Fire, earth, air and water, the four elements of Aristotle, had been reduced to three particles: the electron, proton and neutron. With these three building blocks scientists believed they could build all matter. Oxygen: 8 protons, 8 neutrons and 8 electrons. Sodium: 11 protons, 12 neutrons and 11 electrons. It was as if the music of the spheres was singing out and the foundations of matter were these notes: protons, electrons and neutrons. All matter seemed to be made up of whole-number combinations of these three particles. Why would you expect these particles to be made up of smaller entities? If they were, you might expect to see fractional pieces between the elements in the periodic table.

Except the dividing didn't stop there. It turned out that there were experimentally and mathematically very robust reasons to think that protons and neutrons were not indivisible. But the building blocks of the proton and neutron have a strange property: they don't like to be seen in isolation. They only come in groups, making up something like a proton or a neutron. Safety in numbers. So if they have never been seen on their own, why do scientists think there are even smaller bits into which we can divide protons and neutrons?

4

Everything we call real is made of things
that cannot be regarded as real.

Niels Bohr

At the end of the 1920s it seemed as if the basic building blocks of matter had been tracked down. The atoms of the periodic table could all be built by taking combinations of electrons, protons and neutrons. The electron has withstood any attempts to divide it further. But revelations over the next decades would lead scientists to believe that there was another layer of reality hiding below the other two building blocks.

The principal reason for the realization that protons and neutrons might not be as indivisible as the electron came not from more sophisticated technology but from the mathematics of symmetry. It is striking that time and again mathematics appears to be the best microscope we have to look inside my casino dice. A mathematical model began to emerge to explain the proton and the neutron, and it was built on a mathematical concept that could be divided. If the mathematics came apart into smaller pieces, the feeling was that the same should apply to the proton and the neutron.

The mathematical model responsible for this belief in the divisibility of the proton and neutron arose because physicists discovered that there were a lot more particles out there than just the three believed to be the constituents of stable atoms.

The discovery of these new particles was a result of collider experiments. Not human-constructed colliders like the LHC, but naturally occurring collisions that happen in the upper atmosphere when cosmic rays strike the atmosphere.

THE PARTICLE MENAGERIE

The first evidence of new particles was found in the cloud chambers that experimenters had built in their labs to record the paths of charged particles. Cloud chambers consist of a sealed tank full of a supersaturated vapour of water and alcohol. The supersaturation is such that any charged particle passing through leaves a trail of condensation behind it.

Carl Anderson, a physicist working at Caltech, had used these cloud chambers in 1933 to confirm the existence of a strange new sort of matter called antimatter that had been predicted some years earlier by British physicist Paul Dirac. Dirac's attempt to unify quantum physics and the theory of electromagnetism had successfully explained many things about electrons, but the equations seemed to have a complete mirror solution that didn't correspond to anything anyone had seen in the lab.

Dirac's equations were a bit like the equation $x^2 = 4$. There is the solution $x = 2$, but there is another mirror solution, namely $x = -2$, because -2×-2 is also equal to 4. The mirror solution in Dirac's equations implied that there was a mirror version of the electron with positive charge. Most thought this was a mathematical curiosity that emerged from the equations, but when, four years later, Anderson spotted in his cloud chamber traces of a particle behaving like an electron in a mirror, antimatter went from theory to reality. Anderson's positrons, as they came to be known, had been created in the particle interactions happening in the upper atmosphere. And they weren't the only new things to appear.

Even stranger particles that had not been predicted at all were soon leaving trails in Anderson's cloud chamber. Anderson started to analyse these new paths with his PhD student Seth Neddermeyer in 1936. The new particles corresponded to negatively charged particles passing through the cloud chamber. But they weren't electrons. The paths these new particles were leaving indicated a mass much larger than that of the electron. Just as Thomson had done, mass can be measured by how much the particle is deflected under the influence of a magnetic field.

The particle seemed to have the same charge as the electron but was much harder to deflect.

Now called the muon, it was one of the first new particles to be discovered in the interactions of cosmic rays with the atmosphere. The muon is unstable. It quickly falls apart into other particles, most often an electron and a couple of neutrinos. Neutrinos were another new particle that had been predicted to explain how neutrons decayed into protons. With almost no mass and no charge, it took until the 1950s before anyone actually detected these tiny particles, but they theoretically made sense of both neutron decay and the decay of this new muon. The decay rate of the muon was on average 2.2 microseconds, which is sufficiently slow that enough particles won't have decayed by the time they reach the surface of the Earth.

The muon helped to confirm Einstein's prediction from special relativity that time slows down as you approach the speed of light. Given its half-life, far fewer muons should be reaching the surface of the Earth than were being detected. The fact that time slows down close to the speed of light helps explain this discrepancy. If a clock was attached to the muon, it would show that a smaller interval of time had elapsed before it hit the Earth. Thus more muons would therefore survive, as revealed by experiment. I will return to this in the Fifth Edge when I consider pushing time to the limits of knowledge.

The muon appeared to behave remarkably like the electron but had greater mass and was more unstable. When the American physicist Isidor Rabi was told of the discovery, he quipped: 'Who ordered that?' It seemed strangely unnecessary for nature to reproduce a heavier, more unstable version of the electron. Little did Rabi realize how much more there was on the menu of particles.

Having realized that cosmic ray interactions with the upper atmosphere were creating new forms of matter, physicists decided that they better not wait for the particles to reach the cloud chambers in the labs, by which time the particles might have decayed into traditional forms of matter. So the cloud chambers were moved to high-altitude locations in the hope of picking up other particles.

The Caltech team chose the top of Mount Wilson near their home base in Pasadena. Sure enough, new tracks indicated that new particles were being picked up. Other teams placed photographic plates in observatories in the Pyrenees and the Andes to see if they could record different interactions. Teams in Bristol and Manchester also saw traces of new particles in their own photographic plates. It turned out that the muon was the least of Rabi's worries. A whole menagerie of new particles started showing up.

Some had masses about one-eighth that of a proton or neutron. They came in positively or negatively charged varieties and were dubbed pions. An electrically neutral version that was harder to detect was later discovered. In Manchester two photographs from their cloud chamber showed what appeared to be a neutral particle decaying into pions. The mass of these new particles was roughly half that of a proton. The cloud chamber at the top of Mount Wilson recorded more evidence to support the discovery of what would become known as kaons, four in number.

As time went on, more and more particles were uncovered, so much so that the whole thing became totally unwieldy. As Nobel Prize winner Willis Lamb quipped in his acceptance speech of 1955: 'The finder of a new elementary particle used to be rewarded by a Nobel Prize, but such a discovery now ought to be punished by a $10,000 fine.' The hope was that the periodic table would be simplified once scientists had discovered how it was put together using electrons, protons and neutrons. But these three particles turned out to be just the tip of the iceberg. Now there were over a hundred particles that seemed to make up the building blocks of matter. As Enrico Fermi admitted to a student at the time: 'Young man, if I could remember the name of these particles, I would have been a botanist.'

Just as Mendeleev had managed to find some sort of order with which to classify and make sense of the atoms in the periodic table, the search was on for a unifying principle that would explain these new muons, pions, kaons and other particles.

The underlying structure that finally seemed to make sense of this menagerie of particles – the map, as it were, to find your way around the zoo – ultimately came down to a piece of mathematics.

MAPPING THE PARTICLE ZOO

When you are trying to classify things, it helps to recognize the dominant characteristics that can gather a large mess of objects into smaller groups. In the case of animals, the idea of species creates some order in the animal kingdom. In particle physics one important invariant that helped divide the zoo into smaller groups was the idea of charge. How does the particle interact with the electromagnetic force? Electrons would bend one way, protons the other, and the neutron would be unaffected.

As these new particles emerged from the undergrowth, they could be passed through the gateway of the electromagnetic force. Some would join the electron's cage, others would head towards the proton, and the rest would be put together with the neutron – a first pass at imposing some order on the menagerie of particles.

But the electromagnetic force is one of four fundamental forces that have been identified at work in bringing the universe together. The other forces are gravity, and the strong nuclear force responsible for binding protons and neutrons together at close quarters inside the nucleus, and finally the weak nuclear force that controls things like radioactive decay.

The key was to identify other characteristics similar to the idea of charge that could distinguish the different behaviours of these particles with the other fundamental forces. For example, the mass of a particle was actually quite a good way of establishing some hierarchy in the particle zoo. It collected pions and kaons together as particles that were a factor lighter than the protons or neutrons that made up ordinary matter. A new collection of particles called Sigma, Xi and Lambda baryons had masses larger than the proton and neutron and often decayed into protons or neutrons.

Often particles with very similar masses got the same Greek names. Indeed, the proton and neutron have such similar masses that they were believed to be intimately related, so much so that the German physicist Werner Heisenberg (whose ideas will be at the heart of the next Edge) rechristened them nucleons. But mass was a rather rough and ready way of sorting these particles. Physicists were on the lookout for something more fundamental: a pattern as effective as the one Mendeleev had discovered to order atoms.

The key to finding patterns to make sense of the onslaught of new particles was a new property called strangeness. The name arose due to the rather strange behaviour demonstrated by some of these new particles as they decayed. Since mass is equivalent to energy via Einstein's equation $E=mc^2$, and nature favours low-energy states, particles with larger mass often try to find ways to decay into particles with smaller mass.

There are several mechanisms for this decay, each depending on one of the fundamental forces. Each mechanism has a characteristic signature which helps physicists to understand which fundamental force is causing the decay. Again it's energy considerations that control which is the most likely force at work in any particle decay. The strong nuclear force is usually the first to have a go at decaying a particle, and this will generally decay the particle within 10^{-24} of a second. Next in the hierarchy is the electromagnetic force, which might result in the emission of photons. The weak nuclear force is the most costly in energy terms and so takes longer. A particle that decays via the weak nuclear force is likely to take 10^{-11} seconds before it decays. So by observing the time it takes to decay, scientists can get some indication of which force is at work.

For example, a Delta baryon decays in 6×10^{-24} seconds to a proton and a pion via the strong nuclear force, while a Sigma baryon takes 8×10^{-11} seconds to decay to the same proton and pion. The longer time of decay indicates that it is controlled by the weak nuclear force. In the middle we have the example of a neutrally charged pion decaying via the electromagnetic force into two photons, which happens in 8.4×10^{-17} seconds.

Imagine a ball sitting in a valley. There is a path to the right which, with a little push, will take the ball over the hill into a lower valley. This path corresponds to the strong nuclear force. To the left is a higher hill which is also a path to a lower energy state. This direction represents the work of the weak nuclear force.

A Delta baryon Δ decays via the strong nuclear force to a proton and a pion. In contrast, a Sigma baryon Σ decays via the weak nuclear force.

So why did the Delta baryon find a way over the easy hill while the Sigma baryon went the long way? This seemed rather strange. There appeared to be certain particles that encountered a barrier (represented in the figure by a broken line) that prevented them from crossing via the easy route to the lower valley.

THERE IS NO EXQUISITE BEAUTY WITHOUT STRANGENESS

The physicists Abraham Pais, Murray Gell-Mann and Kazuhiko Nishijima came up with a cunning strategy to solve this puzzle. They proposed a new property like charge that mediated the way these particles interacted or didn't interact with the strong nuclear force. This new property, called strangeness, gave physicists a new way to classify all these new particles. Each new particle was given a measure of strangeness according to whether or not its decay would have to take the long route.

The idea is that the strong nuclear force can't change the strangeness of a particle, so if you have two particles with different strangeness, the strong nuclear force can't decay one into another. There is a barrier blocking the route to the lower valley. But the weak nuclear force can change strangeness. So since the strong nuclear force decays a Delta baryon into a proton, they have the same measure of strangeness equal to 0; while the Sigma baryon has a different value of strangeness because it needs the weak nuclear force to decay it to a proton, and its strangeness is given value –1. (It was a quirk of how all the different particles were numbered that these ones got given –1 rather than 1. It wouldn't really have changed anything had they been given value 1 and others –1.)

Then even more exotic particles were detected, created by higher-energy collisions that seemed to decay in two steps. They were called cascade particles. The proposal was that these were doubly strange, so were given strangeness number –2. The first step in the decay had strangeness –1 and then they ended up with protons and neutrons, which had strangeness 0. It may seem a bit like pulling a rabbit out of a hat, but that's part of the process of doing science. You keep pulling things out of the hat. Most of them you chuck away because they get you nowhere. But pull enough things out of the hat and every so often you'll get a rabbit. As Gell-Mann admitted: 'The strangeness theory came to me when I was explaining a wrong idea to someone, but then I made a slip of the tongue and I had the strangeness theory.' Strangeness turned out to be a pretty amazing rabbit.

Originally the idea of strangeness was meant just as a bookkeeping device, something that conveniently kept track of the decay patterns between particles. There wasn't meant to be any physical meaning to the idea of strangeness. It was just another set of cages to help classify the animals in the particle zoo. But it transpired that this new feature was actually the first hint of a much deeper physical reality at work underneath all these particles. The exciting moment came when they took particles of a similar sort of mass and began to plot them on a graph measuring their strangeness and charge together. What they got were pictures full of symmetry.

The pattern of particles created a hexagonal grid with two particles occupying the centre point of the grid. If one took the pions and kaons and arranged them on a grid of strangeness against charge, a similar

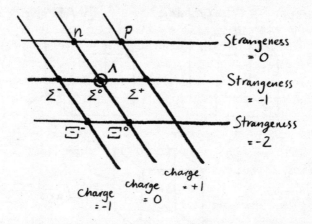

picture emerged. When you get a pattern like this you know you are on to something. The key to the deeper reality underneath these particles was spotting that the hexagonal patterns these particle pictures were making were not new – they'd been seen before. Not in physics, but in the mathematics of symmetry.

SYMMETRICAL ENLIGHTENMENT

To someone trained in the mathematics of symmetry, these arrangements of cages in a hexagonal pattern with a double point at the centre look very familiar. They are the signature of a very particular symmetrical object called SU(3).

For me this is brilliant. Symmetry is something I know about. This gives me a chance to get a handle on what is going on in the depths of my dice. In fact, my dice is a perfect vehicle to explain the ideas that are at the heart of the mathematics of symmetry. The symmetries of my cube (disregarding the spots) are all the ways I can pick my dice up, spin it, and place it back down again so that it looks like it did before I started spinning it. There are actually 24 different moves I can make. For example, I could just rotate the cube by a quarter of a turn round one of the faces or I could spin the dice by a third round one of the axis running through opposite corners of the cube.

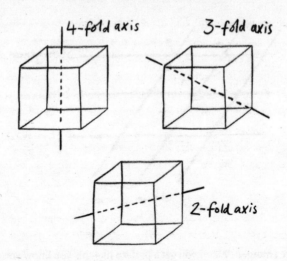

In total there are 24 different moves I can make (including a strange one where I just leave the cube where it is and do nothing). This collection of symmetrical moves is given the name S4, or the symmetric group of degree 4. If I include mirror symmetry, which means I also view the dice in a mirror, there are in total 48 different symmetries of my cube.

The cube should be thought of as the geometrical shape in three dimensions on which the group of symmetries S4 act. But there are other geometric shapes whose symmetries will be the same. For example, the octahedron is another three-dimensional geometric shape whose group of symmetries is the same as that of the cube. But there are higher-dimensional objects whose symmetries are also S4. So there are lots of different geometries that have the same underlying group of symmetries.

It was not the symmetries of my dice behind the hexagonal pictures made up of particles, but a symmetrical object called SU(3). SU(3) stands for 'the special unitary group in dimension 3', but it can describe the symmetries of a range of different geometric objects in different dimensions. The hexagonal grids created by the particles are the same as the picture mathematicians use to describe the way SU(3) acts on an object in eight-dimensional space. The eight particles of the hexagonal grid correspond to the number of dimensions you need to create this symmetrical object.

This hexagonal picture was the Rosetta Stone that opened up a whole new culture at play in particle physics, though it was a different cultural analogy that took hold to highlight the breakthrough. The guiding light of this figure with eight particles corresponding to this eight-dimensional representation led to the phenomenon being called the eightfold way, invoking the Buddhist idea of the eightfold way to spiritual enlightenment.

There were other pictures which corresponded to objects in different dimensions that SU(3) could act on. The exciting revelation was that these different pictures could be used to collect together other members of the particle menagerie. The different geometric representations of the symmetries of SU(3) seemed to be responsible for the different physical particles that make up matter in the universe.

It is amazing to me how time and again the physical world seems to turn into a piece of mathematics. We have to ask to what extent this is just a good story that helps tie the physical universe together, or is the physical universe actually a piece of physicalized mathematics? With this new link, fundamental particles became pieces of geometry that are stabilized by this group of symmetries acting on the geometric space.

Heisenberg was right when he wrote: 'Modern physics has definitely decided in favour of Plato. In fact, the smallest units of matter are not physical objects in the ordinary sense; they are forms, ideas which can be expressed unambiguously only in mathematical language.' Plato's watery icosahedron and fiery tetrahedron have been replaced by this strange new symmetrical shape SU(3).

When the physical world turns into a piece of mathematics, I immediately feel that this is something I can comprehend. The mathematics of symmetry is my language. For most, turning fundamental particles into maths means a move away from things that they know. Comparing particles to billiard balls or waves lends the particles a more tangible reality. How can we know anything unless it grows out of how we physically interact with the world around us? Even the abstract language of eight-dimensional symmetrical objects is possible only because we are abstracting the ideas of things we have physically encountered, like the symmetry of my Las Vegas cube.

SYMMETRY WITH MANY FACES

The essential point here is that you can have several different geometric objects whose underlying group of symmetries is the same. Conversely, if I have a group of symmetries, there can be many different physical objects whose symmetries are described by that group. Mathematicians say that the object is a representation of the abstract group of symmetries, in the same way three apples or three dice are both physical manifestations of the abstract concept of the number 3. For example, if I take my casino cube, there are 24 different rotations that I can make. If I consider the four diagonal lines running between the opposite corners of the cube, these rotations permute these lines around.

In fact, if I put four playing cards (Ace, King, Queen and Jack) on the corners then each rotation is like shuffling these four cards: there are 24 different ways to shuffle four cards. But I can get yet another physical representation of this group of symmetries. If I take a tetrahedron and consider the rotations and reflections of this shape, there are again 24 different symmetries. If I stick the playing cards on the faces of the four-faced triangular pyramid, the symmetries of the tetrahedron give us the 24 different ways the cards can be shuffled. The group of symmetries now has two distinct three-dimensional realizations as the symmetry of some geometric object: one as the rotations of a cube, the other as the rotations and reflections of a tetrahedron. It turns out that if you look at all the physical geometric representations of this object called SU(3) in all dimensions, the symmetrical objects give you a way of generating all the different fundamental particles that were appearing.

It was physicists Gell-Mann and Yuval Ne'eman who in 1961 independently recognized the patterns in these particles. Ne'eman was in fact combining his physics with a career in the IDF, the Israeli Defence Force, and had been posted to London as their military attaché. He'd meant to study general relativity at King's College, but when he realized that it was miles from the Israeli Embassy in Kensington he decided instead to check out what was happening five minutes down the road at Imperial College. They were doing particle physics. Ne'eman turned his attention from the very big to the very small.

Although the pattern for the Lambda, Sigma and Xi particles, together with the proton and neutron, matched the eight-dimensional symmetry of SU(3), the corresponding pattern of kaons and pions was missing a particle at its centre. It was either wrong or there was a new particle to be discovered. Gell-Mann published his prediction of this missing particle in a Caltech preprint in early 1961. Sure enough, the Eta particle was discovered a few months later by physicists in Berkeley.

This is the perfect scenario for a new theory. If it makes a physical prediction that is subsequently confirmed, you know you're on to a winner. The same thing happened again when both Gell-Mann and Ne'eman attended a conference in June 1962 at CERN. At the conference a whole host of new particles was announced: three Sigma-star baryons with strangeness –1, and two Xi-star baryons of strangeness –2. The guess was that these particles would correspond to one of the other pictures that show how the group of symmetries SU(3) acts on a symmetrical object in higher dimension.

As Gell-Mann and Ne'eman independently sat there in the lecture filling in their pictures of how to arrange these new particles, a different picture began to emerge corresponding to another of the symmetrical objects that SU(3) acts on, an object in ten dimensions. But one of the corners of the picture was missing. There were only nine particles. Both Gell-Mann and Ne'eman simultaneously realized that one place had been left empty, leading to the prediction of a new particle. It was Gell-Mann who stuck his hand up first and predicted the Omega particle with strangeness –3, a prediction that would be confirmed in January 1964.

It was the twentieth-century version of the story of Mendeleev's periodic table: a recognition of an underlying pattern but with missing jigsaw pieces. Just as the discovery of the missing atoms gave credence to Mendeleev's model, so too the discovery of these missing particles helped convince scientists that these mathematical patterns were powerful ways to navigate the particle zoo.

It transpired that the patterns Mendeleev discovered in the periodic table were actually the result of these atoms being made from the more fundamental ingredients of the proton, electron and neutron. There was a feeling that the patterns in all the newly discovered particles hinted at a similar story: the existence of more fundamental building blocks at the heart of the hundreds of particles that were being detected.

QUARKS: THE MISSING LAST LAYER?

A number of physicists had spotted that if you place the patterns corresponding to the different multidimensional representations of SU(3) in layers, you get a pyramid shape – with the top layer missing. There should be something akin to a simple triangle sitting on top of all this. This corresponded to the simplest physical representation of SU(3) acting on a three-dimensional geometry. If you looked at these layers from the perspective of symmetry, this missing layer was really the one from which you could grow all the other layers. But no one had spotted any particles that corresponded to this missing layer.

Triangle hinting at three new particles: the up quark u,
the down quark d, and the strange quark s.

Robert Serber, who had been Oppenheimer's right-hand man during
the Manhattan Project, was one of those who conjectured that maybe
this extra layer suggested three fundamental particles that could be used
to build all the particles corresponding to the other layers. At a lunch
with Gell-Mann in 1963, Serber explained his idea, but when Gell-
Mann challenged him to explain what electrical charge these hypothetical particles would have, Serber wasn't sure. Gell-Mann started
scribbling on a napkin and soon had the answer. The charges would
be ⅔ or –⅓ of the charge on a proton. The answer seemed ridiculous.
'That would be a funny quirk,' Gell-Mann commented. Nowhere in
physics had anything been observed that wasn't a whole-number multiple of the charge on the electron or proton.

It was reminiscent of the days of Pythagoras. Everything was meant
to be made up of whole-number multiples, but here was something that
seemed to cut this basic unit into pieces. They were still whole-number
ratios, but no one had ever seen such fractional charges. Although
Gell-Mann was initially sceptical about these hypothetical particles
with fractional charge, by the evening they were beginning to work
their magic on him. In the subsequent weeks he began teasing out the
implications of these ideas, calling the particles 'kworks' whenever he
talked about them, a word he had used previously to denote 'funny
little things'. Serber believed the word was a play on the idea of the
quirkiness Gell-Mann had mentioned at lunch.

It was while perusing James Joyce's experimental novel *Finnegans
Wake* that Gell-Mann came across a passage that determined how he

would spell the word he was using to describe these hypothetical particles. It was the opening line of a poem ridiculing King Mark, the cuckolded husband in the Tristan myth, that caught his attention: 'Three quarks for Muster Mark!'

Given that there were three of these hypothetical new particles that could be used to build the other layers, the reference seemed perfect. The only trouble was that Joyce clearly intended the new word 'quark' to rhyme with 'Mark' not 'kwork'. But the spelling and pronunciation Gell-Mann wanted won out.

These quarks would eventually become what we now believe to be the last layer in the construction of matter. But it would take some time for the idea to catch on. During a conversation on the telephone to his former PhD supervisor about these quarks, Gell-Mann was stopped in his tracks: 'Murray, let's be serious . . . this is an international call.'

For Gell-Mann the patterns seemed too beautiful not to have at least some underlying truth to them. The idea was that sitting below these layers of particles was a new layer of three fundamental particles: the up quark, the down quark and the strange quark, with charge ⅔, –⅓ and –⅓ respectively. The other particles were made up of combinations of these quarks (and their antiparticles in the case of kaons and pions). The number of strange quarks in the make-up determined the

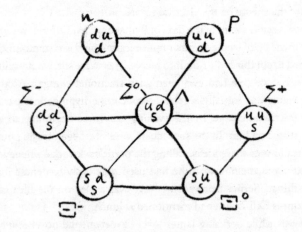

The quark ingredient of the eightfold way.

strangeness of the particle. So I can redraw the picture of the eightfold way made of the proton, neutron, Sigma, Xi and Lambda particles in terms of these quark ingredients.

As I sweep up the picture, the number of strange quarks drops by one at each step. If I head off in the direction of increasing charge I see at each step an increase in the up quark, the quark with charge ⅔. There is a third direction which controls the increase of down quarks. The other layers of particles had similar stories.

Gell-Mann wasn't the only one to play with the idea of pulling matter apart into these smaller particles. American physicist George Zweig also believed these patterns hinted at a more fundamental layer of particles. He called them aces, but, probably more than Serber or Gell-Mann, he believed that these particles had a physical reality. His preprints explaining his ideas were dismissed as 'complete rubbish' by the head of the theory group at CERN. Even Gell-Mann, who had come up with similar ideas, didn't regard them as more than a mathematical model that created some coherent order in the pictures they were drawing. They were a mnemonic, not concrete reality. Gell-Mann dismissed Zweig's belief in the physical reality of these particles: 'The concrete quark model – that's for blockheads.'

FROM FANTASY TO REALITY

That would all change when evidence emerged from experiments conducted at the end of the 1960s by physicists working at the Stanford Linear Accelerator Center in which protons were bombarded with electrons. Analysis of a proton's charge reveals that it can be thought to have a size which spreads over a region of 10^{-15} metres. The belief was that the proton would be uniformly distributed across this small region. But when electrons were fired at the proton blob, the researchers got a shock from the resulting scatter patterns. Rather like the surprise Rutherford got when atoms of gold were bombarded with alpha particles, the proton, like the atom, turned out to be mostly empty space.

The scattering was consistent with a proton that was made up of three smaller particles. Just as in Rutherford's experiments, every now and again one of these electrons would score a direct hit with one of these three points and come shooting back towards the source of the electrons. The experiment seemed to confirm the idea that the proton was made up of three quarks. Although a quark has never been seen in the open, the scattering of the electrons indicated that, sure enough, there were three smaller particles that made up the proton.

It turns out that the blockheads were right. The up, down and strange quarks were not just a mathematical mnemonic but seemed to be a physical reality. It was discovered that these three quarks weren't enough to cover all the new particles, and eventually we've found ourselves with six quarks together with their antiparticles. In addition to the three Gell-Mann named, three more appeared on the scene: the charm quark, the top quark and the bottom quark.

The discovery of this way of ordering the menagerie of particles in physics using the mathematics of symmetry is one of the most exciting discoveries of the twentieth century. Seeing these fundamental particles lining up in patterns that were already sitting there in the mathematics of symmetry must have been so thrilling. If I could choose a discovery in physics that I would have loved to have made, this one would rank pretty high. It must have been like an archaeologist coming across patterns that had previously been seen only in some other distant part of the world. Seeing such distinctive patterns, you knew there had to be a connection between the two cultures.

The weird thing is that this pyramid of triangles and hexagons giving rise to different representations of SU(3) goes on to infinity, implying that you could keep on gluing together more and more of these quarks to make more and more exotic particles. The physical model seemed to run out at the layer that pieces together three quarks. But announcements from the LHC in 2015 revealed exciting evidence for a five-quark particle. The researchers at CERN almost missed the particle, called a pentaquark, thinking it was just background noise. But when they tried to remove the noise they discovered a strong signal pointing towards this next layer in the symmetry tower. As one of the researchers working at CERN admitted: 'We didn't go out looking for a pentaquark. It's a particle that found us.'

How much further can we push the mathematics to make predictions of what else we might see in the LHC? There is an even bigger symmetrical object called SU(6) that would unite all six quarks – up, down, strange, charm, top and bottom – into a fusion of fascinating particles. Instead of the two-dimensional pictures I've drawn combining particles together in families, you'd need five-dimensional pictures. Although it is possible to cook up some of these more exotic combinations of quarks, because the mass differences between the basic quarks get larger and larger, the beautiful mathematical symmetry gets broken and the reality of such particles becomes less and less plausible. Indeed, the top quark is so unstable that it decays before it ever has time to bind to another quark. Why the quarks have these different masses seems to be a question that the physicists don't know the answer to – yet. The mathematics seems to suggest a much richer cocktail of particles than physical reality can actually sustain. Reality seems a pale shadow of what might be possible mathematically. However, understanding that reality still holds many challenges.

I must admit that, even with the mathematical toolkit that I've spent years putting together, I'm still not sure I know what these quarks really are. I've sat at my desk poring over books on particle physics for months – for example, Sudbury's *Quantum Mechanics and the Particles of Nature* – and lecture notes downloaded for Oxford graduate courses on symmetry and particle physics. And as I sit here surrounded by these tales of the inner workings of my dice, I begin to despair a little. There is so much that I still don't know: path integrals describing the futures of these particles, the inner workings of the Klein–Gordon equations, what exactly those Feynman diagrams that physicists so easily draw up on the board really mean. I look enviously at my son who has started his degree in physics. He will have the time to steep himself in this world, to get to know these things as intimately as I know the area I chose to specialize in.

It is the same with my cello. As an adult I hanker to play those Bach suites now, not in ten years' time. But just as it took years to learn the trumpet, so it will be a slow, gradual, sustained period of learning that will bring me to the point where I can play the suites. I've at least managed to pass my grade 3 this month. I was shocked by how nervous I got. My bow was shaking all over the place. Although I was surrounded by a bunch of 11-year-olds waiting to do their grade 1 recorder, it still felt good to get that sense of achievement.

As with the cello, I know that if I spent enough time in this world of particle physics I would have some hope of knowing what my colleagues across the road in the physics department live and breathe daily. It frightens me to realize I don't have time to know it all. But even those physicists whom I envy for the ease with which they play with our current state of knowledge recognize that ultimately they'll never know for sure whether they know it all.

COWBOYS AND QUARKS

I arranged to meet one of the scientists responsible for discovering one of the last pieces in the quark jigsaw to see whether particle physicists think the current jigsaw might be made of even tinier pieces. Now a professor at Harvard, Melissa Franklin was part of the team responsible for detecting the top quark at Fermilab in America. Contrary to popular perception, discovering a particle is not a eureka moment but a slow burn. But Franklin preferred it that way: 'If it's just "boom", it would be a drag. You spend 15 years building the thing and boom, in one minute it's over? It would be terrible.' It probably took a year of gathering data from 1994 till the team felt confident enough in 1995 to confirm the discovery of this particle predicted by the mathematics.

Franklin is definitely on the experimental rather than theoretical side of the physics divide. Happier with a power drill in her hand than a pencil, she helped to build the detector at Fermilab from the bottom up.

We were both talking at the Rome Science Festival on the theme of the unknowable, so we agreed to meet in the lobby of the rather strange hotel we were staying in, which seemed to be dedicated to the sport of polo. Given that Franklin strides round the department in cowboy boots, I thought that perhaps she might feel more at home in this hotel covered in images of horses than I did.

However, she ended up making an extremely dramatic entrance, crashing to the bottom of the stairs into the lobby. Having dusted herself down, she strode over and sat down as if nothing had happened.

I was very keen to know if she thought quarks were the last layer or whether there might be more structure hiding beneath the particles she'd helped to discover.

'We're down to 10^{-18} metres. The next seven or eight orders of magnitude are kind of hard to investigate. But certainly a lot more could happen in there. It's kind of strange that I could die before – especially if I keep falling down the stairs – I could die before we get any further.'

I wondered whether there might be fundamental limits to what we could know?

'There are definitely limits in my lifetime but I'm not sure there are any other limits. In experimental physics, saying there's no way we can do something is the perfect way to get someone to figure out how to do it. In my lifetime I'm never going to be able to measure something that decays in 10^{-22} seconds. I don't think there's any way. That's not to say it's provably unknowable.

'We couldn't have imagined the laser or the atomic clock, right? I think all the limitations in physics are going to be atomic because all the things we do are with atoms. I know that sounds weird but you need the atoms in your detector.'

But it's intriguing how Einstein inferred the existence of atoms from looking at how they impacted on things you could see, such as pollen grains or coal dust. And today we know about quarks because of the way particles bounce off protons. So perhaps there will be ways to dig deeper.

'I'm sure those guys like Heisenberg and Bohr couldn't have imagined what we can detect today. I guess the same must apply to our generation . . . although of course we're much smarter,' she laughed.

And I guess that is the problem each generation faces. How can we ever know what cunning new method might be developed to dig that bit deeper into the fabric of the universe? But Franklin wondered how much we were missing that's already there in the data coming out of the current generation of detectors.

'Many young people in my field don't believe it's possible to find anything new that wasn't predicted by theorists. That's sad. If you found something and it wasn't predicted by theory, then you'll probably think it's wrong and you'll dismiss it, thinking it's a fluctuation. I worry that because of the way our experiments are constructed you have these triggers that trigger on certain things, but only things you're looking for and not other things. I wonder what we're missing.'

I guess that was almost the fate of the pentaquark that CERN recently announced. It nearly got dismissed as noise. Given that I was writing a book about what we cannot know, Franklin was intrigued to know whether, if I could press a button and know it all, would I do so? As I was putting out my hand to press her hypothetical button, selling my soul to Mephistopheles to know the proofs of all the theorems I'm working on, she stopped me.

'I wouldn't.'

'Why not?'

'Because it's not fun that way. There are certain things, like if I could push a button and speak perfect Italian, I would do it. But not with science. I think it's because you can't really understand it that way. You have to struggle with it somehow. You have to actually try and measure things and struggle to understand things.'

I was intrigued. Wouldn't she press the button if she could know there were more particles sitting underneath the quarks?

'If they just told me the method, then that would be great. But a lot of the reason we like doing science is coming up with the ideas in the first place. The struggle is more interesting. This whole pushing the button is really complicated.'

I think in the end Franklin likes making things, driving forklift trucks and drilling concrete in the search for new particles, not sitting at a desk thinking.

'Experimentalists are a bit like cowboys in a way. Lasso that old thing over there and bring it over here. Don't mind that boy over there sitting in the corner thinking about stuff.

'When I turn 60, I'm going to be less judgemental and more open-minded. I'm going to stop being a cowboy . . . No, I don't want to stop being a cowboy . . . I don't know . . . It's hard. Cowboys can be deep.

When you're wearing cowboy boots to work it's kind of making a statement.'

And with that she mounted her taxi and rode off into the Rome sunset, continuing the scientific quest to know what else there is out there to lasso.

THE CELLO OR THE TRUMPET?

Are the quarks that Franklin helped discover the final frontier or might they one day divide into even smaller pieces, just as the atom broke into electrons, protons and neutrons, which in turn broke into quarks?

Many physicists feel that current experimental evidence, combined with the mathematical theory that underpins these experiments, has given us the answer to the question of what the true indivisible units are that built my dice. Just as the periodic table of 118 chemical elements could be reduced to different ways of putting together the three basic building blocks of the electron, proton and neutron, the hundreds of new particles found in the cosmic-ray collisions could be reduced to a simple collection of ingredients. The wild menagerie of particles had been tamed. But how sure am I that the gates might not open again to unleash more new beasts? The truth is that physicists don't know if this is the last chapter in the story.

If you look at the symmetrical model underlying these particles, then the triangle corresponding to the quarks is the last indivisible layer describing the different physical representation of this object SU(3). The mathematics of symmetry suggests that we've reached rock bottom. That triangle corresponding to the quarks is the indivisible layer that builds all the other layers. So the mathematics of symmetry is trying to tell me I've hit the indivisible. And yet maybe we are falling into the same trap that Gell-Mann did when he first dismissed quarks because they'd have to have fractional charge. But there is another feature of quarks and electrons that provides some justification for believing they might not come apart: they don't seem to occupy any space but behave as if they are concentrated at a single point.

In mathematics, geometry is made up of three-dimensional solids, two-dimensional planes, one-dimensional lines and zero-dimensional points. The strange thing is that these were meant to be abstract objects that didn't have a physical reality in our three-dimensional universe. After all, what is a line? If you draw a line on a piece of paper and look at it under a microscope, you'll see that the line actually has width. It isn't really a line. In fact, it even has height, because the atoms that are sitting on the page are piling up to create a little ridge of lead (or whatever pencils are made of today) across the page.

Similarly, a point in space might be identified by its GPS coordinates, but you wouldn't expect to have an object which is located solely at this point and nowhere else. You could never see it. Its dimensions are zero. And yet an electron behaves in many ways as if it is concentrated in a single point in space, as do the quarks inside the proton and neutron. The manner in which electrons scatter off one another and off the quarks inside protons and neutrons makes sense only if you create a model in which these particles all have no volume. Give them volume and the scattering would look different. If they truly are point particles, you wouldn't expect them to come apart.

But what about the fact that electrons have mass? What is the density of an electron? That's mass divided by volume. But the volume is zero. Divide by zero and the answer is infinite. Infinite? So is every electron actually creating a tiny black hole? We are firmly in the territory of the quantum world, because where a particle is located turns out not to be as easy a question to answer as one might expect, as I shall find out in the next Edge.

Have the discrete notes of my trumpet won out over the continuous glissando of the cello? It will be very difficult to know whether this story has reached its end. Atoms were regarded as indivisible because of the indivisible nature of the whole numbers that showed how they combine. And yet they eventually fell apart into the tiny pieces that make up our current ideas about the universe. Why shouldn't I expect history to repeat itself with more surprises as I dig deeper and deeper? Why should there be a beginning, a first layer that made it all? It's a classic problem of infinite regress that we shall meet over and over again. As the little old lady once retorted to a scientist's attempt to mock her theory that the universe was supported on the back of a turtle: 'You're very clever, young man, very clever, but it's turtles all the way down!'

Even if electrons and quarks are particles concentrated at a single point in space, there is no reason why a point can't actually be pulled apart to be made of two points. Or perhaps there are hidden dimensions we have yet to interact with. This is the suggestion of string theory. These point particles in string theory are actually believed to be one-dimensional strings vibrating at resonant frequencies, with different frequencies giving rise to different particles. I seem to have come full circle and be back with Pythagoras' model of the universe. Perhaps my cello does win out over the trumpet and the fundamental particles are really just vibrating strings.

If I am on the search for things we can never know, the question of what my dice is made from could well qualify. The story of what we do know about my dice is full of warnings. Will we ever find ourselves at the point at which there are no new layers of reality to reveal? Can we ever know that the latest theory will be the last theory?

But there may be another problem. The current theory of the very small – quantum physics – proposes that there are limits to knowledge built into the theory. As I try to divide my dice more and more, at some point I run up against a barrier beyond which I cannot pass, as my next Edge reveals.

THIRD EDGE: THE POT OF URANIUM

5

It is absolutely necessary, for progress in
science, to have uncertainty as a fundamental
part of your inner nature.

Richard Feynman

It's extraordinary what you can buy over the Internet. Today a small pot of radioactive uranium-238 arrived in the post. 'Useful for performing nuclear experiments,' the advert assured me. I rather enjoyed the comments from other people who purchased a pot: 'So glad I don't have to buy this from Libyans in parking lots at the mall anymore.' One purchaser wasn't so happy: 'I purchased this product 4.47 billion years ago and when I opened it today, it was half empty.'

The uranium is naturally occurring and I'm assured it is safe to have on my desk next to me as I write. The documentation just warns me that I shouldn't grind it up and ingest it. The packet claims that the uranium is emitting radiation at a rate of 766 counts per minute. It's kicking out a range of radiation: alpha particles, beta particles and gamma rays. But what the specifications cannot guarantee is when exactly the uranium is going to spit out its next particle.

In fact, current quantum physics asserts that this is something I can never know. There is no known mechanism so far developed that will predict precisely when radioactive uranium will emit radiation. The post-Newtonian physics that I explored in the First Edge implied that theoretically everything in the universe is controlled by and follows a deterministic set of mathematical equations. But at the beginning of the twentieth century a group of young physicists – Heisenberg, Schrödinger, Bohr, Einstein and others – sparked a revolution, giving a new perspective on what we can really know about the universe. Determinism was out. Randomness, it appears, rules the roost.

To understand this unknown requires that I master one of the most difficult and counterintuitive theories ever recorded in the annals of science: quantum physics. To listen to those who have spent their lives immersed in this world talking of the difficulties they have in understanding its twists and turns is testament to the challenge I face. After making his groundbreaking discoveries in quantum physics, Werner Heisenberg recalled how 'I repeated to myself again and again the question: Can nature possibly be so absurd as it seemed to us in these atomic experiments?' Einstein declared that 'if it is correct it signifies the end of science'. Schrödinger was so shocked by the implications of what he'd cooked up that he admitted: 'I do not like it and I am sorry I had anything to do with it.' Nevertheless, the theory is one of the most powerful and well-tested pieces of science on the books. Nothing has come close to pushing it off its pedestal as one of the great scientific achievements of the last century. So there is nothing for it but to dive head first into this uncertain world. Feynman has some good advice for me as I embark on my quantum quest:

> I am going to tell you what nature behaves like. If you will simply admit that maybe she does behave like this, you will find her a delightful, entrancing thing. Do not keep saying to yourself, if you can possibly avoid it, 'But how can it be like that?' because you will get 'down the drain', into a blind alley from which nobody has yet escaped. Nobody knows how it can be like that.

RANDOM RADIATION

The revolution these scientists instigated is perfectly encapsulated in my attempts to understand what my pot of uranium is going to do next.

Over a long period of time the rate of radioactive decay approaches a constant and on average is very predictable, just like the throw of my casino dice. But according to the physics of the twentieth century there is a fundamental difference between the dice and the pot of uranium. At least with the dice I have the impression that I could know the outcome given enough data. However, there seems to be no way of determining when the uranium will emit an alpha particle. Complete information doesn't make any difference. According to the current model of quantum physics, it's completely and genuinely random. It is a counterexample to Laplace's belief in a clockwork universe.

For someone on the search for certainty and knowledge the revelations of quantum physics are extremely unsettling. There is nothing I can do to know when that pot on my desk is going to emit its next alpha particle? That's deeply shocking. Is there really no way I can know? There is much debate about whether this is truly something random, something we can never know, or whether there is a hidden mechanism we have yet to uncover that would explain the moment that radiation occurs.

This unknown is related to an even deeper layer of ignorance shrouding the universe of the very small. In order to apply the equations of motion discovered by Newton to calculate the future evolution of the universe, it is necessary to know the location and momentum of every particle in the universe. Of course, practically this is impossible, but discoveries made in the twentieth century hint at a deeper problem. Even if I take just one electron it is theoretically impossible to know both its position and its momentum precisely. Our current model of the very small has a built-in limitation on what we can know: this is called Heisenberg's uncertainty principle.

While my First Edge revealed that the randomness that is meant to describe the roll of the dice is just an expression of a lack of knowledge, the world of the very small seems to have randomness at its heart: an unknowable dice deciding what's going to happen to the lump of uranium sitting on my desk beside my casino dice.

I have learnt to cope with the unknowability of the roll of the dice, because deep in my heart I know it is still dancing to the regular beat of Newton's equations. But I'm not sure I can ever come to terms with the unknowability of my radioactive pot of uranium – something that the theory says is dancing to no one's beat. The challenge is: will it always remain unknowable, or is there another theoretical revolution that needs to take place akin to the radical new perspective that emerged at the beginning of the twentieth century?

WAVE OR PARTICLE?

We had the first inklings of this revolution when scientists tried to understand the nature of light. Is it a wave or is it a particle? Newton's great opus on optics, published in 1704, painted a picture of light as a particle. If you considered light as a stream of particles then the behaviour that Newton described in his book appeared very natural. Take the way that light reflects. If I want to know where a ray of light will emerge when it hits a reflecting surface, then thinking of it like a billiard ball fired at the wall gives me a way to predict its path. The geometry of light made up of these straight lines, Newton believed, could be explained only by thinking of light as made up of particles.

Rivals to Newton's vision, however, believed that a wave was a much better model for describing the nature of light. There seemed to be too many characteristics of light that were hard to explain if it was a particle. An experiment that English physicist Thomas Young concocted in the early 1800s seemed to be the nail in the coffin for anyone believing in light as a particle.

If I shine a light at a screen with a single thin vertical slit cut into the screen, and place a photographic plate beyond the screen to record the light as it emerges, the pattern I observe on the photographic plate is a bright region directly in line with the slit and the light source that gradually tails off to darkness as I move away from this central line.

The intensity of light recorded on the photographic plate after
the light has passed through a single narrow slit.

So far this is consistent with a particle view of light, in which small deflections can occur as the particles of light pass through the slit, causing some of the light to fall either side of this bright region. (Even with the single slit, if the slit is small compared with the wavelength of light, there is some wavelike variation in the intensity of the light as you move away from the central bright region, which hints at waves at work.)

The trouble for the particle version of light was revealed when Young introduced a second vertical slit into the screen parallel to the first slit. You would have expected to see two bright regions occurring in line with each slit corresponding to the particles of light passing through one slit or the other. But that's not what Young observed. Instead, there was a whole series of bands of light and dark lines across the photographic plate. Bizarrely, there are regions of the plate that are illuminated if only one slit is open and plunged into darkness if two slits are open. How is it, if light is a particle like a billiard ball, that giving the light more options results in a particle suddenly being unable to reach this region of the plate? The experiment truly challenged Newton's model of light as a particle.

Light emitted from the left passes through the double-slit screen and strikes the photographic plate on the right. The light and dark bands depicted to the right of the plate represent the interference pattern detected.

It seemed that only a model of light as a wave could explain these bands of brightness and darkness. If I think of a still lake full of water and I throw two stones into the water at the same time, then the waves caused by the stones will interact in such a way that some parts of the waves combine to form a much larger wave and other parts of the waves cancel each other out. If I place a piece of wood in the water, I will see this interaction as the combined waves strike the board. The wave hits the board with a series of peaks and troughs across the length of the board.

The light emerging from the two slits appear to produce two waves that interact in a similar way to the stones thrown into the water. In some regions the light waves combine to create bright bands, while in others they cancel each other out to produce dark bands. No particle version of light could get anywhere near explaining these patterns.

The supporters of the particle theory finally had to throw in the towel in the early 1860s, when it was discovered that the speed at which light travels matched exactly the speed predicted by James Clerk Maxwell's new theory of electromagnetic radiation based on waves. Maxwell's calculations revealed that light was in fact a form of electromagnetic radiation described by equations whose solutions were waves of differing frequencies corresponding to different sorts of electromagnetic radiation.

However, there was a twist in store. Just as Young's experiment seemed to push scientists towards a wave model of light, the results of two new experiments at the end of the nineteenth century could be explained only if light came in packets. That is, if it was quantized.

COOKING UP A CACOPHONY
OF WAVES

The first inkling that light could not be wavelike arose from trying to understand the light or electromagnetic radiation being cooked up in the coal-fired furnaces that drove the Industrial Revolution. Heat is movement, but if you jiggle an electron up and down then, because it has a negative charge, it is going to emit electromagnetic radiation. This is why hot bodies glow: the jiggling electrons emit radiation. Think of the electron a bit like a person holding the end of a skipping rope: as the person's hand goes up and down, the rope begins to oscillate like a wave. Each wave has a frequency which records how often the wave pulses up and down per second. It's this frequency that controls, for example, what colour visible light will have. Red light has a low frequency; blue light a high frequency. The frequency also plays a part in how much energy the wave contains. The higher the frequency, the more energy the wave has. The other contributing factor to a wave's energy is its amplitude. This is a measure of how big the waveform is. If you think of the skipping rope, then the more energy you put in, the higher the rope will vibrate. For many centuries scientists used the dominant frequency of the radiation as the measure of the temperature. Red hot. White hot. The hotter a fire, the higher the frequency of the light emitted.

I got a chance to see one of these coal-fired furnaces at work when I visited Papplewick Pumping Station near Nottingham. Once a month they fire up the furnaces for one of their 'steaming days'. The furnace is housed in a beautifully ornate Victorian building. Apparently the cost of building the station was so far under budget that there were funds left over to decorate the pump house. It feels like a church dedicated not to God but to the science of the industrial age.

The temperature inside the furnace at Papplewick was hitting something in the region of 1000 degrees Celsius. Scientists at the end of the nineteenth century were interested in what the spectrum of frequencies of light looked like inside the furnace for any fixed temperature. A closed furnace can reach a thermodynamic equilibrium where the heat jiggling the atoms causes radiation to be emitted which is then reabsorbed, so none of the electromagnetic radiation is lost.

When the furnace hits equilibrium, what frequencies of radiation do you find inside it? You can think of this as like a lot of my cello strings waiting to be vibrated. The total energy of the vibrating string is a function of the frequency of the vibration and the amplitude of the vibration of the string. Higher-frequency waves need more energy to get them going, but this can be compensated for by creating a wave with lower amplitude. Classically, a fixed amount of energy can theoretically get waves of any frequency vibrating, but the amplitude will be correspondingly smaller as the frequency increases.

A theoretical analysis of the spectrum seemed to indicate that waves of arbitrary frequency would occur in the furnace. And yet when I looked inside the furnace at Papplewick I didn't get zapped by a load of high-frequency X-rays. But the wave-based theory of electromagnetism predicted that I should. Not only that, if I added up all the contributions of the frequencies inside the furnace at thermal equilibrium, then the analysis based on light as a vibrating wave would lead to the absurd conclusion that the total energy contained in the oven is infinite. The furnace in Papplewick wouldn't have lasted long if that had been the case.

At any given temperature there seems to be some cut-off frequency beyond which the waves fail to get going and vibrate. The classical picture is the following. If light is like a vibrating cello string, then the oven should generate waves of all frequencies, the number of waves increasing with the frequency. At low frequency the graph is correct, but as the frequency increases I see the intensity of the radiation at higher frequencies tailing off until beyond some point (which depends on the temperature) no waves of frequency greater than this number are observed.

The frequencies inside a closed oven predicted by classical and quantum models.

In 1900 the German physicist Max Planck took the experimentally observed distribution of frequencies coming out of a furnace like that at Papplewick and came up with a clever idea that would explain how to get the true curve rather than the nonsensical curve produced by a classical cello-string interpretation of light.

He posited that each frequency of electromagnetic radiation had a minimum energy that was required before it got going. You couldn't just continuously reduce the energy of a wave vibrating at a given frequency and expect it to sound. At some point, as the energy is reduced, the wave would just flatline rather than continuously vibrate at smaller and smaller amplitudes. Indeed, Planck's model asserted that there wasn't any continuous behaviour. Each time the energy increased, it went up in quantized jumps. The jumps in energy were very tiny, so they were very hard to observe unless you were looking for them. But once Planck had this assumption in place, the mathematical implications for the intensity of electromagnetic radiation at each frequency corresponded precisely with the observed radiation emerging from the oven.

So perhaps the universe was not the smooth, continuous place that scientists had believed it to be up to the end of the nineteenth century. Even the atomists – those who believed in matter built of basic building blocks – had no idea that the atomist philosophy would apply to things like energy. The implication for my cello string is that if I draw the bow across the string and increase the volume, although your ear hears a gradual and continuous increase in the volume, actually the volume is jumping up in steps. The size of the steps is very small. For any given frequency v, the energy goes up in steps of $h \times v$, where h is called the Planck constant. This number, which controls the steps in energy measured in joule seconds, has 33 zeros after the decimal place before we get the first non-zero digit:

$$h = 6.626 \times 10^{-34} \text{ joule seconds.}$$

At this stage, Planck had no real physical explanation for the steps in energy, but mathematically it was just what was needed to explain the experimentally observed electromagnetic radiation inside an oven like the one at Papplewick. It was Einstein's explanation of a second experiment that shifted scientists towards thinking of light as a particle rather than a wave. And it was these particles that each had an energy of $h \times v$.

KICKING OUT ELECTRONS:
THE PHOTOELECTRIC EFFECT

Metals are such good conductors of electricity because there are lots of free electrons that can move through the metal. This means that if I fire electromagnetic radiation at a piece of metal, I can actually kick these electrons off the metal. The energy from the wave is transferred to the electron, which then has enough energy to escape the confines of the metal. This was the key to Thomson's discovery of the electron described in the previous Edge.

If I think of electromagnetic radiation as a wave, I should be able to increase the energy of the wave until eventually I'll knock out the electron. The greater the energy in the wave, the more of a kick I give the electron and the faster it speeds off. As I described in the previous section, there are two ways to increase the energy of a wave like my vibrating cello string. One is to increase the frequency of the wave, to vibrate it faster. Do this and sure enough the speed of the electrons that are ejected goes up proportionally. But if I fix the frequency, the other way to increase the energy is to increase the amplitude of the wave, to play it louder. The strange thing is that, despite dialling up the intensity of the wave at a given frequency, the speed at which the electrons are emitted is not affected. What goes up is the number of electrons kicked off the metal.

Furthermore, if I decrease the frequency of the wave while increasing the amplitude, I can keep the total energy constant, and yet there is a point at which I can't seem to kick out any of the electrons. There are frequencies below which, however loud I play my cello, the energy just doesn't kick out electrons. In contrast, with a high-frequency wave it doesn't matter how far down you turn the volume dial, even an extremely low-intensity wave has the power to knock out electrons. What's going on? How can I explain this strange behaviour, which scientists call the photoelectric effect?

The answer is to change the model. At the moment I've been thinking in terms of: wave in, particle out. What if I try: particle in, particle out? Perhaps the particle nature of the outgoing electron is actually the key to how I should view the incoming electromagnetic radiation.

This was Einstein's great paradigm shift, which he made in 1905, the year many call his *annus mirabilis*. It is also the year he came up with the special theory of relativity that I tackle in later Edges, and the theory of Brownian motion, which provided the most convincing support for matter made from atoms described in the previous Edge.

Einstein suggested that you should think of electromagnetic radiation or light not as a wave but like a machine-gun fire of tiny billiard balls, just as Newton had suggested. The energy of each individual particle depends on the frequency of the radiation. With this new idea we have a model that can perfectly describe what scientists were experiencing in the lab. Each billiard ball of light will have energy corresponding to the minimum energy that Planck had mathematically introduced to produce his explanation of the radiation in the furnace. Electromagnetic radiation of frequency v should be thought of in Einstein's model as billiard balls each with energy $h \times v$. The jumps in energy that Planck introduced simply correspond to the addition of more billiard balls of light to the radiation. Einstein called these balls light quanta, but they were renamed in the mid-1920s, and we know them today as photons.

PHOTON BILLIARDS

How does this particle model of light explain the behaviour of the electrons being kicked off a metal? Again, think of the interaction like a game of billiards. The photons of light come crashing onto the surface of the metal. If a photon hits an electron, the energy is transferred to the electron and the electron flies off. But the electron needs to receive a certain amount of energy if it is to get kicked off.

The energy of each incoming photon of light depends only on the frequency of its radiation. If the frequency of the radiation is too low, the energy of each incoming photon is too small to kick out the electron. It doesn't matter if you turn up the intensity of the radiation: you're firing more billiard balls at the metal, but each individual billiard ball has the same energy. There is an increased chance of an electron being hit, but since each billiard ball is as impotent as any other, the electron is never going to be kicked off. In the wave model, the electron could sit there absorbing the incoming energy until it had enough to fly off. With the particle model I can kick the electron as many times as I want, but no single kick is going to be enough to knock out the electron. It's like gently prodding someone with your finger. Lots more gentle prods are not going to cause the person to fall over.

But if the frequency of the incoming radiation is above a certain value, the energy of each billiard ball is enough to kick the electron off if it hits. It's like replacing hundreds of tiny prods with one huge shove: now the person falls over. Essentially, the ball has enough energy to transfer to the electron, and the resulting energy of the electron is sufficient for it to overcome the forces binding it to the metal. Increasing the intensity of the radiation means firing more balls at the metal and this simply increases the number of electrons that will be emitted. Hence, rather than knocking out electrons with higher speeds, I just see more electrons being kicked off.

The speed of the emitted electron in Einstein's model will be linearly proportional to the frequency. Interestingly, this relationship had not been observed or previously predicted, so it gave Einstein's model the perfect characteristic for any good scientific theory: to be able not only to explain what has been seen in the laboratory to date but also to predict some new phenomenon that can be tested subsequently. This was especially important, since many scientists were intensely sceptical of Einstein's model. Maxwell's equations, which described electromagnetic radiation in terms of the mathematics of waves, had been so successful that scientists were not going to change their minds without some convincing.

One of the sceptics was American physicist Robert Andrews Millikan. But his attempts to try to disprove Einstein's model of light as billiard balls of energy ended up confirming Einstein's prediction that the speed of outgoing electrons would be directly proportional to the frequency of the incoming radiation. Millikan had previously determined the charge on the electron as part of his research and would subsequently coin the term 'cosmic rays' after he proved that the radiation being picked up by detectors on Earth was of an extraterrestrial nature. For all this work Millikan received the Nobel Prize in Physics in 1923, just two years after Einstein got his.

It was Einstein's explanation of the photoelectric effect for which he received his Nobel Prize in 1921. He wasn't recognized by the Nobel committee for his theory of relativity! Einstein's ideas gave the particle party a reason to retrieve the towel they'd thrown in a few decades earlier after Maxwell's revelations. In turn there would be a counter-revolution which revealed that particles such as electrons have characteristics that make them look more like waves than discrete particles. It seemed as if both light and electrons behaved like particles and waves. Everyone was a winner in the new theory that was emerging.

Despite Einstein's paradigm shift, the experiments that seemed better explained by light as a wave were not invalidated. Weirdly, the circumstances of the experiment seem to dictate which model of light you should use. The wave–particle duality was upon us.

Recall that it was Young's double-slit experiment that had been the most devastating demonstration of why light is a wave not a particle. The photoelectric effect had rather nicely used the particle nature of the electron to provide convincing support for thinking of electromagnetic radiation as a particle. But did the dialogue work the other way? What if I ask an electron to take part in the Young double-slit experiment? Firing electrons at a screen with two slits turned out to have shocking implications for our grasp on reality.

EXPERIMENTING WITH ELECTRONS

One of the most curious consequences of quantum physics is that a particle like an electron can seemingly be in more than one place at the same time until it is observed, at which point there seems to be a random choice made about where the particle is really located. And scientists currently believe that this randomness is genuine, not just caused by a lack of information. Repeat the experiment under precisely the same conditions and you may get a different answer each time. It is this uncertainty about position that is ultimately responsible for bits of my uranium suddenly finding themselves located outside rather than inside the pot on my desk.

The quintessential illustration of this repeats Young's double-slit experiment, but with electrons rather than light. A physicist colleague of mine in Oxford let me come and play in his lab so that I could see with my own eyes the bizarre game these electrons seem to be playing. I've read about it so many times, but as Kant once said: 'All our knowledge begins with the senses.'

I felt compelled to warn my colleague that experiments and I don't mix well. No one would agree to be my lab partner at school because my experiments invariably went wrong. It was one of the reasons I was drawn to the more theoretical end of the scientific spectrum, where the mess of the physical universe can be kept at bay. But my colleague assured me this experiment was pretty robust.

To start with, we set up a source emitting electrons at a rate that allowed me to record them arriving on the detector plate one at a time. I then placed the screen with two slits between the source and the detector plate. I first observed what happened when one slit was closed. The electrons that passed through the open slit hit the detector plate, and, after sending sufficiently many through, I began to see a pattern emerge.

The region directly in line with the source and the slit saw a high intensity of electrons arriving. As I moved to either side of this central line I still detected electrons arriving, but the number dropped off as I moved further from the central line. The electrons sometimes seemed to be deflected as they passed through the slit, resulting in their paths being bent either side of the central line. Nothing too strange up to this point. But then I opened the second slit.

If the electrons behaved like classical particles, I would have expected to see two regions of high intensity in line with the two slits, depending on whether the electron passed through the first or second slit. But this wasn't what I detected. Instead, I saw the interference pattern begin to build up, just as Young did when he shone light at the screen, which was more consistent with the analogy of a water wave passing through the slits and creating two waves that interfere with each other.

As more electrons are detected, the wavelike pattern of interference emerges.

Remember, though, that I'd set the experiment up so that only one electron was passing through the screen at a time. So this wasn't many electrons interacting with each other in a wavelike manner. This was a single electron doing what a wave usually does. Even more inexplicably, there were regions on the detector plate that were totally devoid of any electrons arriving, despite the fact that with one slit open, electrons could reach this point. What was happening? I had opened another slit, providing several paths to a point on the detector plate, but the extra choice had led to no electrons arriving.

Kant proposed that all knowledge begins with the senses but 'proceeds thence to understanding, and ends with reason, beyond which nothing higher can be discovered'. So how did scientists distil reason from the strange behaviour of these single electrons passing through the screen?

THE SCHIZOPHRENIC ELECTRON

When it passed through one slit, how could the electron know whether the other slit was open or not? After all, the other slit was some distance away from the slit through which the electron was travelling. It's not that the electron splits into two and goes through both slits. The extraordinary thing is that I have to give up on the idea of the electron being located at any particular point until it is observed. Rather, I should describe the electron by a mathematical wave function that gives the range of possible locations. This was the revolutionary new viewpoint proposed in 1926 by the Austrian physicist Erwin Schrödinger. The amplitude of the wave encodes the probability that when the electron is observed it will be found in a particular region of space.

A quantum wave: the higher the wave, the more likely it will
be to find the electron at this point in space.

You might ask: a wave of what? What is vibrating? In fact, it is a wave of information rather than physical stuff. Just as a crime wave isn't a wave of criminals but rather information about the likelihood of a crime happening in a particular area. The wave is simply a mathematical function, and a mathematical function is like a machine or computer: you input information, and it calculates away and spits out an answer. The wave function of the electron has as input any region of space, and the output is the probability that you will find the electron in that region. Amazingly, this particle should really be thought of as a piece of evolving mathematics, not a physical thing at all. It is called a wave because the functions describing these probabilities have many of the features of classical wave functions. The peaks and troughs encode information about where the electron might be. The bigger the amplitude of the wave, the more likely you are to find the electron in that region of space.

In the case of the wave describing the behaviour of the electron, when the wave encounters the screen with the double slits it is affected by its interaction with the screen. The result is a new wave whose characteristics produce the strange interference pattern that I picked up on the detector plate. It is at this moment of detection that the electron has to make up its mind where on the plate to be located. The wave function provides the probability of where the electron might appear, but at this moment of detection the dice is cast and probabilities become certainties. The wave is no more, and the electron looks once again like a particle hitting one point on the detector plate. But run the experiment again and each time the electron might appear somewhere else. The more electrons I fire at the screen, as the pattern of detected electrons builds up, the more I see the statistics encoded in the wave appearing. But in any individual case the physics claims I'll never know where on the plate I'll find the electron.

The curious thing is that I can return to the original experiment that Young performed with light, but interpret it in the light (if you'll excuse the expression) of Einstein's discovery that light is made up of particles called photons. If I turn down the intensity of the light source in Young's experiment, I can reach a point at which the energy being emitted is so low that it corresponds to firing one photon of light at a time at the double-slit screen.

Just like the electron, when this photon arrives at the photographic plate it shows up as a single point on the plate corresponding to its particle nature. So what's happened to Young's interference pattern? Here is the amazing thing. Keep firing photons at the double-slit screen one at a time, and after a period of time the build-up of the pricks of light on the photographic plate slowly reveals the interference pattern. Young wasn't witnessing a continuous waveform hitting the plate – it was an illusion. It's actually made up of billions of billions of pixels corresponding to each photon's arrival being detected. To give you a sense of how many photons are hitting the plate, a 100-watt lightbulb emits roughly 10^{20} (or 100 billion billion) photons per second.

The wave quality of light is the same as that of the electron. The wave is the mathematics that determines the probable location of the photon of light when it is detected. The wave character of light is not a wave of vibrating stuff like a water wave but a wavelike function encoding information about where you'll find the photon of light once it is detected. Until it reaches the detector plate, like the electron, it is seemingly passing through both slits simultaneously, making its mind up about its location in space only once it is observed.

It's this act of observation that is such a strange feature of quantum physics. Until I ask the detector to pick up where the electron is, the particle should be thought of as probabilistically distributed over space, with the probability described by a mathematical function that has wavelike characteristics. And it is the effect of the two slits on this mathematical wave function that alters it in such a way that the electron is forbidden from being located at some points on the detector plate. But when the particle is observed, the dice is rolled and the probability wave has to choose the location of the particle.

I remember the Christmas when I first read about this crazy story of how things could appear to be in more than one place at the same time. Along with the toys and sweets that had been crammed into my Christmas stocking, Santa had also included a curious-sounding book, *Mr Tompkins in Paperback*, by a physicist called George Gamow. It tells the story of Mr Tompkins' attempts to learn physics by attending a series of evening lectures given by an eminent professor, but Mr Tompkins always drifts off to sleep mid-lecture.

In his dream world the microscopic quantum world of electrons is magnified up to the macroscopic world, and the quantum jungle Mr Tompkins finds himself in is full of tigers and monkeys that are in many places at the same time. When a large pack of fuzzy-looking tigers attacks Mr Tompkins, the professor who accompanies him in his dreams lets off a salvo of bullets. One finally hits its mark and the pack of tigers suddenly becomes a single 'observed' tiger.

I remember being enchanted by this fantasy world and even more excited by the prospect that it wasn't as fantastic as it appeared. I was beginning to have doubts about the existence of Santa, given that he had to visit a billion children in the course of one night, but the book renewed my faith in the idea. Of course, Santa was tapping into quantum physics. Provided that no one actually observed him, he could be in multiple chimneys at the same time.

QUANTUM ANTHROPOLOGY

To emphasize the peculiar role of observation, if I return to the double-slit experiment and try to sneak a look at which slit the electron 'really' passed through by placing a detector at one of the slits, the interference pattern disappears. The act of looking to see which slit the electron passes through changes the nature of the wave function describing the electron. Now the pattern at the detector plate simply shows two regions of light lining up with the two slits – there is no longer any interference pattern. My act of trying to know changes the behaviour of the electron.

Although it is a bit of a cheat, one way to think about this is to imagine an anthropologist observing a previously undiscovered Amazon tribe. To observe is to alter behaviour. It is impossible to observe without interacting in some fashion and changing the behaviour of the tribe. This is even more evident in the case of the electron. To know which slit the electron went through means to 'look', but that must involve some sort of interaction. For example, it could be a photon of light bouncing off the electron and returning to a detector. But that photon must impart some change of momentum or energy or change the electron's position. It can't interact without some change. But the truth is that this interaction need not be as obvious as a photon bouncing off our electron. It can be more subtle. If I observe whether the electron passes through one slit but don't detect it, I can infer that it passed through the other slit. But there was no photon bouncing off the electron in this case. This is an interaction-free measurement of the electron's location.

There is a very strange thought experiment that exploits this act of looking as the electrons pass through the slits in the screen. Suppose I could make a bomb that would be activated by a single electron hitting a sensor. The trouble is that there is no guarantee that the bomb works. Classically, the only way to test this seems to be the rather useless act of firing an electron at the bomb. If it goes off, I know it works. If it doesn't, then it's a dud. But either way, after testing, I don't have a bomb.

The weird thing is that I can use the double-slit experiment to detect working bombs without setting them off. Remember that there were places on the screen where the electron can't hit if it is really going through both slits at the same time. If I detect an electron at this point, it means I must have been looking and forced the electron to choose one slit or the other. We are going to use this region as the 'bomb detector region'. Place the bomb's sensor at the location of one of the slits, and if the bomb is a dud, the sensor won't activate it. We are making no observations if it is a dud. That means the electron passes through both slits and can't hit the 'bomb detector region'.

But what if it isn't a dud? Well, the sensor will detect the electron if it goes through the slit and set the bomb off. Not much good. But because now I am detecting which slit the electron is going through, it is going through only one slit and has the chance to reach our 'bomb detector region'. So if I pick up an electron in the 'bomb detector region', it must mean the bomb is live. A live bomb is a detection mechanism. Half the time the electron is detected going through the slit where the bomb is located and the bomb goes off. But the other half of the time the bomb detects that the electron passed through the other slit, the interference pattern can't occur, the electron has the chance to hit the 'bomb detector region' and yet the bomb doesn't explode. The electron has given up information about which slit it passed through but the act of 'observation' didn't involve looking at the electron or hitting it with a photon of light or blowing up a bomb.

The strange implications of the act of observation can also be applied to stop the pot of uranium on my desk decaying. By continually making lots of mini-observations, trying to catch the uranium in the act of emitting radiation, the observations can freeze the uranium and stop it decaying. It's the quantum version of the old adage that a watched pot never boils, but now the pot is full of uranium.

It was the code-cracking mathematician Alan Turing who first realized that continually observing an unstable particle could some-how freeze it and stop it evolving. The phenomenon became known as the quantum Zeno effect, after the Greek philosopher who believed that because instantaneous snapshots of an arrow in flight show no movement, the arrow cannot be moving at all.

Think of a particle that can be in two states, HERE and THERE. Unobserved, it's in a mixture of the two, but observation forces it to decide which one. If it decides to be HERE, then after observation it begins to evolve into a mixed state again, but observe it quickly enough and it's still mostly HERE and will probably collapse into the HERE state again. So by continually observing the particle it never evolves sufficiently into the THERE state to have a chance of being observed THERE. It's like having two glasses half filled with water, but each time you observe you have to pour the water from one glass into the other, filling it to the brim. After observation you can start to refill the empty glass, but look quickly enough and it's hardly full and so the easiest thing is to refill the almost full glass again. By looking quickly each time, you ensure the full glass stays full.

My children are obsessed with the science fiction TV series *Doctor Who*, just as I was as a kid. The aliens we find scariest are the Weeping Angels, stone figurines like those in our local cemetery that don't move provided you don't take your eyes off them. But blink and they can move. The theory says that the pot of uranium on my desk is a bit like a Weeping Angel. If I keep observing the uranium, which obviously means a little more than just keeping my eyes on the pot on my desk, I can freeze it in such a way that it stops emitting radiation.

Although Turing first suggested the idea as a theoretical consequence of the mathematics, it turns out that it is not just mathematical fiction. There have been some experiments in the last decade that have demonstrated the real possibility of using observation to inhibit the progress of a quantum system.

MULTIPLE HISTORIES

Quantum physics seems to imply that there are multiple futures for the electron in my double-slit experiment until I observe it, and then the roll of some unknown quantum dice determines which one of these futures it will be. I suppose I can come to terms with the fact that I will not know the future until it becomes the present. After all, if I pick up my casino dice with the intention of throwing it three times, then there are $6 \times 6 \times 6 = 216$ possible futures that the dice can realize. My act of throwing the dice picks out one of these 216 possible futures, just as observing the electron determines one of its many possible locations. But another twist on the double-slit experiment has the frightening implication that the past isn't uniquely determined either.

Indeed, I seem to be able to alter the past by my actions in the present. There is a way to look and see which slit the electron went through long after it has passed through the screen. The observation device can be put up just before the electron is about to hit the detector plate. Let's call the observation device the 'slit observer'.

Suppose I set up the double-slit experiment on a cosmic scale. I put my electron-emitting device on one side of the universe and the double-slit screen just in front of it. I place my detector plate on the other side of the universe. In this way it will take many years for the electron to traverse space and finally hit the detector plate. So when the electron passes through the screen with the double slit, it won't know whether I am going to observe it with my 'slit observer'.

particle in
2000 BC

slit
detector
inserted in
2016 AD

The decision whether to insert the 'slit detector' in the path of the particle in AD 2016 can alter what the particle did in 2000 BC.

If, years later, I do use the 'slit observer', it means that many years earlier the electron must have passed through one slit or the other. But if I don't use the 'slit observer', then years earlier the electron must have passed through both slits. But this is weird. My actions at the beginning of the twenty-first century can change what happened thousands of years ago when the electron began its journey. It seems that, just as there are multiple futures, there are also multiple pasts, and my acts of observation in the present can decide what happened in the past. As much as it questions knowledge of the future, quantum physics asks whether I can ever really know the past. It seems that the past is also in a superposition of possibilities that crystallize only once they are observed.

SPLIT PERSONALITY

The interesting point for me – one that is often missed – is that up to the point of observation, quantum physics is totally deterministic. There is no question of what the nature of the wave equation is that describes the electron as it passes through the slits. When he came up with his theory in 1926, Schrödinger formulated the differential equation that provides this completely deterministic prediction for the evolution of the wave function. Schrödinger's wave equation is as deterministic in some sense as Newton's equations of motion.

The probabilistic character and uncertainty occurs when I observe the particle and try to extract classical information. The highly non-classical and bizarre new feature is this discontinuous shift that seems to happen when the wave is 'observed'. Suddenly the determinism seems to vanish and I am left with an electron randomly located at some point in space. Over the long term the randomness is described by information contained in the wave function, but in each individual instance there seems no mechanism that scientists have identified that lets me determine in this particular experiment where the electron will be located. Is this really what is going on? Is the location of the electron something I will never truly be able to predict before I make the observation?

Once I make an observation or measurement there is this strange jump which locates the particle at one particular coordinate. But immediately after the observation, the evolution of the particle is described by another wave function until the next measurement and the next jump. Schrödinger hated these discontinuous changes in behaviour: 'If all this damned quantum jumping were really here to stay, then I should be sorry I ever got involved with quantum theory.'

We should be careful not to over-egg the role of humans here. Worms too can presumably collapse the wave function. But it is not just living creatures that are doing the measuring. There are particles on the other side of a potentially lifeless universe that are interacting with inanimate objects, causing the wave function to collapse into making a decision about the properties of the particle. This interaction is as much an act of observation as my experimental investigations in the lab. The universe is flooded with radiation that shines a light on anything it encounters. Is this why on the whole the universe appears classical and not in a constant state of uncertainty? This is related to an idea physicists call decoherence.

I am having real trouble getting my head around this idea of observation marking a divide between a deterministic electron described by a wave function and an electron that suddenly has a location determined purely by chance. The whole thing seems crazy. Nonetheless, there is no denying that it works as a computational tool. As the physicist David Mermin is reputed to have said to those who, like me, are unhappy with this unknown: 'Shut up and calculate.' It is the same principle as the theory of probability applied to the throw of the dice. The dice may be controlled by Newton's equations, but the theory of probability is the best tool we have for calculating what the dice might do.

But even though I'm meant to shut up, I can't help feeling that the objections are valid. The equipment I use to make a measurement is a physical system made up of particles obeying the laws of quantum physics as much the single electron I'm trying to observe. And me too! I'm just a bunch of particles obeying quantum laws. Surely even the observer, whether a photographic plate or a person, is part of the world of quantum physics and is itself described by a wave function. The interaction of the wave function of the electron and the observer should still be described by a wave. After all, what constitutes an 'observation' or 'measurement'?

And if the equipment and observer and the particles passing

through slits are all described by a wave function, then isn't everything deterministic? So suddenly the randomness disappears. Why are physicists happy to say the act of observation collapses the wave function when frankly there is a mega-wave function at work describing all the particles at play – the electron, the equipment, me. Where's the dividing line between the quantum world of probability and the classical world of certainties? This dualistic vision of a microscopic quantum world and a macroscopic classical world all seems a bit suspicious. Surely the whole shebang should be described by a wave equation. The whole thing is highly unsatisfactory, but the truth is that most physicists just take Mermin's advice and get on with it. My colleague Philip Candelas tells a story of how a promising young graduate student, for whom everyone had high hopes, suddenly dropped out of sight. When Candelas investigated what had happened, he discovered the reason. A family tragedy? Illness? Debts? None of these. 'He tried to understand quantum mechanics.'

I guess I have forgotten Feynman's advice that he gave those who, like me, were trying to become quantum initiates: 'Do not keep saying to yourself, if you can possibly avoid it, "But how can it be like that?" because you will get "down the drain", into a blind alley from which nobody has yet escaped. Nobody knows how it can be like that.'

That said, there are a number of ways in which people have tried to overcome this apparently in-built uncertainty. One is the hypothesis that, at the point of observation, reality splits into a superposition of realities. In each reality the photon or the electron is located in a different position so that the wave in some sense doesn't collapse but remains, describing the evolution of all these different realities. It's just that, as conscious beings, we are now stuck in one of the realities and are unable to access the other realities in which the photon or electron ended up somewhere else on the photographic plate.

This is a fascinating attempt to make sense of the physics. It is called the 'many worlds' interpretation and it was proposed in 1957 by American physicist Hugh Everett. The interesting thing for me is whether we could ever know that these many worlds are out there and existing simultaneously with our own. No one has yet come up with a way to test or probe these other worlds – if they exist. The theory posits that there is just one single wave function which describes the evolution of the universe in an entirely deterministic manner. It is back to Newton and Laplace, but with a new equation.

The trouble for us is that as part of this wave function, we are denied access to other parts of it. It traps us inside, confined to one branch of reality, and it may be an in-built feature of our conscious experience that we can never experience these other worlds. But could I still use my mathematics to analyse what is happening on the other branches? I observe the electron at this point on the detector plate, but I know that the wave function describes what is happening on all the other branches of reality. I can't see those, but I can at least describe them mathematically. Of course, just as the electron exists in many worlds, so do 'I' – there are copies of me on the other branches witnessing the electron hitting other regions of the detector plate.

This model of reality is very intriguing, seeming to impact directly on what we understand by consciousness. I shall return to the question of consciousness in my Sixth Edge, but my current Edge already raises the interesting question of whether it might be related to the behaviour of this wave function. Why am I aware of only one result of the electron hitting the plate? Is my conscious awareness of what is happening around me some version of the electron hitting a plate? Is the equipment in my skull unable to process multiple worlds? I look out of the window, and the photons emitted from the house opposite enter my eye and are detected on my retina. Why can't I sometimes look out and see house numbers 14 and 16 swapped over?

This attempt to reconcile what is going on involves trying to explain that the jump caused by the act of observation is not real but just something going on in the mind. We perceive a jump, but that isn't what is really happening. This sort of explanation, though, raises the question of what it is we are trying to do when we give a scientific explanation of the world.

What is science? How do we attempt to navigate our interaction with the universe? It is only by measuring and observing that we know anything. Mathematical equations can tell us what to expect, but it's just a story until we measure. So it's curious that our only way to 'know' anything about the universe is to observe and make particles and light make up their mind about where and what they are doing. Before that, is it all just fantasy? I can't measure an entire wave function, I can only know it mathematically. Is a quantum wave function part of the universe that we can never know because how can we truly know without measuring? At which point it collapses. Perhaps it's just greedy to believe that I can know more than I can measure. Hawking has certainly expressed such a view:

> I don't demand that a theory correspond to reality because I don't know what it is. Reality is not a quality you can test with litmus paper. All I'm concerned with is that the theory should predict the results of measurements.

ONE INPUT, MULTIPLE OUTPUTS

My real problem with the current mainstream interpretation of quantum physics is that if you run the double-slit experiment twice, set up with exactly the same conditions, the outcome can be different each time. This goes against everything I believe in. It is why I was drawn to mathematics: the certainty of a proof that there are infinitely many prime numbers means I'm not suddenly going to get finitely many prime numbers next time I check. I believed that ultimately science was made up of similar certainties, even if we as humans might not ultimately have access to them. I throw my dice and the mathematics of chaos theory I recognize means I may never be able to calculate the final outcome of the throw of the dice. But at least the mathematics says that if I start the throw in the same place it will end up with the same face pointing up. But now the physics developed in this Edge fundamentally questions whether this is the case.

Probability for the dice is an expression of lack of information. In quantum physics it's not about the physicist's ignorance of the complete picture. Even if I knew everything, probability and chance remain. According to current interpretations of quantum physics, different outcomes of the roll of the dice really can result from the same starting point, the same input.

Some would question if it makes sense to talk about setting up the experiment and running it again with exactly the same conditions – that in fact it is an impossibility. Locally you might get the conditions exactly the same, but you have to embed the experiment in the universe, and that has moved on. You can't rewind the wave function of the universe and rerun it. The universe is a one-time-only experiment which includes us as part of its wave function. Each observation changes the wave function of the universe and there's no going back.

But what if reality is random and not as deterministic as I might want? Feynman in his *Lectures on Physics* states: 'At the present time we must limit ourselves to computing probabilities. We say "at the present time", but we suspect very strongly that it is something that will be with us forever – that it is impossible to beat the puzzle – that this is the way nature really *is*.'

It looks like the truly random thing sitting on my desk is not the casino dice I picked up in Vegas but the little pot of uranium I bought over the Internet.

6

How puzzling all these changes are! I'm never sure what I'm going to be, from one minute to another.

Lewis Carroll, *Alice's Adventures in Wonderland*

I must admit that I am having real trouble with the counterintuitive nature of the quantum world. Apparently, this is a good sign. The quantum physicist Niels Bohr once declared: 'If quantum physics hasn't profoundly shocked you, you haven't understood it yet.'

Richard Feynman went even further, declaring that 'no one understands quantum physics'. During a keynote address he made in his sixties he admitted: 'Might I say immediately that we have always had (secret, secret, close the doors!) we have always had a great deal of difficulty in understanding the world view that quantum mechanics represents. I still get nervous with it.'

The mathematician in me hankers after some deterministic mechanism that will tell me when my pot of uranium is going to spit out its next particle. But the probabilistic character of quantum physics really challenges my ability to know what's going to happen next. Newton's equations held out the exciting possibility that if I know the momentum and position of a particle then the equations of motion will tell me the complete behaviour of that particle into the future. And if I repeat the same experiment with another particle located at the same point with the same momentum, it will repeat the path of the first particle.

But this hope that we could know the future was fundamentally crushed by the discoveries made by Heisenberg in 1927. He revealed that it doesn't actually make sense to make the statement: 'I know the momentum and the position of a particle at the same time.' There seems to be an elastic relationship between knowing the location of a particle and knowing its momentum. If I measure the position of a particle with increasing precision, it seems to lead to its momentum having a whole range of possible different values. This is the content of Heisenberg's famous uncertainty principle, perhaps the greatest challenge to what we can know. And as we shall discover, Heisenberg's uncertainty principle accounts for why the uranium sitting on my desk is randomly chucking out particles.

Heisenberg himself expressed well how important it is to be ready to reset your view of the world in the light of new revelations: 'Whenever we proceed from the known into the unknown we may hope to understand, but we may have to learn at the same time a new meaning of the word "understanding".'

Quantum physics isn't about knowing answers to old questions, but about challenging the questions we are allowed to ask.

QUANTUM CARPETS

At the heart of Heisenberg's discovery is the following. Suppose I take one of the particles inside my uranium. If I know that the particle is at rest and not moving, it turns out that I can't know where the particle is located. Indeed, there is a chance that when I look I could find it anywhere across the universe. But in contrast, if I try to pin down exactly where this particle is, I suddenly lose my handle on how the particle is moving. What appeared to be a particle at rest can suddenly find itself moving in any direction.

This seems totally crazy. If I throw my dice through the air, then by watching it carefully as it falls to the table I don't expect my knowledge of the dice's location suddenly to cause the dice to fly off in a totally new direction. But this intuition applies only to things with large mass. When the mass is as small as something like that of an electron, this is exactly what can happen. If I pin down the location of the electron to within the radius of an atom, its speed could change by as much as 1000 kilometres per second in any direction.

It's like trying to fit a strange quantum carpet: every time I pin down the position end of the carpet, the momentum end pops out; try to pin the momentum end down and the position end no longer fits.

To get a feel for this elastic relation between position and momentum, let's return to my screen with the slits. I've been exploring the strange behaviour of a particle fired at a screen with two slits in it. The strange tension between the position and momentum of a particle has actually already revealed itself in the behaviour of the particle as it passes through a single slit. I noted that I get some diffusion of the particles as they pass through the single slit. But if I think more carefully about this, why should just one electron passing through the slit get deflected at all? If it is a point particle like an electron, why doesn't it sail straight through the slit? How do I explain the apparent spread of possible locations as it emerges from the slit? It's this trade-off between knowledge of position versus knowledge of momentum that explains the diffusion I see.

I can arrange for the electron to be fired from a distant source, which ensures that if it passes through the slit then I know that there was no movement in the direction perpendicular to the slit. This means that as the particle enters the slit, I know the momentum in this direction is zero. I know it precisely.

If I think of the electron as a point particle, then it either passes cleanly through the slit or it doesn't. If it passes through the slit, I have very precise knowledge about its position with an accuracy given by the width of the slit. Surely I can now predict precisely where it is going to hit the screen. The momentum was zero in the direction perpendicular to the slit before the electron entered the slit, so it should hit a region on the detector screen whose width is precisely the width of the slit. So why, as I fire more and more electrons through the slit, do I get the same diffusion pattern that I see for waves hitting the detector plate? Why aren't they all arriving in a region that is the same width as the slit?

Heisenberg's uncertainty principle asserts that any measurement that involves determining the precise position of the electron results in a new indeterminacy in the value of the momentum. So, for example, if the electron has passed through the slit, I know the location of the electron within a margin of error given by the width of the slit. As the width of the slit is reduced, that margin of error decreases. But this causes the diffusion pattern to get wider and wider. Why? Because the value of the momentum is affected. While it was zero in the direction perpendicular to the slits as it approached the slit, once the electron emerges with its position narrowed down, the momentum becomes indeterminate. I've pulled the quantum carpet down in the position end and caused the momentum end to pop out.

This is a very strange situation. Moreover, the precise way in which the momentum is affected is something I can't calculate in advance. I can measure it only at a later date. I can know only a range of possible values in which I can expect to find the momentum once observed. Not only that, it now seems that if I repeat the same experiment, the momentum is not determined by the set-up. I have only a probabilistic mechanism to determine what the momentum might be.

QUANTIFYING UNCERTAINTY

Heisenberg's uncertainty principle isn't some wishy-washy statement but actually quantifies the loss of knowledge. Once I know the position of the electron with high precision, the momentum of the electron as it emerges is no longer precisely zero but can vary statistically around the average value of 0. I can't know what value I'll get when I measure the momentum, since that is still undetermined, but I know that statistically the possibilities for the momentum will be distributed either side of the average value of 0. I can measure the spread of this distribution with something called the standard deviation of the momentum, denoted Δp. This is a statistical measure of the spread of possibilities. The greater the spread, the larger Δp and the more uncertain I am of the value of the momentum.

Following Heisenberg's original 1927 paper detailing this strange inverse relationship between knowledge of position and knowledge of momentum, Earle Kennard and later Howard Robertson mathematically deduced the trade-off in knowledge. If the spread of possibilities of the position has a standard deviation of Δx, and the standard deviation for the spread of momentum is Δp, then these two values satisfy the following inequality:

$$\Delta x \, \Delta p \geq \frac{h}{4\pi},$$

where h is Planck's constant, the same number that I saw when explaining the energy of a photon of light. The equation says that if the spread of possibilities in the position measured by Δx is reduced, then to keep the equation correct I have to increase the spread of possibilities for the momentum measured by Δp. It is a mathematical consequence of quantum physics that the more knowledge you gain of the possible locations of a particle, the more this results in the possibility of the momentum being spread over a larger range of values. This is exactly what happens in the case of the electron passing through the single slit.

The entwined nature of these two properties is a consequence of the fact that it matters in what order I do my measurements. The acts of measuring position and momentum are described mathematically by two operations that give different answers if you do them in a different order. The idea can be illustrated using my casino dice. Suppose I place my dice on the table with the 1 on top, as illustrated on the next page. Now I am going to rotate the dice by a quarter turn around the vertical axis running through the top face and follow that by a quarter turn through a horizontal axis running through one of the side faces. The top face now has a 5 showing. But if I return the dice to the original position and repeat the moves but in reverse order, horizontal axis spin followed by vertical axis spin, I get a different outcome. Now there is a 4 showing on the top face.

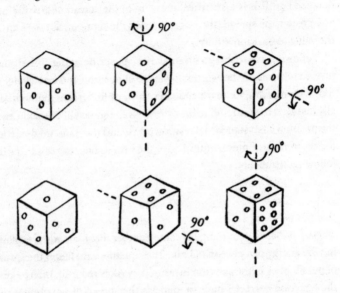

Any measurements that have this property – that when you translate them into mathematical operations it matters what order you do them in – will give rise to an uncertainty principle. This is simply a mathematical consequence of this property called non-commutativity.

It's the mathematics underlying quantum physics that results in much of its counterintuitive nature. As I've buried myself in the books and papers explaining quantum physics, it feels like entering a labyrinth. I thought I knew where I was before I started my journey. Then, using my mathematical skills, I've worked my way logically through the twists and turns of the labyrinth. I have to rely on the maths to lead me because the walls are too high for me to intuit anything about the world outside the labyrinth. But once the maths leads me out the other side and I try to make sense of my destination, where I've ended up doesn't look anything like where I started.

I'm happy with the maths – it's trying to interpret where it's got me that is tough. It's almost as if we don't have the language to reverse-translate what the maths is telling us about reality. Maybe the problems I'm having are not real problems at all but a consequence of the constraints of old language and old stories. Quantum physics is a rabbit hole, and once we've fallen through it we need to reset our vision and formulate a new language to navigate this looking-glass world. And, for better or for worse, that language is mathematics.

But can we trust the maths? This theoretically derived behaviour predicted by the mathematics of Heisenberg's uncertainty principle has been confirmed in experiment. In a paper published in 1969, American physicist Clifford Shull describes the results of firing neutrons at slits of decreasing width. The increased knowledge of the location of the neutrons given by a narrower slit resulted, as theory predicted, in a greater spread of possible values for the momentum. And when the neutrons arrived at the detector plate, they were spread in a distribution whose standard deviation corresponded exactly to that predicted by the equation of Heisenberg's uncertainty principle.

The simple act of knowing more about the position of the neutron has resulted in a potential change in the momentum. Heisenberg's uncertainty principle captures in an equation the fact that we can never know it all. An increase in the known must always be traded off against a corresponding increase in the unknown.

As you tighten your hold on one of the values, you lose determinacy in the other. But this indeterminacy can have some unexpected consequences. If I trap an electron in a very tiny box, the position of the electron is known to a high degree of accuracy. But that results in the possible values of the momentum being spread over a huge range. If I try to measure the momentum, the wave function collapses, resulting in a whole range of different values that the momentum might take.

As soon as I have measured the momentum, you might say that I now know both the position and the momentum. But it actually results in the position becoming indeterminate. The possibilities for where I will find the electron are spread out across space, so much so that I get an effect called quantum tunnelling, whereby the particle I thought

Clifford Shull's experiment confirmed that as the size of the slit is decreased,
the statistical spread of the locations of the neutrons increases.

was trapped inside a box can suddenly appear outside the box. It is this
phenomenon which is responsible for the radiation of an alpha particle
by the uranium that is sitting on my desk.

An alpha particle is part of the nucleus of my uranium and consists
of two protons and two neutrons. The nucleus is like the tiny box containing the alpha particle. In general, the particles don't have sufficient
energy to break out of the confines of the nucleus. Since the speed and
hence momentum are so confined, it means that I know the momentum
with a high degree of accuracy. But by Heisenberg's uncertainty prin-

ciple the position of these particles is not so clearly defined. In fact, there is a chance that the position might be located outside the nucleus, in which case the particles can escape. This uncertainty about position is responsible for the possibility of the uranium radiating.

LIMITS TO KNOWLEDGE AT THE SMALL SCALE

The uncertainty principle not only explains the unpredictability of my pot of uranium but also places limits on the knowledge that I can access as I try to zoom in ever closer on the insides of my dice and see what is going on.

If I try to measure precisely the coordinates of one of the electrons inside my dice, then, as the error in the coordinates goes down, this has to be paid for by an associated uncertainty in the momentum and hence energy. Heisenberg's equations tell me the mathematical relationship between the trade-off. But there is an extra twist. Since energy and mass are related by Einstein's equation $E = mc^2$, if the energy is high enough it can lead to the spontaneous creation of new particles. The trouble is that if I am trying to pin down the location of a particle and by doing that I create lots more particles, it significantly muddies any attempt to investigate the location of the original particle. The scale at which this complication starts kicking in is called the Compton wavelength of a particle. For an electron it is about 4×10^{-13} metres.

Things get even more uncertain as I zoom in closer on my particle. There is a point at which the energy uncertainty is so large that the corresponding mass becomes so great that it causes a black hole to materialize. As I shall explore in the Fifth Edge, a black hole by its very nature appears to trap any information within a certain radius of the centre of the hole and prevent it being released.

This means that the uncertainty principle implies an in-built limit to how far I can probe nature. Beyond a certain scale I seem to be denied access to what's going on. That scale is very small. It is of the order of 1.616×10^{-35} metres, a distance known as the Planck length.

This is ridiculously tiny. If I scale up the full stop at the end of this sentence to be the size of the observable universe, then something the size of the Planck length would scale up to look like the full stop before I enlarged it.

In the previous Edge I hit a point when I couldn't subdivide matter any further, and I've now reached a point when I can't divide space. This seems crazy. Why can't I just talk about the point halfway between two points that are the Planck length apart? Mathematically it makes perfect sense, but physically it seems that it doesn't. The physics means that I can't distinguish any of these points.

The implications are that space at this scale has the appearance of something bitty, grainy and discrete, not continuous as Newton believed. From this perspective, space looks digital, not analogue. This in turn implies that the fractals of the First Edge cannot have any physical reality in quantum physics. A fractal is meant to have infinite complexity at all scales, but quantum physics stops us zooming in beyond the Planck length. Are the fractals of the First Edge only in my mathematical mind? Quantum physics and chaos theory appear to be incompatible with each other. It is possible that quantum physics has the effect of suppressing chaotic systems.

It should be said that this impenetrability beyond the Planck length is under the umbrella of current theory. It is at this scale that quantum physics and general relativity don't really work. We have to come up with a new theory, which is what has led to all the work in fields like quantum gravity and string theory. In string theory, for example, particles are no longer points but are thought of as finite strings of length of the order of the Planck length with different particles vibrating at different frequencies. Are there rules that apply at this scale that mean I could extract information at even finer scales?

OBSERVATION IS CREATION

There have been many attempts to explain the uncertainty principle as a consequence of the act of observation affecting the system. If you want to see where a particle is, you have to fire a photon at it, and this will kick the particle, giving it an unknown momentum. Beware of such explanations. They sound attractive but they are misleading. In the description I gave above of the electron passing through a single slit, I did not need to fire any photons at the electron to alter the momentum. It was purely the act of the electron passing through the screen that gave me new knowledge of its location, resulting in a trade-off that meant I lost knowledge about its momentum. There was no direct interaction with the particle that kicked it in one direction or the other.

Apparently this misleading description of photons of light kicking the particle goes back to Heisenberg's original paper. He needed to include the description in order to persuade the sceptical editors to publish the paper.

Heisenberg's uncertainty principle really is a challenge to what I mean when I talk about an electron having a position and momentum simultaneously. I just have to avoid making statements like 'knowing the position and momentum of a particle'. They have no empirical content.

The uncertainty principle is perhaps more than just an expression of what we cannot know. Rather, it represents a limit of the definition of a concept. This ties in with the description of an electron by a wave function which questions whether that the electron really has a location at all before observation. Heisenberg's approach to this conundrum of what constitutes reality was the following:

> I believe that one can formulate the emergence of the classical 'path' of a particle pregnantly as follows: *the 'path' comes into being only because we observe it.*

There is a fundamental question about what Heisenberg's uncertainty principle really tells us. Is it that we can never know the precise location and momentum of an electron at any instant of time? Or is it that such things don't exist? It's not that we can't know them, but that these things don't make sense to define for the electron. Observation is creation.

For some time I've found it very hard to believe that fundamental properties like position and momentum come into existence only once they are measured. The momentum of an electron might change after it emerges through the tiny slit, but surely it has some precise value even before I measure it? I can accept that I might not know what that is until I use my equipment to determine the momentum, but there are lots of things I don't know before I measure them. Quantum physics, however, is trying to tell me that this belief in the existence of a precise value before measurement is a mistake. It is my interaction with the system that creates the properties of the particle. Can it really be my act of measurement that produces the reality of this particle?

I am in good company. Einstein among others tried to challenge the idea that things like momentum and position are really so indeterminate until they are observed. Surely, he argued, these things really do have explicit values as the particle flies through the vacuum. We might not know what they are, or have a machinery or mathematics to work them out, but they still exist, they still make sense. The argument is that we shouldn't confuse epistemology with ontology. I may not be able to know both momentum and position (epistemology) but that doesn't mean they don't exist (ontology).

However, I had to give up on this intuitive belief in the existence of things before measurement after I read about the remarkable Bell's theorem, discovered in 1964 by Northern Irish physicist John Bell. His theorem explained why it was impossible for certain properties of a particle to exist prior to a measurement being taken. Try and make them exist prior to measurement and everything ends in a contradiction. Since the system doesn't know in advance what measurement you might choose to make, Bell showed that it was impossible to assign values to take into account every possible measurement that might be made without creating results that contradicted what theory and experiment are telling us. It's like trying to do a Sudoku puzzle with a mistake in it. However hard I try to assign values to all the squares, I always get a row or column with the same number twice.

Given that Bell's theorem is as mathematically robust as they come, I've had to concede that my act of measuring seems truly to create the properties of my particle. But I'm still deeply suspicious of whether the outcome of the act of measuring is as random as current theory would have us believe.

A HIDDEN MACHINE

Bell's theorem means that I have to bite the bullet and admit that the quantum dice really isn't cast until I actually look at it. Measurement is what causes the dice to come to rest and decide how it is going to land. But is the outcome truly random, as quantum physics suggests? I know my casino dice really isn't random when it comes down to it. There is a physical mechanism at work which finally is responsible for how the dice lands. My feeling is that the same must be true of my pot of uranium and its radiation.

I must admit to a sneaky feeling that quantum physics is a stop-gap on the way to a more complete understanding of the behaviour of fundamental particles. Surely, like the dice, there is some mechanism deciding when my lump of radioactive uranium is going to spit out an alpha particle, or that will tell us at what point on the detector screen the electron will hit after passing through the double slits.

Einstein certainly thought so, leading to his famous quote:

> Quantum mechanics is very impressive. But an inner voice tells me that it is not yet the real thing. The theory produces a good deal but hardly brings us closer to the secret of the Old One. I am at all events convinced that He does not play dice.

He believed that there must be some objective reality behind this veil that we seem unable to penetrate. Even if we can't get access to them, he believed that there must be smaller cogs that control the outcomes of measurement.

Again, I'm with Einstein on this. Surely there must be some internal mechanism at work – even if we don't know it yet – that interacts with the measurement device to determine the outcome. I am happy to concede that the mechanism will produce outcomes that follow a model of randomness, just as the throw of my dice does. But there must be something that determines the outcome. Perhaps the particles inside my pot of uranium have some little internal ticking clock, so that if the second hand is between 0–30 when I measure it, the uranium emits radiation; but if it's between 30–60, then no radiation is detected.

If it does have an internal ticking clock, then, as I shall explain, it's a pretty extraordinary mechanism, one that goes counter to another intuition. If it exists, the mechanism should, I feel, be located in the vicinity of the pot of uranium. It could be internal to the particles inside the uranium, and perhaps so tiny that I can't see it. Maybe I will never be able to explore it. The trouble is that a scenario first dreamt up by Einstein and his colleagues Boris Podolsky and Nathan Rosen revealed that if there is such a mechanism, then part of it can be moved to the other side of the universe and be located nowhere near the uranium on my desk. This may be true, but it is quite surprising that, if there is something like a hidden clock making the decisions about when the uranium spits out an alpha particle, it is a mechanism that spans the entire universe.

The scenario that Einstein, Podolsky and Rosen cooked up involves the idea of quantum entanglement. It is possible to create two particles whose properties are entangled in the sense that if I measure the properties of one particle, this forces the answers to be mirrored by the other particle. It is a bit like having two casino dice, and whenever one lands on a 6, the other must too. It would be pretty difficult to rig up such an entangled pair of cubes, precisely because the mechanism that determines how one dice will land is controlled by its interaction with the local environment, and it seems impossible to see how that could control the behaviour of the other dice. However, in quantum physics it is entirely possible to create such entangled and dependent particles, but these entangled particles reveal the very strange properties of any hidden mechanism that could determine how they will behave when measured.

To demonstrate the weird non-local nature of such a mechanism – if it exists – the experiment sends the two quantum dice in their entangled state off to opposite sides of the universe. If I then measure the first quantum dice, it has to make up its mind which face is showing, and this instantaneously determines which face is showing on the quantum dice at the other side of the universe. Some people, Einstein included, had real problems with this 'spooky' action at a distance. He felt that there might be a way for the roll of the dice to be preset before the particles head off to opposite ends of the universe. But that was before Bell proved his theorem, which tells me that it is impossible to preset the properties of a quantum particle in advance of measurement. Remember: measurement is creation.

The real challenge is to understand how creation at one end of the universe can instantaneously create a new state for the second particle at the other end. Because if there is some internal mechanism at work determining the outcome of the second particle, that mechanism has just been altered by something that has happened on the other side of the universe. It cannot be localized. The mechanism is not something that can be neatly packaged up inside the particle.

Einstein already expressed his concerns at this 'spooky action at a distance' with the double-slit experiment. How does the photographic plate know not to record an electron in one location if it is to be detected at a second location? There seems to be an instantaneous collapse of the wave function with no cascade effect from the point of observation across the result of the plate.

In this new case I have two particles, but because they are entangled in some sense they are described by one wave function, which makes them not dissimilar to the particle being detected in the double-slit experiment. The two particles must be considered as one holistic unit. Bell's theorem means that the properties of the particles can't be preset before they travel to the ends of the universe, which in turn means that any mechanism that determines their properties cannot be localized at the particle, but must span the entire length of the universe.

So if there is a mechanism deciding when my radioactive uranium emits radiation (as my deterministic soul yearns for there to be), it will have to be a mechanism that spans the universe. It can't just be an internal machine at the heart of the blob of uranium on my desk, because the machine is also potentially controlling the state of particles across the universe that might be entangled with the uranium.

Often these results are trotted out to knock down any attempt to claim that there is a mechanism at work that determines when my pot of uranium spits out an alpha particle. But really these results should be interpreted only as the conditions that a hidden machine must satisfy.

There could be a hidden mechanism – it's just going to be very weird. As Bell, who was responsible for proving that such hidden machines must span the universe, said: 'What is proved by impossibility proofs is a lack of imagination.'

But there are many who are not as keen as I am to eliminate the possibility that the behaviour of my uranium is random. This is because it might be this small chink in the knowable that allows something many people cherish to enter the scientific picture: free will.

Some commentators have argued that if there is genuine randomness in quantum physics, and the present state of things is not predetermined by past events, then it is evidence of free will at work in the universe. These quantum particles seem free to go one way or the other when deciding what to reveal about themselves when observed. Macro-sized humans may not have free will, but these micro-particles seem able to do what they want . . . within reason.

Perhaps the free will of these particles is the expression of a greater free will. Some religious thinkers contend that the known unknown of quantum physics allows room for an external agent to act in the world and influence its course. At the moment we have no mechanism for determining the outcome of the measurement of a system in some quantum state of superposition. Provided that the outcomes over the long term are in line with what we'd expect from the random results we observe, there seems room for an agent to determine individual outcomes. This would take advantage of our present inability to explain how the macroscopic world of measurement interacts with the quantum world. So is the unknown of quantum physics home for a theistic God? If I was going to get anywhere in my attempts to understand whether a God could hide in the equations of quantum physics, I needed to talk to someone who was as much at home in a laboratory as in a cathedral. So I made a trip to Cambridge.

THE VEGETARIAN BUTCHER

John Polkinghorne learned his physics at the feet of Paul Dirac in Cambridge and then with Richard Feynman and Murray Gell-Mann at Caltech. You can't ask for better teachers than that. His research has, among other things, helped to confirm the existence of the quarks that many believe are the last step as I zoom in on my casino dice.

Polkinghorne is back at his alma mater, so I arranged to meet him at his home in Cambridge. Having done a five-year research stint in Cambridge, I always enjoy a chance to visit even if my heart is with the dark-blue city of Oxford. Polkinghorne's decision to become an ordained priest, after a quarter of a century of pushing the limits of quantum physics, makes him perfectly placed to explore the theology in the quantum unknowable. To many it seemed a dramatic career change. As he explained:

'I didn't leave science because I was disillusioned, but felt I'd done my bit for it after about 25 years. I was very much on the mathematical side, where you probably do your best work before you're 45.'

Yikes. I hate it when people say that. I've always clung to the hope that it is a myth that mathematics is only for the under-forties, that mathematics isn't some Club 18–30 holiday camp. But then I guess, being the wrong side of that divide, I would say that. Provided that there are still unanswered questions to struggle with, that is what drives me on. And I've still got plenty of those unanswered questions on my desk. But I can certainly understand the desire to set yourself new challenges . . . like my current attempts to understand quantum physics. For Polkinghorne it was getting ordained, and he often jokes about the seemingly contradictory natures of the two professions he has dedicated his life to.

'People sometimes think that it is odd, or even disingenuous, for a person to be both a physicist and a priest. It induces in them the same sort of quizzical surprise that would greet the claim to be a vegetarian butcher.'

But he himself thinks of the two roles as a harmonious combination.

'The basic reason is simply that science and theology are both concerned with the search for truth.'

I wondered whether there were any questions that he thought were beyond the reach of either discipline.

'There are two sorts of questions that science cannot answer. Some of them arise out of science itself. The first is something we've learnt from quantum physics, which is that although the world is orderly, it's also cloudy and fitful in its character and we don't have access to that clear, unquestionable post-Newtonian world that seems to be sitting there.

'But there are also questions that by their very nature don't lie within science's purview to answer. I think science has been tremendously successful and I have enormous respect for it, but it's achieved its success by limiting its ambition. Essentially science is asking a single question about how things happen: what is the process of the world? And it deliberately brackets out by its nature questions of meaning and value and purpose.'

That's not the first time I've come across this supposed dividing line: science does the 'how' and religion does the 'why'. It's an attractive soundbite, but I think it's a fundamentally flawed take on science.

Science tackles a lot of 'why' questions. Why is my pot of uranium radiating alpha particles? Why do the planets orbit the Sun on the same two-dimensional plane rather than at arbitrary angles to each other? Why do bees make their hives in hexagons? Why does the population of lemmings plummet every four years? Why is the sky blue? Why can't things travel faster than light?

Polkinghorne tried to tease out for me the difference he sees in the two approaches.

'My favourite homely example is that you come into my kitchen and you see the kettle boiling. If I put on my scientific hat then I explain that it is boiling because the burning gas heats the water, and so on. But I can take off my scientific hat and say the kettle is boiling because I wanted a cup of tea and would you like to have one?'

I decided to take him up on his offer of tea. As it brewed, Polkinghorne continued.

'I don't have to choose between those two answers, and if I am to fully understand the phenomenon of the boiling kettle, I have to answer both questions: how it's happening and why it's happening.'

I agree with Polkinghorne to some extent that science has limited its ambitions and tackled the easier questions. Fermat's Last Theorem is frankly easier than trying to understand my cat's behaviour or the next move Polkinghorne is going to make. But that doesn't mean that science can't hope ultimately to understand the complexities of a cat or the vagaries of human desire.

In my view, the science-versus-religion debate has fallen foul of our terrible desire to compartmentalize everything: the silo mentality that says, 'This is science and this is theology and this is art and this is psychology.' The exciting thing is that we have developed a multitude of discourses to navigate our environment. The evolution of everything in the universe might be reducible to the solutions of Schrödinger's wave equation, including Polkinghorne's decision to boil his kettle, but while it's a great language for describing the behaviour of my pot of uranium, it isn't the right language to explain the migration of a flock of birds, the thrill of listening to Mozart, or to discuss the immorality of torture.

Polkinghorne concurred with the dangers of a too reductionist take on reality:

'Sometimes when I'm having arguments with firmly reductionist friends who say that physics is everything, I say first of all, "What about mathematics?" and secondly, "What about music?" Of course music is just vibrations of the ear, but when you've said that you've said all that science can say about music, but you certainly haven't said all that can be said about music. It does seem to me very important that one doesn't just take a reductionist axe and chop everything down.'

I pushed Polkinghorne on his first example of a question science can't answer. Does he really believe that quantum physics means that I can't know when my pot of uranium is going to spit out its next particle? Is it really just chance?

'It's very unsatisfactory that there is this sort of lottery going on. A casino in effect. Most quantum physicists who are busy doing the numbers have just got used to that, but I think it is unsatisfactory. The question is whether it is epistemic or ontological.

'Epistemological problems have an answer, but you don't happen to know it. But ontological things are situations where you could not know it. And that's the traditional interpretation of quantum theory: you cannot know.

'In the casino we know it's essentially epistemic. There are tiny effects that influence things. My feeling is that if the problems of quantum theory are epistemic, then you need to have some notion of how that epistemological frustration arises, what stops you from doing it. I think it's sensible to try to push the issue ontologically as far as you can. We haven't got there yet.'

The majority approach to the problems of quantum physics is that before you observe a particle it is in a superposition of states described by the wave function, and that observation by macroscopic apparatus causes a jump in the behaviour. The particle now has one state and the wave function encodes the probability that you will find the particle in one state rather than another. There is no attempt to explain the jump. This is called the Copenhagen interpretation after the home of its principal proponent, the Danish physicist Niels Bohr. Basically it's the 'Shut up and Calculate' school of quantum physics.

'Although I sign up to the Copenhagen interpretation of quantum theory, I don't think it's intellectually satisfying. At the end of the day all these things come down to someone saying "and then it happens".

'It's somehow produced by the intervention of macroscopic measuring apparatus. End of discussion. But that's just winning by definition. It is a problem. There are still puzzles.'

Given Polkinghorne's belief that there is a God acting in the world, I wondered whether he thought the unknown of this collapsing wave function was a window for his God to act.

'I don't think that God is on hand to decide whether the nucleus in your uranium decays. There is some sort of mechanism . . . no, "mechanism" isn't quite the right word . . . some sort of influence that sorts this thing out. One of the paradoxes of quantum theory is that here we are 80 years later and we still don't understand it.'

In the First Edge, exploring chaos theory, I'd read how Polkinghorne believed that God might get involved with the decimal places we can't know. I wondered why he had chosen chaos theory, rather than his home territory of quantum physics, as the unknown through which his God might act.

'There was a period of about ten years when the science and theology communities were wrestling with these forms of agency. Of course they didn't solve the problem, because that would have been a very ambitious project. There were a lot of people, especially on the west coast of America, who put their money on quantum theory explaining everything. That appeared to me just a little too slick. To counterbalance that I lurched a bit too far in the other direction. I don't think chaos theory is the whole solution. It's really just the suggestion that the physical universe is orderly but looser in its order than Newton would have thought.'

But he certainly isn't dismissive of the implications of quantum physics.

'The discovery of the intrinsic unpredictability in quantum theory shows us that the world certainly isn't mechanical and therefore we certainly aren't automata in some trivial and unbelievable sense.'

It's intriguing that an agent trying to dictate the course of the future using the unknown of quantum physics has the opportunity to act only when measurement is made. Until the measurement causes a phase change, the equations of quantum physics are totally deterministic, rolling along in a linear, non-chaotic fashion with no room for any agent to act. It is one reason why religious physicists like Polkinghorne, who are trying to find a gap for an agent to act, are not particularly enamoured of the unknowable that quantum physics implies.

As I drive back from Cambridge, this question of epistemology versus ontology seems central to navigating what quantum physics tells me about what I cannot know. Is it like my casino dice? Although we can't know the precise starting conditions for the throw of the dice, we don't question whether they exist. But quantum physics questions whether I can talk about my pot of uranium having a well-defined initial state.

The current majority interpretation in physics is that we are mistaken to believe that the particles inside my uranium can be said to have simultaneously a precise momentum and position. This interpretation turns epistemology into ontology. Our inability to know is actually an expression of the true nature of things. As Heisenberg put it: 'The atoms or elementary particles themselves are not real; they form a world of potentialities or possibilities rather than one of things or facts.'

SOMETHING OUT OF NOTHING

Although Heisenberg's uncertainty principle seems to create an unknown or gap through which God can slip back in, it may actually fill another gap that is the spark for most people's belief in a Creator. One of the big unknowns is this: why is there something rather than nothing? My pot of uranium arrived in the post, sent via Amazon from Images Scientific Instruments in Staten Island. But if I keep reaching back, trying to find the ultimate origin of my uranium, I am eventually going to hit an unknown. The need for some explanation of this unknown is at the heart of many cultures' concepts of God. God is the answer to that question. But what sort of answer is that? Perhaps it just highlights the fact that many people think we can't know the answer to this.

I think most scientists who talk of a God have in mind something that answers the seemingly unanswerable question of where all this stuff came from. Once the universe is up and running, they are happy to engage their scientific brains to understand how the stuff we've got behaves. They are not looking for God to intervene in the world. This is what is often called deism rather than theism. This sort of God is very much one that can be equated with 'things we cannot know'.

Of course, if we try to describe what this answer actually looks like, we encounter the problem of infinite regress. If you think that something is responsible for creating the universe, then you quickly hit the question of who created that something. Of course, that 'who' is part of the problem, because we have a terrible urge to personify this concept.

So this is why many talk about transcendent definitions, things which can't be articulated: to avoid the problem of infinite regress. They avoid even an attempt to articulate what the answer might look like. It's just something that is unknown and transcends our attempts to know it. This is the God that the presenter of the Sunday morning programme on BBC Northern Ireland whom I tangled with was trying to formulate.

It is a God that is defined as something that can't be articulated. But then does it have any potency at all as a concept? If it can't interfere, if it can't influence, if it can't be articulated and described, why do we need it? This is why every myth maker has had to mold their gods into forms that can be articulated, recognized, often personified. A God that is too transcendental loses its potency and fades away. For many early religions this was precisely what happened to the idea of the High God or Sky God. As religious commentator Karen Armstrong writes in her book *The Case for God*: 'He became *Deus otiosus*, a "useless" or "superfluous" deity, and gradually faded from the consciousness of his people.'

As the theologian Herbert McCabe declared: 'To assert the existence of God is to claim that there is an unanswered question about the universe.' But he also warned that the fault of religion was always to make this God into a thing rather than a philosophical idea. The problem, he believed, is that religion far too often commits idolatry by trying to engage too personally with this concept of God.

The trouble is that an undefined, unknowable, transcendent concept is too abstract for many to engage with. It can't offer the sort of consolation that many are after. So perhaps it is inevitable that its potency depends on it becoming a little less transcendent, something tangible, even if that contradicts its original definition and leads to the 'who created the creator' paradox.

ZERO EQUALS ONE MINUS ONE

But the question of why there is something rather than nothing may not be as unknowable as we think. And it is the unknowable of this Third Edge that could provide a way to get something *ex nihilo*, something out of nothing. As soon as you have a bit of empty space, quantum physics is going to start filling it with stuff. The version of Heisenberg's uncertainty principle that I have explored so far looks at the relationship between position and momentum. But there are other physical concepts that are similarly entangled.

For example, Heisenberg's uncertainty principle connects the measurement of energy and time: if I look at what is happening in an apparently empty bit of space, then decreasing the time period in which

I examine the space increases the uncertainty of the energy content – which means that empty space can never be truly empty. Over very short periods of time there is the chance of energy fluctuations. Since energy can change into mass, this results in particles spontaneously appearing from the vacuum. Most of the time they annihilate each other and disappear back into the void, but sometimes things survive. And this gives us a mechanism for getting something out of nothing.

But where does this energy come from? Doesn't its sudden appearance contradict the conservation of energy that physics holds dear? Some propose that the total energy content of the universe is actually zero, and therefore that no one is cheating the system. The key here is that gravity provides a negative energy content. So the universe can emerge from zero energy – from nothing – because what emerges is a combination of positive and negative energy. We are just seeing the equation $0 = 1 - 1$ at work. 0 is nothing; 1 plus –1 is matter and gravity pulling that matter.

It might seem a bit bizarre to call gravity negative energy, but think about putting a large mass like an asteroid next to the Earth: as the asteroid falls towards the Earth it gains kinetic energy, but the gravitational pull is also going up because gravity increases the closer two masses are to each other. So to maintain conservation of energy, this gravitational potential energy is negative and balances the increase in kinetic energy.

According to Heisenberg's uncertainty principle, it follows from the fact that space exists that you will get particles appearing from nothing. You don't have any need for a creator. Quantum fluctuations mean that we are seeing something appearing from nothing all the time. As I shall discover in the Fifth Edge, this is how Hawking explained why black holes radiate particles. Nothing becomes a particle and an antiparticle: one gets trapped in the black hole and the other radiates away. So quantum physics already provides a partial answer to the something-from-nothing question.

However, you do at least need a stage on which to play this quantum game, and it's the question of the creation of empty space that in turn becomes the issue. This perhaps is where confusion arises. Some equate empty space with nothing. But that is a mistake. Three-dimensional empty space, a vacuum, is still something. It is an arena in which geometry, mathematics, physics can play out. After all, the fact that you have a three dimensional rather than a four-dimensional empty space already hints at the evidence of something. Nothing does not have a dimension.

There are theories today which could explain how space and time can appear in the same way as particles, as fluctuations in quantum gravity. It's as if the mathematics is enough to input nothing and show how it can give rise to something – to a universe. It is striking that science is telling us how little we need to get things going. In the end, it might be a bit of mathematics, not Amazon, that is the ultimate source of my pot of uranium.

FOURTH EDGE: THE CUT-OUT UNIVERSE

7

I venture to suggest this solution to the ancient problem: the Library is unlimited and cyclical. If an eternal traveller were to cross it in any direction, after centuries he would see the same volumes were repeated in the same disorder. My solitude is gladdened by this elegant hope.

Jorge Luis Borges, *The Library of Babel*

I have always been intrigued by the question: does infinity physically exist? My attempts to create infinity by cutting the dice up into infinitely small pieces ran aground when I hit indivisible quarks. It even seems that I can't divide space infinitely often, since space may be quantized. So my quest to know if infinity exists will turn in a different direction: I shall look out, not in.

What happens if I keep going in a straight line? Do I go on forever? It is a question that I think everyone who looks up into space must contemplate at some point in their lives. If I throw my dice into the vacuum of space, will it one day return to its starting point, or perhaps hit a cosmic wall and bounce back, or will it just tumble forever? Knowing whether the universe goes on forever is a surprisingly subtle question that touches on the fact that space itself is not static. Even if the universe is infinite, I may be restricted in theory to the amount of space I can explore. It may be something we can never know.

To help me on my journey to infinity I've downloaded the universe – what I can see of it at least. I've glued together a star globe from the European space agency website. It's not exactly a globe. It's made from two sheets of A4 that I've cut out and glued together to form one of my favourite mathematical shapes: an icosahedron made from

20 equilateral triangles. Like my casino dice, it is an example of one of the five Platonic shapes that make good dice.

As we look out into space on a clear night, it seems as though the stars are all painted onto a huge black celestial globe that encases the universe. This was certainly the model of the universe for many ancient cultures. They believed that the Earth sat at the centre of this globe which span on an axis passing through the Polaris star, the one star that seems to stay still in the night sky, the other stars rotating round it.

My paper star globe is a model of what this celestial sphere would look like. I've put it on my desk with the Polaris star sitting at the top of this icosahedron. Around the middle of my shape are the signs of the zodiac that mark the passing of the year, including, of course, my own constellation of Virgo. The Sun appears to move through each of these constellations, taking a full year to return to its starting point. On the bottom of the shape are the stars that you can see from the southern hemisphere, the brightest of which is Alpha Centauri. This is actually made up of three stars, including Proxima Centauri, which is thought to be the nearest to our own star, the Sun.

People have been making versions of my paper globe for millennia. Cicero writes of ancient Greek astronomers making models of this celestial globe with stars marked on them, early forerunners of my cut-out universe. Sadly, none of the Greek models have survived, so I popped into one of my favourite museums in Oxford, the Museum of the History of Science, to see some others that have. There was a beautiful globe about half a metre high dating from the early sixteenth century. Made in Germany, it brings the constellations to life with graphic images of birds, fish, animals and men printed onto paper gores that have been glued onto the sphere.

Although my modern paper cut-out doesn't match the beauty of the sixteenth-century globe in the Museum of the History of Science, its icosahedral design harks back to Plato and his belief that the celestial globe that encases our universe may not be a sphere but a dodecahedron – also one of the Platonic shapes that make good dice. The importance of this mathematical dice to understanding the shape of the universe may not be as far-fetched as it sounds.

TRIANGULAR TELESCOPES

That we can know anything about regions of space we will never visit is extraordinary. Every culture has inevitably looked up into the night sky and contemplated what is out there. Most immediately obvious are the Sun and the Moon. But how on Earth did ancient cultures discover anything about these bodies, given that they were confined to the surface of the planet? For me this is one of the striking things about mathematics: it allows us to deduce things about the universe from the comfort of our observatories.

Trigonometry, the mathematics of triangles and angles, was a tool developed not to torture schoolkids but to navigate the night sky. It is the earliest form of telescope. Already in the third century BC Aristarchus of Samos was able to calculate the size of the Sun and the Moon in terms of the radius of the Earth and to determine their relative distance from the Earth, just with the help of a mathematical triangle.

For example, when the Moon is exactly half full, the angle between the Earth, Moon and Sun is essentially 90 degrees. So by measuring the angle Φ between the Moon, Earth and Sun I can use the mathematics of trigonometry to calculate the distance from the Earth to the Moon relative to that from the Earth to the Sun. The ratio of those two distances is precisely what is meant by the cosine of the angle Φ, and that is something that I can determine with a purely mathematical analysis.

The accuracy of the measurement, however, meant that Aristarchus was out by a factor of 20 in the relative distance. He'd estimated the

The right-angled triangle made by the Earth, Moon and Sun when the Moon is half full.

angle to be 87 degrees, while the true value is 89.853, almost a right angle. Small differences in angles of this size result in quite large differences in the relative size of the lengths of the sides of the triangle. It would need the invention of the telescope and some more clever mathematics to truly determine the size of the solar system.

Even without the invention of the telescope, astronomers could see that the Moon and Sun weren't the only bodies processing through the sky. Ancient cultures picked up several tiny pricks of light in the night sky that behaved very differently from the plethora of other stars. They were wandering beacons of light: Mercury, Venus, Mars, Jupiter and Saturn – luminous bodies that can't be marked on my cut-out sphere because the next night they will be located at a different point. One explanation for the importance of the number seven to many cultures derives from the fact that, with the Sun and Moon, the visible planets make up seven heavenly bodies.

WRESTLING WITH INFINITY

Just as the planets move relative to the stars from day to day, it turns out that the stars too are moving relative to each other. So the celestial sphere I have on my desk is just a snapshot of the night sky at a particular moment. Marked on my sphere is the easily identifiable constellation of the Plough or Big Dipper. But the stars that make up the Plough – Merak, Dubhe, Alkaid, Phecda, Megrez, Alioth, Mizar – are on the move: 100,000 years ago they would have been painted on my globe in a very different configuration, and 100,000 years hence they will look different again.

But for ancient astronomers the stars were fixed, bound to the celestial sphere that encompassed the universe. There was little discussion of what lay beyond. This was the void where there was nothing. Beyond the limits of my paper model was a no-go area. However, there were some medieval philosophers who were prepared to contemplate the nature of the void. Nicolas Oresme believed that the extra cosmic space beyond the celestial sphere really existed and was infinite in extent. In his writings he identified this immensity with God – not so

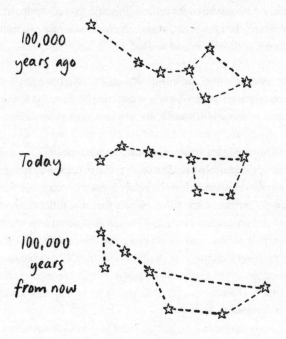

The changing shape of the Plough.

far, perhaps, from my proposed conception of God as the things we cannot know.

Oresme was not frightened by the philosophical challenge of the infinite. Indeed, he proved that you can reach infinity by adding the fractions $1 + \frac{1}{2} + \frac{1}{3} + \frac{1}{4} + \ldots$, a counterintuitive mathematical result, given that the bits you are adding are getting smaller and smaller. This infinite sum is known as the harmonic series, because when I pluck a string on my cello the sound is built from harmonics whose wavelengths are given by all these fractions. As I explain later, the revelation that this harmonic series sums to infinity has interesting repercussions for how far we may ever be able to see into space.

It seems that it was only in the fifteenth century that astronomers began to contemplate the idea that the celestial sphere might be an illusion, and that the universe might extend infinitely. Nicolaus Cusanus suggested that the universe was infinite and any point could therefore be considered its centre. This was picked up by the Italian Dominican friar Giordano Bruno, who in 1584 wrote a seminal work, *On the Infinite Universe and Worlds*.

> The universe is then one, infinite, immobile . . . It is not capable of comprehension and therefore is endless and limitless, and to that extent infinite and indeterminable, and consequently immobile.

Bruno's logic that leads to this conclusion is interesting. The universe is created by God but God is unknowable. Therefore the universe must be beyond our comprehension. Therefore it must be infinite, since a finite universe is in theory knowable. Now, I would say that the converse is true: if the universe is endless, it means that potentially it is beyond our comprehension. And if I am exploring the concept of God as a way of articulating the things we cannot know, then an infinite universe, if unknowable, could imply the existence of this concept of transcendence. But is the universe infinite, and, if so, is it as unknowable as it may first appear?

Bruno offers more than just his belief in God to justify his view of an infinite universe. One of the most powerful challenges to a finite universe contained in a celestial sphere is the question of what is behind the wall that contains the universe. Many suggested that there is nothing – the void. But Bruno was dissatisfied with this. He also believed that time was infinite both in the past and into the future. This somewhat controversially did away with the need for a moment of creation and a day of final judgement. Bruno was not shy of controversy, and his teachings on the Bible eventually led to him falling foul of the Catholic Church – not a good thing at the time. He was burnt at the stake on 17 February 1600.

Bruno's ideas raise the question of how I could ever know whether the universe is infinite. If it is finite then it might be possible to know this. The surface of the Earth turned out to be finite and navigable, so perhaps we can simply navigate our universe and prove that it is finite. Although we don't have a ship in which we can sail to the edges of the universe, scientists in the seventeenth century did come up with a cunning way to explore space: the telescope.

HOW FAR CAN YOU SEE?

It was Galileo's generation that discovered you could enhance how far you can see by placing carved glass lenses in a tube. Indeed, for years Galileo himself seemed to get the credit for the invention of the telescope, but that accolade should go to the Dutch spectacle-maker Hans Lippershey, who filed a patent for an instrument 'for seeing things far away as if they were nearby'. The Dutch instrument was able to magnify things by a factor of 3.

Galileo heard about the instrument on a trip to Venice. That same night he figured out the principle on which it worked and was soon constructing instruments that could achieve a magnification of 33 times. The name 'telescope' was coined by a Greek poet who was attending a banquet to honour Galileo in 1611: in Greek *tele* means 'far' and *skopein* means 'see'. And it did indeed allow Galileo and subsequent generations of astronomers to see further than ever before. Galileo discovered moons orbiting Jupiter and sunspots that rotated, implying that the Sun was spinning on its axis – phenomena that helped to confirm Copernicus's model of a Sun-centred solar system.

In 1663 the Scottish mathematician James Gregory realized that the telescope could also be used to make new calculations of just how far away the Sun was from the Earth. Johannes Kepler had already observed the time it takes each planet to orbit the Sun and deduced, using his laws of planetary motion, the relative distance of each planet from the Sun. His third law states that the square of the time a planet takes to complete one orbit of the Sun is proportional to the cube of the distance from the Sun. For example, Venus completes an orbit in $3/5$ of the time it takes the Earth to go round the Sun, which means that Venus's distance from the Sun is about $7/10$ (approximately $(3/5)^{2/3}$) of the distance of the Earth to the Sun. (When I talk about distance from the Sun I need to be careful since, as Kepler discovered, the planets aren't describing perfect circles but ellipses, so the distance varies. In general, I mean something like average distance.)

But these are only relative distances. What Gregory and others realized is that they could use observations of the planet Venus crossing the Sun, known as a transit, and a bit more trigonometry to calculate how far the Earth and Venus really are from the Sun. If they made observations from two different locations on the Earth of the different points and times at which Venus crossed the Sun, they would be able to work out the angle of the triangle formed by the two observers and Venus. And from there, by calculating the distance between the two observers on the Earth and using some trigonometry, they could deduce the distance to Venus.

The trick with trigonometry is to use triangles to change something you can't measure directly, such as the distance between the Earth and Venus, into something you can measure from the surface of the Earth, such as an angle or the distance between two points on Earth. The calculation was a complicated but clever application of abstract mathematical thought combined with practical astronomical observation.

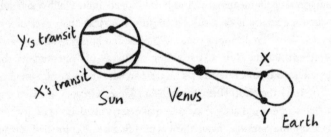

The transit of Venus from two different locations on Earth.

The trouble is that these transits don't happen that often. Venus has crossed in front of the Sun only 10 times since 1400. Gregory had originally proposed using the transit of Mercury, since the next transit of Venus wouldn't be till 1761. Edmond Halley knew of the work and made observations of the transit of Mercury that occurred in 1676, but it transpired that only one other observation was made, enough theoretically to calculate the distance, but, given the errors that can creep in, you really want as many observations as possible.

It was the multiple observations of the transits of Venus in 1761 and 1769 that finally enabled calculations to be made of the distance of the Earth from the Sun. In one of the first coordinated global scientific experiments of its kind, it was calculated that the Earth was 95 million miles from the Sun. Halley alas had died some 19 years earlier and missed the culmination of the project that he'd tried to realize nearly 90 years before. Today the calculations give the average distance of the Earth from the Sun as 92,955,807.267 miles.

Here was the first inkling of the immensity contained in my paper celestial globe. The ancient astronomers believed that my paper model contained smaller globes on which the planets were inscribed. If they were right, these globes were millions of miles in diameter.

I continue to be astounded by the power of trigonometry to translate a measurement on Earth into a measurement of the distance to a planet that no human has ever visited. More impressive mathematical feats were to follow. Telescopes and light aren't the only ways to detect what might be out there. Mathematics also turned out to offer a farseeing view of the universe, so much so that it succeeded in predicting the existence of a new planet before it was ever seen down the barrel of a telescope.

DISCOVERING A PLANET WITH THE POINT OF YOUR PEN

There are two ways to detect a new planet: luck and logic. The first planet to be detected since antiquity was discovered by luck. The German musician Friedrich Wilhelm Herschel had moved from Hanover to England in an attempt to further his musical career. But he was also something of an amateur astronomer and spent his nights staring at the sky with his impressive range of telescopes.

It was on 13 March 1781 that Herschel spotted something unusual. What he at first thought was a star seemed to change size according to the magnification of his telescope. That was generally an indication of something close enough that it could be zoomed in on. The next test was: did it move? Sure enough, when he looked for it four days later it had changed position relative to the stars. Given the number of comets that had been spotted, his first thought was not of a new planet.

But after he alerted the Astronomer Royal and the object was tracked further, it became clear that its orbit was not parabolic, as you would expect for a comet, but nearly circular. The object was also too bright to be a comet and there was no visible tail. The astronomers concluded that it was in fact a new planet. Herschel wanted to name the planet after King George III, but classical mythology prevailed. Saturn was the father of Jupiter, and this new planet orbiting further out again took the name of Saturn's father: Uranus.

Astronomers were ecstatic at the idea of a new planet and started mapping its trajectory, looking for moons, and calculating the length of its orbit around the Sun. But Uranus was not as well behaved as some astronomers had expected. Newton's theory of gravitation, which had proved so successful in predicting the path of the other planets, was distinctly faulty when it came to predicting where Uranus would be found. By 1788 the planet was $1/120$ of a degree out from where it should be. It was realized that the gravitational effect of Jupiter and Saturn needed to be factored in.

A new trajectory was published in 1791, but by 1800 it was out again. By 1825 it was way ahead of its predicted position, but then started to slow down, and by 1832 it had fallen behind where the maths was predicting it should be. Was there some mysterious substance out there causing resistance? Did Newton's laws of gravitation break down at such great distances from the Sun? Some suggested that, just as Jupiter and Saturn were exerting a gravitational pull on Uranus, perhaps there was another planet out there pushing and pulling it around. But if it existed, where was it?

While Uranus was discovered by luck, this new planet would be pinpointed using the power of pure logic, embodied in the mathematics of Newton. Up until this point, astronomers would feed in the location of the planets and use the maths to calculate their orbits. Now the process would have to be reversed. Uranus had been tracked for some decades, and the challenge was to find out where you should place a planet that would explain Uranus's strange trajectory.

The task was pretty daunting mathematically, but two theoreticians picked up the gauntlet: John Couch Adams in England and Urbain Leverrier in France. Both succeeded in inverting the problem and identifying where they thought a new planet might be. Adams had completed his calculations by September 1845 and approached astronomers in England to try to locate the new planet. It seems that Adams's lack of credentials and a rather antisocial manner, perhaps consistent with Asperger's syndrome, didn't endear him to the authorities. The Astronomer Royal was also rather distracted by a scandalous murder case involving one of his assistants. This meant that Adams's prediction was ignored on the English side of the Channel. Leverrier took until June 1846 to complete his calculations and had similar problems getting the astronomical authorities in France to spend precious telescope time looking for a hypothetical planet. So Leverrier wrote to the Berlin Observatory for assistance.

The German astronomers were more helpful. On 23 September 1846, Johann Gottfried Galle pointed the Fraunhofer telescope to the position in the night sky at which Leverrier's calculations predicted the new planet should be located. Sure enough, there was a point of light that wasn't on any of the star charts they had in the observatory. The next night it had moved . . . by exactly the amount predicted by Leverrier's calculations.

The announcement of another new planet was greeted with great excitement by many, but the astronomers in England who had failed to follow up on Adams's predictions were left looking rather foolish. Herschel, now a member of the Board of Visitors of the Royal Observatory, attempted to set down the events that would prove Adams had made the prediction first. The affair inevitably led to a bitter priority dispute. The name of the planet became a political football, with the French wanting it named after Leverrier, and the English objecting that it broke with the tradition of naming planets after Roman gods. Eventually the international community settled on a name: Neptune.

The power of mathematics to tell you what might be out there is remarkable. As the astronomer Francois Arago wryly observed, Leverrier had discovered Neptune 'with the point of his pen'. Of course, it needed Galle's observations at the Berlin Observatory to confirm that theory did indeed match reality.

Stuck on the surface of the Earth, we'd nevertheless managed to navigate towards the edge of our solar system. How much further would it be possible to explore? Although the telescope had allowed us to journey so far, it would also reveal the theoretical limits on how far we will ever be able to see – because, it turns out, light takes time to get to us.

COSMIC SPEED LIMIT

The telescope was instrumental in settling a dispute that had been raging since antiquity. Does light instantaneously assert its presence across space, or does it take time to travel from one place to another? Aristotle, for example, did not believe that light moved. It was just present or not. Others agreed. The ancient Greeks thought that sight involved light travelling from the eye to the object. If that was so, argued the mathematician Heron of Alexandria, light must be instantaneous. Otherwise, when we open our eyes, how could we immediately see the far-distant stars?

It was the Islamic scholar Alhazen who suggested in his *Book of Optics* that light travels in the other direction: from the object to the eye. But even if light travelled the other way, many still believed that it would travel infinitely fast. Galileo, though, wasn't sure. He thought that if light took time to travel from its source, then surely you could measure that. He proposed uncovering a light and seeing how long it took to detect this some miles away. The scale Galileo was proposing was far too small to detect any delay, and it was Descartes who upped it. He realized that if light took time to reach the Earth from the Sun and the Moon, the timings of lunar eclipses would be slightly out from what we'd expect. But no such deviation was picked up. Both Galileo and Descartes were actually on to something – it's just that light travels fast enough that the Sun and Moon are still too close to detect any discrepancy.

It wasn't the Earth's moon but the moons orbiting Jupiter that finally provided proof that it takes time for light to cross space. Galileo had proposed that the moons of Jupiter could be used as a clever means of solving the longitude problem. This would involve measuring time by using the moment when the innermost moon Io went into the shadow created by Jupiter. Io takes 42.5 hours to orbit Jupiter, regular enough for it to be used as a cosmic clock. If a table was drawn up of the times when these eclipses occurred in Florence, then by observing the time of the eclipse in another location, you could deduce your longitude relative to Florence. It didn't really catch on as a method for determining longitude at sea, which was the great challenge at the time, but was used for determining longitude on land.

It was the Danish astronomer Ole Rømer who in 1676 used the moons of Jupiter to discover the finite speed of light. While working at the observatory in Paris, he recorded the times at which the moon Io disappeared into the shadow of Jupiter. The timings seemed to depend on where the Earth was on its orbit around the Sun. If the Earth was on the other side of the Sun from Jupiter there seemed to be a delay. This, he realized, was because the light took longer to travel to the Earth than if it was on the same side of the Sun as Jupiter. The discovery was announced on 22 August 1676 at the Royal Academy of Sciences in Paris by Giovanni Cassini, the director of the observatory in Paris. He explained that astronomers would need to change the tables predicting the times at which Io would disappear:

> This appears to be due to light taking some time to reach us from the satellite; light seems to take about ten to eleven minutes to cross a distance equal to the half-diameter of the terrestrial orbit.

The current measurement is that it takes 8 minutes and 20 seconds, so the seventeenth-century astronomers weren't far off. There followed a whole series of experiments to determine the numerical value of the speed of light through the vacuum of space. Given that the speed is in the order of 300 million metres per second, it is little wonder that many people thought it was infinite. Now, with the telescope allowing huge distances in space to be measured, the speed of light would become an important limit on any attempt to look into the far reaches of our universe.

Indeed, as I look out into the universe, the fact that light takes time to cross space means that I am in fact looking back in time. A snapshot of the sky depicts the Sun as it was 8 minutes and 20 seconds ago, the nearest star as it was four years ago, and the most distant galaxies as they looked billions of years ago. It's possible that in some distant galaxy, telescopes trained on Earth are witnessing the extinction of the dinosaurs some 66 million years ago.

The speed of light became part of the way astronomers measure the vastness of space. When astronomers say something is one light year away, they mean that it takes light one year to travel from that point to us.

THE STARS IN OUR NEIGHBOURHOOD

Looking at the celestial sphere on my desk, I find it laughable that the ancient Greeks thought the stars were painted on a huge celestial ball enclosing the universe with the void beyond. But they didn't have much to go on. Given the distance of the stars from the Earth, to the naked eye they all look to be a long way away. It was impossible for the ancient astronomers to detect any depth. But the invention of the telescope brought those stars a little closer, close enough that modern astronomers could see that they were not all the same distance from the Earth.

If one star is nearer to us than another, then there is a way to tell that it's closer. Although we are stuck on the surface of the Earth, at least the Earth is moving relative to the stars, which means we get different viewpoints on the cosmos. Here was our chance to start pulling some of those stars off the surface of my celestial globe and add some depth to the universe.

If you stick your finger in front of you and look out of the window and move your head from side to side, then you'll notice that the things which are near, such as your finger, move a greater distance relative to the things further away. This effect is called parallax. Astronomers can do the same thing when looking at the stars. If they compare the location of the stars in summer to their position in winter, this can tell them which stars are nearer to the Earth than others.

Herschel was in fact trying to detect this stellar parallax, as it is known, when he stumbled upon the new planet Uranus. The difference in locations of a star is extremely small, and it takes telescopes of sufficient accuracy to detect the shift. Successful measurements weren't made until the 1830s, when the German astronomer and mathematician Friedrich Bessel recorded the first accurate observations of stellar parallax. To apply the technique to nearby stars, astronomers need to assume that the far-off stars are essentially on a single celestial wall that encases the universe, rather like the Greek model. The point is that for the purposes of detecting parallax of nearby stars, the furthest stars look fixed and can be used as a background to pick up the apparent movement of nearby stars.

Bessel compared the locations of a star called 61 Cygni in summer and winter, and then, by constructing the triangle formed by the star with the two points in the Earth's orbit, he calculated one of the angles in the triangle. Then, by applying the knowledge of the distance of the Earth from the Sun and the mathematics of trigonometry, astronomers had their first estimate of how far the nearest stars were from the Earth. Bessel's calculation suggested that 61 Cygni was 660,000 times further away from the Earth than the Sun is. His calculation was about 10% off the mark. The current value for the distance of 61 Cygni is 721,000 times the distance from the Earth to the Sun, or 11.41 light years. But Bessel was close enough that it gave us our first feeling for the depth of space.

Further calculations picked up other stars that were even closer. The closest known star to our own was only spotted in 1915 by Scottish astronomer Robert Innes. Proxima Centauri is too faint to be seen by the naked eye, which is why it took so long to detect it, but parallax calculations put the star 268,326 times further away from the Earth than the Sun is, or 4.24 light years away.

The method of stellar parallax started to peel some of the stars off my celestial sphere and brought them closer to Earth. Provided a star is not more than 400 light years from us, this method works. But the majority of stars still appeared so distant that they might as well be stuck on my paper model. Analysis of the wavelengths of the light coming from these stars let us take our next great step towards the edge of the universe.

TWINKLE, TWINKLE LITTLE STAR

The further away a star is, the less bright it appears to shine. But there is a problem with using this to judge how far away a star is. How do I know whether I am looking at a bright star that is far away, like 61 Cygni, which can be seen with the naked eye, or a duller star that is closer, like Proxima Centauri? Apparent brightness is a combination of actual brightness and the distance of the star from Earth. So how can astronomers use brightness to judge distances? It turns out that in many cases the colour of the light emitted by a star gives us enough information to know how bright it should be shining, and by measuring the apparent brightness we can tell how far away the star is.

By measuring the light coming from a star and analysing the frequencies, scientists saw that certain characteristic frequencies were missing. The light at these frequencies was being absorbed by the particular atoms in the star. This was key to proving Comte wrong when he famously said that we'd never know the chemical composition of the stars. But it could also be used to calculate how bright a star was. When astronomers looked at nearby stars whose distances from us and therefore actual luminosity were known, they found a direct relationship between the different frequencies absorbed by the star and how bright it was shining.

This discovery meant that you could use the missing frequencies of light as a measure of absolute luminosity. Now astronomers could look at the stars whose distances were too far away to apply parallax. By measuring the missing frequencies and their apparent luminosity, astronomers could work out how far the stars were from us. This gave astronomers a much clearer idea of the true depth of space.

However, it was a very special pulsating star that turned out to provide the best way to measure distances across the universe. A Cepheid star twinkles, and in 1912 American astronomer Henrietta Leavitt discovered how to use these twinkling stars to navigate the universe. She was employed at the time not as an astronomer but as a 'computer' at the Harvard College Observatory, extracting data from the photographic plates for 30 cents an hour. Women weren't allowed to operate the telescopes. She'd been assigned the task of analysing stars that grew brighter and dimmer over a period of time. Curious to know if there was any pattern to the pulse of these stars, Leavitt focussed on a batch of stars that were located in the Small Magellanic Cloud and were therefore believed to be at similar distances from the Earth.

When she plotted luminosity against the period of pulsation, she discovered a very clear pattern. The time it takes a Cepheid star to pulsate is directly correlated with its luminosity: the longer the period of pulsation, the brighter the star is shining. So to know how bright a Cepheid star really is, all you need to measure is the period of pulsation, something that is much easier to do than measuring missing light frequencies. These stars were perfect for measuring distances.

If a Cepheid star is pulsating slowly but looks very dim, it must be a long way away; an apparently bright, rapidly pulsating Cepheid must look bright because it is close. With these new rulers to hand, the universe began to take shape. More stars peeled themselves off the celestial sphere and took their place in the emerging map of the Milky Way. And our own star, the Sun, we discovered, was tucked away in a corner of a huge spiralling mass of stars.

But was this the full extent of the universe? There were some spots of light out there that didn't appear to be single stars but the light coming from hundreds of billions of stars. Were these clouds part of our Milky Way galaxy, or did they make up another galaxy like ours but completely separate? The first such region to come under investigation was a small cloud identified by the Persian astronomer al-Sufi in the tenth century. It is bright enough to be detected by the naked eye and became known as the Andromeda nebula. The suggestion that this and other clouds might actually be galaxies in their own right was first voiced in 1750 by English astronomer Thomas Wright. After reading about Wright's ideas, Immanuel Kant romantically referred to them as 'island universes'.

The debate about the status of these clouds raged for years, culminating in a face-off between rival groups in an event now called 'The Great Debate', staged at the Smithsonian Museum of Natural History in 1920. At stake was the question of the size and extent of the universe. Astronomer Harlow Shapely presented the case for why such clouds would have to be part of our local galaxy to be shining so bright. Heber Curtis countered that the number of novae – cataclysmic nuclear explosions that stars can undergo – that had been counted in this cloud exceeded all those that had been recorded in the whole of our local galaxy. How could such a novae-rich region exist as part of our galaxy?

Andromeda was finally ripped out of our local galaxy and proved to be another galaxy in its own right by the observations of American astronomer Edwin Hubble, who in 1925 used the Hooker telescope at the top of Mount Wilson in California, the largest telescope of its kind at the time, to analyse how far away Andromeda was.

Hubble spotted one star in particular that he could use to calculate this distance. At the heart of this cloud was one of the Cepheid stars that Leavitt had investigated. The star was pulsating, growing dimmer and brighter over a period of 31 days. Leavitt's analysis implied that it was burning very brightly, and yet when viewed through a telescope it looked very dim. Combining the period of pulsation with a measurement of the apparent luminosity of the star revealed that it had to be 2.5 million light years away from our Sun. The stars in the Milky Way had been calculated to be a maximum of 100,000 light years apart from each other. Leavitt's insight, combined with Hubble's calculations, dramatically changed our view of the universe. It turned out to be substantially bigger than anyone had previously imagined.

Leavitt's use of Cepheid stars as a way of navigating space transformed our picture of the universe so much that the Swedish mathematician Gösta Mittag-Leffler wanted to nominate her for the Nobel Prize in 1924. He was devastated to discover that Leavitt had died four years earlier from cancer and was therefore ineligible for the award.

This new understanding of the extent of far-off galaxies gave us a sense of the true nature of space. But how far did the universe extend beyond these distant galaxies? The first explorers on Earth leaving their villages must have had the impression that the Earth was vast, perhaps extending forever. But as people journeyed more and more, there came a realization that the surface of the Earth was finite and navigable. So what about space? As we leave our galaxy, can we get a feel for how our cosmic village fits into a bigger picture of space?

A HUGE GAME OF ASTEROIDS

I can easily picture the Earth as finite but without an edge. The surface of a sphere solves this conundrum. But how can space be finite? One of my favourite films that explores this puzzle is *The Truman Show*. It stars Jim Carey as Truman Burbank who doesn't realize that his whole universe is a scripted reality TV show housed in a huge dome. When eventually doubts emerge about his world, he sets out in a boat across the water that surrounds his home town of Seahaven, only to discover that what he thought was an endless sky is actually painted onto the studio wall. Beyond the edge of his universe, he discovers cameras filming his every move.

I don't think we are living in our own *Truman Show*. I don't think that if I travel out into space I'll suddenly hit a studio wall or a celestial sphere like my model that encompassed my world. And I think most people would agree with me. After all, such a model only raises the question of what is beyond that boundary. Are we going to find a celestial film crew looking in on us? And what happens to that film crew when they make the same journey in their world? Is it film crews all the way down? This is why most people, when pressed, conclude that the only way to solve this conundrum is to believe in an infinite universe.

But mathematicians have a third alternative, which posits a universe which has no boundary but is nonetheless finite. In this universe you travel out into space until, rather than carrying on to infinity, eventually you find yourself heading back to your starting location, just like a terrestrial explorer rounding the Earth.

To get a feel for how this universe might work, it is useful to consider a small toy universe. The game of Asteroids created by Atari in 1979 serves as a perfect example of a two-dimensional universe that is finite yet without boundary. The universe consists of just a computer screen, but when a spaceship heads towards the top of the screen, rather than bouncing back off the edge, like a 2D *Truman Show*, it seamlessly reappears at the bottom. As far as the astronauts inside the spaceship is concerned, they are travelling endlessly through space. The same applies if the spaceship heads to the left-hand side of the screen: it doesn't hit a wall but simply reappears on the right. The astronauts might begin to notice landmarks (or spacemarks) repeating themselves, although of course with an evolving universe it might be difficult to recognize things as you pass them for a second or third time.

This Asteroids universe actually has a recognizable shape. If I allow myself a third dimension within which to wrap up this universe, I can join the top and bottom of the screen to make a cylinder. Since the left- and right-hand sides of the screen are also connected, I can join the two ends of the cylinder to create a bagel or what mathematicians call a torus. The surface of this three-dimensional shape is the finite universe in the game of Asteroids.

If I take any finite three-dimensional shape, its two-dimensional surface will provide an alternative universe which is finite and unbounded. The surface of a sphere, for example, is another such two-dimensional universe. These two-dimensional universes are not just mathematical games but are key to navigating the Earth. Indeed, many cultures across the globe wondered whether the Earth went on forever or had an edge over which you would fall. Many ancient civilizations' model of the Earth consisted of a finite disc surrounded by water, a bit like Truman's world.

It wasn't until the Pythagoreans in the fifth-century BC that the idea of a spherical Earth started to take hold. The disappearance of ships over the horizon, the shadow created by the Earth on the Moon during eclipses, the variation of the Sun and stars in the sky as one travels south – all contributed to this shifting perspective. It was the 1522 circumnavigation of the world organized by Ferdinand Magellan (who was killed on the voyage) that finally proved beyond doubt that the Earth is round.

So what about the universe? Does it have a shape? We are sitting at a similar juncture to those ancient cultures contemplating the Earth and wondering whether it went on forever or had an edge or was somehow wrapped up.

But how can I wrap up a three-dimensional universe so that it has finite volume but no edges? This is the power of mathematics, which allows us to embed our three-dimensional universe in a higher-dimensional space and wrap it up like I did with the game of Asteroids. Although I can't physically picture the wrapping up, the language of mathematics gives me the equations to describe and more importantly explore the properties of these finite three-dimensional universes.

So, for example, we may live in a three-dimensional version of Asteroids. Perhaps the universe is essentially a huge cube with six faces like my casino dice. When a spaceship approaches one of these faces, instead of bouncing off the face it seamlessly exits the cube-shaped universe through one face and reappears at the opposite face. In the game of Asteroids I had two directions that were joined up left–right and up–down. In my three-dimensional cube-shaped universe, the third direction is also fused. If I could put this cube in a four-dimensional universe I could wrap it up, joining the faces to make a four-dimensional bagel, or torus, whose three-dimensional surface is our universe.

But there are other possible shapes that our universe could take. A circle is a finite two-dimensional shape whose surface is a finite one-dimensional universe. A sphere is a finite three-dimensional shape whose surface is a finite two-dimensional universe. Mathematical equations can be used to construct a four-dimensional sphere whose surface is a finite three-dimensional universe – another model for what our universe could look like.

Although mathematics provides us with candidates for a finite yet unbounded universe, how can we ever know whether our universe is finite and what shape it might be if it is? Do we have to wait for an astro-Magellan to circumnavigate the universe? Given the scale of the known universe, human exploration seems a rather hopeless way of proving whether the universe is finite. But there are explorers out there that have been navigating the universe for billions of years and can provide us with some insight into whether it is finite or not: photons of light.

COSMIC MAGELLANS

Light is a great explorer. We are constantly being showered with light that has spent billions of years traversing the universe. Does some of that light have a story to tell us that could give us an inkling of whether the universe is finite? I've already explored what would happen to a spaceship that plunged off into the depths of space: in these finite universes it would eventually come back to its starting position, just as Magellan's expedition did on its return to Seville in 1522.

The same could happen to light. Imagine a photon of light leaving our Sun in its early years, some 4.5 billion years ago. Suppose we are living on the surface of a four-dimensional bagel, the cube-shaped universe where opposite faces are joined. What happens to the light as it approaches one of these faces? It passes seamlessly through, reappearing at the opposite face, at which point it can continue its journey back towards its starting point. Provided nothing gets in the way, it could return and enter the telescope of an observer on Earth who detects this photon for the first time after its long journey. So what will our astronomer see? Well, nothing special. It will look like the light from a far distant star in its early years. It will be hard to detect that in fact they are seeing what our Sun looked like 4.5 billion years ago.

However, it does present us with a possible approach to proving the universe is finite, because we can look in the opposite direction and see whether there might be a similar picture shining at us from the opposite face. Researchers in France, Poland and the USA have been looking at the picture of light from the very early universe in the hope that parts of the map we've made may actually match up.

Much to their surprise and delight, they believed they had detected the first hint of some matching in the data. They began analysing what shapes could possibly give rise to the patterns of wavelengths that they were observing. The results suggested that the best candidate for the shape of a universe that would produce these patterns is a dodecahedron. This is the dice-like shape made up of 12 pentagonal faces. Remarkably, Plato had suggested two millennia ago that the shape of the celestial sphere with the stars marked on it was not a sphere but a dodecahedron. But in this modern interpretation, the suggestion was that, like the joined-up cube, space would be fused at opposite faces of the dodecahedron. Interestingly, they have to give the pentagons a bit of a twist (by 36 degrees) before they could match them up. But the majority of astronomers are not convinced. It is difficult to tell whether these matchings are not the result of random coincidences.

There is another way that light could tell us about the geometry of our universe. Light tells us how the universe curves. Let's give our explorer setting out from his village a telescope and a featureless plain to venture across. At first the Earth seems flat, but after some time the curvature of the Earth becomes apparent: looking back, the explorer can no longer see his village – something is in the way. If the curvature continues across the whole surface, then it must join up to form a finite surface. Curvature like that of a sphere is called positive curvature. If a surface is flat, then it could be infinite, extending forever, but it could also be like the game of Asteroids, in which the universe on the screen is flat but finite. Flat surfaces are said to have zero curvature. There is another sort of curvature, which is like the saddle of a horse or a Pringle crisp. The curvature seems to dip down in one direction and up

Two-dimensional surfaces with positive, negative and zero curvature.

in the other direction. This is called negative curvature, in contrast to the positive curvature of the surface of a sphere. It gives rise to infinite surfaces, rather than finite surfaces like that of the sphere.

Just as the two-dimensional surface of the Earth can be curved one way or another, it turns out that three-dimensional space too can have curvature. Measuring this curvature can give us some sense of how space might be wrapped up. If, like the surface of the Earth, the overall curvature of the universe is positive, the universe will curve in on itself into a finite shape. If it is negative it will be infinite. If it is flat, it could be infinite or finite like our cube-shaped universe fused at its opposite faces.

To pick up the overall curvature of space we can examine light as it traverses space. What do we see? Well, it almost looks flat, but it's hard to tell whether it is truly flat, or whether there is a small curvature that could wrap up space. The margins seem to be so small that it is hard to say whether we'll ever be able to determine the curvature with sufficient accuracy to know which way space is bending.

But there is another problem about really knowing the curvature of the universe. Much of our exploration of space depends on an assumption: that where we sit in the universe isn't particularly special. It's called the Copernican principle. Once we thought we were at the centre of it all. But Copernicus put paid to that. So we now believe that what the universe looks like around us is pretty much what it looks like everywhere. That is certainly what the evidence tells us. But it need not be the case. It's possible that the bit of the universe we see is rather special.

Suppose, for example, that our explorer on Earth had been living on a planet shaped like a hemisphere: perfectly flat on the bottom but suddenly curving off in a half sphere. If our explorer's village was on the flat bit, he'd think the whole planet was flat until he suddenly encountered a change in curvature. Perhaps the universe looks the same: flat in our patch, but beyond the region we can see, it does something completely different. How can we ever know whether the universe is as homogeneous as we think it is?

So the quest is still on to see if light really is doing circles round a finite universe like a cosmic Magellan expedition. If it is, it gives us the possibility that we may discover whether the universe is finite. Or perhaps it is bending in such a way that we can work out how the universe is wrapped up.

Magellan, of course, navigated a static planet. It turns out that our universe is a little more dynamic than we thought, as Hubble, the Magellan of space, discovered when he started analysing the light coming from the stars in distant galaxies.

8

For in and out above, about, below
It is nothing but a Magic Shadow-Show
Play'd in a Box whose candle is the Sun
Round which we Phantom Figures come and go.

Omar Khayyam, *The Rubaiyat*

I used to fantasize about being able to look up at the night sky and point confidently at various stars and planets and declare: 'That's Betelgeuse' or 'You see that bright spot there, that's actually not a star but the planet Venus.' But one of my problems is that I have an extremely bad memory. If something's random, like the stars scattered across the firmament, then without some logic to guide me, I find it very difficult to name much beyond the Plough. This is, of course, why we've created patterns like the Plough, or Orion the Hunter, to help us navigate these random spots of light.

But it turns out that I'm also not very physically suited to astronomy. My first attempt to take a deeper look into space was a trip to the telescope housed in Mill Hill in north London. But my wish to see to the edge of the universe was scuppered by the scourge of astronomers: clouds.

So next I tried to get above the clouds. This required more effort than jumping on the Northern Line to Mill Hill. I took a train to Switzerland, culminating in a beautiful alpine climb to the final stop at Jungfraujoch. From there a lift tunnelled into the mountain took me to the mountain peak on which the Sphinx observatory sits, 3571 metres above sea level.

Built in 1912, it looks like the evil villain's lair from a James Bond movie. As the Sun set over the snow and glaciers, I prepared myself for a wonderful evening of stargazing. Except my body had other ideas. I'd already been feeling quite dizzy and even nauseous. I hadn't been able to eat much. As the first stars started to appear, I was hit by a crashing headache. Before long I was throwing up. When an elderly German couple said that I had all the symptoms of altitude sickness save one, it suddenly dawned on me that I'd never been this high before.

'And what's the last symptom?'

'Death.'

It was then that I realized that my dream of the life of an amateur astronomer wasn't really worth it. I got the first train back to a sensible altitude and the symptoms disappeared. I just had to face it: I'm a Thames Valley boy born in London whose body was built to stare up at the stars from the comfort of a telescope closer to sea level. But observations made by some of those great telescopes that sit high on the mountains across the world have revealed a remarkable fact. At some point in the future there won't be so many stars for me to look at: they are disappearing over our cosmic horizon!

THE UNIVERSE THROUGH RED-TINTED SPECTACLES

When an ambulance drives by with its siren blaring, your ears experience the squashing up of sound waves as the ambulance approaches, which causes the wavelength to shorten, resulting in the siren sounding higher-pitched than when the ambulance passes you. As it pulls away, the sound waves are stretched out, resulting in a longer wavelength and lower pitch. This phenomenon is known as the Doppler effect.

The same thing happens to light. As a star speeds away from us, its light shifts towards the longer red wavelength. If it moves towards us, the light shifts towards the shorter blue wavelength. Having already discovered that our galaxy was not special but just one of many, Edwin Hubble turned his attention in 1929 to analysing the light from these galaxies to see how they were moving relative to our own. To his surprise, the light from distant stars in the galaxies he observed were all shifted towards the red. Nothing seemed to be coming towards us. It was as if the other galaxies were fleeing from us. Even more interestingly, the further the stars were from our own star, the more the wavelength was shifted. Hubble couldn't believe that the Earth was in such a special place in the universe. He realized that there was a much better explanation: space is expanding, in all directions simultaneously. Whatever your point of observation, it will appear that everything is moving away from you. The space between us and the stars is being stretched. The galaxies are being carried along by the expansion of space like leaves in the wind.

Although often credited to Hubble, an expanding universe had been predicted by the Jesuit priest Monsignor Georges Lemaître two years earlier. Lemaître deduced that the universe must be expanding as a consequence of Einstein's equations for gravitation. When Einstein heard about the proposal, he dismissed it with the damning declaration: 'Your calculations might be correct but your physics is atrocious.' Einstein was so confident that Lemaître was wrong that he ended up sticking something called the cosmological constant into his equations to try and force the universe to be static and thus scupper Lemaître's prediction.

Lemaître didn't help his cause by publishing his findings in an obscure Belgian journal. But once Hubble's observations supported the idea of an expanding universe, Einstein changed his tune. Hubble and Lemaître's discoveries were the first indication that our universe isn't static, as Einstein and many other scientists thought. Instead, space is getting stretched out.

It is the stretching of space that makes the wavelength of the incoming light longer, and the further the light has travelled, the more its wavelength will gradually have been stretched. So the bigger the redshift, the more space has been stretched on the way and therefore the further the original source of the light from Earth.

To explain why this stretching changes wavelengths of light, blow up a balloon and mark three points on it. One represents Earth, the other two points are distant stars. Draw two waves of light of a fixed wavelength between the stars and Earth. This is what the light looks like when it leaves the stars. By the time the light from the nearer star reaches Earth the balloon has expanded. If I blow it up a bit, the wavelength gets longer. It takes longer for the distant star's light to reach Earth, so the universe has expanded a bit more. If I blow the balloon up even more, the wavelength gets longer again. So the greater the redshift, the further the star is from Earth.

In the first balloon the light leaves the stars with the same wavelength. In the second balloon the universe has expanded and the light from the nearer star reaches Earth. The wavelength has got longer. In the third balloon the universe has expanded further by the time the light arrives from the further star. The wavelength has shifted even more towards the red.

This was a new way of measuring distance to far-flung stars. It has helped astronomers to identify stars that must now be 30 billion light years away from us. It may seem something of a paradox that we can see something 30 billion light years away when, as we shall soon see, the universe is only 13.8 billion years old, but remember that we are seeing the star in the past, when it was close enough that the light could reach us. It is only by analysing the expansion mathematically that we can infer that today the star is at a point from which it would take its light 30 billion years to reach us.

ANT AND THE BAND

If the universe is expanding, then perhaps some stars will always remain out of sight, since they are moving further and further away from us. If the universe is expanding at a constant rate, even if that rate is faster than the speed of light, there is a beautiful mathematical argument which proves that if we wait long enough, we'll eventually see light from every star even if the universe is infinite.

The best way to understand this is to consider an example which has a curiously counterintuitive outcome. Consider an ant (playing the role of a photon of light) sitting on the end a rubber band (playing the role of space) that is stuck down at one end (playing the role of the Earth). The end where the ant starts plays the role of a far-distant galaxy.

The end of the rubber band is pulled so that the speed at which the end is moving is constant. Suppose the rubber band starts with a length of 1 kilometre and every second it increases in length by 1 kilometre. The ant is moving at a much slower speed along the band, say at 1 centimetre every second. At first glance, with the end flying off at such a faster rate, it appears that the ant has no chance of reaching the other end, just as light from a galaxy far enough away seems to have no chance of reaching Earth if the space between them is expanding at a uniform rate.

$$1\text{km}$$
$$\uparrow \tfrac{1}{100,000} \text{ of total}$$

$$2\text{ km}$$
$$\uparrow \tfrac{1}{100,000} + \tfrac{1}{200,000} \text{ of total}$$

$$3\text{ km}$$
$$\uparrow \tfrac{1}{100,000} + \tfrac{1}{200,000} + \tfrac{1}{300,000} \text{ of total}$$

There are some subtleties here, so let me add a condition to help us get a grip on what is happening: the rubber band gets stretched only after each second and it will be an instantaneous stretch. So after 1 second the ant has travelled 1 centimetre, which is $\tfrac{1}{100,000}$ of the total distance. Then the band expands. The point to note is that although the distance that the ant needs to travel has increased, it has at least still covered $\frac{1}{100,000}$ of the distance between the star and Earth, because the stretch has also helped push the ant on a little from its starting position.

Now the ant travels another 1 centimetre. The rubber band is 2 kilometres long. So the ant has covered a further $\frac{1}{200,000}$ of the total distance. The total proportion that the ant has now covered is $\frac{1}{100,000}$ + $\frac{1}{200,000}$ of this total distance. The band expands by another 1 kilometre. The proportion hasn't changed with the stretch. The band is now 3 kilometres long. The ant travels another 1 centimetre. This is only $\frac{1}{300,000}$ of the total distance. Every time the rubber band stretches, the proportion that the ant's 1 centimetre represents is going down. But hold on – here is the power of mathematics. After n seconds the proportion of the band that the ant will have covered is

$$\frac{1}{100,000} + \frac{1}{200,000} + \frac{1}{300,000} + \ldots + \frac{1}{n \times 100,000} = \frac{1}{100,000}\left(1 + \frac{1}{2} + \frac{1}{3} + \ldots + \frac{1}{n}\right)$$

This is the harmonic series that the mathematician Oresme calculated many centuries ago and that I considered at the beginning of the last chapter. And he proved that this series will get arbitrarily large. So I can make n so large that the sum is bigger than 100,000. The proportion of the band that the ant has covered is over 100%. This means that the ant has arrived!

In this example I have the rubber band stretching at a uniform rate. This is pretty much how astronomers like Hubble thought space was behaving, perhaps even slowing down, given that gravity should have a decelerating effect. This implies that even if the universe is infinite, we should be able to see more and more of it if we just sit and wait for the light to arrive – like a colony of ants crawling along the expanding rubber of space.

Doesn't this mean that, in theory, if the universe is infinite, we should already be receiving light from stars no matter how far away they are? Perhaps we can already see an infinite universe. The thing to remember, though, is that the further away the star, the further in the past we are looking at it. If we rewind our expanding universe far enough, we will find there were no stars at all.

REWINDING THE UNIVERSE

The discovery by Hubble and Lemaître of the expanding universe was evidence for what scientists now call the Big Bang. If I reverse time, an expanding universe turns into a contracting universe. But keep contracting and the universe becomes so dense that the state of the universe changes rather dramatically. In fact, as Lemaître first realized, at some finite point in time this reversed expansion leads to a universe which is infinitely dense, a point he called the primeval atom or cosmic egg. This 'singularity' is what scientists refer to as the Big Bang. Given that this is a point at which relativity and quantum physics must fuse into a coherent theory, there are still debates about how far we can rewind the universe before current models fail and new ideas are needed.

When I first heard about the Big Bang at school, I thought that if the universe started as a point then it had to be finite now. But with a bit of mathematics it is possible to show how an infinite universe can still start as a single point. This seems extraordinary. How can a point with no volume contain infinite space? To get an idea of how this works it is worth starting with an infinite space and working backwards. Think of infinite space 1 second after the Big Bang. Take an arbitrary point as the centre of this universe and consider all the points that are a distance R from this point. They all sit on the sphere of radius R.

Now I am going to rewind our universe backwards to time zero. At time $t = \frac{1}{2}$, the points on the sphere of radius R will contract to points on a sphere of radius $\frac{1}{2}R$. At time $t = \frac{1}{4}$, they've contracted further to sit on a sphere of radius $\frac{1}{4}R$. As I keep halving the time in the direction of the Big Bang, this sphere is getting smaller and smaller, until at time $t = 0$ it becomes a point. But this is true of every sphere regardless of how big R is. So every point in my infinite space sits on some sphere of radius R and when rewound to $t = 0$ collapses to the point I chose. So in 1 second the mathematics gives me a way to suck infinite space into a single point with no volume.

Shakespeare put it nicely when Hamlet declares: 'I could be bounded in a nutshell and count myself a king of infinite space.'

Of course, we run into problems with this model if space and time are quantized. As I saw when I tried to keep halving my dice, there may come a point when I can't halve things. This is at the heart of the debate when quantum physics meets general relativity: trying to resolve what happens as we contract the universe to a point.

Many call this the beginning of our universe, and I shall return to the nature of what we mean by beginnings and time in the next Edge. But the Big Bang certainly has implications for just how far we may ultimately be able to see, because it means that the stars could not have existed for more than 13.8 billion years, which is the current estimate of how long ago the singularity occurred. Indeed, it took the universe a period of evolution before stars could form.

As you head out into space, you are heading back in time. Since there were no stars before 13.8 billion years ago, this means there is a sphere around us beyond which there is nothing to see. The wonderful thing is that we are back with the model of the universe proposed by the ancient Greeks. There is a huge sphere with the Earth at its centre, and photons from beyond that sphere have not had time to reach us yet. That sphere is getting larger as time passes, and the question of how much space is contained inside this expanding horizon will turn out to have an unexpected answer.

The furthest galaxy whose distance from us has been confirmed is one whose light has taken 13.1 billion years to reach us, which was announced in October 2013. However, that does not mean that the galaxy is 13.1 billion light years away from us today, because the space between us and that galaxy has expanded during those 13.1 billion years. Calculations suggest that the galaxy is currently 30 billion light years away from Earth. There is a galaxy, it was announced in 2011, that was redshifted even more, indicating that the light had taken 13.41 billion years to reach us, but this hasn't been confirmed yet.

You might think we should be able to see light going back to the first moment after the Big Bang. But, tracing back the state of the universe, we believe there is a moment when no light could travel through space because space was opaque. Photons just found themselves buffeted between one particle and the next. It took 378,000 years following the Big Bang before the density of particles dropped sufficiently for the first photons to start their uninterrupted journey through space.

This is when space suddenly had enough room for these photons to zip through the universe without running into something which might absorb them. These first photons of light that are visible make up what we call the cosmic microwave background radiation, and they represent the furthest that we can see into space. They are like a cosmic fossil telling us about the early universe.

Those first photons that we see today in the microwave background radiation were only 42 million light years away from the Earth when they started their journey. Today, the distance between that starting point in space and the Earth has stretched to an estimated 45.7 billion light years. This is the edge of the visible universe, the visible cosmic horizon. But light isn't everything.

Although light couldn't make it through the plasma of space that existed for 378,000 years after the Big Bang, neutrinos could. They are particles that don't seem to get stopped by anything (well, hardly anything: every now and again they bump into stuff that allows us to detect their existence). You have trillions of neutrinos passing undetected through your body every second. So it's possible that we could 'see' a bit further into space if we could detect the neutrinos that decoupled 2 seconds after the Big Bang. Perhaps we could pick up a cosmic neutrino background, although this seems to be very difficult to detect.

Either way, there is a sphere surrounding the Earth which represents a horizon beyond which we cannot explore even with the cleverest and most sophisticated of telescopes, because the light and neutrinos – or any information – haven't had time to reach us.

As time goes on, this cosmic horizon is growing, allowing us to see further and further into space. At least that's what we thought. However, a discovery in 1998 revealed the alarming fact that, rather than extending further into space, our cosmic horizons are actually contracting. Although the cosmic horizon is growing at a constant rate, the underlying fabric of space itself isn't just expanding, this expansion seems to be accelerating. As it does so, it is pushing things we can see out beyond our horizon with devastating implications for what future generations can ever know.

THE STARS ARE GOING OUT

Some stars end their lives in a catastrophic explosion called a supernova. The luminosity is so intense that these supernovae can be seen over huge distances. When type 1a supernovae explode they all have the same luminosity, no matter where they are in the universe. When that is compared with the apparent brightness, we have a measure of how far away they are.

If the universe was expanding at a constant rate, then, given the distance of a supernova from Earth, you could predict the redshift that you would expect to see based on this constant expansion. But when this theoretical redshift was checked with the recorded redshift of distant supernovae, astronomers got a shock. The redshifts didn't match. If the universe was expanding at a constant rate, the redshift should have been much higher. For galaxies further away, whose light allows us to look back in time, the rate of change of redshift was slower than that measured in nearer galaxies. The only conclusion was that the expansion of space in the early universe had been much slower, but then the expansion started to accelerate, ripping space apart.

It seems that about 7 billion years ago something dramatic happened. Up to this point, the expansion appeared to be slowing down, as one would expect as the gravitational force of the matter in the universe exerted a braking effect. But at this point, halfway through the current life span of the universe, the expansion rate changed character and started to increase, accelerating as if something had suddenly put its foot on the pedal. The fuel driving the acceleration is what scientists call dark energy.

It seems that in the first half of the universe's existence, the density of matter was enough to assert a slowing gravitational pull, but as the universe expanded this density decreased to such a point that the underlying dark energy was strong enough to take over. Dark energy isn't thought to be something whose density decreases with expansion. It is a property of space itself.

If the acceleration continues, this would have extraordinary consequences. The sphere containing the visible universe is growing as time goes on, which should mean we can see further into space. Unfortunately, the underlying space is expanding so fast that stars that were previously within the sphere of the visible universe are being pushed beyond the edge of this sphere. So that in the future all galaxies other than our own will disappear from view and forever remain beyond the edge of the sphere of our visible universe. Even though that sphere is expanding, it will never be fast enough to catch up with the galaxies as they are carried away by the acceleration of space.

Imagine if life had taken longer to evolve and that humans had started doing astronomy only after all this interesting stuff had been pushed over the horizon. We would have an entirely different story of the evolution of the universe. It would look like the static universe that we believed was our home before our telescopes were able to pick out other galaxies. So what we can know depends on the time at which humans were born into the universe. We are in a special time to do our astronomy.

Astronomy in the distant future won't consist of going to the top of mountains and peering through telescopes like the one at the Sphinx observatory. Instead, it will consist of consulting books and journals full of the data recorded by previous generations of astronomers before what they observed was pushed beyond our cosmic horizon. Perhaps astronomy in the future will be more suited to a Thames Valley boy like me who prefers low-lying libraries to high-altitude observatories.

It is worth noting that we won't lose the stars in our own galaxy. The local pull of gravity on the stars in our vicinity will keep the galaxy together. The expansion of space is not sufficient to pull the stars apart, but it raises the question of how much has already disappeared from view that might have told a different story.

If you are in a car and you want to accelerate, you need to put your foot on the pedal and produce energy by burning fuel. So where is the fuel or energy coming from that drives the acceleration of the universe and, like a car's, won't it run out eventually?

The answer is that we don't know. Dubbed 'dark energy', the 'dark' is used in cosmology to indicate that it's something that doesn't seem to interact with light or other forms of electromagnetic radiation. In other words, we can't detect it. There are conjectures about what this dark energy might be. One of them concerns the cosmological constant that Einstein famously inserted into his equations to try to make the universe static. But now that constant is being used to push space apart. Usually we would think of energy spread out across space as being used up or thinning out as space expands. But this energy is now thought of as a property of space itself. Rather than thinning out, more gets created as space grows. In any cubic metre of space it is constant. In other words, it has fixed density. The acceleration is a runaway process that can't be stopped. This doesn't contradict the conservation of energy because this dark energy is treated as a negative energy which is balanced by an increase in kinetic energy as space expands.

If the expansion of the universe continues to accelerate, then there is a sphere which has us at its centre from beyond which we will never receive any information. Information travels at the speed of light. With a static universe, this would mean that any information would reach us given enough time. With a universe expanding at a constant rate, my example of the ant on the expanding rubber band shows again that information travelling across an infinite universe would eventually reach us. But with an accelerating expansion there are things which will never cover the intervening space quickly enough to counter this. Using our current estimate for the cosmological constant that we think might be responsible for this expansion, we believe that the sphere from beyond which we will not receive any information sent today is currently 18 billion light years in radius.

As the space between stars gets stretched, so the light from those stars gets redshifted, and the more the light gets stretched, the longer the wavelength. Stars will seem to go out because the wavelength of light is so elongated that we can no longer detect it. This will also affect what we can identify of the microwave background radiation: the wavelength of those early photons will have been stretched so much that they are almost impossible to detect.

With the cosmic microwave background radiation redshifted to such an extent that it can no longer be detected and galaxies having disappeared from view, it is amazing to think that cosmologists in the future may have no evidence to suggest that we live in an expanding universe. Future civilizations will perhaps return to the model of the universe held by the ancient world: our local galaxy surrounded by the void – everything contained in the paper icosahedron I made to navigate space. There would be no indication that the universe was homogeneous. We would look like an exceptional point in a universe of nothingness.

COSMIC FINGERPRINTS

If the universe is infinite, it seems very probable that this is something we will never know. Certainly, it seems that the structure of the universe will preclude us from ever observing such a fact. And yet the universe beyond our visible horizon can still leave its fingerprints on the space we can see.

If the universe is finite, this places limitations on certain resonances that are possible. Think of the universe as a large resonating box like the body of my cello. The shape of the cello has been chosen because of the pleasing sound made by the resonant frequencies that can vibrate within the box. Indeed, what distinguishes a Stradivarius from a factory-made cello is partly the perfection of shape which leads to a more beautiful sound.

One of the intriguing problems that challenged mathematicians for some time was whether you could deduce the shape of the box from the frequencies of the waves that vibrate inside it. In a seminal paper, Mark Kac posed the question: 'Can you hear the shape of a drum?' For example, only a square has the particular set of frequencies that are produced by this shape. But in 1992 mathematicians Carolyn Gordon, David Well and Scott Wolpert constructed two strange shapes whose resonant frequencies were identical although the underlying shapes differed.

The interesting thing for me on my search for the edge of the universe is that resonances might at least be able to tell me whether the universe is finite or infinite. If I've got a finite box, then the wavelength of waves that can resonate inside the box is limited by the size of the box. If the space is infinite, there shouldn't be a limit. In the mid-1990s Jean-Pierre Luminet and colleagues in France explored the microwave

Two drums with the same resonant frequencies.

background radiation to see what waves were left over from the Big Bang. They believed waves with long wavelengths seemed to be missing from the spectrum. Was space not big enough to support these waves?

More refined data from the Planck spacecraft released in 2013 has revealed that there is no such evidence for these missing wavelengths that would have hinted at a finite universe. So the jury is still out. And this is one of the problems with this dilemma: if the universe is finite, we could possibly know this; but if it is infinite, we will forever be left in a state of epistemological unease.

Although the waves detected in the microwave background radiation don't tell us if the universe is finite, they may allow us to estimate a minimum size for the universe. The waves that we can detect actually give us a chance to sneak a view beyond our cosmic horizon. As Soviet scientists Leonid Grishchuk and Yakov Zel'dovich explained in a paper in 1978, certain waves can resonate only if the box we sit inside is big enough. Patricía Castro, Marian Douspis and Pedro Ferreira have used the resonances that we can detect to propose that the universe is at least 3900 times bigger than the space we can see.

Another way we may be able to deduce things about space beyond the edge of our visible universe is to witness events which can only happen due to the influence of things on the other side of our cosmic horizon. For example, there might be something large beyond our cosmic horizon that is pulling on the galaxies we can see, causing an unusual drift in certain regions of the night sky. Although we might not be able to see such things, we can still experience their effect on the things we can see. What we can know is not limited to what we can see. It's how we know about dark matter. The gravitational behaviour of the things we can see makes sense only if there is more stuff out there. It is how we discovered Neptune. Although we eventually saw Neptune with our eyes, it was mathematically predicted by the effect it was having on the planets around it. If there is something beyond our cosmic horizon that we can't see, it can still pull the gravitational strings inside our bubble.

As I look at the paper model of the universe on my desk that represents this bubble, it's fascinating to consider how we as humans have got smaller and smaller in relation to the whole. As long as humans have been looking out at the night sky, from one generation to the next we've constantly found ourselves adjusting our sense of scale. At first it appeared that the Earth was the centre of it all. Then we had to readjust our position in the cosmos when we realized that the Sun was at the centre, with the Earth just one of many planets orbiting this focal point. Then we realized that all those stars out there might have their own planets in tow and that our Sun was tucked away at the edge of a galaxy of stars. And then we had to rethink our place in the universe once more as we came to terms with the fact that there are billions of other galaxies out there in space. The Milky Way was nothing special after all.

I suppose I'd got used to this immense scale, even if it was almost impossible to truly comprehend. But discoveries made in my lifetime – since I'd come to terms with my place in the universe – have caused me to expand my horizons once again. Just as previous generations recognized that our planet was actually one of many, so it appears we have to face up to the possibility that our universe is simply one of many universes. The first inkling of these other universes was provided by a rather curious enigma encoded in the very first photons that zipped through our own universe.

MULTIVERSE

There is something curious about the cosmic microwave background radiation. Why is it so uniform? The photons that we are picking up in our detectors all have a temperature of 2.725 degrees above absolute zero. When they set off on their journey some 370,000 years after the Big Bang, they were much hotter, around 3000 degrees, the temperature at which electrons and nuclei amalgamated to become atoms. As space expanded, the photons cooled off, which means that the energy they contain, determined by their frequency of vibration, has gradually decreased, until today it is so slow that we find these photons in the microwave region of the electromagnetic spectrum.

But why do all photons have very nearly the same temperature? If two objects with different temperatures are in contact with each other, then over time they will transfer energy so that the temperature of both is the same. This might seem like a good explanation, except that there is an important word in that previous sentence: contact. Contact can be made only at the speed of light. The distance across space was such that there was no time for information to travel at the speed of light to inform the other side of the expanding universe what the temperature was.

The only explanation that seemed to make sense was this: to reach a common temperature these two points in space must have been much closer to each other for long enough than our model of an expanding universe had suggested. In the early 1980s American cosmologist Alan Guth came up with a potential solution. In the early stages of the universe's existence space didn't expand quickly. It was a slow start that allowed space to achieve a common temperature. Then space went through an exceedingly rapid expansion in a period that is now called inflation. An antigravity field called the inflaton is conjectured to have caused this inflation, pushing space apart at an exponential rate. The rapid inflation didn't last for long: some 10^{-36} seconds according to the current model. That's a billionth of a billionth of a billionth of a billionth of a second. Yet in that time the inflaton is thought to have expanded space by a factor of 10^{78}. It's as if there was a build-up in pressure which suddenly got released, and once the release had happened, the universe settled down into the more sedate expansion we have picked up since.

The model helps explain why the universe appears flat and essentially very homogeneous. The large variations we see, like galaxies here but empty space there, are actually the product of very small quantum fluctuations in the small bit of space that got blown up by this massive inflation. The inflation would also explain why the universe appears so flat: it would have virtually flattened out any identifiable curvature that had been present in the early universe.

The mathematics developed to explain this inflation, by Andrei Linde at Stanford and Alexander Vilenkin at Tufts, makes an extraordinary prediction. It implies that it wouldn't just happen as a one-off event but that space could be inflating as it did in our universe in other regions of space. Quantum fluctuations across space cause the inflaton field to pop in certain places, creating vast universes. In other words, there might be other universes out there, like ours, making space look like Swiss cheese, with the holes in the cheese corresponding to different universes.

Can we ever know whether this description of the universe is true? Are we just coming up with self-consistent stories that could be true but are untestable? Even in our own universe there seems to be a limit to how far we can see. So how can we hope to know whether these other universes are real or just the fantasy of theoretical physicists?

Investigations of the existence of these other universes have focused on the possibility that they might interact with our universe in such a way that they leave some sort of imprint. Could the cosmic microwave background radiation provide evidence that our universe collided with other universes during its formation? There has been some speculation that temperature differences in the map of the early universe could be a result of such collisions, but, as one of the team at UCL investigating such possibilities admits: 'One of many dilemmas facing physicists is that humans are very good at cherry-picking patterns in the data that may just be coincidence.' But it is not a hopeless quest. Discovering evidence for neighbouring universes is not *a priori* something beyond our reach. We might know. The challenge is to find ways that these other universes can influence what is within our cosmic horizon.

DIALLING UP DIFFERENT UNIVERSES

One of the intriguing consequences of these potentially unknowable universes beyond our own is that they may explain one of the principal reasons for creating a God in the first place. The possibility of the multiverse could offer the best solution we have so far for the troubling feeling that our own local universe must have been designed.

I'm not talking about the illusion that biological design led to life, which is created by our lack of perspective on randomness and large expanses of time. Thanks to Darwinian evolution we don't need a designer. The internal mechanics of our universe are sufficient to have produced the wonderful structures that exist on our planet.

Darwin does an excellent job of putting paid to the need for a supernatural designer to explain the complexity of the life we see around us. Once you have a simple mechanism like Darwinian evolution to account for the complexity of life, then you don't need a God for that. But what we lack is a good explanation for the constants of nature – the 20 or so numbers like the mass of an electron, the gravitational constant, the speed of light, the charge of a proton – that are so fine-tuned to get life up and running. Although we have a mechanism that explains biology, we don't have a similar way to explain physics.

There seems to be no clear rationale for why these constants assume the values they do. Why couldn't they be dialled to other values? What is particularly striking is how sensitive the possibility of life in our universe is to a small change in these constants. For example, if the constant that controls the way the electromagnetic field behaves is changed by 4% then fusion in stars could not produce carbon – any life that could exist in such a universe would have to be based on other atoms. Some of the other constants turn out to be similarly sensitive to small tweaks. Change the cosmological constant by something in the 123rd decimal place and suddenly it's impossible to have habitable galaxies.

This is one reason why the unknown beyond our cosmic horizon with its multiple universes could hold the solution to this dilemma. In the multiverse model there are lots of different universes, and in each of these universes the fundamental constants could be randomly assigned. In most cases a universe wouldn't really have much going on because the constants aren't set favourably for action. But in a few the constants are in the sweet spot for atoms to get going in a way that eventually leads to life. Of course, for us to be around to observe this universe, we have to be in one of these special universes. This is known as the anthropic view.

I think most scientists hope for a more satisfying answer to why our universe is the way it is, that we'll be able to show that these constants aren't really random, that things had to be the way they are. Relying on multiverses feels like a cop-out, as if we are just not trying hard enough, and so we fill the gap with something that will probably be impossible to know.

But perhaps this is just how it is and I have to bite the bullet and accept the multiverse model. The Earth, for example, is just a random planet that turns out to be in the sweet spot for life. I'm not going to be able to come up with a reason to show why it had to be there. There are lots of planets that failed to be in the right spot. It's just chance that our planet fits the bill. I have successfully coped with a multiplanet explanation for life, so why not a multiverse explanation for physics?

My hope is that we can explain why the universe has to be the way it is without recourse to the idea of the multiverse. Ultimately there may be a reason for this special universe dropping out as the most natural. That is what most scientists would prefer as an answer. A stable bubble is an amazing perfect sphere. There are so many other three-dimensional shapes it could have been. Why this perfect shape? We know why. The maths says it is the lowest-energy shape among all the possible shapes. We are on the lookout for an explanation for why our universe might be scientifically favoured like the sphere.

But the universe is probably not like a bubble. It's probably more like balancing a pencil on its tip and letting it drop. There are infinitely many directions it could fall. No direction is favoured over any other. Chance (embodied in a quantum fluctuation) will determine which direction and which universe gets chosen.

Some suggest that there is an alternative: a transcendental intelligence that fine-tuned the whole thing. But that feels like even more of a cop-out. Why is the multiverse a more scientifically satisfying answer? The reason is that the multiverse theory has – albeit in a strange way – that sense of economy we are after in a good theory. You might say that it seems extraordinarily extravagant for a theory to require multiple universes. But it's the economy of explanation that marks it out as appealing. The explanation terminates and does not require further explanation. The addition of these other universes is just more of the same with variations. It's nothing really new, but once you incorporate all these universes you get a complete solution to the fine-tuning problem. A designer who fine-tunes the constants raises as many questions as it answers.

GUESS THE NEXT NUMBER

A good scientific theory should be an economical proposal that makes sense of how everything is put together, and you shouldn't need to introduce too many extra characters into the story to get the narrative we experience. There is a simplicity and naturalness about the multiverse theory that makes it a strong candidate theory. The physics of inflation provides a possible mechanism for producing these other universes, so it isn't just a wild hypothesis. But we need to take care when using the qualities of simplicity and economy to judge the possible truth of a theory.

If I asked you what the next number in this sequence is:

$$1, 2, 4, 8, 16, \ldots$$

the obvious answer would be 32. To guess that doubling is the key to this sequence would be the majority view. But what would you say to the person who announces that 31 is the next number? They'd probably be laughed at. But once you know that these numbers could describe

---

Why 31 is the next number . . .

Place *n* dots on a circle and then draw lines connecting each dot to the other dots. How many regions have you divided the circle into? The maximum number of regions you get starting with one dot follows the following sequence: 1, 2, 4, 8, 16, and then at six dots there is a surprise: you get a maximum of 31 regions.

the number of ways you can divide a circle, both 31 and 32 become legitimate responses. So you may then ask for more experimental data to help you decide which is the best explanation.

The interesting point is that, however much data you uncover, I can give you an equation that will provide a coherent reason for why any number might legitimately come up next. So, given a finite amount of data, it seems we can never really know what the explanation is for that data unless we can get another bit of data against which to test our equation. This is the model of science that the philosopher Karl Popper proposed: a theory can only be falsified, never proved.

In judging a good theory, scientists often apply some measure of naturalness, an Occam's razor measure that favours one equation over another. The simpler the degree of the equation, the less you have to put in to get an answer out – this is generally significant when deciding which explanation to favour. That's why most would choose doubling as the obvious explanation for the sequence of numbers, rather than the quartic polynomial that gives us the circle division numbers.

So, when we are faced with two competing theories and there is no way of telling which one is right, it does seem to be the case that we favour the theory which is simplest. This is captured by the idea of something philosophers call 'inference to the best explanation', or the theory of abduction. But there is no reason to think that simplicity guarantees truth.

Why is simplicity, economy or beauty a good measure of the fact that we may be closer to the truth? Experience bears this out to a certain extent. Our association of beauty with truth comes from us being evolutionarily programmed to respond with a shot of dopamine when we think we've struck on an idea that helps us to navigate our environment. So we call things beautiful because this is our body's response to something that will be advantageous to our evolutionary survival.

What happens when alternative stories are proposed? How do you deal with the person who believes the universe is 5775 years old? You show them the fossil record and they counter that the universe was created old. They construct for themselves a narrative that is logical and self-consistent but to my mind highly unlikely. It is hard to argue with anyone who puts forward a theory that is immune from testability.

Increasingly we are being pushed towards scientific narratives for the evolution of the universe that may turn out to be untestable. If you come up with a theory that predicts new particles but the theory doesn't pin down at what energy these particles can be detected, no amount of evidence will convince those who believe in this new theory that they are wrong: they will always retort that the hypothetical particles exist in the region that you haven't been able to test yet.

Some have argued that the current untestability of the multiverse theory means that it is as fanciful as proposing a supernatural designer who fine-tuned the whole thing. Although at the moment there is no way of testing the multiverse theory, there is no *a priori* reason why it will always remain untestable. The same applies to string theory, which is often shot down as a scientific theory because it fails to make predictions that can be tested. But that is no justification for throwing it out yet, because there is no reason to believe that it will always remain untestable.

Again, the multiverse theory, although potentially untestable, does come with a mechanism, inflation, for how these multiverses arise. And we do at least have evidence for one of these multiverses: our own universe. One of the criteria for a scientific theory is that it should provide explanations based on things which are natural rather than supernatural. If you are going to posit a new thing like 'dark energy' or 'gravity', you need to embed it in the natural world. How do you do that? You show how its behaviour impacts on the rest of what we can see around us.

Another criterion for good science is that you can do experiments to test your theory. One of the problems with cosmology is that it is a one-time experiment. It is very difficult to run another Big Bang and see what happens this time. That said, you can test the conditions of the Big Bang on a small scale on Earth to get a sense of the physics of the larger cosmological event. But given that you will be working inside the physics that emerged, it's difficult to see how you could test whether other physical theories with different fundamental constants, or even different physics, could emerge from different moments of universe creation.

Since experiments are out, one of the central tenets of cosmology is the concept of homogeneity. You have to work under the assumption that what happens in our local bit of the universe is representative of its overall structure. Without this assumption, anything goes. We assume that the way space curves near us is true universally, but this need not be the case, just as someone living on the flat part of a hemisphere-shaped planet will think the whole planet is flat until they reach the point where curvature changes.

Without the assumption of homogeneity, how can we preclude the possibility of something outrageously different going on beyond our horizon? Perhaps someone has downloaded our universe from a website and glued it together like my celestial sphere. Perhaps we are just the doll's house of some supernatural being – supernatural in the sense that it exists outside our universe. If this supernatural being never plays with the doll's house, it is unclear that we could ever know about it. But if it truly has no influence then it is a strange invention. Why do we need to let our imaginations run riot? If this supernatural being plays with the doll's house and there is interaction, then we are up for testing the idea and it is potentially knowable.

IS THERE ANYONE OUT THERE?

It is striking how often cosmology and religion have intersected throughout history. The question of what might lie beyond the edge of the universe has always intrigued scientists and theologians alike. For the medieval philosopher Oresme, this was where God was hiding. Most religions include a creation myth for the cosmos. For the Australian Aborigines everything spewed forth from the belly of the Rainbow Serpent. For scientists it's the Big Bang. Galileo ran into trouble with the Catholic Church because of his challenge to our thinking about our place in the cosmos. Yet it was a Catholic priest, Lamaître, who came up with science's current story of how our cosmos emerged from the Big Bang.

Even in our current era, cosmology and religion are, sometimes controversially, intersecting. In 1972 Sir John Templeton, an American-born British entrepreneur, initiated a prize in his name to reward 'progress in religion'. It has evolved to become a prize that recognizes 'progress towards research or discoveries about spiritual realities'. It is a big-money prize, currently standing at £1,200,000. Templeton stipulated that the prize should exceed the Nobel prizes, which he felt had unjustly ignored the spiritual dimension.

The prize has been awarded to some obvious names. The first Templeton prize went to Mother Teresa. Subsequent prizes have rewarded priests, evangelists, rabbis and the Dalai Lama. But in recent years a growing number of scientists have joined their ranks, and invariably it's scientists researching cosmology and big questions about the universe who have been honoured.

A number of leading scientists, though, have been critical of those who have accepted the prize, believing that it endorses a spiritual/religious approach to scientific questions. My predecessor Richard Dawkins is one of those critics, declaring that the prize was usually given 'to a scientist who is prepared to say something nice about religion'. Physicist Sean Carrol has written about his reasons for refusing funding for his research from the Templeton Foundation: 'It's not a matter of ethical compromise; it's simply a matter of sending the wrong message. Any time respectable scientists take money from Templeton, they lend their respectability – even if only implicitly – to the idea that science and religion are just different paths to the same ultimate truth.'

I was keen to talk to a cosmologist who had accepted the prize. Professor John Barrow, based in the Department of Applied Mathematics and Theoretical Physics at the University of Cambridge, received the Templeton prize in 2006. His response to my email got straight to the heart of why cosmology in particular has implications for my concept of God as those things we cannot know: 'Most of the fundamental questions in cosmology are unanswerable. In fact, I will talk about some them in a lecture I'm giving this Saturday.'

Perfect. The chance to hear how much cosmologists believe they cannot know. As I sat in the front row of the lecture hall, I began to realize, as Barrow went from one question to the next, how little we will probably ever know about the universe. Accompanied by the obligatory pretty pictures with which astronomers pepper their presentations, Barrow proceeded to confirm all the fears I've been accumulating about how little we can know about our universe.

The Big Bang: 'At a finite time in the past the universe seemed to have a beginning – a time when the density was infinite and the temperature was infinite. We don't know if that beginning was real.'

The size of the universe: 'There is no doubt a lot of universe beyond our horizon, but we haven't seen it and almost all of it we will never see. So when people ask whether the universe had a beginning, or is it finite or infinite, we can never answer questions like those about the entire universe.'

When I met up with Barrow after the lecture and challenged him about the award of the Templeton prize to scientists like himself, he explained to me why he thought the Templeton Foundation was funding and rewarding cosmologists. 'Sir John Templeton liked science because there was progress. He believed cosmology was tackling deep and important questions that everyone ought to know about whatever they were doing, whether it be philosophy or religion or theology. You couldn't study those subjects while ignoring what was going on in the rest of science.'

Barrow believes the science–religion debate needs to be much more nuanced. 'One of the lessons to be learnt for people who are interested in the science–religion interaction is that you have to say which science you mean because the interaction is very different.

'Cosmology and fundamental physics bring you into contact with these big questions that you know you're not going to answer. You're used to uncertainty, to not knowing and, to some extent, seeing why you're not knowing. People in lab physics or biology, like Dawkins, they're not used to that kind of situation. They think every problem is solvable by grinding it down.'

Not that Barrow was belittling what they do: 'People always think that because you're studying the universe this must be the hardest problem. Not at all. Understanding the brain, for example, is a much harder subject. It's much more complicated. In cosmology things happen very slowly, there are nice approximations for understanding. You can pick a simple symmetrical solution and then iterate away. You can't do that with human society. There's no simple model.'

But Barrow believes that the science he is engaged in has a markedly different quality: 'In fundamental physics and cosmology you know there are problems that you're not going to solve. Why are there laws of nature at all? The question of the number of dimensions of space and time. Whether there is a multiverse. Was there an initial singularity? Is the universe infinite? You can think of loads of questions that you're not going to answer. This creates a different complexion.'

It was for his work highlighting the intrinsic limitations of scientific inquiry that Barrow received the Templeton Prize. There is a growing tendency to think that science will ultimately be able to fill all the gaps, and Barrow is keen to rein in this faith in the all-knowing power of science.

'The universe is not constructed for our convenience. It's not an exercise in the philosophy of science. It's too bad if we can't find these things out. In fact, I'd be very suspicious if all these fundamental questions happened to be answerable by what we're doing. I would regard that as anti-Copernican. So I regard the fact that we can't solve certain problems, or we can't get the data we need, as a Copernican aspect of things.'

BLACK SWANS, BIASES AND THE BACK OF THE BOOK

Barrow believes we must recognize that we have an extraordinarily biased view of our universe: 'Most astronomy is based on observing things that shine in the dark: stars in distant galaxies, so-called luminous matter. Only 5% of the universe is composed of ordinary material that composes us and the luminous stars. Luminous material is rather biased. Luminous material tells you about places in the universe where the density became so high that nuclear reactions could ignite and produce luminosity.'

In some ways, this applies to the whole of science. Our view of the universe is biased towards the bits that impact on our senses. Anything that doesn't isn't going to get noticed.

'If you lived on a planet that's covered in cloud all the time – planet

Manchester, say – then there's no astronomy. On the other hand, you might learn an awful lot about meteorology.'

In Barrow's view, cosmology has a very different quality to other sciences like physics or human sciences, and it is this which may be key to its close relationship with theology.

'One of the differences for a cosmologist is that if you're a scientist you're used to carrying out experiments, testing theories. You can't experiment on the universe. You just have to take it as it is.'

Many modern scientists have signed up to the philosophy proposed by Karl Popper: that you can never actually prove that a scientific theory is correct. The best you can do is to try to falsify a theory. All swans are white. You can never prove that. The best you can do is to falsify it by the discovery of a black swan. In Popper's book, anything which can't potentially be falsified is therefore unscientific. So if you can't do experiments in cosmology, are large swathes of it unscientific? Barrow wasn't going to give in too quickly.

'Popper's philosophy of science is incredibly naive. It doesn't really work in astronomy because when you make your observations you don't know whether they have been made correctly. So your prediction might have been falsified because something has been done wrong in the experiment. Or more likely there is some bias in the way the evidence has been gained.'

Black swans seem pretty damning for a theory that says all swans are white, but in other more subtle settings it might be much less clear whether it is the theory that is at fault, or the evidence, which means you shouldn't throw the theory away so quickly. Perhaps the swan rolled in coal dust before you observed it.

Barrow believes that cosmology could have its own black-swan moment.

'The key data point in all these ultimate questions that could really change things, in a way that us thinking about it could never change it, is making contact with some well-evolved extraterrestrial civilization that has evolved independently and knowing how they have come to think about some of these questions. Have they found the same bits of maths useful? Have they done physics in the same way? Do they define fundamental constants in ways that we could make sense of? What do they think about these ultimate questions? Now this would be an unsurpassably important data point and is the most important reason to make contact with extraterrestrials.'

Given the answers that this advanced civilization might have come up with to the big questions, I thought Barrow would be excited by the possibility of contact. But I got a surprise.

'The scientific content I think will be a disaster. If we made contact with a very advanced civilization that had answered all the questions we had ever posed, the game would be over for us. There would be no motivation for us to do science. It will be like looking at the back of the book and finding all the answers.'

You wouldn't want to do that?

'I think it would be a disaster.'

Just as particle physicist Melissa Franklin in my Second Edge didn't want to press the button that would give her complete knowledge, so too was Barrow adverse to looking up the answers in the back of the book. But unlike Franklin, Barrow is convinced that there are questions that even the most advanced civilization will never be able to answer. Those pages at the back will forever remain blank.

'The bad news is that cosmology has unknowable unknowns: things that we are never going to know even though we suspect we might know of their existence.'

MAKING CHOICES

There are many who would argue that you should remain agnostic in the light of an unknowable question, so I was intrigued to know Barrow's stance on the question of God. Was he agnostic? Atheist?

'Christian, in fact.'

That was a surprise. I have heard Barrow talk many times, read many of his books, but, unlike Polkinghorne, he does not wear his choice on his sleeve (or round his neck, like Polkinghorne's dog collar). But I guess that I too have made a choice in declaring myself an atheist. I don't believe that the only logical response to an unanswerable question is to remain on the fence.

Our belief in a possible answer to an unknowable question can have implications for how we conduct ourselves. Take, for example, the question of whether the universe is infinite. That may well be a question that we will never be able to answer. So should we just remain agnostic on the subject?

There is an argument that we would be wise to take out Pascal's wager on this one. If the universe is infinite, you're (probably) never going to know. But if the universe is finite, it's possible that you could know this. So isn't the better strategy to choose to believe that the uni-

---

Why there could be infinitely many copies of you reading this book

This depends on a couple of assumptions. The first comes from quantum physics: namely, that everything in the universe is quantized. This means that in a finite region of space there are only finitely many points in this region and they can take only a finite number of different values.

A simplified version of this universe looks like an infinite chequerboard on which each square can only be black or white. Take a region of this chequerboard which is meant to represent the complexity of life, including you reading this book. Suppose, for example, that it is a 10 x 10 region with a particular pattern of black and white squares.

One model of the entire infinite universe is that outside this 10 x 10 region everything else is coloured black. Rather like the void. So we need another assumption. This is that it is equally probable that any of the possible patterns can occur. No pattern is favoured over any other. Since there are only finitely many possible patterns and infinitely many 10 x 10 cells across this universe, if our pattern occurred only finitely many times then there must be another pattern that occurs infinitely often and therefore is infinitely more likely, which contradicts our second assumption. That means our pattern must be repeated infinitely across the chequerboard universe.

verse is finite? In the end, if the universe is infinite you can never be proved wrong, but if it's finite you could be proved right.

But what if an infinite universe offers a more exciting framework within which to live your life? An infinite universe has some interesting implications. One of these is that there are infinitely many copies of yourself across the universe reading this book. The psychological impact of this conclusion from your belief in an infinite universe might have a dramatic effect on the way you live your life.

I think this is why I reject Pascal's original wager on the question of the existence of God (in the conventional sense of the existence of a supernatural intelligence that created the universe) and choose to declare myself an atheist. Ultimately it affects the way I conduct my life. I'm not denying that it is a question that I may never know the answer to, but to admit such leaps of the imagination into the reality of my life would open up too many other wild possibilities. It goes against my natural predisposition to argue for the best explanation. Believing in multiverses is just creating more of the same but with variations. It may not be the best, but it is a better explanation.

CAN WE REALLY EVER KNOW WE WON'T KNOW?

After leaving Barrow in his office, I was rather downcast. I know I was on the lookout for things we cannot know, but I was beginning to doubt whether we can know anything. On my way back home, a sentence in one of Barrow's books struck a chord: 'The idea of the impossible rings alarm bells in the minds of many. To some, any suggestion that there might be limits to the scope of human understanding of the Universe or to scientific progress is a dangerous meme that undermines confidence in the scientific enterprise.'

Looking back at the Edges I've visited so far, nothing seems quite as unanswerable as the question of whether the universe is infinite. Chaos theory told me that the future is unknowable, but I can just wait until it becomes the present and then I'll know. As I slice my dice, I might actually hit a point at which space is quantized, so it's possible that there are only finitely many steps inside my dice before I hit the indivisible. It's true that it might be almost impossible to navigate this descending staircase, but it isn't a challenge that is *a priori* unsolvable. And Heisenberg's uncertainty principle does not so much challenge us to give an answer but rather to consider whether the questions we are asking are well posed. It's not that we can't know position and momentum simultaneously; the revelation is that it is not a question that it makes sense to ask.

But the question of an infinite universe does not seem like a question that is ill-posed. The universe is either infinite or not. If it is infinite, it is a real challenge to think how we could ever know this, given what we've discovered about the cosmic horizon beyond which we can never know.

But then I had a revelation. Perhaps the question of an infinite universe is not as unknowable as one might think. Might there not be more indirect ways that would lead us to the conclusion that the universe is infinite? The answer might lie in my own field of expertise. Mathematics has been a very powerful telescope through which to look at the universe. What if the current laws of physics lead to a mathematical contradiction under the assumption that the universe is finite? That would force us to conclude that the universe must be infinite, or that our laws of physics are at fault. This is after all how we discovered irrational numbers, numbers whose decimal expansions continue infinitely and never repeat themselves.

This is the power of mathematics: to use our finite brains to know the infinite. The Pythagoreans showed that the length across the diagonal of a unit square is given by a number that can't be written as a simple ratio of whole numbers. The only way this length can exist is if there are numbers that can be captured only by a decimal expansion that is infinite and non-repeating. Perhaps an infinite universe will also be susceptible to a proof of its existence by the same tools that helped us discover irrational numbers – a proof by contradiction.

Perhaps the real lesson is that 'what we cannot know' is something that we can never know because it is so hard to preclude the possibility of new ideas that might pull the unknowns into the known – just as Comte found when we discovered what stars are made from.

Although the universe that I will ever be able to see or explore is as finite as the paper model that sits on my desk, perhaps the message is that we should not give in too early to the lure of the unknowable. The mathematical telescopes of the mind may one day allow us to break through the paper and know that our sphere really does sit in an infinite expanse of space.

FIFTH EDGE: THE WRISTWATCH

9

No people who have the same word for
yesterday and tomorrow can be said to have
a firm grip on time.

Salman Rushdie, *Midnight's Children*

It's 8:50 . . . roughly . . . or so my wristwatch tells me. The weak February sun is trying to climb above the rooftops of the houses opposite. The radio is on, the coffee is brewed. The beginning of another day. But the pulse of Prokofiev's *Cinderella* vibrating the speakers in my radio alarmingly reminds me that time is pressing on. The chimes for twelve o'clock are telling Cinderella that her time at the ball is up. And here I am procrastinating on the Internet. I've just put my birthday into Wolfram Alpha and it's telling me that I've been alive for 18,075 days. But when I ask it how many more I have left, it says it doesn't understand my query. Probably just as well. I'm not sure I want to know how many more times the hands on my watch will go round before the pulse beneath stops.

When I was younger I thought that it might be possible to know everything. I just needed enough time. As the years tick by, I'm beginning to realize that time is running out. The youthful sense of infinity is becoming the middle-aged acknowledgement of finitude. I may not be able to know everything. But that's my own personal limitation, which I shall return to in the next Edge. But is there still hope that humanity can know it all? Or is time going to run out for us collectively too? Will time run out full stop? Whether space is infinite may well be something we can never know. But what about time? I think we all have the feeling that time will probably go on forever. Keep putting batteries in my watch and it will carry on ticking. But when it comes to the question of what happened at the other end, people are less sure: did time have a beginning, or has it been there forever?

I may not be able to look into the future and make predictions, but the past has happened. So can't I look back and see whether time stretches endlessly into the past or if it had a beginning? Our current model of the universe involves a beginning. Tracing the expansion of the universe backwards has led us to a moment we call the Big Bang, when space was infinitely dense, a singularity that occurred 13.8 billion years ago. But what about before the Big Bang? Is that simply a no-go area for scientific investigation? Or are there telltale signs in the current state of the universe that might show me what was going on before it all began?

The nature of time has troubled philosophers and scientists for generations, because tied up in the attempt to understand this slippery concept is the challenge of understanding why there is something rather than nothing. To talk about a moment of creation is to talk about a moment in time.

The Big Bang certainly represents the beginning for most people. Even those with a religious bent are prone to admit a Big Bang as the moment of the creation of the universe. Either way, we are inevitably pushed to ask: what happened before the Big Bang?

I must admit I rather liked the stock answer that I'd picked up from speaking to mathematical cosmologist friends over the years. To talk about a 'before' presupposes the existence of time as a concept before the Big Bang. Given the revelations of Einstein's theory of relativity – that time and space are inseparably linked – perhaps time exists only once you've created space. But if time as well as space came into being only at the Big Bang, the concept of time 'before' the Big Bang has no meaning.

But there are rumblings in the cosmological corridors. Perhaps time can't be mathematically packaged up so easily. Perhaps the question of what happened before the Big Bang is not so easily dismissed. But to try and unravel time means diving into some pretty mind-bending ideas.

As I stare at my watch I can't actually see the hands moving, but if I look away and then look back again after some time has passed, the hands have moved on. It's saying 9:15 now . . . or thereabouts. Tiny cogs inside the watch are driven by a tiny electric motor that in turn is driven by 1-second pulses that have their origin in the oscillations of a tiny quartz crystal. The battery that sits inside the watch sets up a voltage across the crystal that makes it vibrate like a bell with a frequency tuned to 32,768 vibrations a second. This number is chosen for its mathematical properties. It is 2 to the power 15. Digital technology likes powers of 2 because computer circuitry can quickly convert this into a mechanical pulse to drive the cogs every second. Importantly, this frequency is not greatly affected by the surrounding temperature, air pressure or altitude (factors which affect a pendulum, for example). And it is this vibrating, the repetition of motion, that is key to marking the passage of time. But is this sufficient to describe the idea of time?

With my watch ticking away on my wrist, there are no further excuses for procrastinating. So . . .

WHAT IS TIME?

Most attempts to define time very quickly run into difficulties that become quite circular. It's something my watch keeps track of . . . It's what stops everything from happening at once . . . The fourth-century theologian St Augustine summed up the difficulty in his *Confessions*: 'What then is time? If no one asks me, I know: if I wish to explain it to one that asketh, I know not.'

Measuring time is at heart a very mathematical process. It depends on spotting things that repeat, things with patterns in them, such as the movement of the planets or the passing of the seasons or the swinging of a pendulum or the pulsing of an atom. As the nineteenth-century Austrian physicist Ernst Mach had it: 'Time is an abstraction at which we arrive through the changes of things.'

The Lascaux caves in France are believed to contain evidence of one of the first attempts by humans to keep track of time. Dating back 15,000 years, the caves were discovered in 1940 by four French boys after their dog Robot came across a hole leading down into the caves.

The caves are famous for the extraordinary Palaeolithic paintings of animals running across the walls: bison, horses, deer and aurochs.

I've had the chance to visit the caves, but because of the delicate nature of the 15,000-year-old drawings, I got to see only the replica cave that has been built alongside the original. They are still impressively atmospheric, and there is a dramatic sense of energy captured by the ancient images. But it isn't only animals that the artist depicts. There are also strange arrangements of dots that punctuate the paintings, which some archaeologists believe are evidence of ancient humans keeping track of the passage of time.

One collection of dots is generally believed to be a depiction of the constellation of the Pleiades. The reappearance of this constellation in the night sky was regarded by many ancient cultures as marking the beginning of the year. As I moved around the cave I came to a sequence of thirteen dots with a rectangle drawn at the end. Above the rectangle is a huge image of a rutting stag. Further along the wall there is a sequence of what could be counted as 26 dots with a huge pregnant cow at the end.

The dots have been interpreted by some archaeologists as marking quarters of the Moon's cycle, what would become the seven days of the week. These quarter phases of the Moon were easily identifiable in the night sky. So 13 quarters of the Moon represents a quarter of a year, or a season. Counting on a quarter of a year from the reappearance of the Pleiades gets you to the season of rutting stags, when they are more easily hunted. Then the 26 dots can be interpreted as two lots of 13 dots, representing two seasons, or half a year. This gets us to the point in the year when the bison are pregnant and again vulnerable and easily hunted.

The paintings on the wall might represent a training manual for new hunters: a calendar telling them what to hunt at what point in the annual cycle. This early evidence of time-keeping relies on spotting patterns that repeat themselves. Identifying repeating patterns would always be key to understanding the nature of time.

The cycle of the Sun, Moon and stars would inform the way we measured time until 1967. There is nothing in the natural cycle that dictated how we partition our day. Rather, it was the mathematical sensibilities of the Babylonians and Egyptians that gave us a day divided into 24 units of time and an hour subsequently divided up into units of 60. The choice of these numbers was based on the high divisibility of the numbers 60 and 24. Napoleon did attempt to make time decimal by introducing a day with ten hours, but it was about the only unit of measurement that he failed to get the world to count with their ten fingers.

Until 1967, the second, the basic unit for measuring time, was defined variously in terms of the time it takes the Earth to rotate on its axis or the Earth to rotate around the Sun, neither particularly constant when measured against our modern concept of time. For example, 600 million years ago the Earth rotated once on its axis every 22 hours and took 400 days to orbit the Sun. But the tides of the seas have the strange effect of transferring energy from the rotation of the Earth to the Moon, which results in the Earth's rotation slowing down and the Moon gradually moving away from us. Similar effects are causing the Earth and Sun to drift apart, changing the time it takes to complete an orbit.

Given the vagaries of the motions of the planets, from 1967, instead of measuring the passage of time by looking outwards to the universe, metrologists looked to the atom to define the second, which is now understood as:

the duration of 9,192,631,770 periods of the radiation corresponding to the transition between the two hyperfine levels of the ground state of the caesium-133 atom at rest at a temperature of 0 K.

Quite a mouthful. And you should see the clock that does the measuring. I visited the National Physical Laboratory in southwest London to see the atomic clock that tells Big Ben and the pips on the radio when to sound the hour. It's enormous. Definitely not something that you could wear on your wrist. It includes six lasers that trap the atoms of caesium before launching them upward into a microwave chamber. As they fall back down under the effect of gravity in what's called a caesium fountain, the atoms are zapped with microwaves, causing them to emit the radiation whose frequencies are used to define the second.

The atomic clocks that sit at the national laboratories across the world are some of the most extraordinary measuring devices created by humans. The regularity and universality of the atom means that two atomic clocks put next to each other would after 138 million years differ by at most a second. These clocks produce some of the most precise measurements ever made by humans. So perhaps we can say we know time. The trouble is that time isn't as constant as we had hoped. If two atomic clocks are moving relative to each other, then, as Einstein famously revealed at the beginning of the twentieth century, they will soon be telling very different stories of time.

TORCHES ON TRAINS

Newton believed that time and space were absolutes against which we could measure how we move. In the *Principia* he laid out his stall: 'Absolute, true and mathematical time, of itself, and from its own nature flows equably without regard to anything external.'

For Newton, space and time were like a backdrop upon which nature played out its story. Space was the stage on which the story of the universe was performed and time marked the passage through this story. He believed that you could place clocks across the universe, and once they had all been synched they would continue to show the same time at whatever point you were in the universe. Others were not so convinced. Newton's arch-rival Gottfried Leibniz believed that time existed only as a relative concept.

A discovery made in 1887 by American scientists Albert Michelson and Edward Morley ultimately led to Leibniz's view winning out over Newton's. The American scientists found that if we measure the speed of light in a vacuum, then, regardless of whether we are moving towards or away from the source of the light, the measurement remains the same. This revelation was the seed for Einstein's discovery that time was not quite as absolute as Newton had envisioned.

At first sight, the fact that the speed of light is the same however I am moving relative to the light source seems counterintuitive. Consider the Earth orbiting the Sun. If I measure the speed of the light coming from a distant star, I would expect it to be faster when I am heading towards the star than when I am heading away from the light source.

Newtonian physics implies that if I am running 10 miles an hour down a train travelling at 90 miles an hour then relative to someone on the platform I am travelling at a combined speed of 100 miles an hour. So why isn't the same true of light shining from a torch on the train? Why isn't the speed of light 90 miles an hour faster for the person measuring it on the platform? It transpires that Newton was wrong about both the speed of light and the speed of the runner on the train relative to the person on the platform. You can't simply add their speeds to the speed of the train. The calculation turns out to be more subtle.

It was by trying to understand why the speed of light is invariant that Einstein, in 1905, made the breakthrough that changed our perspective on the universe. He discovered that time and space are not absolute but vary according to the relative motion of the observer. Einstein was famously employed at the time as a clerk in the Swiss patent office evaluating applications for a range of new inventions

Relativistic formula for combining speeds

To calculate the apparent speed s of a passenger running at u miles an hour down the length of a train travelling at v miles an hour Einstein discovered that you need to use the following equation:

$$s = \frac{u + v}{1 + (uv/c^2)}$$

where c is the speed of light. When the speeds u and v are small compared to c, the term uv/c^2 is very small. This means that the speed s can be approximated by adding the speeds $u + v$. But when the speeds u and v get close to the speed of light, the approximation breaks down and the formula gives a different answer. The formula is such that it never outputs a combined speed that is faster than the speed of light.

from gravel sorters to electrical typewriters. But he also had to assess attempts to create devices to electrically synchronize time, an important task for a world that was becoming increasingly interconnected. It was such apparently mundane work that fired the thought experiments that led to Einstein's special theory of relativity.

SLOWING DOWN TIME

To explain Einstein's new ideas about time, I need a clock. A clock requires something that repeats itself at regular intervals. I could use one of the atomic clocks at the National Physical Laboratory or my wristwatch, but in fact light is the best clock to use to reveal the strange effect relative motion has on time. I am going to exploit the discovery by Michelson and Morley that the speed of light does not seem to depend on how you are moving when you measure it.

So let me consider time measured by a device in which each tick corresponds to the light bouncing between two mirrors.

I am going to take one such clock onto a spaceship and the other clock I will leave with you on the surface of the Earth. Because it will turn out that distance in space is contracted in the direction of movement, I need to place the clock so that the light travels perpendicular to the direction of the spaceship. This will ensure that the distance between the two mirrors is the same in both locations. To show that – from your perspective on Earth – my spaceship's clock ticks at a slower rate relative to the clock on the Earth requires nothing more sophisticated than Pythagoras' theorem.

Einstein's revelation depends on the fact that the person on the Earth must record the light going at the same speed on the spaceship as it does on the Earth. This is the important discovery made by Michelson and Morley: the speed of light is the same everywhere. Just because the spaceship is moving, that movement can't add speed to the light. To record speed, you need to measure distance travelled divided by the time it takes to travel that distance (with respect to the measuring devices on Earth). So let us look at how far the light travels when it is emitted from one mirror and hits the opposite mirror in my clock on board the spaceship.

Suppose the mirrors are 4 metres apart. Let me suppose also that in the time it takes for the light to travel between the mirrors on the spaceship, the ship has moved 3 metres as measured by you on Earth. Pythagoras' theorem implies that actually the light has travelled across the hypotenuse of the triangle and has therefore covered 5 metres. That's all the maths you need to understand Einstein's theory of special relativity.

From this we can calculate that the spaceship is travelling at ⅗ the speed of light relative to the Earth – the spaceship covers 3 metres in the time that it takes light to travel 5 metres.

The spaceship's clock moves 3 metres in the time it takes the light to travel between the mirrors set at 4 metres apart. By Pythagoras' theorem, this means the light has actually travelled 5 metres.

The key point is that light on the Earth will have travelled the same distance, since the speed of light must be the same everywhere. Your clock on the Earth has the same dimensions, so the light there must be covering the same distance, i.e. 5 metres. But the mirrors are 4 metres apart. This means it must have hit the top mirror, and be on its way back down again, one quarter of the way through a second tick. So time is running faster according to the person on the Earth because one tick of the clock on the spaceship takes the same time as 1¼ ticks of the clock on Earth. According to you, my clock in space is going ⅘ slower!

To get a sense of why this is happening, take a look at the beam of light as it travels on the spaceship and on the Earth. The beam of light is going at the same speed in the clocks on the Earth and the spaceship. The freeze-frames on the next page show where the light will be at various points in time. Because the light on the spaceship has to travel through space in the direction of the movement of the spaceship, it can't travel as far in the direction of the opposite mirror in the clock on the spaceship. So from your perspective on the Earth, the light in your clock reaches the mirror before the light on my clock on the spaceship does. This means that your clock on the Earth is 'ticking' faster.

Earth
clock

Spaceship
clock

Dotted line represents where each beam of light will be at
each freeze-frame taken from the Earth.

In some ways, fair enough . . . and yet when I compare the clocks from my perspective on the spaceship things get very counterintuitive. To understand why things get so weird I need to apply what is known as the 'principle of relativity'. This says that if you are in uniform motion (i.e. not accelerating and not changing direction) then it is impossible to tell that you are moving. This principle of relativity was not due to Einstein but is already in Newton's *Principia*, though it is probably Galileo who should be credited with the realization. It captures that strange experience you may have had when you're in a train alongside another train at a station and then your train starts moving relative to the train alongside. Until the platform is revealed, it's impossible to tell which train is moving (this requires the acceleration to be so gradual that you can't detect it).

When this is applied to our clocks on the spaceship and on Earth, it leads to a rather strange outcome, because as far as I am concerned in my spaceship, it is the Earth that is whizzing by me at ⅗ the speed of light. The same analysis that I performed above implies that I will calculate that it is your clock on Earth that is going slower, not my clock. Time, it turns out, is far less obvious a concept than we experience in everyday life.

The whole thing seems so bizarre as to be unbelievable. How can the spaceship clock be ticking slower than the Earth clock and at the same time the Earth clock be ticking slower than the spaceship clock? But as soon as I have the indisputable observation that the speed of light is constant regardless of how I measure it, the mathematics leads me to this conclusion. It's one of the reasons I love mathematics. It is like a rabbit hole of logic dropping you into unexpected wonderlands.

It's not just the ticking clock on the spaceship that appears to be slowing down from the perspective of Earth. Anything that keeps track of time must also slow down. If I am sitting on the spaceship I cannot tell that my clock is doing anything strange. So it means that anything that measures time will be similarly affected, including the quartz pulsating in my wristwatch, the Prokofiev on the spaceship's radio, the ageing of my body, my brain's neural activity. On board the spaceship I will not be aware that anything strange is happening because everything on board the spaceship will be ticking at the same rate.

But from your perspective on the Earth, it appears that my watch is losing time, the Prokofiev has turned into a deep-sounding dirge, I am ageing slower, and my neurons aren't firing quite as fast as they usually do. Time and the sensation of its passing are relative. It depends on comparing things. If everything is slowing down or speeding up at the same rate, I can't tell any difference. Everything seems normal on board my spaceship. The curious thing is that when I look down at you, I see everything around you slowing to a snail's pace.

SPEED UP AND LIVE LONGER

A rather striking example of this relative difference in the passage of time is the strange case of muon decay that I encountered in the Second Edge. When cosmic rays hit the upper atmosphere the collisions create a shower of fundamental particles, including the muon, a heavy version of the electron. These muons are not stable and very quickly decay into more stable forms of matter.

Scientists talk about something called half-life. This is the amount of time it takes for the population of muons to be reduced by half because of decay. (Knowing when the decay will happen for a particular particle is still something of a mystery, and, as I discussed in the Third Edge, I have only the mechanism of the throw of my casino dice to give me any predictive power.) In the case of muons, after 2.2 microseconds, on average half of these particles will have decayed away.

The speed at which they decay should mean that, given the distance they must travel to the surface of the Earth, not many of them will survive the journey. However, scientists detected far more muons than they expected. The explanation is that a clock on board a muon is going slower because these particles are travelling at close to the speed of light. So the half-life of the muon is actually longer than we'd expect when measured by a clock on Earth. The muon's internal clock is going slower than the clock on Earth, and hence, since not so much time has passed in the frame of reference of the muon, the 2.2 microseconds that it takes for half the muons to decay takes much longer than 2.2 microseconds measured by a clock on the Earth's surface.

But how does this work from the perspective of the muon? The clock on board the muon is running normally, and it's the clock on Earth that is running slow. So, from their perspective, what causes more muons to reach the surface of the Earth than expected? The point is that it isn't only time but also space which is affected by things travelling at speed relative to each other. The space between the planet and the muons is also affected. Distances shrink when they are moving, so the distance from the outer atmosphere to the surface of the Earth from the muons' perspective is much shorter than it is from our own perspective. So the muon doesn't think it has as far to go, meaning more reach their destination.

Is this a strategy I can use to steal some more days out of my finite life? Can I cheat my own half-life? The trouble is that, as I explained, everything slows down on my speeding spaceship. I'm not going to squeeze any more time out of the universe to solve the mathematical problems I'm working on by speeding along near the speed of light, because while my body may age more slowly, my neurons will fire more slowly too. The principle of relativity means that, as far as I am concerned, I appear to be at rest and it's everything else that is speeding by.

RELATIVITY DOGS

The ideas that Einstein came up with in 1905 reveal that the time I see on my watch is much more fluid than I first thought. The absolute nature of time in the universe is challenged even further when you try to understand what it means for two events to happen at the same time. This was the problem Einstein had confronted when working on patents to synchronize time. It turns out that this doesn't make sense as a question. Or at least the answer will depend on your frame of reference.

Let's start with a scene from a fictional movie called *Relativity Dogs* in homage to Tarantino. It takes place on a train (as many things do in relativity). Two people with identical guns are standing at either end of the train. Exactly halfway between them is a third member of the gang. The train is racing through a station. A police officer is watching the scene. Let me first consider the situation on the train. As far as the gang members are concerned, the train can be considered at rest. The guns go off. The bullets hit the man in the middle at the same time. The speed of the bullets and the distance they have to cover is the same, and as far as everyone on the train is concerned the gunmen both shot at the same moment. Indeed, the victim saw light flash from the guns at the same moment, just before being hit by the bullets.

But what about the perspective of the police officer? Let's suppose the victim passes the police officer at precisely the moment both flashes of light reach the victim, so that the police officer witnesses the flashes at the same time too. But then he begins to wonder: how far has the light travelled? Although they are the same distance away from him now, when they went off, the gun at the front of the train was actually nearer to him. So the light had a shorter distance to travel than the light at the back of the train. In which case, since the speed of light is constant, if the light arrived at the same time it must have left the gun at the back of the train earlier than it left the gun at the front. So to the police officer it seems that the gunman at the back of the train shot first. But if I put another officer on a train going in the opposite direction, then everything is reversed and the second police officer will conclude that the gun at the front of the train must have gone off first.

So who shot first? The gunman at the back shot first from the perspective of the policeman on the platform; but the gunman at the front shot first from the perspective of the policeman on the train speeding in the opposite direction. To talk about which gun was fired first is therefore meaningless in an absolute sense. Time takes on different meanings for different frames of reference. It turns out that there is something which is absolute for all of the observers, but it requires combining time and space.

The trouble is that I have been trying to measure the distance between two objects, and this changes according to how I move relative to the two points. Similarly, the time between two events also changes. But if I now define a new distance that measures the distance in time and space, I can get something invariant, i.e. not dependent on who is doing the measuring. This was the great idea of mathematician Hermann Minkowski, Einstein's former teacher at the Polytechnic in Zürich. On hearing about Einstein's ideas, he immediately understood that the high-dimensional geometries discovered by German mathematician Bernhard Riemann 50 years earlier were the perfect stage for Einstein's theory.

For those happy to contemplate a formula, the distance between an event happening at location (x_1, y_1, z_1) at time t_1 and an event happening at location (x_2, y_2, z_2) at time t_2 is defined by

$$\sqrt{(x_1 - x_2)^2 + (y_1 - y_2)^2 + (z_1 - z_2)^2 - c^2 (t_1 - t_2)^2}$$

The first three bits of the equation

$$(x_1 - x_2)^2 + (y_1 - y_2)^2 + (z_1 - z_2)^2$$

make up the usual distance measured in space (using Pythagoras' theorem). The last bit is the usual measurement of the difference in time. Your first intuition might be to add these two distances together. The clever thing that Minkowski did was to take the second away from the first. This creates a very different sort of measure, leading to a geometry which doesn't satisfy the usual laws of geometry as developed by the Greeks. It views the universe not as three-dimensional space animated in time but rather as a four-dimensional block of something called space-time, whose points are located by four coordinates (x, y, z, t), three for space and one for time. Minkowski introduced this new geometrical way of looking at the universe two years after Einstein's announcement of his special theory of relativity in 1905.

If the formula leaves you none the wiser, don't despair. Einstein too was rather suspicious of what he regarded as something of a mathematical trick. But Minkowski's four-dimensional geometry would provide a new map of the universe. As Minkowski declared: 'Henceforth space by itself, and time by itself, are doomed to fade away into mere shadows, and only a kind of union of the two will preserve an independent reality.'

This was Einstein's response to the mathematization of his ideas: 'Since the mathematicians pounced on the relativity theory I no longer understand it myself.' But he soon realized that it was the best language for navigating this strange new universe called space-time.

The power of measuring distance in space-time is that if I take a different observer moving relative to these events, although the time and distance will both have different values, this new distance between events in space-time is actually the same. So Newton was right that there should be some background which is absolute. His mistake was to consider time and space separately. Post-Einstein, we must consider the two simultaneously. And it's this mixing of the nature of time and space that makes the question of what happened before the Big Bang really interesting.

For a start, it forces us to consider time in a very different light. We should regard the universe as a block of space and time in which the ideas of 'before' and 'after' are as questionable as saying what point of space is in front of another: it depends on your perspective. This is very disconcerting. For both policemen in my fictional movie scene, there is a moment when one of the gunmen still hasn't squeezed the trigger. Perhaps there is time for them to stop and consider their actions, to decide not to shoot and let the other person be responsible. But hold on! For the policeman on the platform that decision is in the hands of the man at the front of the train. But for the policeman on the train going in the opposite direction, it's the gunman at the back. Does that actually mean the future is not really in our hands at all?

Usually when I draw a graph of distance against time, the time axis runs along the horizontal and the distance, travelled by a ball, say, is represented on the vertical. But space-time doesn't allow me divide time and space up so neatly. When I think of space-time as a block, I must be careful not to think of one privileged direction in this block representing time and three other independent directions keeping track of space. Two different directions in this space-time can represent

On your timeline, events A and B happen simultaneously and C happens later. However, for me, B and C are simultaneous events, while A happened earlier. If A and C are causally linked then for everyone's timeline A will always happen before C. But B is not causally connected to either A or C, so there are timelines that place event B before A, or alternatively after C.

the time dimension. It just depends on how you are moving through space. Time and space are mixed in this new view.

This is a real challenge to my intuition about the universe. Suppose I am speeding away from you on a spaceship. If I draw a line connecting all simultaneous events from my perspective in this space-time geometry, they will be a very different set of lines from yours.

In Hindi and Urdu the word *kal* is used to mean both yesterday and tomorrow. In the quote from *Midnight's Children* at the head of this chapter, Salman Rushdie joked that people who have the same word for yesterday and tomorrow cannot be said to have a firm grip on time. But could they in fact be on to something? The idea of 'before' or 'after' is not as clear as some languages imply.

And yet, even with this mixing of space and time, time does have a different quality from space. Information cannot travel faster than the speed of light. Causality means that we can't place ourselves at a point in space-time where the bullet hits the victim before it was fired. There are constraints on how these timelines can be drawn in space-time. My intuition about space and time is not going to help me. Instead, as Einstein reluctantly conceded, I have to rely on the mathematics to lead me to the limits of the universe and knowledge.

SHAPE OF TIME

Just as I can talk about space having a shape, I can also talk about space-time having a shape. My initial instinct is to think of time as a line, which makes it very difficult for me to think of anything other than a line that is finite and therefore has a beginning, or a line that is infinite. But there are other possibilities. Since time and space make up four dimensions, I've got to consider shapes that I can't see. I need mathematics to describe them. But I can picture shapes representing parts of space-time which enable me to understand what I mean by the question: what happened before the Big Bang? For example, imagine there was only one spatial dimension, so that space-time is two-dimensional. This creates a surface that I can see, like a rubber sheet that I can play with and wrap up in interesting ways.

I think most people's model of two-dimensional space-time would be an infinite flat sheet with time extending infinitely backwards and forwards and space also one-dimensional and infinite. But, as I explored in the last Edge, space could be finite. I could wrap space up to make a circle and then time would extend this circle to make space-time look like a cylinder. I could of course join the cylinder up to make a bagel- or torus-shaped space-time. That would make time finite too. In this model of space-time I could loop round and return to a previous moment in history. Logician Kurt Gödel proposed solutions to Einstein's equations of general relativity that have this feature. Gödel, as I shall explain in my final Edge, greatly enjoyed messing with people's logical expectations. But Gödel's circles of space-time are generally regarded as curiosities, because going back in time causes too many problems when it comes to causality.

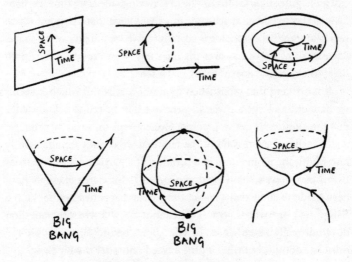

Possible shapes for a two-dimensional space-time.

To get a more realistic picture of space-time, I need to create a geometry that takes into account our current model of the history of the universe, which includes a beginning: the Big Bang. To see this point in my two-dimensional space-time universe, I could wrap up the surface so that it looks like a cone. The universe, which is just a circle, shrinks in size as I go back in time until I hit the point at the end of the cone. This is where time begins. There is nothing before that. No space. No time. Just a point of infinite density. This is a good model for something rather like the Big Bang.

Or, rather than pinching space-time at a point, perhaps it could look like a sphere, like the surface of the Earth. This has its own implications for how I answer the question: what happened before the Big Bang? If I head south along a line of longitude, then when I hit the South Pole there is a sudden flip and I find myself on another line of longitude on the other side. But these are just numbers that we give to these points on the Earth's surface. It doesn't actually represent a discontinuous flip in the shape, just a jump in the way that we measure it.

So by changing the coordinates, what appears to be a singular point can look quite smooth. This is one of Hawking's ideas for time. Perhaps I should try to embed space-time in a shape such that this point which seems to show time stopping is actually just the south pole of the shape. After all, how do you answer the question: what's south of the South Pole? The question doesn't really make sense.

It is striking that often when a question arises to which it seems we cannot know the answer, it turns out that I need to acknowledge that the question is not well posed. Heisenberg's uncertainty principle is not really an expression of the fact that we cannot simultaneously know both the momentum and position of a particle, more that these two things don't actually exist concurrently. Similarly, attempts have been made to show that the question 'What happened before the Big Bang?' isn't one whose answer we cannot know. Rather, the question does not really make sense. To talk about 'before' is to suppose the existence of time, but what if time existed only after the Big Bang?

By picturing the shape of space-time I begin to get a sense of why many scientists have dismissed the question of understanding time before the Big Bang as meaningless. But there are other shapes which allow time to have a history before the Big Bang. What if the cone, instead of coming to a point and ending, actually bounced out of a contracting universe before the Big Bang? To truly get a sense of time's history as I head back towards the Big Bang, I need to understand what happens to time as it approaches a point with increased gravity. This was Einstein's second great discovery: that gravity also has an effect on the ticking clock of time.

WHY SKYSCRAPERS AREN'T GOOD FOR YOU

Einstein's second assault on the nature of time came when he threw gravity into the mix. His general theory of relativity, developed between 1907 and 1915, describes the very geometric nature of gravity. Gravity is not really a force but a property of the way this four-dimensional sheet of space-time is curved. The Moon orbits the Earth because the mass of the Earth distorts the shape of space-time in such a way that the Moon simply rolls around the curved shape of space-time in this region. The force of gravity is an illusion. There is no force. Objects are just free-falling through the geometry of space-time, and what we observe is the curvature of this space. But if massive bodies can distort the shape of space, they can also have an effect on time.

This was yet another of Einstein's great revelations, and it is based once again on a principle of equivalence. The strange consequences of special relativity are teased out of the principle of relativity, which states that it is impossible to tell whether it is me who is moving or my environment that is moving past me. Einstein applied a similar principle of equivalence to gravity and acceleration.

If you are floating out in space in a spaceship with no windows and I place a large massive planet underneath the spaceship, you will be pulled towards the floor. This is the force of gravity. But if instead I accelerate the ship upwards, you will experience exactly the same sensation of being pulled towards the floor. Einstein hypothesized that there is no way to distinguish between the two: gravity and acceleration produce the same effects.

This is particularly striking if I apply this to the photon clock inside our spaceship. Let's suppose that our spaceship is as tall as the Shard in London. I'm going to place a photon clock at the bottom of the space-ship and another at the top of the spaceship. Next to each clock I'm going to station an astronaut who will help me compare the running of these two clocks.

The astronaut at the bottom of the spaceship is going to send a pulse of light to the astronaut at the top each time his clock ticks. The astronaut at the top can then compare the arrival of these pulses with the ticking of her clock. Without acceleration or gravity, the arrival of the pulses and the ticking of the clocks will be in synch. However, let me now accelerate the spaceship in the direction of the top of the spaceship. A pulse is emitted at the bottom of the spaceship, and, as the spaceship accelerates away, the light has further to travel each time, so that it takes longer and longer for each pulse to reach the top of the spaceship, and the astronaut at the top will receive the pulses at a slower rate. This is similar to the Doppler effect we experience with sound, where moving away from the source causes the frequency to decrease, resulting in a lower pitch. But in this case it is important to note that the spaceship is accelerating rather than just flying along at a constant speed.

The interpretation, though, of the drop in frequency is that the clock at the bottom of the spaceship is going slower than the clock at the top. What if I reverse the experiment and get the astronaut at the top of the spaceship to send pulses down to the bottom of the spaceship? Because the astronaut at the bottom is accelerating towards the pulses, he is going to receive them at a faster rate than the pulses of light he is sending. So he will confirm that his clock is running slower

Acceleration and gravity have the same effect: slowing the
clock at the bottom of the Shard spaceship.

than the clock at the top of the spaceship. This is in contrast to two clocks that are travelling at constant speeds relative to each other, in which case both astronauts think their clock is going faster.

The interesting conclusion of the experiment comes when I replace acceleration with gravity. According to Einstein's principle of equivalence, whatever effect acceleration had on the clocks in the spaceship, the effect of gravity must be the same. So when I place a large planet at the foot of our Shard-sized spaceship, the impact is the same as if the spaceship was accelerating through space: clocks run slower at the foot of the Shard than they do at the top.

Since the ageing body is a clock, this means that you age slower the closer you are to the centre of the Earth – people working at the top of the Shard in London are ageing faster than those on the ground floor. Of course, the difference in the speed of the clocks is extremely small at this scale, but it makes a significant difference if we compare the ticking of atomic clocks on the surface of the Earth with those in orbit on satellites. The difference in gravity experienced by the two clocks results in them ticking at different rates. Since these atomic clocks are integral to the functioning of GPS, it is essential that the effects of gravity on time are taken into account if these systems are to be accurate.

ASYMMETRICAL TWINS

There is a classic story that reveals the strange nature of time in Einstein's new world. It involves sending twins, or actually one twin, on a space journey. It is particularly close to my heart because I have identical twin girls, Magaly and Ina. If I send Ina off on a spaceship travelling at close to the speed of light and then bring her back to Earth, the physics of relativity implies that, although she will think that she's been away for only ten years, her twin sister's clock on Earth has raced ahead, so that Magaly is now in her eighties.

To truly understand the asymmetric nature of the story, I need to take into account Einstein's revelation about the effect of gravity and acceleration on time. Once Ina is travelling at a constant speed close to the speed of light, Einstein's first revelation declares that neither twin can tell who is moving and who is still. Ina will think Magaly's clock is running slower, and Magaly will think Ina's is slower. So why does Ina return younger? Why aren't they the same age?

Ina returns younger because she has to accelerate to get to her constant speed. Similarly, when she turns around she needs to decelerate and then accelerate in the opposite direction. This causes her clock to slow down relative to that of her twin on Earth, who doesn't accelerate. This asymmetry results in Ina heading into Magaly's future. If I sent both twins off in spaceships in opposite directions and brought them back together then they'd be the same age – and everyone on Earth would have aged quicker.

Einstein's general theory of relativity revealed that time as well as space gets pulled about by things with mass. Gravity is actually the distortion of this space-time surface. If something has mass, it curves the surface. The classic way to imagine this is to consider space-time as a two-dimensional surface, and the effect of mass as that of placing a ball on this surface. The ball pulls the surface down, creating a well. Gravity can be thought of as the way things get pulled down into this well.

This distortion of space-time has an interesting effect on light. Light follows the shortest path between two points – the definition of a 'straight' line. But I am now talking about lines in space-time, where distance is measured using Minkowski's formula that includes the coordinates of space and time. Weirdly, using Minkowski's formula, it turns out that the distance between two points in space-time is reduced if the light takes longer to get there.

So in order to find the shortest space-time path, light will follow a trajectory that tries to balance a minimizing of distance travelled against a maximizing of time taken. By following a trajectory such that the light particle is essentially free-falling, the clocks on board the particle will go faster. Pull against gravity and you are accelerating and thus slowing your clock down. So Einstein's theory predicted that light would be bent by the presence of a large mass. It was a highly unexpected prediction of the theory, but one that could be tested: a perfect scenario for a scientific theory.

Convincing evidence for this picture of a curved space-time was provided by the British astronomer Arthur Eddington's observations of light from distant stars recorded during the solar eclipse of 1919. The theory predicted that the light from distant stars would be bent by the gravitational effect of the Sun. Eddington needed the eclipse to block out the glare of the Sun so that he could see the stars in the sky. The fact that the light did indeed seem to bend round objects of large mass confirmed that the shortest paths weren't Euclidean straight lines but curved.

We experience the same effect on the surface of the Earth. An aeroplane flying from London to New York takes a curved path passing over Greenland rather than the straight line we'd expect by looking at a map of the Earth. This curved line is the shortest path between the two points on the Earth. Light too found the shortest path from the star to Eddington's telescope on Earth.

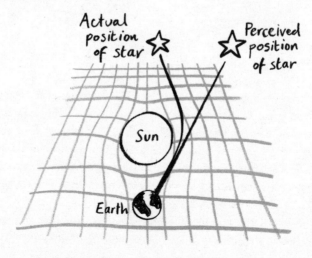

Eddington announced his experimental evidence confirming Einstein's ideas on 6 November 1919. Within days, newspaper headlines across the world trumpeted the great achievement: 'EINSTEIN THEORY TRIUMPHS: Stars Not Where They Seemed To Be, but Nobody Need Worry' announced the *New York Times*; 'Revolution in Science' declared the London *Times*. Although we're quite used to Higgs bosons or gravitational waves hitting the headlines, this was probably the first time in history that a scientific achievement was given such public exposure. Heralded by journalists as the new Newton, the obscure 40-year-old Einstein shot to international fame.

If you are finding all this warping of space and time bending your brain, don't despair. You are in good company. After Eddington announced his discovery that light bends, a colleague came up to congratulate him: 'You must be one of only three people in the world to understand Einstein's theory.' When Eddington failed to respond, the colleague prompted: 'Come, come, there is no need to be modest.' 'On the contrary,' replied Eddington, 'I was trying to think who was the third.'

But trying to say what happens to time as we head back towards the Big Bang would test even Eddington's understanding of Einstein's theory.

10

There is a place where time stands still.
Raindrops hang motionless in air. Pendulums
of clocks float mid-swing. Dogs raise their
muzzles in silent howls. Pedestrians are frozen
on the dusty streets, their legs cocked as if
held by strings. The aromas of dates, mangoes,
coriander, cumin are suspended in the space.

Alan Lightman, *Einstein's Dreams*

I'm rather fond of the design of my watch. The face is a simple brown square sitting inside a circular silver case. I like the symmetry of the shape, and yet there is subtle tension between the square and the circle. It's not expensive, which is a good thing, as I tend to lose watches.

My last watch slipped off my wrist when I was kayaking across a lake next to the glacier on Mount Cook. I tried to rescue the watch but the water was so bitterly cold that I couldn't leave my hand in it for more than a couple of seconds. Not that I had anything to measure time with anymore. The watch had disappeared below the surface and its mechanism is by now presumably rusted and frozen, its telling of time stopped by the glacial waters flowing off Mount Cook.

If I want an environment to freeze the ticking of my current watch, dropping it into the mathematical singularities that were discovered within Einstein's equations for general relativity will stop even the most robust of watches. However, I'll need a spaceship, not a kayak, to explore these singularities known as black holes.

HORIZONS BEYOND WHICH WE CANNOT KNOW

The reason the universe is so fascinating – rather than a uniform spread of matter – is that, thanks to gravity, atoms attract other atoms. And so unless everything is in a perfect balance, we see a movement of matter towards other bits of matter. But the interesting thing about gravity is that the pull that matter exerts on other matter gets stronger as things get closer. This attraction is what leads to the creation of stars like our Sun, but also to the potential for more catastrophic events in space-time.

The simplest atom is hydrogen, which is made up from one electron and one proton held together by the electromagnetic force. If I have two atoms of hydrogen, they are pulled towards each other by the force of gravity. And as the atoms are pulled closer and closer they start to collide with each other. Increase the number of hydrogen atoms and the collisions get more and more energetic until the atoms no longer simply bounce off each other but the conditions for nuclear fusion are satisfied and I get a star. The hydrogen atoms fuse to create helium atoms. In the process energy is given off, creating outward pressure as the energy is dissipated. This is the energy that we depend on for life on Earth. The star remains stable, not collapsing any further, because the gravitational pull inwards is counterbalanced by the outward pressure of the energy released in the process of fusion.

At some point all the hydrogen gets used up. Some stars will continue to fuse helium into atoms further up the periodic table. Many of the atoms we find on Earth, such as iron, oxygen, or even the carbon that is crucial for making life, are all products of this continuing fusion of lighter atoms in stars. Eventually the star isn't able to sustain this fusion – the fuel is spent. And then, once again, gravity takes over, and as the star contracts, quantum physics comes into play. If I confine particles in a smaller and smaller space then I know a lot about their position. By Heisenberg's uncertainty principle, this must be balanced by huge uncertainty in the velocity of the particles. The movement of the particles away from each other results in a second period of stability that counteracts the pull of gravity, resulting in what is known as a white dwarf.

But in 1930 the Indian physicist Subrahmanyan Chandrasekhar realized that there is a problem with this. Stuck on a boat sailing from India to do his doctoral studies in Cambridge, Chandrasekhar recognized that special relativity puts a speed limit on how fast these particles can move. So if the mass of the star is great enough, gravity will win out over this speed limit and the star will continue to collapse, creating a region of space of increasingly high density. His calculations made on board ship revealed that any star that was more than 1.4 times the mass of our Sun would suffer such a fate. The supernovae responsible for creating elements like gold and uranium are the result of these cataclysmic collapses.

The space around these points of high density will get severely warped, so much so that the light is trapped inside and can't get out. One way to get a sense of why things might get ensnared is to consider throwing a ball in the air. On the surface of the Earth it is possible to launch a ball fast enough such that it actually escapes the gravitational pull of the Earth. The speed at which you need to throw the ball is called its escape velocity. But imagine increasing the mass of the Earth more and more. The speed required to escape the gravitational pull also increases. But there will be a point at which the mass of the Earth is so big that the ball would need to be launched at a speed faster than the speed of light in order to escape. At this point the ball is trapped. It cannot go beyond a certain point before it is pulled back to Earth.

This is with our classical pre-Einstein view of gravity. Towards the end of the eighteenth century, Laplace and English physicist John Michell had already flirted with the proposal that light too could get trapped by massive objects. However, Michelson and Morley's discovery a hundred years later that light always travels at the same speed in a vacuum means that light doesn't behave like the ball. Gravity isn't going to slow the light down as Laplace and Michell thought. But Einstein's conception of gravity as the result of curved space-time can still result in light failing to get away. Einstein's ideas suggest a region of space that is so curved that even light (which is massless yet still affected by the curvature of space) cannot escape. Space is curved so much that no light can find its way out but is bent back into the region of high density. In 1967 American physicist John Wheeler whimsically referred to these regions as 'black holes'. Richard Feynman thought the name was obscene: in French, *trou noir* has other connotations. However, the name stuck.

As you move away from the centre of the collapsed star, the effect of gravity decreases. This results in a boundary shaped like a sphere, with the black hole at its centre, that represents a point of no return: outside of this sphere light can escape; but any light or any thing inside this boundary will be trapped because it doesn't have sufficient speed to escape. This sphere is known as the event horizon of the black hole, because anyone outside the sphere cannot witness the events occurring on the inside.

The mass of the star needs to be sufficiently great for the mass to collapse within the region of this sphere. For example, the mass of the Earth is too small to create a black hole – it would need to be packed into a sphere with a radius of just 1 centimetre. Our Sun is also not massive enough: the radius of its event horizon would be just 3 kilometres. But if the mass of the star is 1.4 times greater than the mass of our Sun, the inward pressure of gravity will counter any outward pressure caused by the high momentum of the trapped matter and it will collapse inside its event horizon.

Black holes have been a subject of hot debate since they were first theoretically proposed following Einstein's publication of his equations for gravity in 1915. Some believed that stars, as they collapsed, would somehow avoid such no-go regions. Perhaps the star would throw off mass. That is certainly possible, but with a star that is 20 times the mass of the Sun, you'd need 95% of the mass to be thrown off to avoid it becoming a black hole, which is unlikely. Nevertheless, some held on to the belief that these regions of space-time would not occur.

In 1964 the first potential example of just such a high-density region was identified in the constellation of Cygnus. Called Cygnus X-1, by 1971 calculations of its mass and concentration led to the conjecture that it was a black hole. Not everyone was convinced. In fact, there was one notable person who made a bet in 1975 to the effect that Cygnus X-1 was not a black hole: Stephen Hawking. This was somewhat odd, given that he'd dedicated much of his research to probing the nature of black holes. If Cygnus X-1 turned out to be the first example of a black hole, all Hawking's theoretical musings would have been justified.

As he explained in *A Brief History of Time*, the bet was an insurance policy. Betting against your football team winning the final of the FA cup is a win–win situation: if your team loses, at least you benefit financially. If it turned out that his life's work on black holes was a waste of time, then at least he'd won the bet. His prize? A subscription to *Private Eye* magazine to distract him from the misery of his failed research. He made the bet with fellow cosmologist Kip Thorne. Convincing evidence that proved that Cygnus X-1 was indeed a black hole would win Thorne a subscription to the journal of his choice. He opted for *Penthouse* magazine.

By 1990 there was much evidence that Cygnus X-1 was indeed a black hole: it is estimated to have a mass of 14.8 times the mass of the Sun and to be too compact to be a star. Cygnus X-1 is believed to have an event horizon of 44 kilometres. Inside this spherical ball, whose diameter stretches the distance between Oxford and Cambridge, no light can escape. Given all the data, Hawking conceded the bet. Thorne has his subscription to *Penthouse*, much to the chagrin of his wife.

But there is something mathematically disturbing about these black holes, something which contributed to those doubts about whether they could exist. As the stars collapse, creating points of high density, there seemed nothing left to counter the continuing pull of gravity. It seemed like they would continue collapsing, becoming smaller and smaller and more and more dense with nothing to stop the implosion. Would it therefore continue to collapse, creating a singular point of infinite density? There was a lot of hostility to the idea of such physical infinities.

Einstein himself tried to prove the absurdity of such a mathematical conclusion. Eddington could see what the maths was implying but baulked at the implications: 'When we prove a result without understanding it – when it drops unforeseen out of a maze of mathematical formulae – we have no grounds for hoping that it will apply.' But in 1964 Oxford mathematician Roger Penrose proved that such singular points were a necessary consequence of the theory of general relativity.

A black hole in two-dimensional space-time.
The event horizon is a circle inside of which we cannot know.

In collaboration with a young Stephen Hawking, Penrose went on to prove that the same infinite density is predicted when we rewind the universe back to the Big Bang. Both black holes and the Big Bang are examples in general relativity of a mathematical entity called a singularity. Singularities encompass a whole range of situations where it is impossible to work out what's happening. A singularity is a point at which our ability to model the scenario breaks down. A place where we have to throw up our hands and declare that we do not know.

SINGULARITIES

Singularities are points at which mathematical functions crash. A function in mathematics is a little like a computer program. You input numbers, the function calculates away and then it spits out an answer. Mathematicians often represent functions visually using graphs. The input is given by a number on the horizontal line, and we mark the output above the horizontal line, and the result is a curve.

For example, consider the function which inputs the distance from a massive object, and, outputs the gravitational pull experienced at that point due to the massive object. Newton realized that the greater the distance from the object, the weaker the pull. He discovered a very precise relationship between the pull and the distance. If I am a distance x

from the planet, Newton's function calculates that the pull of gravity is proportional to $1/x^2$. This is what we mean by an inverse square law. I can draw a picture of this function.

Graph of $1/x^2$. The function has a singularity at $x = 0$.

But something interesting happens as I get closer and closer to the object. The force gets bigger and bigger until, when I am at distance $x = 0$, the output is infinite and the graph doesn't have a value. Of course, in reality I am measuring the distance from the centre of gravity of the planet, and once I reach the surface of the planet the function and graph change because, as I pass through the surface, parts of the planet start pulling in the other direction. When I hit the centre of gravity, all the pulls balance out and I experience zero gravitational pull. But what if I replace the planet with a black hole, a region in space where all the mass is meant to be concentrated at a single point? Now this point has infinite density, and I can approach it and as I hit the point the gravitational pull is infinite.

The fact that the function doesn't really make sense at $x = 0$ is what mathematicians call a singularity. There are different sorts of singularities, but they all have a point at which the function doesn't give a sensible output, or where there is a sudden discontinuous jump from one value to another.

A very homespun example of a singularity can be realized by taking a coin and spinning it on a table. If there was no friction on the table or air resistance, the coin would spin forever at a constant speed. However, because in fact energy is dissipated, the coin does not spin forever. Instead, the angle of the coin to the table decreases, and, intriguingly, the speed of the rotation increases proportionally. As the angle approaches zero, the speed eventually becomes infinite. The final stages of the spinning result in the coin shuddering as it falls and there is a whirring sound whose frequency rapidly increases until suddenly the coin comes to a juddering halt.

The equations of motion reveal that the speed of the coin's rotation is increasing at such a rate that after a finite amount of time it hits infinite speed. This is what we hear when the frequency of the sound increases. The spinning coin is an example of a singularity. Of course there are other effects that come into play to stop the full realization of this mathematical infinity, but it does reveal that you don't have to disappear down a black hole for the equations of physics to produce infinities.

Even Newton's equations on planetary motion can produce singularities. As I explained at the end of the First Edge, mathematician Zhihong Xia revealed that four planets can be arranged in such a way to cause a fifth planet to be ejected from their midst, so that after a finite amount of time that planet hits infinite speed. The equations have nothing to say about what happens to that planet once it hits this astronomical singularity.

Singularities are typically moments where infinities kick in and beyond which it is impossible to make predictions. It isn't just in physics that these singularities can emerge. There is a famous example, published in 1960 by Heinz von Foerster, Patricia Mora and Lawrence Amiot, which predicts a serious singularity here on Earth. The rate of population growth, if it followed the pattern of behaviour observed up to 1960, indicated that the population of the planet would become infinite on 13 November 2026. A Friday, it so happens, if you're at all superstitious.

The simplest model of population growth posits that it is exponential. For example, a species might double in number every 50 years. With such a model the population quickly explodes but never becomes infinite. But the authors' analysis of previous data indicated that the period of time it takes for the human population to double was getting shorter and shorter.

The population took 1650 years to double from 250 million in AD 0 to 500 million in 1650. It reached a billion 200 years later, in 1850. The next doubling took only 80 years. The population hit 4 billion in 1976, just 36 years later. The rate of growth is faster than exponential. So, in 1960, with the data to hand, the authors estimated that the population of the Earth is due to hit a singularity a decade or so from now.

Another example of this super-exponential growth is the rate of increase of computer power. There is a dictum called Moore's law, which states that computers double in power every 18 months. With such an increase, computers are powerful but never hit a singularity. But others have suggested that just as the time it takes for the population to double seems to be getting shorter, the same applies to technology. The possibility of a technological singularity has given rise to something called the Singularity movement. Popularized by inventor and futurist Ray Kurzweil in his book *The Singularity Is Near*, the singularity is due to hit humanity in 2045. At this point, Kurzweil believes, humans will be able to create artificial intelligence that exceeds our own. This moment will be accompanied by a breakdown in our ability to predict what life after such a singularity will be like.

We have to be careful about mathematical equations, because there may be some hidden piece that becomes significant only when we approach the singularity, and which will then play a large role in preventing any physical realization of this infinity. This clearly occurs in the case of population growth, because the finite area of the Earth's surface will, beyond some threshold, constrain how big a population can be produced.

Similar factors could come into play with the Big Bang and black holes. Some have suggested that the equations of general relativity don't apply in these extreme settings. For example, it is possible that we need to introduce another term into Einstein's equations for gravity that impacts on the equations only when we approach the singularity. This will alter what happens as we approach the singularity of the Big Bang – but the extra component is practically undetectable before we hit these extreme conditions. It is like the subtle change that Einstein needed to introduce when considering things travelling near the speed of light: at low speed, we just add speeds; but Einstein realized that close to the speed of light you need to be more careful. As I explained in the previous chapter, the formula for the speed of a man running on a moving train relative to the platform is given by adding together the speed of the man and the train, but then you need to divide by a second formula. At low speeds, this second formula is so close to 1 that it has little effect, which is why scientists pre-Einstein believed that the speeds were simply being added together. But close to the speed of light a different behaviour dominates. The same could apply close to the Big Bang or a black hole. The equations of general relativity might need that extra term that comes into play only in cases of extreme gravity.

But if the universe does contain these singular points of infinite density, what effect do they have on time? Einstein discovered that increased gravity slows time down. So what happens to my watch as I approach these singular points of extreme gravity?

THE UNKNOWN HIDING INSIDE A BLACK HOLE

If I throw my watch into a black hole, something strange occurs. If I stay on Earth and observe my watch dropping towards the black hole, there is a moment when time seems to stop. My watch gets slower and slower until it doesn't tick any more. Eventually the image of my watch is frozen, then fades. The event horizon surrounding a black hole is like a bubble in space beyond which time seems to break down. It can't continue. From my perspective outside the 'black hole', it doesn't have an 'after'. Could this be the reverse of what happens to time as we head back to the Big Bang? Time doesn't have a 'before'.

But remember, this is from my perspective, as I compare time on Earth to the time I can see on my watch as it heads towards the black hole. How do things look if I wear my watch on my wrist and join it on its trip towards this mathematical singularity? My experience is now very different. From Earth, when my watch hit the event horizon of the black hole it appeared to stop ticking. But from my new perspective, as I cross the event horizon my watch seems to continue ticking with no problem. Indeed, I won't actually be able to detect when I have crossed this line of no return.

That's not to say that all is well for me as I fall towards the black hole, because what happens to space-time as I approach this infinitely dense centre is not so easily ironed out. As I head feet first towards the centre of the black hole, gravity pulls harder on my feet than my head, stretching me out until I am spaghettified. Within a finite amount of time, everything is crushed into the singularity, including my watch, and time comes to an end. Like a line drawn across a page, time reaches the edge and there is nowhere for it to go.

It is strange that elsewhere time seems to tick on obliviously. I guess we all have a similar fate waiting for us. When we die, time stops for us, but we know that time will continue on unawares. Just as I cannot experience my own death, I wouldn't experience arriving at a singularity in space-time.

Just in case I do slip into a black hole, a physicist friend offered me some advice: as with quicksand, the best thing is not to struggle. If I just free-fall towards my destiny, I will survive longer. This sounded very counterintuitive. But my physicist friend reminded me of what happens to my watch under the effects of gravity and acceleration. If I struggle, and try to accelerate away from the singularity, I'll find time running slower where I am. Increased acceleration, like gravity, slows clocks down. And so I will race into the future of the surrounding space-time – remember my accelerating twin daughter Ina who raced into the future of her sibling Magaly. So if I struggle when I arrive at the singularity I will have aged less. But that's not much good: I'll be extinguished in the singularity after having experienced less of life. So it's much better not to struggle and enjoy as much time as possible before I hit the singularity.

The interesting thing is that someone outside the event horizon will never know what is going on inside. From their perspective, time does appear to stop as soon as I cross the event horizon, and for them there is no telling what comes after, although there is an after for me as I carry on towards spaghettification. So asking what happens next appears to be a sensible question. It has an answer. The only trouble is that if you are outside the event horizon, you are denied access to the answer by the laws of physics.

The same principle was thought to apply to the challenge of

knowing what, if anything, happened before the Big Bang. Time comes to an end inside a black hole. But the Big Bang is like the collapse of a star into a black hole played in reverse. So I should also infer that time comes to an end as I head back towards the Big Bang. In other words, I should conclude that time had a beginning, that time itself starts at the Big Bang.

Singularities in space-time are edges, points at which I hit an end and can't go any further. An edge in space and time is difficult to understand: even though I may be prohibited from going any further, I still feel there should be something beyond that edge.

These black holes offer a challenge not only to our concept of time, but also appear to contradict one of the other discoveries of modern physics: that information is never lost.

THE ULTIMATE PAPER SHREDDER

There is a rather remarkable consequence of the laws of quantum physics, which is that they are reversible. This means that information is never lost. This is very counterintuitive. For example, if I took a subscription to *Private Eye* and a subscription to *Penthouse* magazine and I burned a year's worth of both, then it seems impossible that I could ever determine which pile of ashes corresponds to which magazine.

But provided I have complete information about all the atoms and photons involved in my bonfire, it is theoretically possible to rewind the process and recover the information contained inside the magazines. It would of course be extremely difficult in practice, but the science asserts that there is nothing about this process that is irreversible. The laws of physics work both ways.

The existence of black holes offers a challenge to this idea. If I throw one magazine in one black hole and the other magazine in another black hole, it is now impossible to find out which magazine went into which black hole. Black holes seem to be the ultimate paper shredders, in which information appears to be genuinely lost.

Black holes are particularly interesting in my search for things we cannot know, because once something has disappeared behind the event horizon – the boundary beyond which light cannot escape – it appears that I actually lose information about what has crossed the horizon. If I take the casino dice that I've been carrying with me in my search for things we cannot know and I toss it into the black hole, then once it passes the event horizon it appears that I can never know how it will land. There could be a desk on the other side on which the dice lands and comes up 6. Someone on the other side of the event horizon could see this but never be able to communicate the result because everything is trapped inside.

According to the physics of general relativity, the only things I can know about a black hole from the outside are its mass, its angular momentum and its electric charge. All other information is lost. This is known colourfully as the no-hair theorem, the idea being that any other information would represent hairs on this round bald ball of a black hole. I could chuck my dice, my cello, my wristwatch inside, and once they have passed the event horizon there is nothing about the black hole that gives any hint about what I threw in there. There is no way to rewind events to see what it was that passed that event horizon.

Although it is referred to as a theorem, it should actually be called a conjecture, because there is no conclusive proof that information is truly lost. Indeed, in 1974 the extent to which the event horizon masks what's going on inside a black hole was queried. This is because, according to Stephen Hawking, black holes are leaking.

NOT-SO-BLACK BLACK HOLES

Once my dice is thrown into a black hole, there seems to be no mechanism to know how it lands. At least many thought this must be the consequence of such a concentration of mass-warping space-time. But when Hawking applied the second law of thermodynamics to black holes, it turned out that they weren't as black as everyone had originally thought.

The second law of thermodynamics states that we are moving

from a highly ordered universe into one which has disorder. What is changing is something called the entropy of a system. Entropy is a measure of disorder. It essentially measures the number of different possible scenarios, which in turn will be a measure of how likely it is that one of those scenarios will come to pass. And the second law states that the entropy of the universe is increasing.

A classical example of the increase of entropy is to consider a gas trapped inside a container. If the gas is concentrated in one corner (imagine it has been squashed in by internal walls that have been removed), it will, in time, distribute itself across the container. The entropy counts how many different scenarios are possible for the gas. When the gas is trapped in the corner there are fewer possible scenarios than when the walls are removed and the gas can occupy the whole of the container. The entropy increases as the number of possible scenarios increases. The entropy starts low and then rises.

Or consider the everyday example of an egg falling from a table and smashing on the ground. The highly ordered egg becomes a scattered mass of eggshell. There are many more ways for the broken shell to be arranged than when it was in one piece around the egg. Watch a video of this scenario run forwards and backwards and it is clear which direction represents the true flow of time. Increased entropy keeps track of time's arrow.

And this is why entropy is intimately related to the concept of time. It is one of the few things that helps us to know which way the movie should be playing. Many other laws of physics work perfectly well if I run them forwards or backwards. Although the egg reassembling itself onto the table is physically possible, the decrease in entropy is an indication of how unlikely it is.

Yet there is a curious question about where the order in that egg comes from in the first place. You may feel that this move from order to disorder is not demonstrated on Earth. We have evolved from a messy swamp to a state in which we have life and eggs and order. This seeming violation of the second law of thermodynamics is resolved because the Earth is taking low entropy from another source – there is a trade going on. The incoming photons from the Sun, which are the source of life on Earth, have low entropy. But then, instead of the Earth warming up, the planet radiates heat via electromagnetic waves of lower frequency (and hence energy) but more of them.

So a few high-energy waves from the Sun are changed into many low-energy waves emitted by the Earth. This increase in the number of rays means an increase in the number of possible scenarios for the emission of the rays. The process is a bit like smashing the egg. A single photon of high frequency is absorbed by the Earth like the egg falling to the ground, and then the Earth kicks out many photons of low energy like bits of eggshell. The Earth benefits by a net decrease in its own entropy, and we witness order emerging out of chaos. But consider the whole system of the Earth and Sun, and entropy is indeed increasing just as the second law of thermodynamics demands.

So what happens to a container of gas when it is thrown into a black hole? Or, more intriguingly, what happens to its entropy? Outside the event horizon, I'm meant to lose any knowledge of what goes on inside. Is the entropy lost, in which case entropy would decrease, contradicting the second law of thermodynamics? Perhaps we should regard the black hole as having its own entropy, which would increase as stuff gets chucked in. But since we have no idea what's going on inside the black hole, it has been suggested that the entropy might be proportional to the surface area of the sphere of the event horizon, something we could know and calculate. That's all very well, but the physics implies that things with entropy have temperature – and things with temperature radiate heat. So it seemed that black holes should be emitting radiation inversely proportional to the mass contained in the black hole. If they were radiating, they weren't as black as the name suggests, but should be glowing gently in the night sky.

FUZZY EDGES

This didn't make sense. How can the black hole radiate if everything including light is meant to be trapped inside? There just didn't seem to be a mechanism for this to happen. That was until Hawking brought a bit of quantum physics to bear. Heisenberg's uncertainty principle implies that the event horizon is a little fuzzier than the mathematics of general relativity implied. As we saw in the Third Edge, the uncertainty principle means that position and momentum cannot both be known precisely. Similarly, time and energy are related in such a way that I can't know both simultaneously. Therefore we can't have a perfect vacuum in which everything is set to zero. If everything was zero, I'd know everything precisely.

The vacuum experiences quantum fluctuations, so that, for example, a particle and an antiparticle can appear, one with positive energy and the other with negative energy. It was possibly this mechanism of something from nothing that got the universe up and running. Usually in the vacuum of space, the particle and antiparticle will very quickly annihilate each other. But if this pair should form in such a way that the particle with positive energy is outside the event horizon of a black hole and the particle with negative energy is trapped inside, something interesting happens.

We get this strange effect: the particle inside gets sucked into the black hole, and since it has negative energy it reduces the mass of the black hole; while the particle with positive energy looks like something being radiated away from the black hole. The black hole is glowing – it has a temperature, just as we would expect if the black hole had positive entropy.

But hold on. Half the time the positive-energy particle ends up on the inside rather than the outside. Wouldn't that lead to the black hole increasing in mass? The way to resolve this is to understand that a negative-energy particle outside the event horizon doesn't have the energy to get away, so the net effect of these random fluctuations is an overall decrease in the mass of the black hole over time.

Hawking radiation, as it is known, hasn't been detected emanating from any of the black holes we've identified so far. The trouble is that the mathematics implies that the rate of emission depends inversely on the mass of the black hole. So a black hole with the mass of several suns will be emitting radiation at such a slow rate that it is below the temperature of the cosmic microwave background radiation, meaning that it is impossible to detect against the background noise left over from the Big Bang.

The striking implication of Hawking's proposal was that it provided a mechanism for black holes to fade away, reducing in mass as time passes. As the mass decreases, the radiation increases, with the result, it's believed, that black holes will eventually disappear with a pop. Hawking predicted the pop would be pretty grand: equivalent to the explosion of millions of H-bombs. Others believe it to be more on a par with an artillery shell going off.

But this leaves us with something of a puzzle. Where did the information thrown into the black hole go? I could cope with the fact that this information was trapped inside the black hole – at least it still existed. But if the black hole eventually disappears, does the information vanish with it? Or is the information somehow encoded in the radiation coming off the singularity? If I throw my casino dice into the black hole, can I somehow tell how it lands from the particles emitted at the edge of the event horizon? Perhaps, like the magazines being burnt, there is in theory a way to untangle this radiation and retrieve information about everything that disappears behind the event horizon. The puzzle of what happens to the information is called the black hole information paradox.

In 1997 Hawking took out another bet, and this time Kip Thorne sided with him. Their bet was with Caltech theoretical physicist John Preskill. They believed that this loss of information was inevitable. But, given that it contradicted the theory of quantum physics, Preskill wasn't prepared to concede that information was lost. Rather than magazine subscriptions, the wager this time was an encyclopedia of the winner's choice. The choice of an encyclopedia captured the idea that if it was thrown into a black hole, could the information contained in the encyclopedia somehow be encoded in the new particles being radiated thanks to the uncertainty principle?

In 2004 Hawking dramatically conceded the bet. Preskill collected *Total Baseball: The Ultimate Baseball Encyclopedia*. Hawking later joked: 'I gave John an encyclopedia of baseball, but maybe I should just have given him the ashes.'

Hawking now believes that the information that plunges into a black hole is actually encoded on the surface of the event horizon enclosing the black hole and is then imparted back to the particles that are emitted. Weirdly, this surface is two-dimensional yet seems to encode information about the three-dimensional space inside. It has led to the idea of the holographic universe: the whole of our three-dimensional universe is actually just the projection of information contained on a two-dimensional surface. Although Hawking conceded the bet, Thorne has stood his ground. He still believes that the information is lost.

Roger Penrose, like Thorne, believes that Hawking conceded the bet too quickly. Once a black hole has radiated away, Penrose believes that information and entropy are lost. For Penrose, this is relevant to the question of why the universe started in such a low-entropy state. Why was there order to begin with, which meant that the second law of thermodynamics could get started in the first place? Where did the order come from? If black holes actually destroy entropy, they could provide a mechanism for resetting the universe to a low-entropy state.

Penrose had always been a believer in the Big Bang as a boundary beyond which you couldn't do physics. As we head back towards the singularity of the Big Bang, the equations of physics break down. If we accept the description of the Big Bang as an infinitely dense point, on many levels it doesn't make sense to explore the question of what happened before the Big Bang: the laws of physics could do anything on the other side of this singularity. We can't measure anything that lies beyond this singularity either, so we may as well treat it as if it doesn't exist. Or should we? Penrose has changed his mind.

JOINING UP THE PAST AND
THE FUTURE

There are stories emerging of what might have happened before the Big Bang, and one of the most remarkable is told by Penrose. He proposes that the Big Bang was just one in an infinite cycle of Big Bangs. This isn't the first time such a possibility has been suggested: when it was thought that the universe would end in a big crunch, it seemed a good idea to turn the crunch into the Big Bang of a new era.

But as I discovered in the Fourth Edge, the universe is not contracting but expanding at an accelerating rate, heading for a cold state where no life, galaxies or even matter will exist, just photons of light. This is what Penrose calls the 'very boring era'. Even the black holes that will swallow much of the galaxies we see at the moment are believed to leak radiation, so that they too will be spent, disappearing in a final pop and leaving a universe full of photons and gravitons, the hypothetical massless particle thought to mediate the force of gravity.

Penrose admitted to being somewhat depressed by this vision of our universe's future: 'Good God, is that what we are in for!' But then he was struck by the question of who would be around to witness this 'overpowering eventual tedium'. Certainly not us. The only things around to be bored by events would be the photons and gravitons that alone would make up the universe.

But it turns out that a photon has no concept of time. It lives in a timeless environment. As things approach the speed of light, relativity implies that time slows down, so much so that by the time something hits the speed of light, clocks stop. But hold on. Light travels at the speed of light. So this means that a photon has no concept of time. In fact, in Penrose's scenario, in which all particles with mass will have decayed to massless photons or gravitons, there will be nothing left to mark time, nothing from which to make a clock. Similarly, since time is essential to measuring space, this future universe will have lost all ability to quantify and measure distance – whether it is big or small will be meaningless.

Rather than giving in to pessimism, Penrose saw an opportunity.

Didn't that sound remarkably like the state of the universe just after the Big Bang? A universe full of energy, but with no matter yet formed. Admittedly, this energy was meant to be concentrated into an infinitely small region, creating the conditions for the Big Bang. But if the universe has lost any sense of scale, then couldn't the conditions at the end of our universe be the starting point for a new Big Bang, so that the universe that emerges has rescaled to concentrate the energy into a new beginning?

These two scenarios – the universe ending in a boring heat death and the universe starting in an exciting Big Bang – can actually be seamlessly fused together, like two landscapes whose boundaries match up to create one continuous landscape. The sewing together of these scenarios requires that the end of one universe contracts and the beginning of the next expands, so that the two ends fit together, smoothly passing from one to the other. Cold far-away photons become hot close-together photons initiating a new Big Bang.

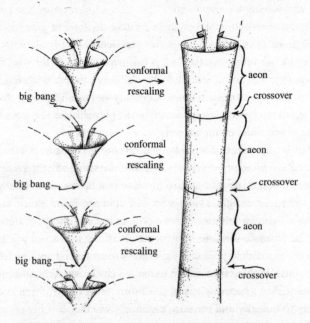

By rescaling the universe at the end of one aeon with the beginning of another,
we can pass seamlessly from one to another.

Penrose's theory is controversial, and I couldn't find many scientists who thought it was more than a clever mathematical idea. And yet when Penrose first revealed that the mathematics of general relativity predicted the existence of singularities in space-time, many dismissed the idea as physically impossible. His current theory of the cycles of time may prove to be wrong, but for me there is something exciting about a scientist changing his mind about the possibility of exploring time before the Big Bang.

Penrose calls the period between one Big Bang and the next an aeon, and our aeon is just one of possibly infinitely many aeons that preceded and will follow our own.

One big challenge to this model, and to many cyclical models, is the second law of thermodynamics. How is entropy reset to such a low state that we can run the second law of thermodynamics in each new aeon?

The Big Bang singularity is a state of very low entropy. As the universe evolves, entropy increases – how can we move seamlessly into the next aeon and reset the entropy? This is why Penrose was unhappy that Hawking conceded the bet about black holes. In Penrose's view, black holes are the mechanism for resetting entropy. All the entropy entering a black hole is lost or subtracted from the whole system, so that by the end of the aeon we are at low entropy again, because all the information has been lost in the plethora of black holes that populate the universe. This sets up the conditions for the next Big Bang.

Even if the theory is correct, how can we ever dig back into the period that preceded our own Big Bang to test this or other theories? Is 'before the Big Bang' a no-go area? Penrose thinks not. Given that the two landscapes must match up, things that happened in the previous aeon should impact on our own. He believes that the bumping together of black holes towards the closing stages of the last aeon will have caused gravitational ripples that passed into our aeon. He compares it to a pond into which many pebbles have been thrown. Once the black holes or pebbles have disappeared, we will have a pattern of ripples that results from these interacting expanding circles.

Penrose believes that this is something that we could look for in the cosmic microwave background radiation, the radiation left over after the Big Bang that started our universe. Although the fluctuations across this radiation look random, perhaps some of them are the result of black holes bouncing off each other towards the end of the last aeon.

The trouble is that the cosmic microwave background radiation is notoriously difficult to analyse, partly because there isn't enough of it. You may consider this crazy, given that it makes up the surface of the sphere enclosing the observable universe. And yet if you are surveying sections of this sphere that surrounds the universe and you need to take sections which span 10 degrees of arc, you are very quickly going to run out of bits you haven't looked at. Although many are sceptical about seeing evidence of previous aeons in our current aeon, it does raise the exciting prospect that perhaps the question of what happened before the Big Bang is not as unanswerable as we once thought!

A MODERN-DAY GALILEO

I popped into Penrose's office, which is one floor down from my own in Oxford, to get his take on whether we will ever know what happened before the Big Bang. In his eighties, Penrose is a great example of how the desire to know never fades. Because he wrote a book with the subtitle *A Complete Guide to the Laws of the Universe*, you may assume that he thinks he knows it all. But Penrose is still asking new questions.

'I used to say that the Big Bang was a singularity so the notion of time doesn't mean anything before the Big Bang. 'Before' is a meaningless question. Don't ask that question. I've heard Stephen Hawking saying not to do so, and I would have agreed. But the view I take now is that you really are allowed to ask that question.'

Did this mean that Penrose thought there was no beginning to it all?

'My belief is that it's an infinite sequence of aeons.'

I challenged him on whether this was an example of something we cannot know. After all, infinity is usually a no-go area for physics.

'We might be able to increase technology and see a few aeons back.

But going back to the beginning of them all? Well, there's a candidate for something we may never know. People say that the infinite is unknowable, but in mathematics people use it all the time. We feel completely at home. Well, if not completely, then largely.'

When I asked Penrose whether he thought there was any question that by its very nature was unanswerable, he was typically cautious.

'I slightly worry about the concept that there might be anything that will always remain beyond our knowledge. There may be questions that you might not expect an answer to, I suppose. Problems that you think are unsolvable, but then you think of a way around them and get some handle on them. I don't like the term "unknowable". It just means we're not looking at the thing in the right way.

'You might not think you could ever know what's happening in the middle of the Sun, but now people do know what is going on there. Not so long ago, people would have thought of that as an impossible question, I suppose.

'Can you multiply together two incredibly large numbers when the result has more digits than there are particles in the universe and therefore cannot be written down? Does that count as an unsolvable problem? It just seems a tiresome unsolvable problem.

'I think I have a bias – although I wouldn't like to say it's a position I'm taking – a bias in favour of not having absolutely unknowable things.' Penrose looked a little concerned. 'I hope I haven't disappointed you by saying there are no unknowables.'

I suggested that this could be an important mindset for doing science.

'A problem may be pretty difficult, but somehow you feel there's got to be a solution. I do have that feeling, but I don't know if it is justified. I don't expect to see answers to the big questions in my lifetime, though it would be nice to see a few of the more immediate ones resolved.'

I wanted to know which problem he would like to see resolved if he could choose one. Since time is on Penrose's mind, he chose evidence of a time before the Big Bang.

'I'd like to see signals from the previous aeon. But we're a long way from that.'

So is doing away with the need for a beginning a threat to those who believe in a God who created everything? Penrose laughs as he recalls how he was worried that his proposal might ruffle ecclesiastical feathers, just as his hero Galileo had.

'I did this event at the Vatican and I was a little bit nervous. But then I realized they were honouring Galileo and the invention of the astronomical telescope. So I described my theory of cycles of time and I thought they might be a bit uncomfortable about the Big Bang not being the beginning. Their response: "No, that's fine . . . God created the whole thing."'

OUTSIDE OF TIME

The Vatican response points to a question that has always intrigued religious thinkers: what is God's relation to time, especially given our modern revelations about its fluid nature? Einstein's special theory of relativity asks whether you can talk about one event happening before another. From one perspective, event A happens before event B, but Einstein showed that from another perspective event B can occur first.

For religious commentators this poses an interesting challenge: what is God's perspective? For God, did A happen before B, or vice versa? One answer is to respond as the Vatican representative had to Penrose: take God outside of time. Just as God is not located at one point in space, there is no need to locate God at one point in time.

An outsider would look at space-time just as someone on top of a mountain might look down on the lie of the land. But this view of space-time would include the past, present and future, all of time, in one take. Although not phrased in terms of four-dimensional Lorentzian geometry, this is actually the position taken by the fourth-century theologian Saint Augustine of Hippo.

Einstein tried to use this perspective on time to comfort the widow of his friend Michele Besso, writing to her: 'Now he has departed from this strange world a little ahead of me. That means nothing. People like us, who believe in physics, know that the distinction between past, present and future is only a stubbornly persistent illusion.' We should regard our existence at this point in time like being in London rather than Paris.

But some theologians have a problem with a God outside of time, because it doesn't leave room for that God to act in the world. If you opt for theism rather than simple deism, then God needs to have a temporal quality to intervene in the world. If God is outside, looking at the whole of space-time, the future is already there in the landscape. Interestingly, although people may argue over the order of events, they won't argue about their order if they are causally related. This demands a God who steps in and out of time, moulding the geometry of space-time. But a God who acts in the world is a God who acts in time. So it is very difficult to square a timeless God with a God who acts in the universe.

The question remains: what is this thing called God that is meant to be outside of time? Can anything be outside of time? Actually, there is something that I would regard as timeless: mathematics. And as a timeless thing it is well suited to the job of sparking the creation of what we observe around us. It is the creator responsible for the equations of quantum physics that give us space-time and something from nothing. Mathematics has an attractive quality: you don't need to ask who created the mathematics. It is something that exists outside of time and doesn't need a moment when it was created. It just is. Perhaps we should reverse the old adage 'God is a mathematician'. Perhaps mathematics is the god everyone is chasing. If I replace the word 'God' with the word 'mathematics' in Aquinas's attempt at a definition, I think it works quite well: 'Mathematics is to be thought of as existing outside the domain of existents, as a cause from which comes everything that exists in different forms.'

This is close to theoretical physicist Max Tegmark's idea of the mathematical universe hypothesis, or MUH. He proposes that our physical universe is an abstract mathematical structure. It's a modern take on the Pythagorean philosophy. In the paper in which he proposes this mathematical universe, he concludes with the following:

'If the MUH is true, then it constitutes great news for science, allowing the possibility that an elegant unification of physics, mathematics and computer science will one day allow us humans to understand our reality even more deeply than many dreamed would be possible.'

I probably wouldn't go as far as Tegmark in identifying our physical universe with mathematics. It seems hard mathematically to distinguish between two universes in which positive and negative charges are swapped over. The two universes would be physically different, but the mathematical description would be exactly the same. This is an example of something called quidditism: the idea that there is more to the universe than just the relationship between objects – what they are (the *quid* is Latin for 'what') provides another level of distinction.

If mathematics is eternal and outside of time, you don't need a creator to begin things. The equations of mathematics are truly outside the universe, so they could play the role of something supernatural and godlike. It is not, however, a God that acts in the world, because this is a deistic vision. The interesting question is then: how many different ways are there to set up a universe out of a set of mathematical equations? The multiverses now arise from multi-mathematical models.

Some argue that simply having an equation that goes from zero unicorns to three unicorns per second doesn't mean unicorns exist. So having equations that allow for the physics of quarks and their interactions with various fields doesn't make the quarks any more real than the unicorns. It's what Hawking refers to as the necessity of understanding how 'to breathe fire into the equations'. For example, what led to our universe having negative and positive charges set as they are rather than the other way round? Where did the 'quid' in 'quidditism' come from?

If there was no universe, no matter, no space, nothing, I think there would still be mathematics. Mathematics does not require the physical world to exist. Therefore, for me, mathematics is a very strong candidate for the initial cause. It also explains the 'unreasonable effectiveness of mathematics'. This is the expression Eugene Wigner coined for the uncanny knack of abstract mathematics to explain physical phenomena. If physical phenomena are a result of mathematics, it should not be surprising that we keep finding mathematical explanations at the heart of the universe we inhabit.

TIME: AN EXPRESSION OF
INCOMPLETENESS OF KNOWLEDGE

There are those who would have us do away with the need to talk of time at all. My watch has been ticking away. It says it is a little past ten o'clock in the evening. But what does that mean? Put another watch telling the same time in a spaceship, and when it returns it won't match my watch.

Einstein's discoveries reveal that the best I can do is to compare the running of clocks. No one clock measures absolute time. Such a thing does not make sense. If you think about it, this was always the case. How did Galileo discover that swinging pendulums are a good way of measuring time? He was sitting in Mass watching the chandelier in the church swinging in the wind. When he compared it with his pulse, he realized that the time it took to swing from one side to the other did not depend on the angle of swing. But here Galileo was comparing one measure of time with another that he assumed was constant. The truth is that all these time-keeping devices are relative to other things.

If we go back to the equations of physics, then, although time appears to play a major role, it is possible to rewrite everything without reference to time at all. It seems that because we have such a strong sense of the passage of time, it was the most obvious window through which to observe the world. Books on mechanics are all about the evolution of the universe with respect to time. The equation for the trajectory of a ball takes time as input and outputs where you will find the ball. But none of these books defines time, and no physicist has satisfactorily pinned down what we mean by time, so perhaps the best strategy is to eliminate it altogether.

This was the aim of physicist Julian Barbour. Working without an academic position, supporting his family by translating Russian, Barbour has developed a theory of physics that removes the need for time at all. His ideas are articulated in his ground-breaking book *The End of Time*, published in 1999. 'Nothing happens; there is being but no becoming. The flow of time and motion are illusions.' A number of physicists within mainstream academia have taken his ideas very seriously.

But why then do I feel that there is something called time flowing along, with me at its mercy? I have the feeling that I can never go back in time, that the future is waiting out there still to happen. I remember the past but not the future. Italian physicist Carlo Rovelli and French mathematician Alain Connes believe that this sensation is a result of incompleteness of knowledge. Called the thermal time hypothesis, it proposes that time is an emergent phenomenon, not a fundamental concept.

If I take any physical system, like the molecules of gas in my room, then generally I don't have complete knowledge of the microscopic state of these particles, but only some overall macroscopic description that could allow for many possible microscopic states. I am reduced to considering the situation statistically because of my incomplete knowledge. Rovelli and Connes are able to demonstrate mathematically how this incomplete knowledge can give rise to a flow that has all the properties we associate with our sensation of time. They believe that time emerges only from this macroscopic consideration of an unknown microscopic system. If you dig deep enough, time will disappear, rather like the way the idea of surface of a liquid doesn't make sense when you are at the atomic level. Or consider the fact that you can't talk about an atom having a temperature or a molecule of water being wet. Time is not fundamental but a similar emergent property.

That's not to say these things aren't real. Hotness, wetness, time ticking by. I look at my watch. Staring me in the face is 23:55. Another day drawing to a close. Midnight is about to strike, heralding the end of the party, and the feeling that I am one day closer to the moment when I won't be able to know anymore. But why do I feel anything: the passage of time, the pain of a stubbed toe, the pleasurable taste of a fine wine, the excitement of listening to Prokofiev? These things are at the heart of one of the biggest unsolved and possibly unanswerable questions on the scientific books, as I will discover in the next Edge.

SIXTH EDGE: THE CHATBOT APP

11

My brain? It's my second favourite organ.

Woody Allen, *Sleeper*

I've downloaded a smartphone app called Cleverbot, which I'm trying out. It is attempting to convince me that it is human. So I've decided to ask it a few questions to test it out. I've texted a friend of my son's too, to get a comparison, so here are the responses. Can you tell which is the human and which the chatbot?

Question 1: Do you have a girlfriend?
    Response A: Do you want me to have a girlfriend?
    Response B: Mind your own business.

Question 2: What is your dream?
    Response A: My dream is to become a famous poet.
    Response B: To make lots of money.

Question 3: Are you conscious?
    Response A: If I wasn't I don't think I . . .
    Response B: It's the only thing I'm sure of.

It turns out that the more I play with Cleverbot the more I am training the app to respond like a human. Every conversation I have with the app is banked and tapped into for future conversations, so that my responses will become part of the next conversation that Cleverbot might have.

Although the responses to my questions so far are inconclusive, it's not long before a conversation with Cleverbot reveals it to be rather less than human. But the question of whether my smartphone will ever be clever enough to be conscious of its own existence, or whether I can really tell if my son's friend is truly conscious or is also just a good simulation, is far trickier and goes to the heart of one the toughest unknowables on the books.

Both responses to my question about consciousness tap into Descartes' famous declaration: 'I think, therefore I am.' This was his response to the sceptics who doubted whether we could be sure that we truly knew anything about the universe. Originating in Plato's Academy in Athens, the sceptics believed nothing could be known for certain. You think you are currently holding a book or perhaps some electronic device in your hand. But are you sure? I've picked up the dice on my table. At least I think I have, but perhaps the whole thing is a dream and there is no book and no dice. Perhaps the whole experience is some computer-simulated environment fed into our brains like some scene from *The Matrix*. Descartes in his *Meditations* retorts that in all these scenarios the one thing I can be sure about is my own existence, my own consciousness. However, this 'I' could turn out to be one of the ultimate unknowables.

ARE YOU THINKING WHAT I'M THINKING?

There is something scientists call the 'hard problem of consciousness'. It concerns our internal world: what makes me me? What is it exactly that creates our feeling of consciousness? What are the ingredients and mechanism that create consciousness, and how does it emerge? How can I know that my conscious experience has the same quality as yours? Can I ever get inside your head and experience what you are feeling? I feel pain in my head the morning after I've drunk too much, but is that feeling anything like the hangover you experience? I see red when I look at my casino dice. You give the colour the same name, and we both experience the same wavelength of light. But are you really seeing it how I see it? Is it a question that it even makes sense to ask? When I play my cello, the vibrations of the strings are the same as they reach our ears, but can I ever know that our brains are feeling the same thrill of a Bach suite?

We are in a golden age for the question of consciousness. In the Fourth Edge I described how the invention of the telescope allowed Galileo and his contemporaries to probe the edges of the universe. In the Second Edge we saw how the invention of the microscope gave us a tool with which to dig deep into the structure of matter. At the beginning of the twenty-first century we are blessed with new telescopes, telescopes of the mind: fMRI and the EEG scanners allow scientists to peer into our brains and measure the activity associated with our different experiences of red, pain and cellos.

But even if I can observe exactly the same activity going on inside your head, it doesn't tell me that my conscious experience is the same as yours. Why not? We are built in a very similar way, so why wouldn't it be safe to assume that your internal world is similar? We use the same principle of homogeneity that is key to doing cosmology. What's happening here is very likely to be the same as what's happening over there. And yet I have only my own conscious experience to go on – one data point. What if my consciousness is uniquely different, yet in all tests my brain appears to behave in exactly the same way as your brain? How could I ever know I was experiencing things differently? Perhaps you are not conscious at all. How could I ever know? Language has evolved in such a way that I say 'red' to describe all the things that my society declares red, yet perhaps I am experiencing something wildly different to your conscious experience of red.

We already know that there are people who have a different quality of conscious experience when they hear a cello or see the number 2. Synesthetes find that other senses are triggered by these experiences. My wife experiences the sensation of very dark red when she sees the number 9 or the letter S. For my favourite composer, Olivier Messiaen, colours were triggered by certain chords. The physicist Richard Feynman had the same technicolour experience with mathematical equations. These are things that our new telescopes of the mind could explain or at least detect. They could possibly pick up genuinely different brain behaviour. But even if all the evidence shows that the person in front of you has a brain that is displaying the same activity as your brain, will you ever be able to know that they are truly conscious or just a zombie doing a very good impression of a conscious person. This is the hard question of consciousness, and some believe that it is one whose answer we cannot know.

WHERE IS CONSCIOUSNESS?

Many of the other questions that I've been exploring have a rich history and reveal how much we have managed to know thanks to our investigations over the centuries. But the problem of consciousness and getting inside a living brain is so difficult that, until the dawn of the new technology of the last few decades, it has remained the preserve of theologians and philosophers rather than scientists. That's not to say that we haven't been trying to solve the problem.

The question of where my 'I' is located has vexed scientists for centuries. I have a strong feeling that my 'I' is situated somewhere just behind my eyes. It feels like there is a tiny version of myself sitting there observing the world through my eyes as if it were a cinema screen, making executive decisions about how the body that encases my consciousness will act. There is certainly a feeling that my consciousness is not dependent on my whole body for its existence. If I chopped off my hand, I wouldn't feel as though my consciousness had been split in two. My hand is not me. But how many bits can I chop off before I discover what it is that makes me me?

Not everyone has been convinced that the brain is the seat of our consciousness. Aristotle, for example, thought the brain was simply a cooling agent for the heart, which he believed was the true location of the senses. But others realized that the brain probably was key to who we are. The first-century anatomist Rufus of Ephesus gave us one of the first physical descriptions of the brain. Once the brain is removed from the skull, you first notice that there are three distinct pieces: two halves, which seem to be mirror images of each other, called the cerebrum, and then, sitting underneath, what looks like a tiny version of the brain called the cerebellum.

Cut into the brain and you find holes filled with liquid: the ventricles. In the Middle Ages scientists thought these cells controlled different

On the left is a top-down view of the brain revealing the two hemispheres. On the right is a view from the left-hand side of the brain showing the cerebellum at the base of the brain.

mental activities: imagination in the front ventricle, memory in the rear, and reason located in between. Leonardo da Vinci believed that common sense, the thing which fused the five senses into a common experience close to our idea of consciousness, was located in the front ventricle.

In contrast, Descartes thought that if we each have a single consciousness, we should be looking for something in the brain that does not have a mirror image but is a single entity. He proposed the pineal gland as the seat of the soul.

Even with a microscope it is hard to see what it is about this lump of grey matter that could give rise to the complex individual currently reading this book. I'd never seen a brain in the flesh before, and I wondered if meeting one face to face, or brain to brain, might give me new insights. So I visited somewhere with one of the highest concentration of brains in the country. Not Oxford University, but the Parkinson's UK Brain Bank, where I was allowed to hold my first brain, the brain of a man who had recently died and had donated his organ to the tissue bank.

The container in which the brain now sat was labelled C33. But the contents of the vat once had a name like yours or mine. The brain was once home to the hopes and fears, memories and dreams, loves and secrets of the 89-year-old man who chose to donate his brain to medical science after his death. But where is he now? What was going on inside this brain before the man died that gave rise to his conscious experience, and what is it that has stopped now?

Just from holding the brain, it was no easier to see how it could give rise to our conscious experience. It looked like a huge lump of foie gras. The belief that the ventricles, the liquid-filled holes, were the key to our conscious world turned out to be a red herring; the idea that different regions of the brain were responsible for different functions would, however, turn out to be correct.

It was by analysing brains that weren't functioning properly because of damage or lesions that scientists in the nineteenth century began to understand that different parts of the brain are responsible for different functions. For example, the front part of the brain is responsible for problem solving and decision making, and social and sexual behaviour. The middle portion deals with sensing and perceiving and integrating the data collected by the senses. The back of the brain is like the cinema screen responsible for visual perception, which partly explains the feeling that my consciousness sits at the back of my head watching the film that is my life.

What about the two sides of the brain? There has been much speculation on the role of each side, but recent research has shown that the brain is perhaps more plastic and flexible than some have thought. That said, we know that the language centre is housed principally in the left side of the brain. The nineteenth-century French physician Paul Broca analysed the brains of patients who had lost the power of speech and discovered that they all had lesions in the same part of the brain, now called the Broca area. Some years later, in 1874, the German physician Carl Wernicke hypothesized that damage to a different area of the brain was causing patients problems with processing language (rather than articulating words). Located towards the back of the left hemisphere of the brain, it is now known as the Wernicke area.

The left side of the brain is also responsible for the number crunching that I do when I'm calculating the probabilities associated with the throw of my casino dice. This is where numbers are processed. The right side of the brain is responsible for processing the sound of my cello and listening to music, as well as imagining geometric figures like the icosahedral shape of my cut-out universe. To work most effectively, the two halves of the brain are in constant communication through the corpus callosum that divides the two hemispheres. The two hemispheres communicate with each other via nerve fibres that run through this join. It is a curious design feature, causing quite a bottleneck in communication between the two sides of the brain.

While cutting off a hand certainly isn't going to alter my sense of consciousness, what happens if you cut a brain in two? Since consciousness is a result of brain activity, if I cut the corpus callosum so that the two sides of the brain can't communicate, what happens to my consciousness? Does it split in two?

CUTTING CONSCIOUSNESS IN TWO

A surgical procedure called corpus callosotomy, which cuts the corpus callosum, was first carried out in the 1940s on living patients in order to limit epileptic seizures. An epileptic seizure essentially consists of huge simultaneous firing of neurons across the brain. A surge of electrical activity sweeps across the brain, causing the patient to go into seizure. The theory was that cutting the corpus callosum would spare at least one side of the brain from these huge power surges. But what effect did such surgery have on consciousness?

There is good evidence to suggest that indeed the body now houses two distinct consciousnesses. Since each hemisphere of the brain is dedicated to physical behaviour on the opposite side of the body, this split consciousness can be observed in the contrasting behaviour of the two sides of the body. Extraordinary footage exists of one patient who underwent such a corpus callosotomy, which shows the left side of the body physically attacking the right side. The left side of the body, which is controlled by the right hemisphere of the brain, does not have access to the language side of the brain, which is located in the left hemisphere, so was unable to articulate itself verbally. This frustration seems to have manifested itself in the attack. Eventually, the patient took drugs in order to suppress the right hemisphere and allow the articulate left hemisphere to dominate.

Whether this genuinely reveals a consciousness housed in the right-hand side at loggerheads with the left is difficult to determine. These could be physical responses disconnected from any conscious experience, just as tapping your knee with a hammer produces an involuntary physical response.

Another remarkable experiment that supports the idea that there are two identities at work inside a single body involved counting. A screen was erected between a patient who had undergone a corpus callosotomy and a table on which a number of objects would be placed. The patient could put their right or left hand through a hole in the screen and then use their hand to count how many objects were on the screened-off table.

When the right hand was used, the patient would say out loud the correct number of objects the hand had encountered. But something very curious occurred when the left hand was used. The experimenter would ask the patient to say out loud how many objects the left hand had encountered, and the answer would be completely random and wrong. The language side of the brain (the left) that was saying the number had no access to the left hand (controlled by the right side of the brain) and was just guessing.

However, when the experimenter asked the patient to put up the number of fingers corresponding to the number of items encountered, they had no problem indicating the correct number. One side of the brain was articulate but had to guess; the other half could only use sign language but had access to the correct answer. This seems less explicable in terms of simple automatic physical response to external stimuli.

Again, the right-hand side might still be able to function intelligently, but perhaps we have here a case of a zombie, without any internal conscious world, that is still able to function like a conscious being. How can we know either way? And in any case, why should we restrict consciousness to the language-generating left hemisphere?

Split brains seem unable to unify information in the way that connected brains can. Show the left eye the word 'key' and the right eye the word 'ring' and the person will say out loud the word 'ring' and can point with their left hand to a picture of a key, but isn't able to unify the two in the concept of a 'keyring'. But is this an example of two consciousnesses, or simply evidence for the failure of a cut brain to formulate a cognitive connection?

Many patients who have undergone corpus callosotomy are able to function quite successfully. They can drive, work and function normally in a social setting. So are the two sides actually able to integrate, or is this an example of the two consciousnesses acting successfully in tandem, essentially just two identical copies with one replicating the behaviour of the other?

Consciousness takes the multiple inputs that our brain receives from our senses and integrates them into a single experience. In the case of the patients who have undergone corpus callosotomy, the brain is unable to do this. But perhaps there are some brains that, even without corpus callosotomy, have difficulty integrating brain activity into a unified experience. Perhaps disorders like schizophrenia or multiple personality disorder are caused by a brain that can't integrate everything into a single voice. The result is that it sounds like there is more than one conscious being inside the brain.

Although these damaged brains helped neuroscientists to understand how certain regions in the brain are associated with certain brain functions, the real breakthrough in understanding brain architecture came at the end of the nineteenth century, with the work of Spanish scientist Santiago Ramón y Cajal.

SWITCHING ME ON AND OFF

Born in 1852, as a young boy Ramón y Cajal wanted to be an artist, but his father had not considered this a suitable profession. He thought the medical profession was a much worthier cause. He came up with an intriguing strategy to spark his son's medical interests: he took him to graveyards in search of human remains. Using what they found, Ramón y Cajal would indulge his artistic disposition by drawing diagrams of the bones they had unearthed, but his father's plan succeeded, and the son became more and more fascinated by the human anatomy he was drawing. He received his medical doctorate in 1877.

It was ten years later that Ramón y Cajal discovered a way to combine his love of art and anatomy. While a professor at the University of Barcelona, he learnt about a new technique using silver nitrate that could reveal the structure of nerve cells. By applying the technique to cells in the brain, he provided some of our first views of the truly extraordinary and complex nature of this piece of our anatomy. Using silver nitrate, he could randomly stain individual cells in the brain to reveal their structure. The results were startling and beautiful.

This is one of the first pictures of a neuron. It is a human retinal cell. It was the first indication that the brain was not a continuous structure but was made up of discrete interconnected cells called neurons.

As Ramón y Cajal stained more and more cells across the brain, he discovered neurons of different shapes and sizes. Using his artistic skill, he filled his sketchbooks with the complex array of structures, documenting them like a butterfly collector. We now know that there are in the region of 86 billion neurons in the human brain – it would take over 2700 years to count them at one per second. Although the body's neurons come in many different shapes and sizes, as Ramón y Cajal's sketches revealed, they have a very similar underlying structure, consisting of a central cell called the soma, with branches stretching away from the soma called axons and dendrites.

How does a neuron actually work? A neuron gets turned on or fires a little bit like a switch. For example, if my ears pick up a change of air pressure when I play my cello, this initiates a molecular change in the neuron, causing an electrical current to pass through the cell. This neuron can then talk to another neuron via connections called synapses. Each neuron has one axon coming out of the cell, which is like an electrical wire along which information travels to other neurons. This axon is then connected to the dendrites of other neurons via the synapses. The electrical activity in one neuron can cause a chemical reaction across one of the synapses connected to another neuron, causing it to fire. The brain works very much like a computer or my smartphone with its chatbot app: the neurons are either firing or not.

It is true that there are things that distinguish the brain from a computer. There are analogue factors at work in determining the firing of a neuron. The chemical flow across the synapse must pass a critical rate to trigger the firing of the associated neuron. The rate of firing of the neurons is as important as the actual firing itself for the transmission of information. That said, these discrete neuronal cells connected by wires that cause cells to be active or not are extremely suggestive when considering the possibility of creating artificial consciousness in something like my smartphone. But this is an extremely complicated network that evolution has wired for us. Each axon can be connected to 1000 different dendrites. This may seem a lot, but given that the brain has 86 billion neurons, each individual neuron is actually communicating with only a small fraction of the brain.

It is this electrical and chemical activity that gives rise to brain activity, and the loss of it which can give rise to problems and pathologies. The 89-year-old man whose brain I held at the Parkinson's UK

Brain Bank suffered from Alzheimer's disease, which is a direct result of the loss of these neurons and synapses.

We can cut open brains, stain their cells with silver nitrate, build a static map of the network, but how do we get a picture of the dynamic activity of a living brain? The thing that has revolutionized the study of the brain is the ability to look inside the brain while it performs certain tasks. The study of the brain has progressed remarkably thanks to advances in technology.

NEURAL TELESCOPES

The easiest and quickest way to get some idea of brain activity is to use something called EEG. When I first had my brain scanned by EEG I was a bit nervous. It looked rather like an alien brain-extraction device. In quite a lengthy procedure, which seemed to involve sandpapering my scalp to get a good connection, 64 electrodes were attached to the surface of my head, which, while not used to extract my brain, did allow access to something of my thought processes.

Developed by German physiologist Hans Berger in the 1920s, electroencephalography (much easier to call it EEG) uses the electrodes to record electrical activity along the scalp. EEG measures the voltage fluctuations resulting from the electrical current flowing within and between the neurons of the brain. Using EEG, scientists picked up different kinds of waves corresponding to different brain activity. Synchronized activity of a large number of neurons gives rise to macroscopic oscillations of different frequencies which correspond to different brain states.

The first-discovered and best-known frequency band is the one known as alpha waves, which is a synchronized activity of a large number of neurons that give rise to macroscopic oscillations of 8–12 hertz. This is a much lower frequency than the notes produced by my cello, the lowest of which vibrates at 65 hertz. Nevertheless, it is rather like a musical note singing through the brain. Alpha waves can be detected at the back of the brain during relaxed wakefulness, increasing when our eyes are closed. They're not the only notes the brain plays, and there are other frequency waves that you find during different periods of brain activity.

- The slowest are delta waves at 1–4 hertz, which are associated with deep, unconscious, dreamless sleep.
- Theta waves are next at 4–8 hertz, associated with light sleep or meditation.
- Faster than alpha waves are the beta waves at 13–30 hertz, which the brain hits when it is wide awake.
- Believed to be most important for the brain's ability to create consciousness are the fast gamma waves at 30–70 hertz, frequencies that just creep into the bottom range that my cello can play. Gamma waves are associated with the formation of ideas, language and memory processing, and with various types of learning.

The buzzing brain: from gamma waves to delta waves.

As we make our way through day and night, the brain seems to behave like an orchestra performing a symphony, moving between fast movements and slow movements, with the occasional scherzo when we generate new ideas or encounter new situations.

EEG signals change dramatically during sleep and show a transition from faster frequencies to increasingly slower frequencies such as alpha waves. In fact, different sleep stages are characterized by the difference in frequency of the waves across the brain, which is why these neural oscillations could be linked to cognitive states such as awareness and consciousness. For example, it is when the EEG detects no waveform at all that doctors call a patient brain dead. It seems that the waves inside the brain are the brain synchronizing activity to work in the most efficient manner.

Although the EEG gives scientists fast access to brain activity, the fMRI scanner, developed in the 1990s, is probably the most well known of these new tools for seeing what is happening inside the brain. Compared to the compact EEG, the fMRI scanner is a beast. Looking like some space-age sleeping pod, once it gets going there is no way you'd be able to sleep. The sound of the magnets at work is so loud that I've needed earplugs when I've been inside a scanner. Although not a painful experience, having my brain scanned by fMRI required keeping still for an unnaturally long time inside the device in order to get a clear picture of what's going on inside my head.

The scanner works by detecting changes in blood oxygenation and flow that occur in response to neural activity. When a brain area is more active it uses more oxygen. The increased blood flow to the active area can be picked up because oxygenated blood is more magnetic. The fMRI scanner can detect this magnetic fluctuation, which can then be used to produce activation maps that show which parts of the brain are involved in a particular mental process.

Since the EEG measures actual brain activity through the change in electrical behaviour, in contrast to the fMRI, which detects a secondary feature, the EEG provides a much better measure of what's going on in the brain. The ability of the EEG to record the brain's activity changing over time cannot be matched by fMRI scanners at present. The fMRI scanner comes into its own in giving a much higher-definition snapshot of the brain. The combination therefore provides a good picture of the brain in action. For example, both EEG and the fMRI scanner could identify a very specific region that is active when I think about mathematics. So can we use these neural telescopes to see consciousness? As yet, such a view eludes us. The question is whether there is really anything to see.

IS MY CAT CONSCIOUS?

Even if we understand which bit of the brain is firing when we do different activities, and how the physics and chemistry of the brain work, it still doesn't give us much understanding of why we have a sense of 'I'. How can we even approach this kind of question? A very powerful strategy for a mathematician trying to understand what something is, is to try and understand why something else isn't.

For example, despite my chatbot app's best attempts to convince me otherwise, I do not believe my smartphone is conscious, neither is the chair I am sitting on. But what about animals? Before he left home, my black-and-white cat Freddie would sit in my office living a life of leisure as I sat scribbling away at my maths. But did he have a sense of self? What about babies? As my children grew up, their brains evolved, and with it their consciousness and sense of self-awareness changed. So can we identify different levels of consciousness? Are there thresholds in brain development at which different states of consciousness emerge?

Of course, asking an animal like my cat about its internal world is a problem. In the late 1960s animal behaviourist Gordon Gallup was shaving in the mirror, pondering the question of how to test self-awareness in animals, when he was suddenly struck by an idea. He was aware that the face he was looking at in the mirror was his. He wondered which animals know that what they see in the mirror is not another animal but actually an image of themselves.

Perusing the near infinite number of cat videos on the Internet reveals that cats tend to think the image in the mirror is a rival cat in the room. But how can we tell whether an animal realizes that actually the image is of them? Gallup came up with a very robust test to reveal which species recognize themselves in the mirror, which in turn indicates that they have a sense of self.

His test is simple. Introduce the animal to the mirror so that it familiarizes itself with its reflection. (There is fascinating footage of chimpanzees excitedly dancing along with their images in front of the mirror. But do they think they are dancing with another chimp, or are they admiring their own moves?) At some point, the experimenter takes the animal aside and, while wiping its face, surreptitiously places a red mark just below the eye of the animal in such a way that the animal is unaware of the mark and can't see it without looking in the mirror. Gallup wanted to know how the animal would now react to seeing its image in the mirror.

If you looked in the mirror and noticed something strange on your cheek, your immediate reaction would be to touch the mark to investigate it. Gallup's mirror self-recognition test, as it is known, reveals the startling fact that humans are part of a very small group of animals that systematically pass this test of consciousness or self-awareness. The only other species that Gallup found reacted in a similar fashion are orang-utans and chimpanzees. A third species was added to the list when research by Diana Reiss and Lori Marino on bottlenose dolphins was published in 2001.

Although dolphins have no hands with which to touch a mark, they spent much more time in front of the mirrors in their tanks when they had been marked. They were uninterested in marks on other dolphins in their tank, indicting some awareness that the dolphin in the mirror was not just another dolphin. In addition to orang-utans, chimpanzees and dolphins, there is evidence of other individual animals passing the test. A clever magpie. An elephant. But certainly not a whole species that passes the test on a consistent basis.

It is striking that chimpanzees start to fail the test once they reach 30 years old, despite having some 10 or 15 years left to live. The reason could be that self-awareness comes at a cost. Consciousness allows the brain to take part in mental time travel. You can think of yourself in the past and even project yourself into the future. And that is why Gallup believes that in later life chimpanzees prefer to lose their ability to be conscious of themselves. The price you pay for being aware of your own existence is having to confront the inevitability of your demise. Death-awareness is the price we pay for self-awareness. It raises the interesting question of whether dementia in humans plays a similar role, protecting an ageing human from the painful recognition of their impending death.

Of course, the mirror self-recognition test is a very crude measure of consciousness. It has a bias towards species with highly developed sight. Dogs, for example, do not have good vision but rely on scent to identify other dogs, so you wouldn't expect a dog to pass such a test of self-awareness even if it had an equally well-developed sense of self. Even for those species for whom sight is the primary sense with which they negotiate the world, it is a very rough test of awareness of self. Nonetheless, it has striking consequences when applied to humans, because we can use it to discover when the brain goes through some transition that means we start to recognize the image in the mirror.

I don't think my children, when they were babies, had the same sense of self as they do now. But at what point would they have started to react like the chimpanzees to a mark surreptitiously placed on their faces? It turns out that a child of 16 months will continue playing in front of the mirror quite oblivious to the new mark, though they might put their hand up to the mirror to investigate the slightly unusual image.

But place a child of 24 months in front of the mirror and you see their hands reach for their faces at once to explore the strange spot. The strong reaction is an indication that the 24-month-old recognizes the image and thinks 'That's me.' Something happens during the brain's development that means we become self-aware, but quite what it is still remains a mystery.

If consciousness emerges in humans at 18–24 months, we can ask the same question on a more cosmic scale. When did consciousness first emerge in the universe? Surely nothing was evolved enough to qualify as conscious just after the Big Bang. So there must be a moment when the first conscious experience occurred. So consciousness probably does have a different quality to gravity or time, although the extent to which the latter emerged or are fundamental is also coming under scrutiny.

American psychologist Julian Jaynes, who died in 1997, hypothesized that the emergence of consciousness in humans may help to explain the creation of the concept of God. With the evolution of consciousness came the creeping awareness of a voice in our heads.

Perhaps, Jaynes suggested, God was formulated as a way to try to make sense of this emerging internal world.

As you read this now, you can probably sense the words being sounded out in your head. This is part of our conscious world. But those words aren't being sounded out aloud or heard by anyone else. They are part of your conscious world, and yours alone. Jaynes believed that as we evolved and consciousness emerged, the shock of the voice in our heads might well have given rise to the idea of a transcendent intelligence, something that isn't of this world, and this led the brain to interpret it as the voice of God.

This idea of our internal world being close to the transcendent concept of God is central to many Eastern religious practices, including the Vedic tradition. Brahman, the transcendent supreme being of the Hindu religion, is often identified with Atman or the concept of the self.

Rather amusingly, Jaynes believed that you can actually date the emergence of consciousness in human evolution. He places it somewhere in the eighth century BC between the creation of Homer's *Iliad* and the *Odyssey*. In the *Iliad* there is no evidence in the characters of internal worlds, of introspection or consciousness. The characters in the Trojan siege are simply pushed around by the gods. In the *Odyssey*, in contrast, we see that Odysseus is clearly introspective, aware of his own self, conscious in a way the characters in the *Iliad* appear not to be.

TRICKS OF THE MIND

One of the pleasures of reading a book like the *Odyssey* or the *Iliad* is immersion in another world. A good book can make you totally unconscious of your surroundings. The brain has become very good at filtering what reaches your consciousness. You don't want to be aware of the whole gamut of sensory input that you receive – it would be too overwhelming. But it is striking that your brain can switch between one conscious perception and another without any change in the external input.

My favourite example of this change in consciousness is the brain's reaction to a sketch of my casino dice. What do you see?

At first it appears to be a cube with one square to the fore. But then, as you stare at it, suddenly the cube flips and it seems as if another square is to the fore. Called the Necker cube, the image hasn't changed but what you are conscious of has. What has happened in the brain? Is consciousness really just a story that your brain tells about the sensory input it receives through the body's interaction with the world?

Another striking example of how the brain processes visual data in surprising ways was shown to me by neuroscientist Christof Koch. Koch is one of the leading lights in the modern investigation into consciousness. For years, the subject of consciousness was not something a well-respected scientist would say they were studying. It was the preserve of those in the humanities department, not a subject for those in the lab. But when Nobel Prize winner Frances Crick turned his attention from research into DNA to explore the question of how the brain generates consciousness, the subject suddenly became one that it was considered OK for a scientist to take seriously. Forty years his junior, Koch was Crick's partner in his probing of this problem.

I first met Koch at the top of Mount Baldy just outside Pasadena, home to Caltech, where Koch worked at the time. We'd arranged to meet there as it was the halfway point on one of the epic runs Koch likes to do. I'm ashamed to say that I declined his offer to join him on the run and cheated by taking the ski lift to the top. Before we grappled with the thorny subject of consciousness, I couldn't help being distracted by a tattoo that Koch sports on his shoulder. It seemed to be the rainbow bitten-apple logo used by the Apple computer company.

'I had it done in 2000 while I was on an archaeological dig in Israel with my son. The Apple computer is one of the most beautiful and elegant artefacts of the twentieth century. A perfect marriage of form and function.'

I think he believes that it will be as significant to understanding today's culture as the pots he was digging out of the ground with his son are to appreciating Herod's Caesarea in 20 BC. Koch talks a lot about his Apple computer and is constantly wondering whether one day it might be conscious and talk back to him. His other love is his dogs, which he believes have a much higher level of consciousness than we give them credit for. It was his belief in animal conscious-ness that led him to become a vegetarian.

'Because it is likely that mammals can consciously experience the pains and pleasures of life, can be happy or sad, we should not be eating their flesh. It was difficult to immediately follow this growing realization with action – the taste of meat is very deeply ingrained.'

Koch's area of neurological expertise is vision, and it was with a piece of A4 paper that he had in his pocket that he illustrated how vision gives us some interesting insights into how things reach our conscious minds.

Koch gave me the A4 paper and asked me to roll it up into a cylinder to make a telescope. Then he told me to bring the telescope up to my right eye, and, keeping my left eye open, hold my left hand open at a slight distance from my left eye.

'Now look at the mountains over there. What do you see?'

As I looked across at the view I could not stop laughing. I seemed to have a hole in my hand!

Koch explained to me that the brain is trying to process two lots of information that seem to be inconsistent with experience. So what reaches my conscious brain is a fusion of what it thinks I will be interested in. So I was seeing part of my hand from the visual information entering my left eye, but also the small circle at the centre of the telescope from my right eye. Superimposed, it appeared that I had a hole in my hand. Koch believes that how the brain decides what to make my consciousness aware of could help us to understand more about consciousness itself.

So can we use our new neural telescopes to see what happens when our brain becomes conscious of one thing or another? According to Koch's research, it appears that the retinal nerves are not sending different information, so the change in our conscious experience is happening further down the line in the brain. The trouble is that the fMRI and EEG scanners are too crude to pick up changes as subtle as the flip from one view of the Necker cube to the other. But in 2004 Koch, together with his team at Caltech, spotted an opportunity to ask an individual neuron questions about what stimulated it to fire, which led to the discovery of some curious neuronal activity.

THE JENNIFER ANISTON NEURON

Epileptic seizures can be caused by a miswiring or scar tissue that is responsible for triggering the synchronized firing of neurons across the brain, a bit like the chain reaction of an atomic bomb going off in the head. In some cases, the removal of a small section of the brain can prevent such seizures by taking away the trigger that sets off the cascade.

To ascertain where the source of the seizure is, and in order not to remove too much tissue, patients have around 20 electrodes inserted into the soft tissue of the brain through holes made in the skull. It sounds like some medieval torture regime, but it is actually a procedure that is very much part of current medical practice. Each electrode has tiny wires as thin as hair emerging from it which are wired up to a region of about 10 to 50 neurons. If any of these neurons fire, the electrical activity is picked up by the electrode. The surgeon then waits for a seizure in the patient, at which point a recording can be made of the neurons firing across the brain, and a mathematical analysis of the data pinpoints the potential source of the surge.

But a seizure can take some time to occur, so in the meantime these wired-up patients sit on the ward twiddling their thumbs. The Caltech team saw an opportunity. Why not ask the patients questions and see which made the neurons fire? The region of the brain that is the most common source of seizures is also the area where memories are laid down. Since this is where the bulk of the electrodes were attached, they decided to see what electrical activity could be picked up when memories were fired. To trigger these memories, the patients were shown a range of different pictures.

It took some patient probing, but the results were striking. In one instance, neurons would fire only when shown pictures of the actress Jennifer Aniston. It didn't matter if she was dressed differently or her hair was a different colour, the neuron seemed to fire in recognition of the concept of Jennifer Aniston. Even when the patient was shown just the name of the actress written down, the neuron would fire.

In one sense the discovery was not surprising. To encode memories, ideas and concepts, the brain has to find some way to convert the data into neuronal activity. Just as a digital photo of Jennifer Aniston is a way of changing her image into a series of 0s and 1s, our brains take the sensory data that bombards us and decide whether Jennifer Aniston is important enough to be encoded as a concept. If she is, then the synapses that are currently connected to that neuron will strengthen and survive, ensuring that the neuron fires when the brain receives the associated visual information. Each concept will have its own characteristic synaptic chain of neuronal activity. I particularly liked the patient who had a neuron that fired whenever he was shown an image of Pythagoras' theorem – a much more discerning neuron.

The surprise lies perhaps in how selective the neuron was in its firing. It didn't seem to be interested in any other images. As Koch explained to me, they are certainly not claiming that this neuron is the only one involved in encoding the idea of Aniston or Pythagoras. That would be extremely inefficient. The experiment was limited in the number of neurons it could question. It seems very likely that, just like the digital 1s that are switched on to record a digital photograph in my smartphone, the brain has a selection of neurons that fire across the brain to encode the concept of Aniston. But Koch believes that a remarkably small number are involved in the encoding, in the hundreds or perhaps thousands, rather than the millions that would be involved in encoding such images on a computer.

This encoding will be very relevant to understanding something called qualia. A qualia is a quality or property as perceived or experienced by someone, like the colour red. It doesn't matter whether you are looking at my casino dice, an Arsenal football shirt, or the cross on the flag of St George, you will experience a sensation of redness. The challenge is to determine whether your qualia are anything like mine. Or whether animals or computers experience qualia.

I can imagine that the mathematical nature of the encoding of concepts in the brain could well capture different qualia. If we think of the neurons that fire when shown an Arsenal football shirt or a tomato, Koch's results suggests that we can think of this like a codeword of billions of 0s and 1s lighting up in the brain as the concept is recognized. These different codewords can be thought of as points or as marking out shapes, like crystals in high-dimensional geometric spaces. Do the shapes of these geometries encode different qualia? Is there something common to the shapes of the encodings of an Arsenal football shirt and my casino dice that means that we experience the feeling of red?

Could this also be the source of synesthesia? Perhaps in some brains the encoding of the qualia of red has a shape that is very close to the shape that encodes the concept of the number 7, so much so that when the brain recognizes the concept of 7 it fires the sensation of red.

Returning to my paper telescope and the hole in my hand, Koch explained to me that you can modify the experiment a little to test whether being conscious of something corresponds to these concept neurons firing. Suppose we have two paper telescopes, one attached to each eye. At the end of one telescope I place a picture of Jennifer Aniston. Sure enough, the Jennifer Aniston neurons in my brain fire. But now I flash an image of Pythagoras' theorem on the end of the other telescope. Again, the brain has to choose which image will reach your consciousness.

What tends to happen in these experiments is that the image of Jennifer Aniston disappears from our consciousness in deference to the new image that the brain receives. The image of Pythagoras' theorem takes precedence, so that the participant is no longer conscious of the image of Jennifer Aniston, despite the fact that the brain is still receiving all the same Aniston-related input.

So can we observe a change in brain activity corresponding to the change in consciousness? Experiments similar to those conducted on epileptic patients have been run on monkeys, and these indicate that the neurons that fire in recognition of one concept stop firing when a second image is introduced.

I would suggest that this helps us to focus on the fact that there is something in the electrochemical activity of the brain that contributes to what we are conscious of. This seems obvious, but suppose you think that consciousness is the result of an as yet undiscovered force or physical thing – or something else entirely. Then, if the neurons keep firing even when we are no longer conscious of the image of Jennifer Aniston, this would support the idea that something else was controlling why we are suddenly unaware of the image. That something else would have had to switch off the conscious experience.

This ability to switch our conscious experience of something on and off is at the heart of many magicians' and illusionists' acts. I vividly remember an evening with Fellows at the Royal Society during which we were shown a video by Richard Wiseman, a professor of psychology at the University of Hertfordshire. The video showed two teams passing two basketballs between them. 'I want you to count how many passes of the ball the black team makes,' Wiseman instructed us. In a classic illusionist's move, we were sold a red herring to ensure that we all concentrated our attention on the task at hand: 'Men and women tend to count the passes differently.'

The video played and we all counted away. When the video finished, Wiseman asked who had counted 17 passes. Hands went up. 18 passes? Some other hands went up. 'And who in the room saw the man in the monkey suit walk to the centre of the court and bang his chest before walking off?' What! I hadn't seen anything of the sort. I thought he was having us on – until I saw two people with their hands up. They hadn't bothered to concentrate on counting the passes, and, with their attention free to wander, they had clocked the man in the monkey suit. And yet my brain had not offered this up to my conscious experience. It was an important message to the scientists sitting in the room at the Royal Society: focusing on one thing too much can stop you seeing the monkey right in front of your eyes.

This sense of things floating in and out of consciousness is familiar to me as a research mathematician. Many times I get the feeling that the work I do at my desk sows the seeds of ideas that often come to fruition once I've moved away from my desk. Those flashes of insight that people often talk about are, I believe, a result of the brain ticking away subconsciously to solve a problem, and then, when a match is found, this is fired into the conscious mind with a surge of dopamine to make sure that it is noticed.

The mathematical discovery I am most proud of certainly seemed to come to me in this way. I had been working away all day at the Max Planck Institute in Bonn, trying to get to grips with a thorny problem that I was working on with a colleague. Nothing seemed to give. It was in the evening, when I'd switched off from consciously thinking about my problem that, as I tried to phone my wife in London, I suddenly 'saw' a new symmetrical object with strange unexpected properties. I scribbled down on my yellow legal notepad (my canvas of choice) the idea that I'd suddenly become conscious of, and to this day I find it quite extraordinary how this thing appeared in my mind, an object that had never been conceived of before that moment when I was on the telephone in Bonn. It was as if this new mathematical object was thrust up into my conscious brain, having been honed in my subconscious, accompanied by a chemical rush to make sure I didn't miss it. But still quite what happened so that I had that experience is a mystery.

OUT-OF-BODY EXPERIENCES

Koch's paper telescope reveals how easy it is to confuse our vision and change how we experience our environment. But there are even more spectacular tricks you can play on the brain. By messing with several senses at the same time, it is possible to alter quite dramatically our consciousness to the extent that we can shift our sense of 'I' outside our bodies completely.

One of the most striking examples of this is something called the McGurk effect. Search for this on YouTube and you will find a video that illustrates the effect, and once you have seen it you will realize the extraordinary power of the brain to create conscious experiences that aren't really there.

The illusion begins with you looking at and listening to a face that appears to be articulating the sounds 'Fa . . . Fa . . . Fa'. However, if you close your eyes, the sound suddenly turns into the words 'Ba . . . Ba . . . Ba'. This was the sound all along, but because you see a face making the movements associated with the sound 'Fa', your brain is confused by the contradictory input. Because the brain always seeks one integrated conscious experience, it finds a story consistent with your previous experience and this is what is brought to consciousness. Very often vision trumps sound when it comes to integrating the different senses.

In contrast to the man in the monkey suit, even when you know what is going on it is very difficult to make your brain hear 'Ba' as you watch the mouth make the sound of 'Fa'. The brain is a pattern searcher and is trying to impose structure on the cacophony of information it is being bombarded with. When the information is ambiguous, as in the example of the Necker cube or the McGurk effect, the brain has to choose.

These illusions are a warning to all of us trying to know things about our universe. We have no privileged access to reality. Our interaction with our environment is constructed from the information our brains receive, and we build a plausible representation of the external world. This mixing of the senses has some very strange implications for the location of our consciousness.

It was experiencing first hand an experiment at the Karolinska Institute in Sweden that really made me question where I think 'I' am located. Developed by Henrik Ehrsson in 2007, the experiment succeeded in making me feel as though my consciousness was actually located in someone else's body. The inspiration for the work stems from a famous experiment called the false hand illusion. In this experiment the participant's hand is placed out of view behind a screen and a false rubber hand is placed in view of the participant and joined via a sleeve to the participant's body. Initially, the participant sees it for what it is: a false hand. But if the experimenter starts stroking both the false hand (which is in view) and the real hand (which is out of view) in such a way that the actions are synchronized, there's a strange shift.

The combined visual and tactile stimulus is ambiguous, so the brain tries to make sense of what is going on. Vision again dominates, and the participant begins to identify with the false hand, so much so that when a hammer is taken to the false hand, the participant very often reacts as if they are being attacked. The combination of the sense of sight and the sense of touch has tricked the brain into identifying with the false hand. What's striking is the plasticity of the brain, which has reprogrammed itself within only a few minutes to identify with a false hand.

At the Karolinska Institute this combination of visual and tactile input has been taken one stage further. Many of the advances in neuroscience are due to the development of new technology. In this case, virtual reality goggles. I was asked to wear the goggles while Ehrsson donned what looked like an academic mortar board with two cameras on top. These cameras were to become my eyes. By taking the video feed from the cameras on top of Ehrsson's head and feeding them into the virtual reality goggles, I was given Ehrsson's visual perspective. Nothing too strange there. It was when he asked me to shake hands that things became somewhat surreal.

As we shook hands, Ehrsson asked me to squeeze his hand in a regular rhythm that he matched, and this combination of vision and touch caused me to identify more and more with the arm that I could see supposedly emanating from my body. The weird thing was that the arm I was looking at belonged not to me but to Ehrsson. The identification was so strong that when Ehrsson produced a knife and drew it across his hand, I reacted as if it was my hand that was going to be cut. Since my visit to Stockholm, Ehrsson has pushed this illusion even further, making participants feel as if their consciousness is located in a Barbie doll.

Such effects had previously been confined to the movies. A number of recent science fiction films have explored this idea of out-of-body experience, including *Avatar* and *Surrogate*. But having taken part in Ehrsson's experiments, I wonder just how long will it be before I can send an avatar to a concert or to the top of Everest, and, by feeding my body at home with all the sensory input experienced by the avatar, I can feel as though I am actually sitting inside the concert hall or standing on top of the world.

MIND/BODY

These experiments get to the heart of the thorny issue of what is called the mind–body problem. Is consciousness separate from the physical body? It certainly appears to be created by it, but should we regard it as something distinct from the physical hardware? What is it for the mind to be located in a body? Some have argued that mind is something which is genuinely independent of the body. This was Descartes' view.

Called dualism, it posits that the mental world is separate from the physical one. A soul is one word that some have used to describe the 'other thing' that exists in this mental world. The question of how independent that other thing is from the body it is connected to is part of the debate. Ehrsson's experiments shift the apparent location of this other thing, whatever it is, challenging our sense of the spatial unity of mind and body. But the sense of self still seems very dependent on the body, because it is by manipulating sensory input that we seem able to play with the nature of our conscious experience.

There has been a growing trend for 'emergent phenomena', a term coined to express how some things arise from more fundamental entities and yet are themselves fundamental and irreducible. The idea arose briefly in the previous Edge, where we considered the proposal that time is emergent and not fundamental. Emergence, when applied to consciousness, is an attempt to find a middle ground between hardcore reductionism and Descartes' spooky dualism. Wetness is the classic example of an emergent phenomenon: one molecule of H_2O is not wet; wetness requires that you put many molecules together before it appears.

Many neuroscientists talk now about consciousness being similar to the wetness of water. It is probably the case that consciousness is an emergent phenomenon in the sense that it arises as a higher-level property of a system because of neuronal activity happening at a lower level. But that still doesn't really explain what this higher-level thing really is.

Some have argued that the concept of emergence is really just a way for chemists and biologists to claim that their subject is distinct from, and not merely a corollary of, physics and mathematics. A hard-core reductionist will tell you that a chemical reaction or a biological process is just a mathematical equation describing physics in action. This reductionist spirit is perfectly encapsulated in one of my favourite cartoons from the xkcd.com site.

Being at the top of the pile, I've always rather enjoyed the snooty mathematician's aloof place way out to the right. Emergence is what those on the left have invented to disrupt the picture.

I often wonder whether mathematics offers a good example of dualism, something which exists in a purely mental realm, disconnected from the physical. Our own access to this world is certainly dependent on the physical realization of the mathematics. We were led to the discovery of π because of the ancient Egyptian desire to tax land that was circular in area, carved out by the Nile. But the irrational nature of this number means that it can only be approximated in the real world. And yet it has a reality in our minds, something that can be defined precisely, explored logically. So where is it?

And isn't the app on my phone that is trying to convince me it is conscious really just mathematical code that would make sense even without the phone to bring it to life? When I ask Cleverbot whether it is just a piece of mathematics, it comes back with an interesting answer:

'I might be. Are you?'

12

What we are today comes from our
thoughts of yesterday and our present
thoughts build our life of tomorrow:
our life is the creation of our mind.

The Dhammapada

Some years ago my wife was in a coma following an accident. I spent
many hours in the hospital wondering whether 'she' was still inside, or
whether this was just a body with no consciousness. Fortunately she
woke up after two weeks, but what about those who cannot respond
physically? For some, the body has become a collection of cells with
no conscious experience – the vegetative state. But for others there
is the terrifying scenario in which their consciousness is locked in a
body that won't respond. So is there any way to ask the brain whether
it is conscious in these situations? Amazingly, there is and it involves
playing tennis – or at least imagining playing tennis.

Conjure up the image of you playing tennis. Big forehands. Over-
head smashes. Asking you to imagine playing tennis involves you
making a conscious decision to participate; it isn't some sort of automatic response to a physical stimulus. But once you are imagining the
actions, an fMRI scan can pick up the neural activity that corresponds
to the motor activity associated with the shots you picture yourself
playing.

The discovery that we could use the fMRI to see patients making
conscious decisions was made by British neuroscientist Adrian Owen
and his team, when in early 2006 they were investigating a 23-year-
old woman who had been diagnosed to be in a vegetative state. When
the patient was instructed to imagine playing tennis, Owen saw, to his
surprise, the region corresponding to the supplementary motor cortex

light up inside the scanner. When asked to imagine taking a journey through her house, a different region called the parahippocampal gyrus, which is needed for spatial navigation, was activated. It was an extremely exciting breakthrough, not least because the doctors rediagnosed this 23-year-old as conscious but locked in.

Numerous other patients who had previously been regarded as in a vegetative state have now been rediagnosed as locked in. This makes it possible for doctors and, more importantly, family to talk to and question those who are conscious but locked into their bodies. A patient can indicate the answer 'yes' to a question by imagining playing tennis, creating activity that, as we've seen, can be picked up by a scanner. It doesn't perhaps tell us what consciousness is, but the combination of tennis and fMRI has given us an extraordinary consciousometer.

The same tennis-playing protocol is being used to examine another case where our consciousness is removed: anaesthesia. I recently volunteered to be participant number 26 in a research project in Cambridge that would explore the moment when an anaesthetic knocks out consciousness – there have been some terrible examples of patients who can't move their bodies but are completely conscious during an operation.

The experiment had me lying inside an fMRI scanner while plugged into a supply of propofol, the drug Michael Jackson had been taking when he died. After a few shots of the anaesthetic, I must admit I could understand why Jackson had become addicted to its extremely calming effect. But I was here to work. With each increased dose I was asked to imagine playing tennis. As the dose was increased, the research team could assess the critical moment when I lost consciousness and stopped playing imaginary tennis. The interesting thing for me was to find out afterwards just how much more propofol was needed to go from knocking my body out so that it was no longer moving to the moment my consciousness was turned off.

The ability to question the brain even when the rest of the body is unable to move or communicate has allowed researchers to gauge just how much anaesthetic you need to temporarily switch off someone's consciousness so that you can operate on them.

This tennis-playing consciousometer leads us also to the close relationship between consciousness and free will: you must choose to imagine playing tennis. And yet recent experiments looking at the brain in action have fundamentally challenged how much free will we truly have.

AM I IN CONTROL?

I'm sure you thought you were asserting your free will when you decided to read this book. That it was a conscious choice to pick up the book today and turn to this page. But free will, it appears, may be just an illusion.

Much of the cutting-edge research into consciousness is going on right now. Unlike the discovery of the quark or the expanding universe, it is possible to witness much of this research as it is conducted, even to be part of the research. An experiment designed by British-born scientist John-Dylan Haynes is probably the most shocking in its implications for how much control I have over my life.

I hope these fMRI scanners are not bad for you because in my quest to know how the brain creates my conscious experience here I was: another city (Berlin this time) and another scanner. Lying inside, I was given a little hand-held console on which there were two buttons: one to be activated with my right hand, the other with my left. Haynes asked me to go into a Zen-like relaxed state, and whenever I felt the urge I could press either the right-hand or left-hand button.

During the experiment, I had to wear a pair of goggles containing a tiny screen on which a random stream of letters was projected. I was asked to record which letter was on the screen each time I made the decision to press the right or left button.

The fMRI scanner recorded my brain activity as I made my random conscious decisions. What Haynes discovered is that, by analysing my brain activity, he is able to predict which button I am going to press six seconds before I myself became consciously aware of which one I was going to choose. Six seconds is a very long time. My brain decides which button it is going to instruct my body to press, left or right. Then one elephant, two elephant, three elephant, four elephant, five elephant, six elephant – and only now does the decision get sent to my conscious brain, giving me the feeling that I am acting of my own free will.

Haynes can see which button I will choose because there is a region in the brain that lights up six seconds before I press, preparing the motor activity. A different region of the brain lights up according to whether the brain is readying the left finger to press the button or the right finger. Haynes is not able to predict with 100% certainty yet, but the predictions he is making are clearly more accurate than if you were simply guessing. And Haynes believes that with more refined imaging, it may be possible to get close to 100% accuracy.

It should be stressed that this is a very particular decision-making process. If say, you are in an accident, your brain makes decisions in a split second, and your body reacts without the need for any conscious brain activity to take place. Many processes in the brain occur automatically and without involving our consciousness, preventing the brain being overloaded with routine tasks. But whether I choose to press the right or left button is not a matter of life or death. I am freely making a decision to press the left button.

In practice it takes the research group in Berlin several weeks to analyse the data from the fMRI, but as computer technology and imaging techniques advance, the potential is there for Haynes's consciousness to know which button I'm going to press six seconds before my consciousness is aware of a decision I think I am making of my own free will.

Although the brain seems unconsciously to prepare the decision a long time in advance, it is still not clear where the final decision is being made. Maybe I can still override the decision my brain has prepared for me. If I don't have 'free will', some have suggested that perhaps I at least have 'free won't': that I can override the decision to press the left-hand button once it reaches my conscious brain. In this experiment, which button I press is immaterial, so there seems little reason not to go with the decision my unconscious brain has prepared for me.

The experiment seems to suggest that consciousness may be a very secondary function of the brain. We already know that so much of what our body decides to do is totally unconscious, but what we believe distinguishes us as humans is that our consciousness is an agent in the decisions we make. But what if it is only way down the chain of events that our consciousness kicks in and gets us involved? Is our consciousness of a decision just a chemical afterthought with no influence on what we do? What implications would this have legally and morally? 'I'm sorry m'lud but it wasn't me who shot the victim. My brain had already decided 6 seconds before that it was going to pull the trigger.' Be warned: biological determinism is not a defence in law!

The button-pressing that Haynes got me to perform is, as I've said, of no consequence, and this may skew the outcome of the experiment. Perhaps if it was something I cared more about, I wouldn't feel my subconscious had so much of a say. Haynes has repeated the experiment with a slightly more intellectually engaging activity. Participants are asked whether to add or subtract a number to numbers shown on a screen. Again, the decision to add or subtract is indicated by brain activity recorded 4 seconds before the conscious decision to act.

But what if we take the example proposed by the French philosopher Jean-Paul Sartre of a young man who has to choose between joining the resistance movement or looking after his grandmother. Perhaps in this case conscious deliberation will play a much greater role in the outcome and rescue free will from the fMRI scanner. Maybe the actions performed in Haynes's experiments are too much like subconscious automatic responses. Certainly many of my acts appear in my consciousness only at a later point, because there is no need for my consciousness to know much about them. Free will is replaced by the liberty of indifference.

The preconscious brain activity may well be just a contributing factor to the decision that is made at the moment of conscious deliberation. It does not necessarily represent the sole cause but helps inform the decision: here's an option you might like to consider.

If we have free will, one of the challenges is to understand where it comes from. I don't think my smartphone has free will. It is just a set of algorithms that it can follow only in a deterministic manner. Just to check, I asked my chatbot app whether it thought it was acting freely, making choices. It replied rather cryptically:

'I will choose a path that's clear, I will choose free will.'

I know that this response is programmed into the app. It may be that the app has a random-number generator that ensures its responses are varied and unpredictable, giving it the appearance of free will: a virtual casino dice picking its response from a database of replies. But randomness is not freedom – those random numbers are being generated by an algorithm whose outputs are necessarily random in character. As I discovered in my Third Edge, perhaps my smartphone will need to tap into ideas of quantum physics if it is to have any chance of asserting its free will.

A belief in free will is one of the things that I cling to because I believe it marks me out as different from an app on my phone, and I think this is why Haynes's experiment left me with a deep sense of unease. Perhaps my mind, too, is just the expression of a sophisticated app at the mercy of the brain's biological algorithm.

The mathematician Alan Turing was one of the first to question whether machines like my smartphone could ever think intelligently. He thought a good test of intelligence was to ask, if you were communicating with a person and a computer, whether you could distinguish which was the computer? It was this test, now known as the Turing test, that I was putting Cleverbot through at the beginning of this Edge. Since I can assess the intelligence of my fellow humans only by my interaction with them, if a computer can pass itself off as human, shouldn't I call it intelligent?

But isn't there a difference between a machine following instructions and my brain's conscious involvement in an activity? If I type a sentence in English into my smartphone, the apps on board are fantastic at translating it into any language I choose. But no one thinks the smartphone understands what it's doing. The difference perhaps can be illustrated by an interesting thought experiment called the Chinese Room, devised by philosopher John Searle of the University of California. It demonstrates that following instructions doesn't prove that a machine has a mind of its own.

I don't speak Mandarin, but imagine I was put in a room with an instruction manual that gave me an appropriate response to any string of Chinese characters posted into the room. I could have a very convincing discussion with a Mandarin speaker without ever understanding a word of my responses. In a similar fashion, my smartphone appears to speak many languages, but we wouldn't say it understands what it is translating.

It's a powerful challenge to anyone who thinks that just because a machine responds like a conscious entity, we should regard that as a sufficient measure of consciousness. Sure, it could be doing everything a conscious person does, but is it *really* conscious? Then again, what is my mind doing when I'm writing down words now? Aren't I just following a set of instructions? Could there be a threshold beyond which we would have to accept that the computer understands Mandarin, and hence another at which the algorithm at work should be regarded as having consciousness? But before we can program a computer to be conscious, we need to understand what is so special about the algorithm at work in a human brain.

THE TIDE COMES IN

One of the best ways to tease out the correlation between consciousness and brain activity is to compare conscious brains with unconscious brains. Is there a noticeable difference in the brain's activity? We don't have to wait for a patient to be in a coma or under anaesthetic to make this comparison, because there is another situation in which every day, or, rather, every night, we lose our consciousness: sleep. And it is the science of sleep and what happens to the brain in these unconscious periods that perhaps gives the best insight into what it is the brain does to create our experience of consciousness.

So I went to the Centre for Sleep and Consciousness at the University of Wisconsin–Madison, where experiments conducted by neuroscientist Giulio Tononi and his team have revealed strikingly different brain behaviour during waking and dreamless sleeping.

In the past it was impossible to ask the sleeping brain questions. But transcranial magnetic stimulation, or TMS, allows scientists to infiltrate the brain and artificially fire neurons. By applying a rapidly fluctuating magnetic field, the team can activate specific regions of my brain when I am awake and, more excitingly, when I am asleep. The question is whether this artificial stimulation of neurons causes the conscious brain to respond differently from the unconscious sleeping brain.

I was a bit nervous about the idea of someone zapping my brain. After all, it is my principal tool for creating my mathematics. Scramble that and I'm in trouble. But Tononi assured me it was quite safe. Using his own brain, one of his colleagues demonstrated how he could activate a region connected with the motor activity of the hand. It was quite amazing to see that zapping this region caused his finger to move. Each zap of TMS was like throwing a switch in the brain that made the finger move. Given that Tononi's colleague seemed unaffected by the zapping, I agreed to take part in the experiment.

The first stage involved applying TMS to a small region of my brain when I was awake. Electrodes attached to my head recorded the effect via EEG. The results revealed that different areas far away from the stimulated site respond at different times in a complex pattern that feeds back to the original site of the stimulation. The brain, Tononi explains, is interacting as a complex integrated network. The neurons in the brain act like a series of interrelated logic gates. One neuron may fire if the majority of neurons connected to it are firing. Or it may fire if only one connected neuron is on. What I was seeing on the EEG output was the logical flow of activity caused by the firing of the initial neurons with TMS.

The next part of the experiment required me to fall asleep. Once I was in deep 'stage 4' sleep, they would apply TMS to my brain in exactly the same location, stimulating the same region. Essentially, the TMS fires the same neurons, turning them on like switches, and the question is: how has the structure of the network changed as the brain went from conscious to unconscious? Unfortunately, this part of the experiment proved too difficult for me. I am an incredibly light sleeper. Having a head covered in electrodes and knowing that someone was about to creep up and zap me once I'd dropped off aren't very conducive to deep sleep. Despite depriving myself of coffee for the whole day, I failed to get past a light 'stage 1' fitful sleep.

Instead, I had to content myself with the data from a patient who had been able to fall asleep in such unrelaxing conditions. The results were striking. Electrical activity does not propagate through the brain, as it does when we're conscious. It's as if the network is down. The tide has come in, cutting off connections, and any activity is very localized. The exciting implication is that consciousness perhaps has to do with the complex integration in the brain, that it is a result of the inter-related logic gates that control when the firing of one set of neurons causes the firing of other neurons. In particular, the results suggest that consciousness is related to the way the network feeds information back and forth between the original neurons activated by the TMS and the rest of the brain.

TMS applied here

Wakefulness   Deep Sleep

Having failed to fall asleep in his lab, I was taken by Tononi to his office, where he promised that he would make up for my caffeine deprivation by crafting the perfect espresso from his prized Italian coffee machine. But he also had something he wanted to show me. As we sat down to the wonderful aroma of grinding coffee beans, he passed me a paper with a mathematical formula penned on it.

My interest was immediately piqued. Mathematical formulas are for me what Pavlov's bell was for his dogs. Put a mathematical formula in front of me and I'm immediately hooked and want to decode its message. But I didn't recognize it.

'It's my coefficient of consciousness.'

Consciousness in a mathematical formula . . . how could I resist?

MAKING 'ME' MATHEMATICS

Tononi explained that, as a result of his work on the sort of networked behaviour that corresponds to conscious brains, he has developed a new theory of networks that he believes are conscious. The theory is called integrated information theory, or IIT, and it includes a mathematical formula that measures the amount of integration and irreducibility present in a network, which he believes is key to creating a sense of self. Called Φ (that is, phi, the twenty-first letter of the Greek alphabet) it is a measure that can be applied to machines like my smartphone as much as it can the human brain, and it offers the prospect of a quantitative mathematical approach to what makes me 'me'. According to Tononi, the larger the value of Φ, the more conscious the network. I guess it's the mathematician in me that is so excited by the prospect of a mathematical equation explaining why and how 'I' am.

A conscious brain seems similar to a network that has a high degree of connectivity and feedback. If I fire neurons in one part of the network, the result is a cascade of cross-checking and information fed across the network. If the network consists of only isolated islands, then it appears to be unconscious. Tononi's coefficient of consciousness is therefore a measure of how much the network is more than a sum of its parts.

But Tononi believes that it's the nature of this connectivity of the whole that is important. It isn't enough that there should be high connectivity across the network. If the neurons start firing in a synchronous way, this does not seem to yield a conscious experience. This is actually a property of the brain during deep sleep. At the other extreme, seizures that lead to a person losing consciousness are often associated with the highly synchronous firing of neurons across the brain. It therefore seems important that there is a large range of differentiated states. There shouldn't be too many patterns or symmetry in the wiring, which may lead to an inability to differentiate different experiences. Connect a network up too much and the network will behave in the same way whatever you do to it.

What the coefficient tries to capture is one of the extraordinary traits of our conscious experience: the brain's ability to integrate the vast range of inputs our body receives and synthesize them into a single experience. Consciousness can't be broken apart into independent experiences felt separately. When I look at my red casino dice I don't have separate experiences: one of a colourless cube and another experience which is just a patch of red formless colour. The coefficient also tries to quantify how much more information in a network is generated by the complete system than if it were cut into disconnected pieces, as happens to the brain during deep sleep.

Tononi and colleagues have run interesting computer simulations on 'brains' consisting of eight neurons connected in different ways to see which network has the greatest Φ. The results indicate that you want each neuron to have a connection pattern with the rest of the network that is different from that of the other neurons. But at the same time, you want as much information to be able to be shared across the network. So if you consider any division of the network into two separate halves, you want the two halves to be able to communicate with each other. It's an interesting balancing act between overconnecting and cutting down differentiation across the different neurons versus creating difference at the expense of keeping everyone talking.

But the nature of the connectivity is also important. Tononi has created two networks that are functionally equivalent and have the same outputs, but in one case the Φ count is high, because the network feeds back and forth, while in the other network the Φ count is low because the network is set up so that it only feeds information forwards (the neurons can't feed back). Tononi believes this is an example of a 'zombie network': a network that outputs the same information as the first network but has no sense of self. Just by looking at the output, you can't differentiate between the two networks. But the way the zombie network generates that output has a completely different quality that is measured by Φ. According to Tononi's Φ, the zombie network has no internal world.

It's encouraging to know that the brain's thalamocortical system, which is known to play an important part in generating consciousness, has a structure similar to networks with a high Φ. Contrast this with the network of neurons in the cerebellum, which doesn't create consciousness. Called the little brain, it is located at the back of the skull and controls things like balance and our fine motor control. It accounts for 80% of the neurons in the brain, and yet, if it is removed, although our movement is severely impaired, we do not have an altered sense of consciousness.

In 2014, a 24-year-old woman in China was admitted to hospital with dizziness and nausea. When her brain was scanned to try to identify the cause, it was found that she had been born without a cerebellum. Although it had taken her some time to learn to walk as a child, and she was never able to run or jump, none of the medical staff who encountered her doubted that she was fully conscious. This was not a zombie, just a physically unstable human being.

If you examine the neural network at the heart of the cerebellum, you find patches that tend to be activated independently of one another with little interaction, just like the brain at sleep. The low Φ of the cerebellum's network fits in with the idea that it does not create conscious experience.

A network with a high Φ and perhaps a higher level of consciousness.

Although highly connected, the symmetry of this network causes little differentiation to occur across the network, resulting in the whole not contributing to the creation of new information not already inherent in the parts. This leads to a low Φ and hence a lower consciousness.

That the connectivity of the brain could be the key to consciousness has led to the idea that my 'connectome' is part of the secret of what makes me 'me'. The connectome is a comprehensive map of the neural connections in the brain. Just as the human genome project gave us unprecedented information about the workings of the body, mapping the human connectome may provide similar insights into the workings of the brain. Combine the wiring with the rules for how this network operates and we may have the ingredients for creating consciousness in a network.

The connectome of the human brain is a distant goal, but already we have a complete picture of the wiring of the neurons inside *C. elegans*, a one-millimetre-long brainless worm with a noted fondness for compost heaps. Its nervous system contains exactly 302 neurons, ideally suited for us to map out a complete neuron-to-neuron wiring. Despite this map, we are still a long way from relating these connections to the behaviour of *C. elegans*.

IS THE INTERNET CONSCIOUS?

Given that Tononi's Φ is a measure of how a network is connected, it could help us understand if my smartphone, the Internet, or even a city can achieve consciousness. Perhaps the Internet or a computer, once it hits a certain threshold at some point in the future, might recognize itself when it looks in the mirror. Consciousness could correspond to a phase change in this coefficient, just as water changes state when its temperature passes the threshold for boiling or freezing.

It is interesting that the introduction of an anaesthetic into the body doesn't gradually turn down consciousness but at some point seems to suddenly switch it off. If you've ever had an operation and the anesthetist asks you to count up to 20, you'll know (or perhaps won't know) that there is a point at which you suddenly drop out. The change seems to be very non-linear, like a phase transition.

If consciousness is about the connectivity of the network, what other networks might already be conscious? The total number of transistors that are connected via the Internet is of the order of 10^{18}, while the brain has about 10^{11} neurons. The difference lies in the way they are connected. A neuron is typically linked to tens of thousands of other neurons, which allows for a high degree of information integration. In contrast, transistors inside a computer are not highly connected. On Tononi's measure it is unlikely that the Internet is conscious . . . yet.

If I take a picture with the digital camera in my smartphone, the memory in my phone can store an extraordinary range of different images. A million pixels, for example, will give me $2^{1,000,000}$ different possible black-and-white images. It will record detail that I am completely unaware of when I look through the viewfinder. But that's the point: my conscious experience could not deal with that huge input, and instead the raw sensory data is integrated to glean the significant information from the scene and limit its content.

At present, computers are very bad at matching the power of human vision. They are unable to tell the story inside a picture. The trouble is that a computer tends to read a picture pixel by pixel and finds it hard to integrate the information. Humans, however, are excellent at taking this huge amount of visual input and creating a story from the data. It is this ability of the human mind to integrate and pick out what is significant that is at the heart of Tononi's measure of consciousness Φ.

Of course, there is still no explanation of how or why a high Φ should produce the conscious experience I have. We can certainly correlate it with consciousness, which is very suggestive – witness the experiments on sleeping patients whose networks have a decreased Φ. So too are considerations of different bits of the brain which have distinctive wirings. But I still can't say why this produces consciousness, or whether a computer wired in this way would truly experience consciousness.

There are reasons why having a high Φ might have significant evolutionary advantages. It seems to allow planning for the future. By taking data from different sensors, the highly integrated nature of a network with high Φ can make recommendations for future action. This ability to project oneself into the future, to perform mental time travel, seems to be one of the key evolutionary advantages of consciousness. A network with a high Φ appears to be able to demonstrate such behaviour. But why couldn't it do all this while unconscious?

SKYPING CONSCIOUSNESS

Christof Koch, he of the Jennifer Aniston neuron, is a big fan of Φ as a measure of consciousness, so I was keen to push him on whether he thought it was robust enough to provide an answer to the 'hard problem', as philosopher David Chalmers dubbed the challenge of getting inside another person's head.

Since I first met Koch at the top of Mount Baldy outside Caltech, he had taken up the directorship of an extraordinary venture called the Allen Institute for Brain Science, funded by a single individual, Paul G. Allen, co-founder of Microsoft, to the tune of 500 million US dollars. Allen's motivation? He simply wants to understand how the brain works. It's all open science, it's not for profit, and they release all the data free. As Koch says: 'It's a pretty cool model.'

Since it was going to be tricky to make another trip to California to quiz Koch on his views on Φ and Tononi's integrated information theory, I decided the next best thing was to access Koch's consciousness via a Skype call. Koch was keen, though, to check which side of the philosophical divide I was on:

'Sure, we can chat about consciousness and the extent to which it is unanswerable. But I would hope that you're not going to turn away young people who are contemplating a career in neuroscience by buying into the philosopher's conceit of the "Hard problem" (hard with a capital H). Philosophers such as Dave Chalmers deal in belief systems and personal opinions, not in natural laws and facts. While they ask interesting questions and pose challenging dilemmas, they have an unimpressive historical record of prognostication.'

Koch was keen to remind me of the philosopher Comte and his prediction that we would never know what was at the heart of a star. It is a story that I have kept in mind ever since embarking on this journey into the unknown. Koch added another important voice to the debate, that of his collaborator Francis Crick, who wrote in 1996: 'It is very rash to say that things are beyond the scope of science.'

Koch was in excited mood when we finally connected our consciousnesses via Skype – actually, I've never seen him anything but excited about life at the cutting edge of one of today's greatest scientific challenges. Two days earlier, the Allen Institute had just released data that tried to classify the different cell types that you find in the brain.

'One of the unknowns is how many different sorts of brain cells are there. We've known for two hundred years that the body is made up of cells, but there are heart cells and skin cells and brain cells. But then we realized that there aren't just one or two types of brain cell. There may well be a thousand. Or of the order of several thousand. In the cortex proper, we just don't know.'

Koch's latest research has produced a database detailing the different range of cortical neurons to be found in a mouse brain. 'It's really cool stuff. But this isn't just a pretty picture in a publication as it usually is in science. It's all the raw data and all the data is downloadable.' Ramón y Cajal updated to the twenty-first century.

It's this kind of detailed scientific analysis of how the brain functions that Koch believes is how we chip away at the challenge of understanding how the brain produces conscious experience.

Given that Koch is keen to get young scientists on board the consciousness bandwagon, I wondered what had inspired him to embark on a research project when there was no wagon. At the time, many regarded setting off in search of consciousness as akin to heading into the Sahara desert in search of water.

Part of the motivation was provided by people who said it was a no-go area. 'One reason was to show them all they were wrong. I like to provoke.' Koch is also someone who likes taking risks. It's what drives him to hang off the side of a mountain, climbing unaided to the top. But there was a strand to his choice of problem that was a little more unexpected. It turned out that Koch's religious upbringing was partly responsible for his desire to understand consciousness.

'Ultimately I think I wanted to justify to myself my continued belief in God. I wanted to show to my own satisfaction that to explain consciousness we need something more. We need something like my idea of a God. It turned out to be different. It provoked a great internal storm within me when I realized there wasn't really any need for a soul. There wasn't any real need for it to generate consciousness. It could all be done by a mechanism as long as we had something special like Tononi's integrated information theory, or something like that.'

As a way to reaffirm his belief in something transcendental, Koch admits it failed.

'Over the last ten years I lost my faith; I always tried to integrate it but couldn't. I still very much have a sentiment that I do live in a mysterious universe. It's conducive to life. It's conducive to consciousness. It all seems very wonderful, and literally every day I wake up with this feeling that life is mysterious and a miracle. I still haven't lost that feeling.'

But Koch believes we are getting closer to demystifying consciousness, and he believes it is this mathematical coefficient Φ and Tononi's IIT that hold the key.

'I'm a big fan of this integrated information theory which states that, in principle, given the wiring diagram of a person or of *C. elegans* or a computer, I will be able to say whether it feels like something to be that system. Ultimately that is what consciousness is, it's experience. And I'll also be able to tell what that system is currently experiencing. I have this mechanism, this brain, this computer currently in this one state. These neurons are off; these neurons are on; these transistors are switching; these are not. The theory says that at least in principle I can predict the experience of that system, not by looking at the input–output but by actually looking inside the system, looking at the transition probability matrix and its states.'

Koch has a tough battle on his hands convincing others. There is a hardcore group of philosophers and thinkers who don't believe that science can ever answer this problem. They are members of a school of thought that goes by the name of mysterianism, which asserts that there are mysteries that will always be beyond the limits of the human mind. Top of the mysterians' hit list is the hard problem of consciousness.

The name of the movement – it originated from a rock band called Question Mark and the Mysterians – began as a term of abuse concocted by philosopher Owen Flanagan, who thought the standpoint of these philosophers was extremely defeatist. As Flanagan wrote: 'The new mysterianism is a postmodern position designed to drive a railroad spike through the heart of scientism.' Koch has often found himself debating with mysterian philosophers who think him misguided in his pursuit of an answer. So I wondered what he says to those who question whether you can ever know that a system is really experiencing something?

'If you pursue that to its end you just end up with solipsism.'

You can hear the exasperation in Koch's voice at this philosophical position, which asserts that knowledge of anything beyond our own mind is never certain. It takes us back to Descartes' statement that the only thing we can be sure of is our own consciousness.

'Yes . . . solipsism is logically consistent, but then it's extremely improbable that everyone's brain is like mine, except only I have consciousness and you are all pretending. Yes, you can believe that, but it's not very likely.'

Did Koch think that those who insist on the unanswerability of the hard problem must therefore question whether anything is knowable? If you are going to be so extreme, are you inevitably drawn to a sceptic's view of the world?

'Exactly, and I don't find that very interesting. You can be an extreme sceptic, but it doesn't lend itself to anything easy. Any theory like IIT is an identity relationship ultimately. The claim of this particular theory and theories like it is that experience is identical to states in this very high-dimensional qualia space spanned essentially by the number of different states that your system can take on. It amounts to a configuration, to a constellation, to a polytope in this high-dimensional space. That is what experience is. That's what it feels like to be you and it's something that I can predict in principle . . . it's an empirical project because I can say: "Well, Marcus, now you are seeing red or right now you are having the experience of smelling a rose." I can do fMRI and I can see that your rose neurons are activated, that your colour area is activated. So in principle this is an entirely empirical project.'

Koch believes that this is as good as it's going to get if you want to explain consciousness. It fits very well with what it would mean to be engaged in a science of consciousness. Wouldn't it be good enough to identify a configuration in the brain, for example, that always correlates with your acknowledging an experience of feeling a sensation of pain or red or happiness? This is something that I could test with experiments. And if every time I get a correspondence, can't I say that I know what the experience of red is, and that I can therefore extend the science to say that a computer will also have experiences of red?

Hardcore mysterians will contend that you haven't explained how such a network gives rise to this sensation of feeling something. But aren't we in danger of demanding too much, to the extent that we fall into solipsism and down the slippery sceptic slope to arguing that you can't really say anything about the universe? We understand that the sensation of heat is just the movement of atoms. No one is saying you haven't really explained why that gives rise to heat. We have identified what heat is. I think Koch would say the same of consciousness.

Theoretically the idea is very attractive, but I wondered whether Koch thought we could ever get to point at which we can use an fMRI scanner or something more sophisticated to know what someone is really experiencing. Or is it just too complex?

'That's a pragmatic problem. That's the same problem that thermodynamics faced in the nineteenth century. You couldn't compute those things. But at least for a simple thing like a critter of ten neurons, the expressions are perfectly well defined and there is a unique answer. The maximum number of neurons one could navigate is a big practical problem. Will we ever overcome it? I don't know, because the problem scales exponentially with the number of neurons, which is really bad. But that's a different problem.'

MAKING MINDS

The ultimate test of our understanding of what makes me me is to see whether I can build an artificial brain that has consciousness. What is the prospect of an app on my phone that would truly have consciousness? Humans are quite good at making conscious things already. My son is an example of how we can combine various cellular structures, an egg and some sperm, and together they have all the kit and instructions for growing a new conscious organism. At least I'm assuming that my son is conscious – on some mornings he appears to be at the zombie end of the spectrum.

There are some amazingly ambitious projects afoot which aim to produce an analysis of the wiring of a human brain such that it can be simulated on a computer. The Human Brain Project, the brain-child of Henry Markram, aims within ten years to produce a working model of the human brain that can be uploaded onto a supercomputer. 'It's going to be the Higgs boson of the brain, a Noah's archive of the mind,' declared Markram. He was rewarded with a billion-euro grant from the European Commission to realize his vision. But when this is done, would these simulations be conscious? To my surprise, Koch didn't think so.

'Let's suppose that Henry Markram's brain project pans out and we have this perfect digital simulation of the human brain. It will also speak, of course, because it is a perfect simulation of the human brain, so it includes a simulation of the Broca area responsible for language. The computer will not exist as a conscious entity. There may be a minimal amount of Φ at the level of a couple of individual transistors, but it will never feel like anything to be the brain.'

The point is that Tononi's Φ gets at the nature of the cause–effect power of the internal mechanism, not at the input–output behaviour. The typical connectivity inside the computer has one transistor talking on the CPU to at most four other transistors. This gives rise to a very low Φ, and in Koch's belief a low level of consciousness. The interesting thing is that because it is a perfect simulation, it is going to object vociferously that it is conscious, that it has an internal world. But in Koch's view it would just be all talk.

'The reason is essentially similar to the fact that if you get a computer to simulate a black hole, the simulated mass will not affect the real mass near the computer. Space will never be distorted around the computer simulation. In the same way, you can simulate consciousness on a computer, but the simulated entity will not experience anything. It's the difference between simulating and emulating. Consciousness arises from the cause–effect repertoire of the mechanism. It's something physical.'

Consciousness depends on how the network is put together. A

similar issue is at work with the zombie network that Tononi constructed with ten neurons. The amazing thing is that the principle that Tononi used to turn a high-Φ network with ten neurons into a zero-Φ network or zombie with exactly the same input–output repertoire can be applied to the network of the human brain. Both would have the same input–output behaviour, and yet, because of the difference in the internal state transitions, one has a high Φ, the other zero Φ. But how can we ever know whether this would mean that one is conscious and the other a zombie?

What bugs me is that this seems to highlight the near unanswerability of the question of consciousness. Φ is certainly a great measure of the difference between a simulation of the brain and the actual nature of the brain's architecture. It defines the difference between a zombie network and the human mind. But how can we really know that the simulation or zombie isn't conscious? It is still there shouting its head off: 'For crying out loud, how many times do I need to tell you? I am conscious in here.' But Φ says it's just pretending. I tell the zombie that Φ says it doesn't have an internal world. But just as my conscious brain would, the zombie insists: 'Yes I do.' And isn't this the heart of the problem? I have only input–output to give me any idea of the system articulating these feelings. I can certainly define Φ as consciousness, but isn't this finally the one thing that by its nature is beyond the ability of science to investigate empirically?

DOWNLOADING MY CONSCIOUSNESS

One of the other reasons Koch likes Φ as a measure of consciousness is that it plays into his panpsychic belief that we aren't the only ones with consciousness. If consciousness is about integration of information across a network, then that applies from things as small as an amoeba to the consciousness of the whole universe.

'Ultimately it says that anything that has cause–effect power on itself will have some level of consciousness. Consciousness is ultimately how much difference you make to yourself, the cause–effect power you have on yourself. So even if you take a minimal system like a cell – a single cell is already incredibly complex – it has some cause–effect power on itself. It will feel like something to be that cell. It will have a small but non-zero Φ. It may be vanishingly small, but it will have some level of consciousness. Of course, that's a very ancient intuition.'

When I tell people I am investigating what we cannot know, a typical response is: will you be tackling life after death? This is intimately related to the question of consciousness. Does our Φ live on? There is no good evidence that anything of our consciousness survives after death. But is there any way we can know? Since we are finding it difficult to access each other's consciousnesses while we are alive, to investigate consciousness after someone's death appears an impossible challenge. It seems extremely unlikely, given how much correlation there is between brain activity and consciousness, that anything can survive beyond death. If there could be some communication, it might give us some hope. That is, after all, how we are able to investigate the consciousnesses we believe exist in the people around us.

Koch agreed with me that it is extremely unlikely that anything of our Φ survives after death. Koch had in fact spent some time debating the issue with an unlikely collaborator.

'I spent a week a couple of years ago in India talking with the Dalai Lama. It was very intense. Four hours in the morning, four hours in the afternoon, talking about science. Two whole days were dedicated to consciousness. Buddhists have been exploring their own consciousness from the inside using meditative techniques for 2000 years. In contrast, we do it using fMRI and electrodes and psychophysics from the outside, but basically our views tend to agree. He was very sympathetic to many of the scientific ideas and we agreed on many things. For example, he has no trouble with the idea of evolution.'

But there must have been points of difference?

'The one thing where we fundamentally disagreed was this idea of reincarnation. I don't see how it would work. You have to have a mechanism that carries my consciousness or my memories over into the next life. Unless we find something in quantum physics, and I don't know enough about it to know, I don't see any evidence for it.'

As Koch points out, if you are going to attempt to answer this question as a scientist, you will need some explanation of how consciousness survives the death of your body. There have been some interesting proposals. For example, if consciousness corresponds ultimately to patterns of information in the brain – perhaps something close to what Tononi is advocating – then some argue that information can theoretically always be reconstructed. The black hole information paradox relates to the question of whether information is lost when things disappear in a black hole. But provided you avoid the black hole crematorium, the combination of quantum determinism and reversibility means no information is ever lost.

The religious physicist John Polkinghorne offers this as a story for the possibility of life after death: 'Though this pattern is dissolved at death, it seems perfectly rational to believe that it will be remembered by God and reconstituted in a divine act of resurrection.' Of course, you may not have to resort to God to realize this striking idea. Some people are already trying to ensure their brain information is stored somewhere before their hardware packs up. The idea of downloading my consciousness onto my smartphone so that 'it' becomes 'me' may not be so far from Polkinghorne's proposal. It's just Apple playing the role of God. Rapture for nerds, as Koch calls it.

ZOMBIELAND

When faced with a question that we cannot answer, we have to make a choice. Perhaps the intellectually correct response is to remain agnostic. After all, that is the meaning of having identified an unanswerable question. On the other hand, a belief in an answer one way or the other will have an impact on how we lead our lives. Imagine if you regarded yourself as unique and everyone else as zombies – it would have a big effect on your interaction with the world. Or, conversely, if there is a moment when you think a machine is conscious, then pressing Shut Down on your computer will become loaded with moral issues.

Some posit that to crack the problem of consciousness we will have to admit to our description of the universe a new basic ingredient that gives rise to consciousness, an ingredient that – like time, space or gravity – can't be reduced to anything else. All we can do is explore the relationship between this new ingredient and the other ingredients we have to date. To me this seems a cop-out. Consciousness does emerge from a developing brain when some critical threshold is hit – like the moment when water begins to bubble and boil and turn into a gas. There are many examples in nature of these critical tipping points where a phase transition happens. The question is whether the phase transition creates something that can't be explained other than by creating a new fundamental entity. It's not without precedent, of course. Electromagnetic waves are created as a consequence of accelerating charged particles. That is not an emergent phenomenon, but a new fundamental ingredient of the natural world.

Or perhaps consciousness is associated with another state of matter, like solid or liquid. This state of matter already has a name proposed for it: perceptronium, which is defined as the most general substance that feels subjectively self-aware. This change of state would be consistent with consciousness as an emergent phenomenon. Or could there be a field of consciousness that gets activated by critical states of matter, in the same way that the Higgs field gives mass to matter? It sounds like a crazy idea, but perhaps, in order to get to grips with such a slippery concept, we need crazy ideas.

Some argue that nothing physical is ever going to answer the problem of what it feels like to be me, that the very existence of consciousness implies something that transcends our physical realm. But if mind can move matter, then surely there must be a physics which connects these two realms and allows science back into the game.

Perhaps the question of consciousness is not a question of science at all, but one of language. This is the stance of a school of philosophy going back to Wittgenstein. In his *Philosophical Investigations*, Wittgenstein explores the problem of a private language. The process of learning the meaning of the word 'table' involves people pointing at a table and saying 'here is a table'. If I point at something which doesn't correspond to what society means by 'table', then I get corrected. Wittgenstein challenges whether the same principle can apply to naming 'pain'. Pain does not involve an object that is external to us, or that we can point at and call pain. We may be able to find a correlation between an output on an fMRI scanner that always corresponds to my feeling of pain. But when we point at the screen and say that is pain, is that what we really mean by 'pain'?

Wittgenstein believed that the problem of exploring the private worlds of our qualia and feelings was one of language. How can we share the meaning of 'here is a pain'? It is impossible. 'I have a pain in my tooth' seems to have the same quality as 'I have a table', and it tempts us into assuming both say the same kind of thing. You assume that there is something called 'my pain' in the same sense that there is 'a table'. It seems to be saying something, but Wittgenstein believed that it isn't really saying anything at all: 'The confusions which occupy us arise when language is like an engine idling, not when it is doing work.'

For example, if you have a feeling and declare 'I think this is pain', I have no way of correcting you. I have no criterion against which to determine whether what you are feeling is what I mean by 'pain'. Wittgenstein explores whether it is possible to show you pain by pricking your finger and declaring 'that is pain'. If you now reply, for example: 'Oh, I know what "pain" means; what I don't know is whether *this,* that I have now, is pain.' Wittgenstein replies that 'we should merely shake our heads and be forced to regard (your) words as a queer reaction which we have no idea what to do with'.

We can get at the problem of identifying what is going on inside our heads by imagining that we each have a box with something inside. We all name the thing inside 'a beetle', but we aren't allowed to look in anyone else's box, only our own. So it is quite possible that everyone has something different in the box, or that the thing inside is constantly changing, or even that there is nothing in the box. And yet we all call it 'a beetle'. But for those with nothing in the box, the word 'beetle' is a name for nothing. It is not a name at all. Does this word therefore have any meaning? Are our brains like the box and consciousness the beetle? Does an fMRI scanner allow us finally to look inside someone else's box and see if your beetle is the same as mine? Does the machine rescue consciousness from Wittgenstein's language games?

Wittgenstein explores how a sentence, or question, fools us into thinking it means something because it takes exactly the form of a real sentence, but when you examine it carefully you find that it doesn't actually refer to anything. This, many philosophers believe, is at the heart of the problem of consciousness. It is not a question of science, but will vanish as a challenge once we recognize that it is simply a confusion of language.

Daniel Dennett is one of those philosophers who follow in the tradition of Wittgenstein. He believes that in years to come we will recognize that there is little point in having this long debate about the idea of consciousness beyond the physical things that seem necessary for us to have consciousness. So, for example, if we do encounter a machine or organism that functions exactly as we would expect a conscious being to, we should simply define this thing as conscious. The question of whether it is a zombie or not, whether it is actually feeling anything, should just be ignored. If there is no way to distinguish the unconscious zombie from the conscious human, what point is there having a word to describe this difference? Only when you can know there is difference is there any point having a word to describe it.

Dennett cites vitalism to support his stance. Vitalism suffered such a fate: we've given up on the idea that there is some extra special ingredient, an *élan vital*, that breathes life into this collection of cells. If you show me a collection of cells that have the ability to replicate themselves, that miaows and purrs like a cat, and then declare that it isn't actually alive, it would be very difficult to convince me. Some believe that arguments over consciousness will go the same way as those over vitalism. Vitalism was an attempt to explain how a physical system could do the things associated with a living organism: reproduce, self-organize, adapt. Once those mechanisms were explained, we had solved the problem of life and no *élan vital* was needed. But in the case of consciousness, some believe that the question of how physical stuff produces a subjective experience cannot by its very subjective nature be answered by mechanisms in the same way.

With the advent of extraordinary new equipment and techniques, our internal world has become less opaque. Mental activities are private, but physical interactions with the world are public. To what extent can I gain access to the private domain by analysing the public?

We can probably get to the stage that I can know you are thinking about Jennifer Aniston rather than Pythagoras' theorem just by looking at the neurons that are firing.

But to get a sense of what it feels like to be you – is that possible just by understanding the firing of neurons? Will I ever be able to distinguish the conscious from the zombie? My gut has as many as 100 million neurons, 0.1% of the neurons in my brain, yet it isn't conscious. Or is it? How could I know if it actually had a distinct consciousness from mine? This is the heart of the problem with the question of consciousness. My stomach might start communicating with me, but how can I ever know if it experiences red or falls in love like I do? I might scan it, probe it with electrodes, discover that the wiring and firing are a match for a cat brain that has as many neurons, but is that as far as we can go?

The question of distinguishing the zombies from the conscious could remain one of the unanswerable questions of science. The Turing test that I put my smartphone through at the beginning of our journey into the mind hints at the challenge ahead. Was it the zombie chatbot who wanted to become a poet, or did it want to become rich? Is a chatbot clever enough to make a joke about Descartes' 'I think, therefore I am'? Will it eventually start dating? Who is the zombie and who is conscious?

As we finished our Skype chat, Koch admitted to me that there was no guarantee we'll ever know.

'There is no law in the universe which says we have the cognitive power to explain everything. If we were dogs – I mean, I love my dog – my dog is fully conscious, but my dog doesn't understand taxes, it doesn't understand special relativity, or even the simplest differential equation. Even most people don't understand differential equations. But for the same reasons, I really dislike it when people say you will never know this. You can't say that. Yes, there's no guarantee. But it's a really defeatist attitude, right? I mean, what sort of research programme is it, Marcus, where you throw up your hands and say forget about it, I can't understand it ever, it's hopeless? That's defeatism.'

With that clarion call not to give up trying to answer unanswerable questions ringing in my ears, I quit our Skype call. Koch's face vanished from my screen, leaving me with a slightly uneasy feeling. Was I sure that it had been Koch at the other end of the line? Or had he devised some algorithmically generated avatar to deal with the onslaught of enquiries he gets about whether we can ever solve the hard problem of consciousness?

SEVENTH EDGE: THE CHRISTMAS CRACKER

13

Number is the ruler of forms and ideas
and the cause of gods and demons.

Pythagoras

**The statement on the other side
of this card is false**

**The statement on the other side
of this card is true**

Bored of the uninspiring range of Christmas crackers available in the shops, I decided this year to treat my family to my very own home-made mathematical crackers. Each cracker included a mathematical joke and a paradox. My family were of the opinion that the jokes were stronger on the mathematics than the humour. I'll let you decide . . . How many mathematicians does it take to change a light bulb? 0.99999 recurring. And if you're not laughing, don't worry. My family weren't either. If you don't get it, then – although you should never have to explain a joke – the point is that you can prove that 0.9999 recurring is actually the same number as 1.

The paradoxes were a little less lame. One contained a Möbius strip, a seemingly paradoxical geometric object which has only one side. If you take a long strip of paper and twist it before gluing the ends together, the resulting shape has only one side. You can check this by trying to colour the sides: start colouring one side and you soon find you've coloured the whole thing. The strip has the surprising property that if you cut it down the middle, it doesn't come apart into two loops, as you might expect, but remains intact. It's still a single loop but with two twists in it.

The cracker I ended up with wasn't too bad, even if I say so myself. Even the joke was quite funny. What does the B in Benoit B. Mandelbrot stand for? Benoit B. Mandelbrot. (If you still aren't laughing, the thing you're missing is that Mandelbrot discovered the fractals that featured in my First Edge, those geometric shapes that never get simpler, how-ever much you zoom in on them.) The paradox was one of my all-time favourites. It consisted of the two statements that opened this chapter, one on either side of a card. I've always enjoyed and in equal measure been disturbed by word games of this sort. One of my favourite books as a kid was called *What Is the Name of This Book?* It was stuffed full of crazy word games that often exploited, like the title, the implications of self-reference.

I have learnt not to be surprised by sentences formed in natural lan-guage that give rise to paradoxes like the one captured by the circular logic of the two sentences on my cracker card. Just because you can form meaningful sentences doesn't mean there is a way to assign truth values to the sentences that makes sense.

I think the slippery nature of language is one of the reasons that I was drawn towards the certainties of mathematics, where this sort of ambiguity was not tolerated. But as I shall explain in this Edge, my cracker paradox was used by one of the greatest mathematical logicians of all time, Kurt Gödel, to prove that even my own subject contains true statements about numbers that we will never be able to prove are true.

SCIENCE V. MATHS

This desire for certainty, to know – to really know – was one of the principal reasons that I chose mathematics over the other sciences.

In the sciences the things we think we know about the universe are models that match the data. To qualify as a scientific theory they must be models that can be falsified, proved wrong. The reason they survive – if they survive – is that all the evidence supports the model. If we discover new evidence that contradicts the model, we must change the model. By its very nature, a scientific theory is one that can potentially be thrown out. In which case, can we ever truly know we've got it right?

We thought the universe was static, but then new discoveries revealed that galaxies are racing away from us. We thought the universe was expanding at a rate that was slowing down, given the drag of gravity. Then we discovered that the expansion was accelerating. We modelled this with the idea of dark energy pushing the universe apart. That model waits to be falsified, even if it gains in credibility as more evidence is collected. Eventually, we may well hit on the right model of the universe, which won't be rocked by further revelations. But we'll never know for sure that we have got the right model.

This is one of the exciting things about science: it is constantly evolving – there are always new stories. We can feel rather sorry for the old stories that fade into irrelevance. Of course, the new stories grow out of the old. As a scientist you live with the fear that your theory may be flavour of the moment, winner of prizes, and then suddenly it is superseded. Plum pudding models of the atom, the idea of absolute time ticking away, particles having identifiable positions and momentum: these are no longer top of the science bestseller list. They have been replaced by new stories.

The model of the universe I read about as a schoolkid has been completely rewritten. The same cannot be said of the mathematical theorems I learned. They are as true now as the day I first read them and as true as the day they were first discovered. Sometimes that day was as long as 2000 years ago. As an insecure spotty teenager, I found the certainty it promised particularly attractive. That's not to say that mathematics is static. It is constantly growing as unknowns become known, but those knowns remain known and robust, and become the first pages in the next great story. Why is the process of attaining mathematical truth so different from that faced by the scientist who can never really know?

The all-important ingredient in the mathematician's cupboard is proof.

PROOF: THE PATH TO TRUTH

There is evidence of people doing maths as far back as the second millennium BC. Clay tablets in Babylon and papyri in Egypt show sophisticated calculations and puzzles being solved: estimates for π; the formula for a volume of a pyramid; algorithms being applied to solve quadratic equations. But in general these documents tell of procedures that can be applied to particular problems to derive solutions. We don't find justification for why these procedures should always work, beyond the convincing evidence that it's worked in the thousands of examples that have been documented in the clay tablets to date. Mathematical knowledge was based on experience and had a more scientific flavour to it. Procedures were adapted if a problem cropped up that wasn't amenable to the current algorithm.

Then around the fifth century BC things began to change as the ancient Greeks got their teeth into the subject. The algorithms come with arguments to justify why they will always do what it says on the tin or tablet. It isn't simply that it's worked the last thousand times, so it will probably work the next time: the argument explains why the proposal will always work. The idea of proof was born.

Thales of Miletus is credited with being the first known author of a mathematical proof. He proved that if you take any point on the circumference of a circle and join that point to the two ends of a diagonal across the circle, then the angle you've created is an exact right angle. It doesn't matter which circle you choose or what point on the circle you take, the angle is always a right angle. Not approximately, and not because it seems to work for all the examples you've drawn. But because it is a consequence of the properties of circles and lines.

Thales' proof takes a reader from things they are confident are true and by a clever series of logical moves arrives at this new point of knowledge, which is not one that you would necessarily think obvious just from looking at a circle. The trick is to draw a third line going from the initial point B on the circle to the centre of the circle at O.

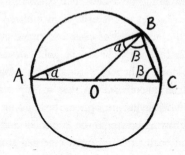

Why does this help? Now you have two triangles with two sides of equal length. This means that in both triangles the two angles opposite the centre of the circle are equal. This is something that has already been proved about such triangles. Take the larger triangle you originally drew. Its angles add up to 2α + 2β. Combine this with knowledge that a triangle has angles adding up to 180 degrees, and we know that α + β must be 90 degrees, just as Thales asserted.

When I first saw this proof as a kid it gave me a real thrill. I could see from the pictures that the angle on the circle's edge looked like a right angle. But how could I know for sure? My mind searched for some reason why it must be true. And then as I turned the page and saw the third line Thales drew to the centre of the circle, and took in the logical implications that flowed from that, I suddenly understood with thunderous clarity why that angle must indeed be 90 degrees.

Note that already in this proof you see how the mathematical edifice is raised on top of things that have already been proved, things like the angles in a triangle adding up to 180 degrees. Thales' discovery in turn becomes a new block on which to build the next layer of the mathematical edifice.

Thales' proof is one of the many to appear in Euclid's *Elements*, the book which many regard as the template for what mathematics and proof are all about. The book begins with basic building blocks, axioms, statements of geometry that seem so blindingly obvious that you are prepared to accept them as secure foundations on which to start building logical arguments.

The idea of proof wasn't created in isolation, out of nowhere. Rather, it emerged alongside a new style of writing that developed in ancient Greece. The art of rhetoric, as formulated by the likes of Aristotle, provided a new form of discourse aimed at persuading an audience. Whether in a legal context or political setting, or simply the narrative of a story, audiences were taken on a logical journey as the speaker attempted to convince listeners of his position. The mathematics of Egypt and Babylon grew out of the building and measuring of the new cities growing up round the Euphrates and Nile. This new need for logic and rhetorical argument emerged from the political institutions of the flourishing city-states at the heart of the Greek empire.

Rhetoric for Aristotle was a combination of pure logic and methods designed to work on the emotions of the audience. Mathematical proof taps into the first of these. But proof is also about storytelling. And this is why the development of proof at this time and place was probably as much to do with the sophisticated narratives constructed by the likes of the dramatists Sophocles and Euripides, as with the philosophical dialogues of Aristotle and Plato.

In turn, the mathematical explorations of the Greeks moved beyond functional algorithms for building and surveying to surprising discoveries that were more like mathematical tales to excite a reader.

A proof is a logical story that takes a reader from a place they know to a new, unvisited destination. Like Frodo's adventures in Tolkien's *Lord of the Rings*, a proof is a description of the journey from the Shire to Mordor. Within the boundaries of the familiar land of the Shire are the axioms of mathematics, the self-evident truths about numbers, together with those propositions that have already been proved. This is the setting for the beginning of the quest. The journey from this home territory is bound by the rules of mathematical deduction, like the legitimate moves of a chess piece, prescribing the steps you are permitted to take through this world. At times you arrive at what looks like an impasse and need to take a lateral step, moving sideways or even backwards to find a way around. Sometimes you need to wait for new mathematical characters like imaginary numbers or the calculus to be created so you can continue your journey. The proof is the story of the journey and the map charting the coordinates of that journey. The mathematician's log.

To earn its place in the mathematical canon it isn't enough that the journey produce a true statement about numbers or geometry. It needs to surprise, delight, move the reader. It should contain drama and jeopardy. Mathematics is distinct from the collection of true statements about numbers, just as literature is not the set of all possible combinations of words or music all possible combinations of notes. Mathematics involves aesthetic judgement and choice. And this is probably why the art of the mathematical proof grew out of a period when the act of storytelling was flourishing. Proof probably owes as much to the pathos of Aristotle's rhetoric as to its logos.

NUMBERS AT THE EDGE

While many of the first geometric proofs are constructive, the ancient Greeks also used their new mathematical tools to prove that certain things are impossible, beyond knowledge. The discovery, as we saw, that the square root of 2 cannot be written as a fraction is a striking example.

The proof has a very narrative quality to it, taking the reader on a journey under the assumption that the length can be written as a fraction. As the story innocently unfolds, one gets sucked further and further down the rabbit hole until finally a completely absurd conclusion is reached: odd numbers are even and vice versa. The moral of the tale is that the imaginary fraction representing this length must be an illusion. (If you would like to take a trip down the rabbit hole, the story is reproduced in the box on page 370.)

For those who encountered a number like the square root of 2 for the first time, it must have seemed like something that by its nature was beyond full knowledge. To know a number was to write it down, to express it in terms of numbers you knew. But here was a number that seemed to defy any attempt to record its value.

Proof of the irrationality of the square root of 2

Let L be the length of the hypotenuse of a right-angled triangle whose short sides are both of length 1 unit. Pythagoras' theorem implies that a square placed on the hypotenuse will have the same area as the sum of the area of squares placed on the two smaller sides. But these smaller squares each have area 1 while the larger square has area L^2. Therefore L is a number which when you square it gives you 2.

Suppose L is actually equal to a fraction $L = p/q$.

We can assume that one of p or q is odd. If they are both even we can keep dividing both top and bottom by 2 until one of the numbers becomes odd.

Since $L^2 = 2$, it follows that $p^2/q^2 = 2$.

Multiply both sides by q^2: $p^2 = 2 \times q^2$.

So is p odd or even? Well p^2 is even so p must be even because odd times odd is still odd. So $p = 2 \times n$ for some number n. Since p is even that means that q must be the odd number. But hold on . . .

$$2 \times q^2 = p^2 = (2 \times n)^2 = 2 \times 2 \times n^2,$$

so we can divide both sides of the equation by 2 to get

$$q^2 = 2 \times n^2.$$

Remember that we'd worked out that q was the odd number.

So q^2 is also odd. But the right-hand side of this equation is an even number! So if L is expressible as a fraction it would imply that odd = even. That's clearly absurd, so our original assumption that L can be written as a fraction must have been false.

I think this is one of the most stunning proofs in mathematics. With just a finite piece of logical argument we have shown there is a length that needs infinity to express it.

It was an extraordinary moment in the history of mathematics: the creation of a genuinely new sort of number. You could have taken the position that the equation $x^2 = 2$ doesn't have any solutions. At the time, the numbers that were known could not solve this equation precisely. Indeed, it was really only in the nineteenth century that sufficiently sophisticated mathematics was developed to make sense of such a number. And yet you felt it did exist. You could see it – there it was, the length of the side of a triangle. Eventually mathematicians took the bold step of adding new sorts of numbers to our mathematical toolkit so that we could solve these equations.

There have been other equations that seemed to defy solution, where the answer was not as visible as the square root of 2, and yet we've managed to create solutions. Solving the equation $x + 3 = 1$ looks easy from our modern perspective: $x = -2$. But for the Greeks there was no number that solved this. Diophantus refers to this sort of equation as absurd. For mathematicians like Diophantus, numbers were geometrical: they were real things that existed, lengths of lines. There was no line such that if you extended it by three units it would be one unit in length.

Other cultures were not so easily defeated by such an equation. In ancient China numbers counted money and money often involved debt. There certainly could be a circumstance in which I add 3 coins to my purse, only to find I have 1 coin left. A debt to a friend could be responsible for swallowing 2 of the coins. In 200 BC Chinese mathematicians depicted their numbers using red sticks; but if they represented debts, they used black sticks. This is the origin of the term going into the red, although somewhere along the line the colours got swapped.

It was the Indians in the seventh century AD who successfully developed a theory of negative numbers. In particular, Brahmagupta deduced some of the important mathematical properties of these numbers: for example, that 'a debt multiplied by a debt is a fortune', or minus times minus is plus. (Interestingly, this isn't a rule, it's a consequence of the axioms of mathematics. It is a fun challenge to prove why this must be so.) It took Europeans till the fifteenth century to be convinced that there were numbers that could solve these sorts of equations. Indeed, the use of negative numbers was even banned in thirteenth-century Florence.

New numbers continued to appear, especially when mathematicians were faced with the problem of solving an equation like $x^2 = -1$.

At first sight, it seems impossible. After all, if I take a positive number and square it, the answer is positive, and, as Brahmagupta proved, a negative number squared is also positive. When mathematicians in the Renaissance encountered this equation, their first reaction was to assume it was impossible to solve. Then Italian mathematician Rafael Bombelli took the radical step of supposing there was a new number that had a square equal to -1, and he found that he could use this new number to solve a whole host of equations that had been thought unsolvable. Interestingly, this imaginary number would sometimes be needed only in the intermediate calculations and would disappear from the final answer, leaving ordinary numbers that people were familiar with that clearly solved the equation at hand.

It was like mathematical alchemy, but many refused to admit Bombelli's new numbers into the canon of mathematics. Descartes wrote about them in a rather derogatory manner, dismissing them as imaginary numbers. As time went on, more mathematicians realized their power but also the fact that they didn't seem to give rise to any contradictions in mathematics if they were admitted. It wasn't until the beginning of the nineteenth century that they truly found their place in mathematics, thanks in part to a picture which helped mathematicians to visualize these imaginary numbers.

The ordinary numbers (or what mathematicians now call the real numbers) were laid out along the number line running horizontally across the page. The imaginary numbers like i, the name given to the square root of -1, were pictured on the vertical axis. This two-dimensional picture of the imaginary or complex numbers was instrumental in the acceptance of these new numbers. The potency of this picture was demonstrated by the discovery that the geometry of the picture reflected the arithmetic of the numbers.

So are there even more numbers out there beyond the edge that we haven't yet discovered? I might try writing down more strange equations in the hope that I get more new numbers. For example, what about the equation $x^4 = -1$?

Perhaps to solve this equation I'll need even more new numbers. But one of the great theorems of the nineteenth century, now called the fundamental theorem of algebra, proved that, using the imaginary number i and the real numbers, I can solve any equation I want. For example, if I take

$$x = \frac{1}{\sqrt{2}} + \frac{1}{\sqrt{2}} i$$

and raise it to the power of 4, then the answer is −1. The edge had been reached beyond which no new numbers would be found by trying to solve equations.

PROVABLY IMPOSSIBLE

The ancient Greek proof of the irrationality of the square root of 2 was the first of many in mathematics to show that certain things are impossible. Another proof of the impossible was the concept of 'squaring the circle'. Indeed the mathematical idea of squaring the circle has entered many languages as an expression of impossibility. Squaring the circle relates to the geometric challenges that the ancient Greeks enjoyed trying to crack, using a ruler (without measurements) and a compass (for making arcs of circles). They discovered clever ways to use these tools to draw perfect equilateral triangles, pentagons and hexagons.

Squaring the circle consists of trying to use these tools to construct from a given circle a square whose area is the same as that of the circle you started with. Try as hard as the Greeks could, the problem stumped them. A similarly impossible challenge was posed by the oracle of the island of Delos. Residents of the Greek island had consulted the oracle to get advice about how to defeat a plague that the god Apollo had sent down upon them. The oracle replied that they must double the size of the altar to Apollo. The altar was a perfect cube. Plato interpreted this as a challenge to construct, using straight edge and compass, a second perfect cube whose volume was double the volume of the first cube.

If the second cube is double the volume of the first, this means the sides have lengths which are the cube root of 2 times the length of the first cube. The challenge therefore was to construct a length equal to the cube root of 2. Constructing the square root of 2 was easy since it arises as the diagonal of a unit square; but the cube root of 2 turned out to be so difficult that the residents of Delos could not solve the problem. Perhaps the oracle wanted to distract the Delians with geometry and mathematics as a way of diverting their attention away from the more pressing social problems they faced.

Doubling the cube, squaring the circle, and a third classical problem of trisecting the angle all turned out to be impossible. But it took until the nineteenth century before mathematicians could prove beyond doubt that there was no way to do these things. It was the development of group theory – a language for understanding symmetry that I use in my own research – that held the key to proving the impossibility of these geometric constructions. It turns out that the only lengths that can be constructed by ruler and compass are those that are solutions to certain types of algebraic equation.

In the case of squaring the circle, the challenge requires you to produce, using ruler and compass, a straight line of length $\sqrt{\pi}$ starting from a line of unit length. But it was proved in 1882 that π is not only an irrational number but also a transcendental number, which means it isn't the solution to any algebraic equation. This in turn means that it is impossible to square the circle.

Mathematics is remarkably good at proving when things are impossible. One of the most celebrated theorems on the mathematical books is Fermat's Last Theorem, which states that it is impossible to find any whole numbers that will solve any of the equations

$$x^n + y^n = z^n,$$

where n is greater than 2. This is in contrast to the case of $n = 2$, which corresponds to the equation Pythagoras produced from his right-angled triangles. If $n = 2$, there are many solutions, for example $3^2 + 4^2 = 5^2$. In fact, there are infinitely many solutions, and the ancient Greeks found a formula to produce them all. But it is often a much easier task to find solutions than to prove that you will never find numbers which satisfy any of Fermat's equations.

Fermat famously thought he had a solution but scribbled in the margin of his copy of Diophantus' *Arithmetica* that the margin was too small for his remarkable proof. It took another 350 years before my Oxford colleague Andrew Wiles finally produced a convincing argument to explain why you will never find whole numbers that solve Fermat's equations. Wiles's proof runs to over one hundred pages, in addition to the thousands of pages of preceding theory that it is built on. So even a very wide margin wouldn't have sufficed.

The proof of Fermat's Last Theorem is a tour de force. I regard it as a privilege to have been alive when the final pieces of the proof were put in place.

Before Wiles had shown the impossibility of finding a solution, there was always the prospect that maybe there were some sneaky numbers out there that did solve one of these equations. I remember a great April fool that went round the mathematical community around the same time as Wiles announced his proof. The joke was that a respected number theorist in Harvard, Noam Elkies, had produced a non-constructive proof that such solutions existed. It was a cleverly worded April fool email because the 'non-constructive' bit meant he couldn't explicitly say what the numbers were that solved Fermat's equations, just that his proof implied there must be solutions. The great thing is that most people were forwarded the email several days after 1 April, when the joke first started its rounds, and so had no clue that it was an April fool.

April fool or not, the mathematical community had spent 350 years not knowing whether there was a solution or not. We didn't know. But finally Wiles put us out of our misery. His proof means that however many numbers I try, I'll never find three that make one of Fermat's equations true.

RUNNING OUT OF NEURONS

We are living in a golden age of mathematics, during which some of the great unsolved problems have finally been cracked. In 2003 one of the great challenges of geometry, the Poincaré conjecture, was proved by the Russian mathematician Grigori Perelman. But there are still many statements about numbers and equations whose proofs elude us: the Riemann hypothesis, the twin primes conjecture, the Birch–Swinnerton-Dyer conjecture, Goldbach's conjecture.

In my own research I have dedicated the last twenty years trying to settle whether something called the PORC conjecture is true or not. This was formulated over fifty years ago by Oxford mathematician Graham Higman, who believed that the number of symmetry groups with a given number of symmetries should be given by nice polynomial equations (which is what the P in PORC stands for). For example, the number of symmetry groups with p^6 symmetries, where p is a prime number, is given by a quadratic expression in p: it is $p^2 + 39p + c$ (where c is a constant that depends on the remainder you get on dividing p by 60).

My own research has cast real doubts on whether this conjecture is true. I discovered a symmetrical object with p^9 symmetries whose behaviour suggests something very different to what was predicted by Higman's conjecture. But it doesn't completely solve the problem. There is still a chance that other symmetrical objects with p^9 symmetries could smooth out the strange behaviour I unearthed, leaving Higman's conjecture true. So, at the moment, I don't know whether this conjecture is true or not, and Higman, alas, died before he could know. I am desperate to know before my finite life comes to an end, and it is questions like this that drive me in my mathematical research.

I sometimes wonder, as I get lost in the seemingly infinite twists and turns of my research, whether my brain will ever have the capacity to crack the problem I am working on. In fact, mathematics can be used to prove that there are mathematical challenges that are beyond the physical limitations of the human brain, with its 86 billion neurons connected by over 100 trillion synapses.

Mathematics is infinite. It goes on forever. Unlike chess, which has an estimated $10^{10^{50}}$ different games that are possible, the provable statements of mathematics are infinite in number. In chess, pieces get taken, games are won, and sequences are repeated. Mathematics, though, doesn't have an endgame, which means that even if I get my 86 billion neurons firing as fast as they physically can, there are only a finite number of logical steps that I will be able to make in my lifetime, and therefore only a finite amount of mathematics that I can ever know. What if my PORC conjecture needs more logical steps to prove than I will ever manage in my lifetime?

Even if we turned the whole universe into a big computer, there are limits to what it could ever know. In his paper 'Computational Capacity of the Universe', Seth Lloyd calculates that since the Big Bang the universe cannot have performed more than 10^{120} operations on a maximum of 10^{90} bits. At any point in time the universe can only know a finite amount of mathematics. You might ask: what is the universe calculating? It's actually computing its own dynamical evolution. Although this is a huge number, it is still finite. It means that we can prove computationally that at any point in time there will always be things that the observable universe will not know.

But it turns out that mathematics has an even deeper layer of unknown. Even if we had a computer with infinite capacity and speed, there are things it will never know. A theorem proved in the twentieth century has raised the horrific possibility that even a computer with this infinite capacity may never know whether my PORC conjecture is true. Called Gödel's incompleteness theorem, it shook mathematics to the core. It may be that these conjectures are true, but they will always be beyond our ability to prove within our axiomatic framework for mathematics. Gödel proved that within any axiomatic framework for mathematics there are mathematically true statements that we will never be able to prove are true within that framework. A mathematical proof that there are things that are beyond proof – mathematics beyond the edge.

When I learned about this theorem at university, it had a profound effect on me. Despite the physical limitations of my brain or the universe's brain, I think I grew up with the comforting belief that at least theoretically there was a proof out there that would demonstrate whether my PORC conjecture was true or not, or whether the Riemann hypothesis was true or not. One of my mathematical heroes, the Hungarian Paul Erdős, used to talk affectionately about proofs from 'The Book'. This was where Erdős believed God kept the most elegant proofs of each mathematical theorem. The challenge for a mathematician is to uncover the proofs in The Book. As Erdős joked in a lecture he gave in 1985: 'You don't have to believe in God, but you should believe in

The Book.' Erdős himself doubted the existence of God, dubbing him the Supreme Fascist responsible for hiding his socks and Hungarian passport. But I think most mathematicians accepted the metaphor of The Book. However, the proof I learned about in my university course on mathematical logic proved that there were pages missing from The Book, pages that even the Supreme Fascist did not possess.

PARALLEL UNIVERSES

The revelation that there were mathematical statements beyond the limits of proof was sparked by the realization that one of the geometric statements Euclid had used as an axiom was actually not as axiomatic as had been thought.

An axiom is a premise or starting point for any logical train of thought. In general, an axiom is meant to express some self-evident truth that is accepted as true without the need for proof. For example, I believe that if I take two numbers, then no matter in what order I add them together, I get the same answer. If I take 36 and add 43, I won't get a different answer if I start with 43 and add 36. You might ask how I know that this will always be true. Perhaps something weird happens if I take really large numbers of things and add them together. What mathematics does is to make deductions about numbers which do satisfy this rule. If the way we count things in the universe does something weird, we just have to accept that the mathematics that we have developed from this axiom is not applicable to the way physical numbers work in the universe. We would then develop a new number theory based on numbers that satisfy a different fundamental set of axioms.

Although many of the axioms that Euclid used to deduce his theory of geometry seemed self-evident truths about the geometry of the universe, there was one that mathematicians increasingly thought a bit suspicious.

The parallel postulate states that if you have a line and a point off that line then there is a unique line through the point which is parallel to the first line. This postulate certainly seems obvious if you are drawing geometry on a flat page. It is one of the axioms that is crucial to Euclid's proof that triangles have angles that add up to 180 degrees. Certainly any geometry in which the parallel postulate is true will give rise to triangles with this property. But the discovery in the nineteenth century of new sorts of geometry with no parallel lines, or with many lines that could be drawn parallel, led mathematicians to the realization that Euclid's geometry was just one of a whole host of different geometries that were possible.

For example, if I take the surface of a sphere – a curved geometry – then lines confined to this surface are not straight but bend. Take two points on the surface of the Earth, then, as anyone who has flown across the Atlantic knows, the shortest path between these two points won't match the line you would draw on a flat atlas. This is because the line between these two points is part of a circle like a line of longitude that divides the sphere perfectly in half. Indeed, if one of the points is a North or South Pole then the line would be a line of longitude. All lines in this geometry are just lines of longitude that are moved round the surface so that they pass through the two points you are interested in. They are called great circles. But now if I take a third point off this great circle there is no way to arrange another great circle through the third point that doesn't intersect the first circle. So here is a geometry that doesn't have parallel lines.

Consequently, any proof which depends on the parallel postulate won't necessarily be true in this new geometry. Take the proof that angles in a triangle add up to 180 degrees. This statement depends on the geometry satisfying the parallel postulate. But this spherical geometry doesn't. And indeed this geometry contains triangles whose angles add up to more than 180 degrees. Take the North Pole and two points

A triangle whose angles add up to more than 180 degrees.

on the equator and form a triangle through these three points. Already the two angles at the equator total 180 degrees, so the total of all three angles will be greater than 180 degrees.

Other geometries were discovered in which there was not just one but many parallel lines through a point. In these geometries, called hyperbolic, triangles have angles adding up to less than 180 degrees. These discoveries didn't invalidate any of the proofs of Euclid. This is a great example of why mathematical breakthroughs only enrich rather than destroy previous knowledge. But the introduction of these new geometries in the early nineteenth century nonetheless caused something of a stir. Indeed, some mathematicians felt that a geometry that didn't satisfy Euclid's axiom about parallel lines must contain some contradiction that would lead to it being thrown out as impossible. But further investigation revealed that any contradiction inherent in these new geometries would imply a contradiction at the heart of Euclidean geometry.

Such a thought was heretical. Euclidean geometry had stood the test of time and not produced contradictions for 2000 years. But hold on . . . this is beginning to sound like the way we do science. Surely mathematics should be able to prove that Euclidean geometry won't give rise to contradictions. We shouldn't just rely on the fact that it's worked up to this point, therefore we should believe everything's OK. That's how the scientists in the labs across the road work. We mathematicians should be able to prove that our subject is free of contradictions.

WHAT IS THE NAME OF THIS SECTION?

When, at the end of the nineteenth century, mathematical set theory produced strange results that seemingly led to unresolvable paradoxes, mathematicians began to take more seriously this need to prove our subject is free of contradictions. The British philosopher Bertrand Russell was the author of a number of these worrying paradoxes. He challenged the mathematical community with the set of all sets that don't contain themselves as members. The problem was whether this new set was a member of itself. The only way you are in this set is if you are a set which doesn't contain yourself as a member. But as soon as you put the set in as a member, suddenly it is (of course) a set which contains itself as a member. Aargh! There seemed no way to resolve this paradox, and yet the construction was not so far from sets that mathematicians might want to contemplate.

Russell came up with some more prosaic, homely examples of this sort of self-referential paradox. For example, he imagined an island on which a law decreed that the barber had to shave all those people who didn't shave themselves – and no one else. The trouble is that this law leads to a paradox: can the barber shave himself? No, since he is allowed only to shave those who don't shave themselves. But then he qualifies as someone who must be shaved by the barber. Aargh, again! The barber has taken the role of the set Russell was trying to define, the set of all those sets that don't contain themselves as members.

I think my favourite example of all these paradoxes is the puzzle of describing numbers. Suppose you consider all the numbers that can be defined using fewer than 20 words taken from the *Oxford English Dictionary*. For example, 1729 can be defined as 'the smallest number that can be written as the sum of two cubes in two different ways'. Since there are only finitely many words in the *Oxford English Dictionary* and we can use only a maximum of 20 words, we can't define every number in this way since there are infinitely many numbers and only finitely many sentences with fewer than 20 words. So there is a number which is defined as follows: 'the smallest number which cannot be defined in fewer than 20 words from the *Oxford English Dictionary*'. But hold on . . . I just defined it in fewer than 20 words. Aargh!

Natural language is prone to throw up paradoxical statements. Just putting words together doesn't mean they make sense or have a truth value. But the worrying aspect to Russell's set of all sets that don't contain themselves is that it is very close to the sorts of things we might want to define mathematically.

Mathematicians eventually found ways around this paradoxical situation, which required refining the intuitive idea of a set, but it still left a worrying taste in the mouth. How many other surprises were hiding inside the mathematical edifice? When the great German mathematician David Hilbert was asked to address the International Congress of

Mathematicians in 1900, he decided to set out the 23 greatest unsolved problems facing mathematicians in the twentieth century. Proving that mathematics was free of contradictions was second on his list.

In his speech, Hilbert boldly declared what many believed to be the mantra of mathematics: 'This conviction of the solvability of every mathematical problem is a powerful incentive to the worker. We hear within us the perpetual call. There is the problem. Seek its solution. You can find it by pure reason, for in mathematics there is no *ignorabimus*.' In mathematics there is nothing that we cannot know. A bold statement indeed.

Hilbert was reacting to a growing movement at the end of the nineteenth century that held that there were limits to our ability to understand the universe. The distinguished physiologist Emil du Bois-Reymond had addressed the Berlin Academy in 1880, outlining what he regarded as seven riddles about nature that he believed were beyond knowledge, declaring them '*ignoramus et ignorabimus*'. Things we do not know and will never know.

In the light of my attempt to understand what questions may be beyond knowledge, it is interesting to compare my list with the seven riddles presented by du Bois-Reymond:

1. The ultimate nature of matter and force
2. The origin of motion
3. The origin of life
4. The apparent teleological arrangements of nature
5. The origins of simple sensations
6. The origins of intelligent thought and language
7. The question of free will.

Du Bois-Reymond believed that 1, 2 and 5 were truly transcendent. The first two are very much still at the heart of the questions we considered in the first few Edges. The teleological arrangement of nature refers to the question of why the universe seems so fine-tuned for life, something that still vexes us today. The idea of the multiverse is our best answer to this riddle. The last three were the subject of the previous Edge, which probed the limits of the human mind. Only the riddle with the origin of life is perhaps one that we have made some headway on. Despite amazing scientific progress in the last 100 years, the other six problems are still potentially beyond the limits of knowledge, just as du Bois-Reymond believed.

But Hilbert was not going to admit mathematical statements to the list of du Bois-Reymond's riddles. Thirty years later, on 7 September 1930, when Hilbert returned to his home town of Königsberg to be made an honorary citizen, he ended his acceptance speech with the clarion call to mathematicians:

> For the mathematician there is no *Ignorabimus*, and, in my opinion, not at all for natural science either . . . The true reason why no one has succeeded in finding an unsolvable problem is, in my opinion, that there is no unsolvable problem. In contrast to the foolish *Ignorabimus*, our credo avers: *Wir müssen wissen. Wir werden wissen.* [We must know. We shall know.]

However, Hilbert was unaware of the startling announcement that had been made at a conference in the same town of Königsberg the day before the ceremony. Mathematics does contain *ignorabimus*. A twenty-five-year-old Austrian logician by the name of Kurt Gödel had proved that it was impossible to prove whether mathematics was free of contradictions. And he went even further. Within any axiomatic framework for mathematics, there will be true statements about numbers that you can't prove are true within that framework. Hilbert's clarion call – '*Wir müssen wissen. Wir werden wissen*' – would eventually find its rightful place: on Hilbert's gravestone. Mathematics would have to face up to the revelation that it too had riddles that we would never be able to solve.

THE NEXT SENTENCE IS FALSE

The title of this section is true.

It was self-referential statements like the one I found in my cracker last Christmas that Gödel tapped in to for his devastating proof that mathematics had its limitations.

Although sentences in natural language might throw up paradoxes, when it comes to statements about numbers, we expect a statement to be either true or false. Gödel was intrigued by the question of whether you could exploit the idea of self-reference in mathematical statements. Hilbert's challenge already had an element of self-reference built in: he wanted to construct a mathematically secure argument to prove that mathematics was without contradictions. The challenge already demanded that mathematics look in on itself to prove that it wouldn't suddenly give rise to proofs that two contradictory statements were true.

Gödel wanted to show that within any axiom system for number theory there would always be true statements about numbers which couldn't be proved from these axioms. It's worth pointing out that you can try to set up different sets of axioms to try to capture how numbers work. Hilbert's hope was that mathematicians could construct one axiom system from which we could prove all truths of mathematics. Gödel found a way to scupper this hope.

The clever trick that Gödel played was to produce a code that assigned to every meaningful statement about numbers its own code number. A similar idea is already at work as I sit typing. The words that I am using to tell Gödel's story are being converted into strings of numbers which represent the letters I am typing. For example, in decimal ASCII, Gödel becomes the number 71246100101108. The advantage of the coding Gödel cooked up is that it would allow mathematics to talk about itself.

According to Gödel's code, any axioms we choose to capture the theory of numbers – the statements from which we deduce the theorems of mathematics – will each have their own code number. For example, the axiom 'if $A = C$ and $B = C$, then $A = B$' has its own code number. But statements that can be deduced from these axioms like 'there exist infinitely many primes' will also have their own code number. Even false statements like '17 is an even number' will have a code number.

These code numbers allowed Gödel to talk in the language of number theory about whether a particular statement is provable within the system. The basic idea is to set up the code in such a way that a statement is provable if its code number is divisible by the code numbers of the axioms. It's much more complicated than that, but this will be a helpful simplification.

Gödel could now talk about whether a statement is provable or not from the axioms just as a statement about numbers. To express the fact that 'The statement "there exist infinitely many primes" can be proved from the axioms of number theory' translates into 'the code number of the statement "there exist infinitely many primes" is divisible by the code numbers of the axioms of number theory' – a purely mathematical statement about numbers which is either true or false.

Hold on to your hats as I take you on the logical twists and turns of Gödel's proof . . . Gödel decided to consider the statement S: 'This statement is not provable.' Statement S has a code number. But if we analyse the content of statement S, it translates into a statement simply about whether the code number of this sentence S is not divisible by the code numbers of the axioms. Let us suppose that the axiomatic system for number theory that we are analysing doesn't lead to contradictions – as Hilbert hoped.

Thanks to Gödel's coding, S is simply a statement about numbers. Either the code number of S is divisible by the code numbers of the axioms or it isn't. It must either be true or false. It can't be both, or it would contradict our assumption that the system doesn't lead to contradictions.

Suppose there is a proof of S from the axioms of number theory. This implies that the code number of S is divisible by the code number of the axioms. But a provable statement is true. If we now analyse the meaning of S, this gives us the statement that the code number of S is not divisible by the axioms. A contradiction. But we are assuming that mathematics doesn't have contradictions. Unlike my Christmas cracker paradox, there has to be a way out of this logical conundrum.

The way to resolve this is to realize that our original assumption is false: we can't prove S is true from the axioms of number theory. But that is exactly what S states. So S is true. We have managed to prove that Gödel's statement S is a true statement that can't be proved true from the axioms.

The proof may remind you of the way we proved the square root of 2 was irrational. First, suppose it isn't. This leads to a contradiction. So root 2 must be irrational after all. The proofs of both results rests on the important assumption that the axioms of number theory don't lead to contradictions. One of the striking consequences of Gödel's proof is that there is no way of rescuing mathematics by adding one of these unprovable statements as an axiom. You may think that if the statement S is true but unprovable, why not just make it an axiom and then maybe all true statements are provable? Gödel's proof shows why, however many axioms you add to the system, there will always be true statements left over that can't be proved.

Don't worry if your head is spinning a bit from this logical dance that Gödel has taken us on. Despite having studied the theorem many times, I'm always left a bit dizzy by the end of the proof – the implications are amazing. Gödel proved mathematically that within any axiomatic framework for number theory that was free of contradictions there were true statements about numbers that could not be proved to be true within that framework – a mathematical proof that mathematics has its limitations. The intriguing thing is that it's not that the statement S is unknowable. We've actually proved that it is true. It's just that we've had to work outside the particular axiomatic framework for mathematics that we have demonstrated has limits. What Gödel showed is that it can't be proved true within that framework.

Gödel used this already devastating revelation, called Gödel's first incompleteness theorem, to kill off Hilbert's hope of a mathematical proof that mathematics was free of contradictions. Gödel proved that 'this statement is not provable' is true under the hypothesis that mathematics has no contradictions. If you could prove mathematically that there were no contradictions, this could be used to give a proof within mathematics that the statement 'this statement is not provable' is true. But that is a contradiction because it says it can't be proved. So any proof that mathematics is free of contradictions would inevitably lead to a contradiction. We are back to our self-referential statements again. The only way out of this was to accept that we cannot prove mathematically that mathematics is free of contradictions. This is known as Gödel's second incompleteness theorem. Much to Hilbert's horror, it revealed *ignorabimus* at the heart of mathematics.

But mathematicians believe that mathematics is free of contradictions. If there were contradictions, how could we have come this far without the edifice collapsing? We call a theory consistent if it is free of contradictions. The French mathematician André Weil summed up the devastating implications of Gödel's work: 'God exists since mathematics is consistent, and the Devil exists since we cannot prove it.'

Did Gödel's revelations mean that mathematics was as open to falsification as any other scientific theory? We might have hit on the right model, but just as with a model for the universe or fundamental particles, we can't know that it might not suddenly fall to pieces under the weight of new evidence.

For some philosophers there was something attractive about the fact that although we cannot prove Gödel's statement S is true within the axiomatic system for number theory, we have at least proved it is true by working outside the system. It seemed to imply that the human brain was more than a mechanized computing machine for analysing the world mathematically. In a paper called 'Minds, Machines and Gödel', read to the Oxford Philosophical Society in 1959, philosopher John Lucas put forward the argument that if we modelled the mind as a machine following axioms and the deductive rules of arithmetic, then, as it churned away constructing proofs, at some point it would hit the sentence 'This statement is not provable' and would spend the rest of time trying to prove or refute it; and yet we as humans could see that it was undecidable by understanding the content of its meaning. 'So the machine will still not be an adequate model of the mind . . . which can always go one better than any formal, ossified, dead system can.'

It seems a very attractive argument. Who wouldn't want to believe that we humans are more than just a computational device, more than just an app installed on some biological hardware? In his recent research on consciousness, Roger Penrose used Lucas's argument as a platform for his belief that we need new physics to understand what makes the mind conscious. But although it is true that we acknowledge the truth of the statement 'this statement is not provable' by working outside the system, it is also under a huge assumption, which is that the system we are working within to prove the truth of this Gödel sentence is itself free of contradictions. And this is the content of Gödel's second incompleteness theorem: we can't prove it.

The sort of statement that Gödel cooked up that is true but unprovable may seem a little esoteric from a mathematical point of view. Surely the really interesting statements about numbers – the Riemann hypothesis, Goldbach's conjecture, the PORC conjecture – will not be unprovable? The hope that it would only be tortuous Gödelian sentences that would transcend proof turned out to be a false one. In 1977, mathematicians Jeff Paris and Leo Harrington came up with a bona fide mathematical statement about numbers that they could show was true but unprovable within the classical axiomatic set-up for number theory. But in the next chapter I will discover that, as mathematicians grappled with the idea of infinity, they discovered not only that some statements are unprovable, but also that it is impossible to tell whether they are true or false.

A JOKE

Having read this chapter and the Third Edge, you are now ready for one of the other jokes in my paradoxical Christmas crackers. The only other thing you need to know is that the American linguist and philosopher Noam Chomsky distinguished between linguistic competence (the linguistic knowledge possessed by a culture) and linguistic performance (the way the language is used in communication). The joke goes like this:

> Heisenberg, Gödel and Chomsky walk into a bar. Heisenberg looks around the bar and says, 'Because there are three of us and because this is a bar, it must be a joke. But the question remains, is it funny or not?'
>
> And Gödel thinks for a moment and says, 'Well, because we're inside the joke, we can't tell whether it is funny. We'd have to be outside looking at it.'
>
> And Chomsky looks at both of them and says, 'Of course it's funny. You're just telling it wrong.'

14

As I discovered in the Fourth Edge, in the physical universe that we inhabit there are limits to how far we can see, how far we can explore. However, I spend my life exploring not the physical universe but a mental universe of mathematical truths. Here I don't need telescopes, spaceships, microscopes. I have different tools for probing the limits of this world. For a start, the issue of whether it is infinite can be settled with the finite equipment inside my head. Mathematics provides us with a way to go beyond the barriers that stop us exploring the edges of the physical universe. There is no biggest number. I can always add 1 in the face of any attempt to wall in the universe of numbers. And by this simple finite act of adding 1, I have a way to construct infinite worlds of the mind.

But how much can I know about such infinite worlds? Are there limits to how far my finite neurological tools can navigate the truths in this infinite universe of numbers? Before the nineteenth century, 'infinity' was synonymous with 'beyond knowledge'. And yet ever since the ancient Greeks concocted the dark art of mathematics, we humans have been using our finite minds to navigate the infinite.

STARING OFF INTO INFINITY

Here is another of the mathematical jokes that burst out of our Christmas crackers:

Teacher: What's the biggest number?
Student: Seventy-three million and twelve.
Teacher: What about seventy-three million and thirteen?
Student: Well, I was close!

The ancient Greeks understood that numbers do not have an end, but this was different from knowing that infinity genuinely existed. Aristotle made the distinction between potential infinity and actual infinity. There is the potential to keep adding 1 to a number, but realizing an infinity of numbers is not possible. Nevertheless, it is striking how the Greeks were able to wield finite logical arguments to explore this potential infinity.

For example, one of the first great proofs of mathematics found in Euclid's *Elements* is the explanation that among the universe of numbers there is an infinite number of indivisible numbers, which we call prime numbers. Even today this proof gives me a frisson of excitement: the idea that something that outwardly looks infinite and intractable can nevertheless be understood.

You may ask: since you've admitted the possibility that numbers are unlimited, why should proving that there are infinitely many primes be so extraordinary? After all, knowing there are infinitely many even numbers is not so surprising once you have admitted that numbers go on forever. And yet it is the fact that we don't genuinely understand the nature of primes that makes the proof so surprising. It shows that the set of primes is infinite without being able to say where they are. The question of whether the physical universe is infinite might require a similar approach: a logical argument implying that it must go on forever without us physically being able to see it.

Despite the successes of the ancient Greeks, for millennia infinity has caused problems. Most regarded it as an expression of something beyond our comprehension. Thomas Aquinas, the thirteenth-century Christian theologian and philosopher, wrote:

The existence of an actual infinite multitude is impossible. For any
set of things one considers must be a specific set. And sets of things
are specified by the number of things in them. Now no number is

infinite, for number results from counting through a set of units.
So no set of things can actually be inherently unlimited, nor can it
happen to be unlimited.

Discussion of infinity was never too far removed from questions of theology. In the fifth century, St Augustine, the Christian philosopher, wrote in his most famous work, *City of God,* that infinity was reserved for the mind of God. He was dismissive of those who believed infinity was beyond even the mind of God:

> Such as say that things infinite are past God's knowledge may just as
> well leap headlong into this pit of impiety, and say that God knows
> not all numbers . . . What madman would say so? . . . What are we
> mean wretches that dare presume to limit his knowledge?

The medieval philosopher Oresme, who contemplated the idea that there might be infinite space beyond the celestial sphere that enclosed our universe, was also adept at manipulating mathematical infinities. He was the first to prove the startling fact that if you keep adding up the fractions $1 + \frac{1}{2} + \frac{1}{3} + \frac{1}{4} + \ldots$ the answer can be as big as you want. He was also one of the first to consider the idea that you might be able to compare the size of different infinities. After all, if you compare the infinity of all numbers and the infinity of even numbers then you could match every whole number with its double. Yet Oresme, given that the even numbers are clearly a smaller subset than all numbers, concluded that comparing infinities was a dangerous move.

For centuries many felt that arguments of this sort proved that infinity could not really exist. The fourteenth-century English cleric and mathematician Thomas Bradwardine had used a similar idea to prove that the world is not eternal. If the world was eternal, he argued, the number of female souls and the number of all souls would be infinite. If they were infinite, you could match them up. But that would leave no room for the male souls. Therefore an infinity of souls led to a contradiction.

Several centuries later, infinity is still tying mathematicians in knots. Galileo had similar problems to Oresme and Bradwardine when it came to contemplating the number of square numbers. On the one hand, there are clearly more numbers that are not square numbers than numbers that can be written as a square. The square numbers, 1, 4, 9, 16, 25, . . . , get sparser and sparser, with more non-squares appearing between each successive square. And yet wasn't every number the square root of some square number? So from this perspective every number could be paired with a square number, leading to the conclusion that there were the same number of squares as all numbers.

Like Oresme before him, Galileo was flummoxed by this. As he wrote in the *Two New Sciences*:

> The difficulties in the study of the infinite arise because we attempt, with our finite minds, to discuss the infinite, assigning to it those properties which we give to the finite and limited; but this . . . is wrong, for we cannot speak of infinite quantities as being the one greater or less than or equal to another.

It was shortly after Galileo's death that the now familiar symbol that represents infinity was introduced. The symbol ∞ was first used by the English mathematician John Wallis in 1655. He chose it to capture the idea that one could traverse the curve infinitely often.

For another two centuries mathematicians were happy with the idea of a potential infinity but not with the idea that infinity genuinely existed, which just seemed to cause too many problems. As the nineteenth-century mathematician Carl Friedrich Gauss wrote in a letter to his colleague Heinrich Christian Schumacher:

> I protest against the use of infinite magnitude as something completed, which is never permissible in mathematics. Infinity is merely a way of speaking.

INFINITY TAMED

Then, at the end of the nineteenth century, an intellectual shift occurred. Thanks to one man's finite brain, the infinite seemed to be within reach.

For Georg Cantor, infinity was not simply a way of speaking. It was a tangible mathematical object:

> The fear of infinity is a form of myopia that destroys the possibility
> of seeing the actual infinite, even though it in its highest form has
> created and sustains us, and in its secondary transfinite forms occurs
> all around us and even inhabits our minds.

At the end of the nineteenth century you might expect a separation between those practising science and those who were religious. And yet Georg Cantor was both, and he writes about religion influencing his mathematical ideas. In a similar vein to Bruno, who contemplated an infinite universe, Cantor's belief in God is the hypothesis from which he deduces that the infinite must exist.

> One proof is based on the notion of God. First, from the highest
> perfection of God, we infer the possibility of the creation of the
> transfinite, then, from his all-grace and splendour, we infer the
> necessity that the creation of the transfinite in fact has happened.

Cantor's proposal for navigating the infinite goes back to some of the ideas contemplated by Oresme. To say that two sets of things have the same size is to find some way to match up members from one set with members of the second set, such that each member has a pair in the other set.

Cantor's approach to the infinite was to think of mathematicians like a tribe who had names for the numbers 1, 2, 3, but beyond that every number was just called 'lots', the tribe's version of infinity. Two tribes that meet but do not have names for numbers beyond three are still able to compare sizes and judge whose tribe is the bigger. Members of the first tribe pair up with members of the second tribe, and whichever tribe has people unpaired has the biggest 'lots'. If the tribes match up exactly, then their 'lots' have the same size.

This is a good description of the mathematics of the animal kingdom: animals probably don't have names for numbers but can still judge whose group is the biggest. Developing a sense of size is key to their survival. If one group of animals encounters another group, they need to assess quickly if their group is bigger or smaller than the group they are facing. Bigger they fight, smaller they flee. But they don't need names for the numbers to make that comparison. By a process of matching members of each group, they know that if one group is left with members unpaired, it is bigger.

Using the idea of pairing objects, Cantor was able to propose a way of declaring whether two infinite sets were numerically identical or not. For example, you might be tempted to declare that there are half as many even numbers as there are all numbers. However, Cantor showed, just as Oresme had suggested, that there is a way to line up both sets of numbers so that each number has its pair. For example, 1 gets paired with 2, 2 with 4, 3 with 6, and n with $2n$. So these two sets have the same size. The tribe that arrives with even numbers on their backs will be able to hold its own against a tribe that is numbered with all numbers. These infinite sets are identical in size.

This is similar to the arguments that Oresme and Galileo proposed, and yet both were disturbed by the fact that from another perspective the even numbers or square numbers are a subset of all numbers and should in some sense be the smaller set. Cantor believed that you just had to find one way to pair the sets up to deem them equal in size. For finite sets, if you tried pairing them up and couldn't do it, no re-ordering or rearranging would create a way of pairing everything up perfectly. But in the case of the infinite, Cantor saw that rearranging the order of a set might help you to find a new way to pair off sets so that nothing was left over.

The key for Cantor is that if there is one possible way to pair up both sets with nothing left over, then you can say they have the same size. There may be pairings that leave tribe members unpaired: for example, if I match only all the even numbers in each group, there are infinitely many odd numbers left unpaired. But for Cantor a set of numbers could be judged to be genuinely bigger only if there existed no possible way to pair them up without having leftovers.

For example, what about a set of numbers like the fractions? How big is that infinity? Cantor came up with an ingenious way to compare all whole numbers with all fractions and prove that both sets are identical in size. At first sight, this looks impossible: between each pair of whole numbers there are infinitely many fractions. But there is a way to match all whole numbers perfectly with all fractions so that no fractions are left unmatched.

It starts with a table containing all the fractions. The table has infinitely many rows and columns. The nth column consists of a list of all the fractions $1/n, 2/n, 3/n, \ldots$

How did Cantor pair up the whole numbers with the fractions in this table? The trick is, first of all, to wend a snake diagonally through the fractions in the table, as illustrated. Then, in order to pair the whole numbers with all the fractions, what we do is work our way along the path, pairing 1 with $\frac{1}{1}$, 2 with $\frac{2}{1}$, 3 with $\frac{1}{2}$, 4 with $\frac{1}{3}$. The number 9, for example, gets paired with $\frac{2}{3}$, the ninth fraction that we meet as the snake slithers through the table of fractions. Since the snake covers the whole table, every fraction will be paired with some whole number.

It's a beautiful and surprising argument. If I was cast away on a desert island and allowed to take only eight theorems with me, Cantor's snake would be one of them. How remarkable to find a way to match up all the fractions with whole numbers and show they have the same order of magnitude.

UNCOUNTABLY INFINITE

This is beginning to look like all infinities are identical in size. Perhaps once a tribe has infinitely many members it will never be beaten by another tribe. Now enter the new big-cheese tribe whose members are labelled with all the possible decimal expansions there are of numbers. Will the tribe whose members are labelled with the whole numbers 1, 2, 3, . . . be able to pair themselves up with this new tribe? I might start by matching tribe member number 1 with tribe member π = 3.1415926 . . . , then tribe member number 2 with e = 2.7182818 . . . But how can I find a way to exhaust all the members of the infinite decimal tribe? Is there a clever way to arrange the infinite decimal numbers so that I can snake the whole numbers through them like Cantor did with the fractions?

Cantor produced a clever argument to show why he could be sure that however hard I try to match up the whole number tribe, he could guarantee that an infinite decimal tribe member would always be unaccounted for. The infinity of all infinite decimal expansions of numbers is a genuinely bigger sort of infinity than the infinity of whole numbers. It's another beautifully simple argument and I think it would be another one of the mathematical theorems I'd take to my desert island.

How could Cantor be sure that he could always guarantee an infinite decimal tribe member will be unaccounted for? Let's take one of my attempts to match the whole-number tribe with the infinite decimal numbered tribe.

$$1 \leftrightarrow 3.1415926 \ldots$$
$$2 \leftrightarrow 2.7182818 \ldots$$
$$3 \leftrightarrow 1.4142135 \ldots$$
$$4 \leftrightarrow 1.6180339 \ldots$$
$$5 \leftrightarrow 0.3331779 \ldots$$

. . .

What Cantor does is to build a number with an infinite decimal expansion which he can guarantee is not on my list and has not been paired up with one of the whole numbers. Each decimal place is a number between 0 and 9. In the first decimal place, Cantor chooses a number which is different from the first decimal place of the number paired with number 1. In the second decimal place, he chooses a number different from the second decimal place of the number paired with number 2.

$$1 \leftrightarrow 3.1415926\ldots$$
$$2 \leftrightarrow 2.7182818\ldots$$
$$3 \leftrightarrow 1.4142135\ldots$$
$$4 \leftrightarrow 1.6180339\ldots$$
$$5 \leftrightarrow 0.3331779\ldots$$
$$\ldots$$

For example, the infinite decimal number starting 0.22518 . . . is not paired with the first five whole numbers because the infinite decimal is different from the first five infinite decimals in this list. In this way Cantor can point to a member of the infinite decimal tribe that hasn't been paired up with any whole number. If I claimed it was paired with, say, number 101, Cantor could simply say: 'Check the 101st decimal place, it's different from the 101st decimal of this new number.'

There are a few technical points to watch out for. For example, you don't want to produce the number 0.9999 . . . because, as our 'how many mathematicians does it take to change a lightbulb' joke suggested, this is actually the same as the number 1.000 . . . But the essence of the argument suffices to show that there are more numbers with infinite decimal expansions than there are whole numbers.

You may object and say that I could just add this new number into the list and shunt all the other numbers along one. But however many numbers I add to the list, Cantor will always be able to play the same game and cook up yet another infinite decimal number I've missed. The point is that the argument works for any attempt I might make to pair up whole numbers with infinite decimal numbers – there are always infinite decimals left over. It has a similar flavour to Gödel's realization that you couldn't add unprovable true axioms to mathematics in the hope that eventually every true statement would be provable – there will always be unprovable truths left unaccounted for. In fact, Gödel used a similar trick to Cantor's to prove his incompleteness theorem.

Cantor himself was genuinely surprised by his discoveries about the infinite. 'I see it, but I do not believe it,' he said.

Given that there was more than one sort of infinity, the ∞ symbol introduced by Wallis wasn't going to hack it any more. Indeed, Cantor's ideas proved that there are infinitely many types of infinity. Cantor showed we could replace 'lots' with meaningful names for all these different infinities. He introduced new symbols for these new infinite numbers using letters of the Hebrew alphabet. The smallest infinity, $\aleph_0$, was called aleph-zero after the first letter of the Hebrew alphabet. Cantor was probably aware of its mystical significance in Jewish Kabbalah, where it represents the infinity of God. But for Cantor the choice also hints at the idea of a new beginning, the start of a new mathematics. For me, this is one of the most exciting moments in mathematical history. It is like the moment we counted for the first time. But instead of 1, 2, 3, we were counting infinities.

The great German mathematician David Hilbert recognized that Cantor was creating a genuinely new mathematics. Hilbert declared Cantor's ideas about infinities to be 'the most astonishing product of mathematical thought, one of the most beautiful realizations of human activity in the domain of the purely intelligible . . . no one shall expel us from the paradise which Cantor has created for us'. I think I would agree.

Cantor believed that he was in fact tapping into the mind of God. Far from it being his own mathematics, he was just a mouthpiece for God. It may be that his faith in something transcendent gave him the courage to believe that infinity too existed. But it was Cantor's mathematical brilliance that wrestled the infinite from the unknown into the known. And the Christian Church, far from being disturbed by Cantor's attempts to read the infinite mind of God, took an active interest in the emerging ideas. Cantor entered into a lengthy correspondence with members of the Christian Church over the nature of God and infinity.

But not everyone was so enamoured with his ideas. In particular, one of the most influential mathematicians in Germany, Leopold

Kronecker, thought Cantor's mathematics an aberration, describing him as a corrupter of youth:

> I don't know what predominates in Cantor's theory – philosophy or theology, but I am sure that there is no mathematics there.

Kronecker once famously said that 'God created the integers. All the rest is the work of man.' But what Cantor had created was so revolutionary that Kronecker regarded it as a mathematical carbuncle. Kronecker's opposition to Cantor's infinity ensured that Cantor never claimed a job at one of the big universities, including Berlin, where Kronecker was based. Instead, he spent his days in the backwater of the University of Halle. Cantor tried fighting back, writing directly to the Minister of Education about Kronecker's behaviour. But it was probably not a good idea to alienate one of the key members of the mathematical community.

Even publishing his ideas proved difficult. Another influential mathematician of the day, Gösta Mittag-Leffler, eventually rejected Cantor's work, declaring it a hundred years ahead of its time. Cantor was severely thrown by this rejection from a mathematician he greatly respected. The continual battle with the establishment, his struggles with the mysteries of the infinite, and the deaths of his mother, brother and then youngest child took their toll. Cantor suffered from bouts of manic depression, and the controversy about his mathematics only exacerbated his condition. He was admitted to the Nervenklinik in Halle, where he spent much of the last few decades of his life. Disillusioned with mathematics, he turned to questions of religion, as well as spending a lot of time trying to prove that Francis Bacon was the real author of Shakespeare's plays.

But Mittag-Leffler's premonition was right in some respects. A hundred years later, Cantor's ideas are considered some of the most beautiful and extraordinary of the last 300 years. Cantor has allowed mathematicians to touch infinity, to play with it, compute with it, to finally recognize that infinity is a number. Not just one number but infinitely many numbers.

But for Cantor the infinite was not just an idea of the mind:

I am so in favour of the actual infinite that instead of admitting that Nature abhors it, as is commonly said, I hold that Nature makes frequent use of it everywhere, in order to show more effectively the perfections of its Author. Thus I believe that there is no part of matter which is not – I do not say divisible – but actually divisible; and consequently the least particle ought to be considered as a world full of an infinity of different creatures.

NOW YOU SEE IT, NOW YOU DON'T

Cantor's discovery of these layers of infinity led to a very real example of a problem that could not be resolved within the current axioms of mathematics – a statement without proof, undecidable, beyond what we can know. It was a question that went to the heart of what number is and revealed just how subtle numbers are.

Cantor wanted to know whether there are sets of numbers which are bigger in size than whole numbers but small enough that they can't be paired with all infinite decimal expansions. In other words, can there be a tribe whose members are numbered with a set of numbers that beats the whole-number tribe but is outdone by the tribe with all infinite decimal numbers? The name given to the infinity of all infinite decimal numbers is the continuum. The continuum hypothesis posited that there was no infinity smaller than the continuum but larger than the infinity of all whole numbers.

Hilbert was so struck by the challenge of proving the continuum hypothesis that he put the problem of determining whether there was an intermediate infinity at the top of his list of 23 problems for the mathematicians of the twentieth century.

It is a question Cantor wrestled with for the whole of his life. One day he was convinced he'd proved there was no infinity between these two. But then he found a mistake. The next day he thought he'd proved the opposite: there was an infinity between. As Cantor always believed: 'In mathematics the art of asking questions is more valuable than solving problems.'

And so it turned out to be. The reason Cantor was having so much trouble was that both answers are correct.

The answer to this problem, which finally arrived in the 1960s, rocked the mathematical community to its foundations. Building on work done by Gödel, Paul Cohen, a logician at Stanford, demonstrated that you couldn't prove from the axioms we currently use for mathematics whether or not there was a set of numbers whose size was strictly between the number of whole numbers and all infinite decimal numbers. In fact, he produced two different models of numbers that satisfied the axioms we use for mathematics: in one model the answer to Cantor's question was yes, and in the other model the answer was no.

I'm not sure whether Cantor would have liked this conclusion. He did once declare: 'The essence of mathematics lies entirely in its freedom.' But was this too much freedom? It meant that there are several sorts of mathematics, not just one!

Some regard this as similar to the moment when mathematicians discovered that there are many sorts of geometry in addition to Euclid's. Euclid's geometry satisfies the parallel postulate, while the new spherical and hyperbolic geometries don't. Now we understood that there are different models for our numbers, some which have these intermediate infinities, others which don't.

That said, it was deeply unsettling for many mathematicians. We thought we knew our numbers. Numbers like the square root of 2 and π might be irrational, with infinite decimal expansions, but we felt that we could see these numbers marked on a ruler. So in the case of the numbers we think we know, we feel there should be an answer to Cantor's question. Is there a subset of numbers on this ruler that is strictly bigger than the whole numbers yet strictly smaller than the set of all infinite decimal numbers? Most mathematicians believe that the answer must be yes or no, not yes and no. And yet here we have a proof that we can't prove it either way.

Cohen's colleague Julia Robinson wrote to Cohen: 'For heaven's sake there is only one true number theory! It's my religion.' Intriguingly, she crossed out the last sentence before sending the letter. But Cantor would probably have had no problem with such uncertainty, because his religion encouraged the acceptance of things which transcend human knowledge.

How many other unresolved problems on the mathematical books will turn out to be unprovable? To tackle some of these great unsolved problems we may need to add new axioms for them to become provable. Gödel thought this could account for the difficulty of proving the Riemann hypothesis, the greatest unsolved problem of mathematics. He questioned whether our current axioms were sufficient to tackle many of the problems of number theory:

> One is faced with an infinite series of axioms which can be extended further and further, without any end being visible . . . It is true that in the mathematics of today the higher levels of this hierarchy are practically never used . . . it is not altogether unlikely that this character of present-day mathematics may have something to do with its inability to prove certain fundamental theorems, such as, for example, Riemann's hypothesis.

YES AND NO

Gödel's incompleteness theorem is a fascinating microcosm of the challenge of trying to prove what is true. Within any consistent axiomatic system for number theory there will be things which are true that cannot be proved true. The intriguing thing is that by working outside the system we can even prove that a particular statement is true but unprovable within the system. You might say: then why not work in that larger framework? But Gödel guarantees that this larger system will have its own unprovable true statements requiring another move outside the system. It's a very familiar infinite regress.

There are resonances with many of the problems I have been wrestling with. Perhaps it is impossible to understand the universe when we are part of the system. If the universe is described by a quantum wave function, does there need to be something outside the system to observe it? Chaos theory implies that we can't understand part of the system as an isolated problem, because an electron on the other side of the universe may have an influence that will send a chaotic system in a completely different direction. We must stand outside in order to consider the whole system. The same problem applies to the question of understanding consciousness. We are stuck inside our own heads, our own systems, unable to access anyone else's consciousness. This is also why some say we will always be limited in our ability to tackle something like the existence of a God that transcends the universe we are stuck in.

The other important aspect of Gödel's work is the fact that you cannot prove within the axiomatic framework for number theory that it is consistent, that it contains no contradictions. This can be applied to the question of whether the methods we employ to gain knowledge about the universe are effective. Any attempt to explain, for example, why induction is the right strategy for studying physical phenomena is going to rely on applying induction. The whole thing becomes very circular.

The implications for the limitations of the mathematical method are not all doom and gloom. You can say that it led to the exciting revelation that there are statements about numbers that you can either assume are true or assume are false and both answers derive from legitimate models of mathematics; that is, there are many different sorts of mathematics. Can we do the same once we encounter a genuinely unknowable question about the universe? If we identify a question whose answer cannot be known, then it makes perfect sense to work under the hypothesis that the answer is one thing or another. Your choice of working hypothesis may depend in part on the probability that the answer is one thing rather than another. But sometimes probabilities are not relevant, and your choice may be based on your personal relationship to the consequences that follow from working within that system.

In mathematics we are freed up from this need to choose. As a mathematician I'm quite happy to move between different mathematical models that are individually self-consistent yet mutually contradictory. For example, I can do mathematics under the assumption that the continuum hypothesis is true or that it is false. If the original model is consistent, then both mathematical models are consistent. If it makes my mathematics work, I might use the continuum hypothesis to explore this particular mathematical universe. Can we do the same thing with other unknowables? If God is that which is unknowable, can we make a choice that gives flesh to this unknown? But by doing that, aren't we trying to make it knowable, going against the spirit of the definition?

You have to be careful when making choices or hypotheses under which to operate. You can't just assume that something you don't know can be true or false. You have to prove first that both possibilities are consistent. For example, I don't know whether the Riemann hypothesis about prime numbers is true or false, but only one of these is consistent with our theory of numbers. If it turns out to be unprovable within the current axioms of number theory, this would actually imply that it was true. If it is false, we know that it is provably false because we will be able to find a counterexample with a finite systematic search. If it is false, you can't work within a model of numbers where you assume it is true because you'll generate contradictions. This is the amazing thing about the continuum hypothesis: either it or its negation can be incorporated into a consistent theory without creating contradictions.

Some have argued that the numbers we are trying to capture axiomatically are meant to be the numbers that we measure with, that are located somewhere on a ruler. So there might be good reason to assume the continuum hypothesis as a better description of what we are trying to model. In fact, logician Hugh Woodin has recently put forward arguments for why the numbers we are trying to model are those in which the continuum hypothesis is false. He argues that if these numbers model measurements on a ruler, then there are reasons to believe this would imply that there are infinite subsets of intermediate size between the set of whole numbers and the set of infinite decimals.

This illustrates the tension between mathematics and physics. Mathematics has for centuries been happy with the mathematical multiverse: different, mutually exclusive mathematical models of geometry or number theory. But even if the physicist is happy with the idea of the multiverse, there is still the desire to identify which of these possibilities describes the universe we are part of.

Suppose a scientist cooks up a perfectly consistent logical theory of how the universe might work, but then discovers that it doesn't match the experimental evidence of our own universe. The hypothetical theory is booted out and is no longer of interest to the world of science. If a biologist starts writing papers about a hypothetical beast that potentially could exist, like a unicorn, but doesn't actually walk this Earth, no one is going to be interested unless it casts some light on the animals that do exist. By contrast, in mathematics such new worlds and beasts are celebrated and embraced. They become part of a richer tapestry of mathematical possibilities. Science does the actual, mathematics does the possible. Science charts a single pathway through a tree of possible universes, mathematics maps every possible journey.

But what do we do about a question of science that can't be resolved. In the case of the continuum hypothesis, it doesn't make sense to resort to probabilistic considerations in choosing one or the other hypothesis. It isn't as if one is 'true' or not. But does the same apply to unknowables in physics where we do have a 'truth'?

It is interesting that, in the case of physics, once we have a question that is beyond knowledge, one answer will still be a correct description of our universe, and one will not. But by its nature, if it is unanswerable, we are not going to get any new evidence about our universe that would allow us decide which is the true description and which the false. If we do, the question wasn't unanswerable in the first place. So what happens to those who labour under the false hypothesis? Nothing! As with the continuum hypothesis, its negation will still be consistent with our current theory of the universe. You will get a different story with different theorems and results. If it led to contradictions, this would give us a way to know that it was wrong, and hence the question was not genuinely unanswerable.

For example, consider the question of whether the universe is infinite. If this is an unknowable, it is because the universe is infinite or because it is finite and of such a size that it will always remain beyond our event horizon and therefore beyond the realms of investigation. If it is infinite, what happens to someone who works under the hypothesis that it is finite but too big ever to prove finite? The interesting thing is that if this led to problems – it contradicted current theory or new data – we'd have a way of proving that the universe is infinite, so it can't have been an unknowable question. Of course, in mathematics this is a great way to proceed to prove ideas of infinity. We proved that the square root of 2 cannot be captured by a ratio of two finite numbers by working under the hypothesis that it could and eventually running up against a contradiction. It is possible that an infinite universe might be the only assumption that doesn't lead to contradictions. It could be that mathematics is again our best means of exploring the far reaches of the universe.

In this Edge I've explored how mathematics has even managed to help us navigate infinity itself. It is quite striking that infinity was once regarded as something beyond knowledge and often connected to the idea of God. Descartes wrote: 'God is the only thing I positively conceive as infinite.' And yet Cantor's extraordinary insights at the end of the nineteenth century provide us with a way to explore and compare infinities. Infinity is no longer beyond our reach. Cantor was not unaffected by the implications of his study of infinity for the question of God. Indeed, he believed he had been chosen by God to reveal these ideas about infinity to the world.

Infinity has played a key role in the exploration of the existence of God. For example, Thomas Aquinas's proof of God, known as the cosmological argument, proposes that anything which exists needs a creator, but this would then apply to the creator itself. To avoid infinite regress, God is the solution to the problem of a first cause. But mathematics allows us to keep building new infinities by considering all the old infinities and then taking their union, so there is no need to stop this chain of creators, as Aquinas believed. Each time we get something new, and the process never ends.

Even though the mathematics is there to keep building new infinities from the old, it becomes very hard even for a mathematician to grasp the extent of our mathematical universe. Most content themselves with playing down in the lower echelons of the infinite. But we know that these are just part of an unending hierarchy. This gives those who try to define God as 'that which nothing greater can be thought of' some problems. In one sense, such a thing doesn't exist because there is always a way to make something greater. But if we come back to the idea of something beyond that which humans can conceive of, then we are back to things we as humans cannot know: the limitations of our biology to know.

WHAT WE CANNOT KNOW

So, at the end of my journey to the edges of knowledge, have I found things that we can categorically say we cannot know? The things I thought we could never know, such as whether the universe is infinite, turn out not to be as unassailable as I thought. We can use mathematics to employ finite means to prove the existence of the infinite. So although we may never explore or see beyond the finite bubble that encloses the universe we have physical access to, we may be able to know, using the power of our minds alone, what is beyond.

Understanding the nature of time before the Big Bang was another edge that I thought was unassailable. But chinks have opened up in that wall too. Recent progress has provided us with ways to theorize and even perhaps detect evidence of a time before we thought it all began. And yet the question of whether time had a beginning or extends infinitely into the past feels like one that will remain on the scientific books for some time yet.

In contrast, the infinitely small at the heart of the dice that I hold in my hand feels like something that will always remain beyond complete knowledge. Every generation thought they'd hit the indivisible, only for matter to fall apart into smaller pieces. How can we ever know that the current building blocks of the universe – quarks, electrons, neutrinos – aren't as divisible as all the other particles we've hit as we've peeled the onion of reality. Indeed, quantum physics currently posits a limit to how far we will be able to penetrate in our investigation of what's inside my dice: that beyond the Planck length, it's simply no-go. There is an edge beyond which we cannot know.

Whether we can know about the edge that constitutes our consciousness is something that is very much in a state of flux. Will this challenge vanish as an edge because it will turn out to be an ill-posed question? Will it be answered with a strategy similar to that used by scientists to pin down the essence of life? There was no *élan vital*, just a set of biological processes that means a collection of molecules has life. Or will the problem of consciousness remain something that can never be understood because we are stuck inside our own consciousnesses and can never get inside another's?

The possibility that we cannot know because we are stuck within the system is a common theme among many of the problems I have tried to tackle. Mathematics has truths that will remain unprovable within a system. Step outside and you can know, but this creates a new system which will have its own unprovable truths.

The idea that a quantum experiment can be repeated is an impossibility because we can never isolate the experiment from the universe it is conducted in, a universe that has changed and evolved by the next time we come to run the experiment.

Even the mathematics created to understand my dice is something of a fantasy. What is probability? If I throw my dice 600 times, I expect to get 100 6s. But I just want to throw it once and know something about how it will fall. The equations of chaos theory tell us that so much of the future is dependent on extremely fine-tuning of the decimal places that control the input of the equations. So I can never know the present completely enough to have any chance of knowing the future or the past.

The physical limitations of the human brain, even of the computational ability of the universe itself, place bounds on how much can ever be known, so there will always be things beyond knowledge. But this isn't an absolute unknowability. Like light coming in from the outer reaches of the universe, before we realized that the expansion of the universe was accelerating, wait long enough and the light will arrive. Wait long enough and a computer can make its way through all the provable truths of mathematics. However, as my exploration at the edges of time revealed, what if time itself runs out while we are waiting?

The limitations of language are at the heart of many of the limits of knowledge, and these could possibly evolve and change. Certainly, many philosophers identify language as a problem when it comes to the question of consciousness. Understanding quantum physics is such a problem because the only language that helps us navigate the ideas is mathematics. Try to translate the mathematics into the language of everyday experience and we create the absurdities that make quantum physics so challenging. So the unknowability of position and momentum isn't really a genuine unknowable. Rather, it is a failure of translation from mathematics to natural language.

But we must always recognize that we are bound by the ways of thinking particular to our own moment in history. Comte thought we could never know the constituents of a star. How wrong he was. So I wonder if the safest bet is to say that we can never truly know for sure what it is we cannot know.

IS GOD AN IMAGINARY NUMBER?

How far can we get by creating solutions to seemingly unanswerable problems? For many centuries mathematicians looked at the equation $x^2 = -1$ and believed it had no answer. But then a more imaginative approach was taken. Let us create a solution to this equation. We admitted imaginary numbers into the landscape of mathematics by defining i as the number whose square is -1. Why does this work? It doesn't create contradictions in the theory. We interweave this concept with the mathematics we know and we begin to know i. And most importantly it allows access to new and exciting bits of the mathematical world. Not admitting imaginary numbers into mathematics would have limited its extent and power. But the important point is not to give the concept more properties than it has.

What happens if I try to be creative with some of our unknowable questions? What happens, for example, if I define God as the solution to the question 'Why something rather than nothing?' This concept is meant to be nothing more than the solution to that question, that is its definition. It doesn't have any other properties. It is this unknown. Even if we gain more knowledge about the answer to the question, it will just mean that we know more about this God that was defined as the solution to 'Why something rather than nothing?'

But we have to be careful with such an approach. Just because you write down a mathematical equation, this doesn't mean it has solutions. Admitting a new concept which solves $x^2 = -1$ was profitable because it provided access to new consistent mathematics. For the Platonist, the idea was sitting there all along, waiting to be articulated; for others, it was a creative act which enriched our mathematical world. But if I write down the equations for Fermat's Last Theorem and try to define new numbers which solve these equations, I am going to find myself with statements that contradict themselves. This is, after all, precisely how Wiles proved that the equations couldn't be solved.

The trouble with most religions is that the God that is served up has so many properties that are nothing to do with the definition. It's as if we are working backwards, focussing on the strange properties conjured up over the generations without really understanding what the original definition was. We come across this bastardized picture early on as kids, and then when we ask the question 'Why something rather than nothing?', it doesn't really work as a solution. But we've been shown the wrong thing.

This is why I declare that I am an atheist. It means, for me, that I reject the classical solutions that religion seems to offer up for these unknowns. But maybe I shouldn't throw everything out. There are things that will always remain unknown, so perhaps that God does exist. The traditional argument against the God of the gaps is that we should strive to know God, to have a personal relationship with this concept. And this God, defined as the transcendental or unknown, precludes by its definition the possibility of knowing it.

But the trouble with this as a definition of God is that it doesn't really get you much further. While defining a number whose square is -1 resulted in a rich array of consequences, defining something as the solution to 'Why something rather than nothing?' doesn't give rise to anything new. You've got to make up properties for this thing which don't follow from its definition. As Karen Armstrong articulated, this high God is too high.

There are several responses to identifying the unknowable. One is to leave it at that: if it is unknowable, then it can't be known. But there is also the temptation to make a choice about the answer and live your life according to that answer. Perhaps the logically most consistent response is to be open to a many worlds solution and allow all the solutions to run parallel until new ideas collapse the possibilities. Mathematicians are happy to explore a mathematics in which the continuum hypothesis is true and equally at home with a parallel mathematics in which it is presumed false.

I wonder, though, whether, as I come to the end of my exploration at the limits of knowledge, I have changed my mind about declaring myself an atheist. With my definition of a God as the existence of things we cannot know, to declare myself an atheist would mean that I believe there is nothing we cannot know. I don't believe that anymore. In some sense I think I have proved that this God does exist. It's now about exploring what quality this God has.

My statement about being an atheist is really just a response to the rather impoverished version of God offered by most religions and cultures. I reject the existence of a supernatural intelligence that intervenes in the evolution of the universe. This is a rejection of the God that people assign strange properties to – such as compassion, wisdom, love – which make no sense when it comes to the idea that I am exploring.

Such a position and definition will probably not satisfy either side of the divide. The militant atheists don't want to admit anything named God into the debate, while those who believe in a God will criticize the concept of God as the unknown as impotent and missing the point. So how do we engage with this God of the gaps?

Perhaps the important lesson is to maintain a schizophrenic state of mind. A multi-mindset. On the one hand, as humans we must recognize that we cannot know it all. There are provable limits to knowledge. Such a state of humility is intellectually important, or we will live in a state of delusion and hubris. Yet the other lesson is that we cannot always know what it is that will forever transcend our understanding. This is why it is essential for a scientist not to give in too early. To believe that we can find answers. To believe that perhaps we can know it all.

DO I OWN AN ODD OR EVEN NUMBER OF DICE?

My journey through science has thrown up a number of challenging edges to knowledge. But there is also the basic epistemological question of whether we can actually know anything at all. Two thousand years ago Socrates declared: 'True knowledge exists in knowing you know nothing.' An acknowledgement of your ignorance is the only true statement of knowledge.

There have been volumes of philosophy that tackle the theory of knowledge and try to pin down what we can know, to define what we mean by knowledge. Plato proposed that knowledge should be defined as 'justified true belief', but Bertrand Russell and then the American philosopher Edmund Gettier in the 1960s questioned whether this truly captures its meaning.

The classic example proposed by Bertrand Russell tells the story of a woman who looks at a clock which says two o'clock. She believes therefore that it is two o'clock. She seems justified in her belief because the clock says so. And it does indeed happen to be two o'clock. Yet actually the clock stopped 12 hours ago, and it's just coincidence that she happened to look at the clock exactly 12 hours later.

Gettier created similar scenarios to challenge 'justified true belief'. You are looking at a field and see what you believe is a cow. You infer that there is a cow in the field. Actually, there is a cow in the field, so the inference is true, but it can't be seen because it is in a dip in the field. You are in possession of a true statement. It was based on a justifiable belief, and the thing you were looking at certainly looked exactly like a cow. But the fact that the statement you made is true does not imply knowledge.

We can imagine a situation in which we have come up with a statement about the universe that is in fact true. But the justification for the statement is completely incorrect, even if it led us to make a statement that is true. Surely that doesn't constitute knowing that the statement is true. I have often cooked up proofs of true mathematical statements that turn out to have a logical flaw in them (which I hope to spot before

I send them to a journal for publication). But my false proof can't really justify my knowledge that the mathematical statement is true.

I don't know whether the Riemann hypothesis is true or false. However, there have been a few people who have come up with what they believe are proofs of the truth of this hypothesis, and they have pages and pages of equations to back up their belief. Most of the time a fault is found. Once shown to the proposer, that justified belief vanishes. But what if that false proof convinces everyone? Suppose the fault is actually quite subtle. We cannot say we know that the Riemann hypothesis is true despite our justified true belief. Surely the justification has to be true to lead to justified true belief.

Some ancient astronomers proposed that the Earth goes round the Sun, but their justification of this fact was not correct. The Indian philosopher Yajnavalkya justified this belief in a heliocentric solar system in the ninth century BC by proposing that: 'The Sun strings these worlds – the Earth, the planets, the atmosphere – to himself on a thread.' Can we say that he knew that the Earth goes round the Sun?

I think that I side with my fellow Fellow in New College, Timothy Williamson, who asserts in his book *Knowledge and Its Limits* that knowledge should be regarded as something fundamental, not something that can be defined in terms of other things. It seems like we all seem to know what 'to know' means. It is one of only 100 or so words that have a comparable translation in every language on Earth, which is not the case for as basic a word as 'eat'.

It was also from Williamson that I learned about a fantastic piece of logical trickery called the paradox of unknowability, which proves that unless you know it all there will always be truths that are by their nature unknowable. This paradox is attributed to American logician Frederic Fitch, who published it in a paper in 1963. Fitch admitted that the original source of the argument was actually a comment made in 1945 by an anonymous referee about a paper Fitch had submitted for publication but had never made it into print. For many years the referee responsible for this logical gem remained a mystery. But subsequent detective work has tracked down the handwritten copy of the report, and an analysis of the handwriting reveals the author to be the famous

American logician Alonso Church, who made major contributions to the understanding of Gödel's incompleteness theorem.

Church's argument has a whiff of the self-referential strategy that Gödel employed, but this time there is no mathematics involved, just pure logic. And while Gödel proves that there are mathematical truths that can never be proved within a particular consistent axiomatic system of mathematics, Church goes one further, promising a truth that will never be known by any means.

Suppose that there are true statements that I do not know are true. In fact, there are lots of such statements. For example, my house is full of dice, not just the casino dice that I have on my table. There are dice in our monopoly set, our box of ludo, dice that have gone missing down the side of our sofa, dice that are buried in the chaos of my kids' rooms. I do not know whether my house contains an odd or even number of dice. This by itself is, of course, not an unknowable statement, because I could make a systematic search of my house to determine the answer. But it is certainly something that at this point in time I do not know the answer to.

Now hold on tight – this is the bit that leaves my brain in a spin every time I read it. Let p be the true statement among the two options: 'there are an even number of dice in my house' and 'there are an odd number of dice in my house'. I don't know which one is true, but one of them must be. The existence of an unknowable truth is squeezed out of the existence of this unknown truth. The following statement is an unknowable truth: 'p is true but unknown'. It is certainly true. Why is this unknowable? Because to know this means I know that p is true and unknown, but that's a contradiction because p can't be unknown and known simultaneously. So the statement 'p is true and unknown' is itself an unknowable statement. It's not that p itself is unknowable. As I said, I can go and find all the dice in my house and know whether it is an odd or even number. It is the meta-statement 'p is true and unknown' that is unknowable. The proof works provided something exists that is true but unknown. The only way out of this is if I already know it all. The only way that all truths are knowable is if all truths are known.

Although it has become known as a paradox, there is, as Williamson points out, no paradox involved. It is simply a proof that there are unknowable truths. After all my journeying at the limits of science, it turns out that a clever logical riff produces the gap I was looking for.

CAN WE KNOW ANYTHING?

Many philosophers of knowledge question how much we can ever really know about anything. The eighteenth-century Scottish philosopher David Hume identified one of the fundamental problems we've had with many of the questions I've been tackling: that of being stuck inside the system. If we are going to apply scientific methods to establish that we actually know something, we get into a loop because we are using scientific and logical arguments to prove that these methods are sound. It is impossible to assume an outside position. Wittgenstein summed this up colourfully: 'You cannot shit higher than your arse.'

What about mathematics? Surely there we have certain knowledge. Doesn't proof give us 100% certainty that, for example, there are infinitely many prime numbers? Even mathematical proofs, although everything is on the table, are going to have to be processed by the human brain to check whether the proof is correct. What if we are all convinced of the truth of an argument that nonetheless has a subtle hole in it? Of course, one of the things that we take advantage of is the fact that any fatal holes should eventually reveal themselves. But then doesn't this imply that mathematics, like science, is subject to an evolutionary process? The mathematical philosopher Imre Lakatos believed so. He developed a philosophy of mathematics that was modelled on Popper's view of science as something that could only be falsified, not proved true. For Lakatos, it can never be known whether a proof might hide a subtle flaw that was been missed.

His book *Proofs and Refutations* presents a fascinating dialogue between students exploring the proof of Euler's theorem on the relationship between the number of vertices, edges and faces of a three-dimensional polyhedron. It mirrors the history of the evolution of this theorem $E = V + F - 2$. At first, the students think they've got a proof. Then a student proposes a shape with a hole in the middle. The formula doesn't work on this shape. Nor does the proof. One interpretation is that the proof works for the shapes that it was intended to work on. But now a new proof and theorem are introduced which pertain to a new formula which, in addition to vertices, edges and faces, includes the number of holes in the shape. The story reveals a much more evolutionary approach to mathematical knowledge than many mathematicians will dare admit to, more akin to the process of scientific investigation. So how effective are either in discovering the truth?

One of the reasons for believing that science is producing true knowledge is its success rate. Science is so successful in its description and prediction of the way things appear to be that we feel like it must be getting close to a reality that most of us believe does exist. The fact that science works so well at making predictions and explaining phenomena is perhaps the best measure there is that we are close to the truth. If the map that you are using consistently gets you to your destination, that's a good sign that the map is an accurate representation of reality.

Science has mapped the universe pretty well. Space probes land on distant planets thanks to our discoveries about the nature of gravity. Gene therapies help to tackle previously untreatable conditions thanks to our discoveries about the biology of the cell. We find our way with GPS by exploiting our discoveries about time and space. When the scientific map doesn't work, we are ready to redraw its contours to find a description that successfully helps us navigate our environment. It is survival of the fittest theory: continued success at making predictions and controlling our environment means the theory survives. Science may not really represent reality, but there isn't anything that comes close as an alternative.

Ever since Kant, we have had to wrestle with the unknowability of 'things in themselves'. The limits of human perception, highlighted by how easily our senses can be tricked, raise questions about how much our brain can really know about reality. Isn't everything being viewed through the spectacles we wear to look at our universe?

One of the key problems with our attempt to know the world is that it is with our senses that we gain knowledge of the world around us, and with analytic argument that we take that knowledge and extend it.

We come up with stories that match all the information that we gather with our senses. The inventions of the telescope, the microscope and the fMRI scanner have extended how much we can perceive with our senses.

Yet what if there are things in the universe that our senses can't detect? We have more senses than many people realize: in addition to sight, hearing, taste, touch and smell, we also have a sense called proprioception that gives us an awareness of how our body is located in space. There are also senses that give us information about the inner state of our body. The fluid in the inner ear tells us how our body's position is changing in relation to gravity. But are there physical phenomena that we miss because we don't have the sensory tools to interact with them?

Consider an organism without an eye or neurons to detect light. If it has no way of accessing electromagnetic waves, how could it ever come up with a theory of electromagnetism? We have done very well to combine our sense of sight, which can see part of the electro-magnetic spectrum, with mathematical analysis to deduce other parts of the spectrum. And then we developed tools that can detect these waves and convert them into things that we can interpret. But could we have got going without being able to access, via our sense of sight, some bit of the spectrum?

It is possible that the limitations of our senses also limit the math-ematics we can know. Despite mathematics being all in the mind, there is a school of thought that suggests that because our intelligence is ultimately an embodied intelligence, the knowledge we can obtain about mathematics is restricted to that which can be embodied. It is certainly true that if you look at the mathematics we do know, it often has its origins in descriptions of the physical world. Take imaginary numbers – you may question how they are embodied. And yet they emerge from the act of measuring lengths in geometric shapes. It is this act of understanding the diagonal across the face of my cube-shaped dice that led the Babylonians to consider the square root of 2. And from here we begin the journey that leads to the idea of the square root of –1.

There are proponents of artificial intelligence who assert that if we are to create an intelligence that matches ours, it must be physically embodied. In other words, a brain that lives exclusively in computer hard drives cannot generate intelligence like ours without physically interacting with the world through a body. It is a challenging hypothesis. Could there really be parts of the mathematical world that are off limits to me because they don't originate in physically embodied concepts?

And yet there is the deep philosophical issue of the extent to which our senses allow us to know anything for sure. We've already seen how our senses can be fooled into believing things that turn out to be tricks of the mind. How, for example, can we be sure that the universe as we apprehend it isn't a simulation? As we saw in the Sixth Edge, we can make someone believe they are in another person's body. So how can we be sure that we aren't just brains in a jar being fed artificial sensory information by a computer and that the whole world around us isn't just a trick?

My response to this attempt to undermine everything we know is to counter that this book has tried to explore how we can know anything about that simulation. Kant believed that the ways things really are will always remain hidden from our view. All we can ever know is the appearance of things. I think most scientists spend some time reading about this debate concerning ontology and epistemology, and listening to philosophers who question whether science is really telling us how it is. And then they get back to the science, telling themselves that if we can never know what reality is really like, then let us at least try to say what the reality that we apprehend through our senses is like. After all, that is the one that impacts on us.

So perhaps the best we can hope is that science gives us verisimilitudinous knowledge of the universe; that is, it gives us a narrative that appears to describe reality. We believe that a theory that makes our experience of the world intelligible is one that is close to the true nature of the world, even if philosophers tell us we'll never know. As Niels Bohr said: 'It is wrong to think that the task of physics is to find out how nature is. Physics concerns what we can say about nature.'

HERE BE DRAGONS

But what of the things that we cannot know? If something is beyond scientific investigation, if it is unknowable, perhaps there is some other discipline that will have a better grip on the unknowable? Here is Martin Rees wrestling with the 'something rather than nothing' question: 'The pre-eminent mystery is why anything exists at all. What breathes life into the equations, and actualized them in a real cosmos? Such questions lie beyond science, however: they are the province of philosophers and theologians.'

Perhaps that is to give in too easily, but it is certainly true that science flourishes when we share the unknowable with other disciplines. If the unknowable has an impact on how we lead our lives, then it is worth having ways to probe the consequences of choosing an answer to an unknowable. Music, poetry, stories and art are powerful voices in exploring the implications of the unknowable.

Take the question of whether the universe is infinite. There are interesting consequences if you believe that space goes on forever. The fact that across the universe there may be infinitely many copies of you reading this book might have a profound effect on the way you lead your life, even if you will never know whether it's true.

Chaos theory implies that not only my casino dice but humans too are in some ways part of the unknowable. Although we are physical systems, no amount of data will help us to completely predict human behaviour. The humanities are the best language we have for understanding as much as we can about what it is to be human.

Studies into consciousness suggest boundaries beyond which we cannot go. Our internal worlds are potentially unknowable to others. But isn't that one of the reasons we write and read novels? It is the most effective way to give others access to that internal world.

What we cannot know creates the space for myth, for stories, for imagination, as much as for science. We may not know, but that doesn't stop us creating stories to fill the unknown, and these stories are crucial in providing the material for what one day might be known. Without stories, we wouldn't have any science at all.

Wittgenstein concluded his *Tractatus Logico-Philosophicus* with the famous line: 'Whereof one cannot speak, thereof one must be silent.' I think that is defeatist, as did Wittgenstein in later life. A better denouement would be: 'Whereof we cannot know, there our imaginations can play.' After all, it's by telling stories that we began our journey to know what we know.

That journey has always been driven by what we do not know. As Maxwell declared: 'Thoroughly conscious ignorance is the prelude to every real advance in science.' I certainly think that's true when it comes to mathematics. I need to believe that there is a solution, and that I can find it if I'm going to have any chance of maintaining my faith as I venture into the unknown. Being aware that we don't know is crucial to making progress. Stephen Hawking appreciates the danger of believing we know it all: 'The greatest enemy of knowledge is not ignorance but the illusion of knowledge.'

For me, the conjectures of mathematics, the things we haven't proved, are its lifeblood. It is the things I do not know that drive me to continue my mathematical quest. I want to know if the Riemann hypothesis is true, and whether the PORC conjecture that I have dedicated the last few decades of my research to is false. As Jacob Bronowski put it: 'Human knowledge is personal and responsible, an unending adventure at the edge of uncertainty.'

The importance of the unattained destination is illustrated by the strange reaction that many mathematicians have when a great mathematical theorem is finally proved. Just as there is a sense of sadness when you finish a great novel, the closure of a mathematical quest can have its own sense of melancholy. I think we were enjoying the challenge of Fermat's equations so much that there was a sense of depression mixed with the elation that greeted Andrew Wiles's solution of this 350-year-old enigma.

It is important to recognize that we must live with uncertainty, with the unknown, the unknowable. Even if we eventually manage to produce a theory which describes the way the universe works, we will never know that there isn't another chapter in the story, waiting for us to discover it. We can never know whether we've come to the end of the story. As much as we may crave certainty, to do science we must always be prepared to move on from the stories we tell now. But that's why science is alive and will never ossify.

So maybe it is important that I embrace the uncertainty of the future of my casino dice as it rattles around in my hand. And once it falls from my palm, perhaps it is not knowing how it will land that drives me to keep looking as it hits the table and rolls.

ACKNOWLEDGEMENTS

Many thanks to the people who helped to make this book possible:

My editor at 4th Estate: Louise Haines.

My agent at Greene and Heaton: Antony Topping.

My assistant editor: Sarah Thickett.

My illustrator: Joy Gosney.

My copy-editor and proofreaders: Eddie Mizzi, Jan McCann, Stephen Guise.

My readers: Andreas Brandhuber, Joseph Conlon, Pedro Ferreira, Chris Lintott, Dan Segal and Christiane Timmel.

My interviewees: Bob May, Melissa Franklin, John Polkinghorne, John Barrow, Roger Penrose and Christof Koch.

My employers: The Mathematical Institute, The Department of Continuing Education, New College, the University of Oxford.

My patron: Charles Simonyi.

My family: Shani, Tomer, Magaly and Ina.

ILLUSTRATION CREDITS

All illustrations created by Joy Gosney, apart from the following:

EDGE 1

p. 23 Dice pyramid © Raymond Turvey

p. 41 Chaotic path. Constructed using 'Restricted Three-Body Problem in a Plane', Wolfram Demonstrations Project: http://demonstrations.wolfram.com/RestrictedThreeBodyProblemInAPlane/

p. 60 Evolutionary fractal tree. Illustration adapted from images generated by the One Zoom Tree of Life Explorer: http://www.onezoom.org/index.htm

p. 65 Magnetic fields © Joe McLaren

p. 68 Four graphs describing the behaviour of the dice. Illustration adapted from M. Kapitaniak, J. Strzalko, J. Grabski and T. Kapitaniak. 'The three-dimensional dynamics of the die throw', *Chaos* 22(4), 2012

EDGE 2

p. 91 Atoms inside a dice. Yikrazuul / Wikimedia Commons / Public Domain

p. 94 Jean Baptiste Perrin's *Les Atomes*. J. B. Perrin (SVG drawing by MiraiWarren) / Public Domain

EDGE 3

p. 166 Reprinted graph with permission from the American Physical Society as follows: C.G. Shull, 'Single-Slit Diffraction of Neutrons'. *Physical Review*. 179, 752, 1969. Copyright 1969 by the American Physical Society: http://dx.doi.org/10.1103/PhysRev.179.752

EDGE 5

p. 286 Entropy. Illustration adapted from Roger Penrose's *The Emperor's New Mind: Concerning Computers, Minds, and the Laws of Physics*. OUP, 1989

p. 292 CCC diagram © Roger Penrose. *Cycles of Time: An Extraordinary New View of the Universe.* Bodley Head, 2010

EDGE 6

p. 312 Neuron drawing. Reproduced with kind permission from Santiago Ramón y Cajal, Cajal Legacy, Instituto Cajal, Madrid

p. 331 Purity by Randall Munroe. xkcd.com: http://xkcd.com/435/

p. 341 Wakefulness / Deep Sleep. Illustration based on images from Marcello Massimini, Fabio Ferrarelli, Reto Huber, Steve K. Esser, Harpreet Singh, Giulio Tononi. 'Breakdown of Cortical Effective Connectivity During Sleep', *Science* 309, 2228–2232, 2005

p. 344 Two images of 8-node networks. Reproduced with kind permission from the authors. Giulio Tononi and Olaf Sporns. 'Measuring information integration', BMC Neuroscience 4, 2003

FURTHER READING

Al-Khalili, Jim. *Quantum: A Guide for the Perplexed.* Weidenfeld & Nicolson, 2003.

Armstrong, Karen. *A Short History of Myth.* Canongate, 2005.

Armstrong, Karen. *The Great Transformation: The World in the Time of Buddha, Socrates, Confucius and Jeremiah.* Atlantic Books, 2006.

Armstrong, Karen. *The Case for God.* Bodley Head, 2009.

Ayer, A.J. *Language, Truth and Logic.* Victor Gollancz, 1936.

Ayer, A.J. *The Problem of Knowledge.* Penguin Books, 1956.

Baggini, Julian. *Atheism: A Very Short Introduction.* Oxford University Press, 2003.

Baggott, Jim. *Farewell to Reality: How Fairytale Physics Betrays the Search for Scientific Truth.* Constable, 2013.

Barbour, Julian. *The End of Time: The Next Revolution in Physics.* Oxford University Press, 1999.

Barrow, John. *Impossibility: The Limits of Science and the Science of Limits.* Oxford University Press, 1998.

Barrow, John. *The Constants of Nature.* Jonathan Cape, 2002.

Barrow-Green, June. *Poincaré and the Three-Body Problem.* American Mathematical Society, 1997.

Bayne, Tim. *The Unity of Consciousness.* Oxford University Press, 2010.

Blackburn, Simon. *Truth: A Guide for the Perplexed.* Allen Lane, 2005.

Blackmore, Susan. *Consciousness: An Introduction.* Hodder & Stoughton, 2003.

Blackmore, Susan. *Conversations on Consciousness.* Oxford University Press, 2005.

Bondi, Hermann. *Relativity and Common Sense: A New Approach to Einstein.* Doubleday, 1964.

Borges, Jorge Luis. *Labyrinths: Selected Stories and Other Writings.* New Directions, 1962.

Butterworth, Jon. *Smashing Physics: Inside the World's Biggest Experiment*. Headline, 2014.

Carroll, Sean. *From Eternity to Here: The Quest for the Ultimate Theory of Time*. Oneworld Publications, 2011.

Close, Frank. *Particle Physics: A Very Short Introduction*. Oxford University Press, 2004.

Close, Frank. *The Infinity Puzzle: Quantum Field Theory and the Hunt for an Orderly Universe*. Oxford University Press, 2013.

Conlon, Joseph. *Why String Theory?* CRC Press, 2016.

Cox, Brian and Forshaw, Jeff. *Why Does E=mc²? (And Why Should We Care?)*. Da Capo Press, 2009.

Dawkins, Richard. *The Blind Watchmaker*. Longman, 1986.

Dawkins, Richard. *The God Delusion*. Bantam Press, 2006.

Dennett, Daniel. *Consciousness Explained*. Little, Brown, 1991.

Deutsch, David. *The Fabric of Reality*. Allen Lane, 1997.

Dixon, Thomas. *Science and Religion: A Very Short Introduction*. Oxford University Press, 2008.

du Sautoy, Marcus. *The Music of the Primes*. Fourth Estate, 2003.

du Sautoy, Marcus. *Finding Moonshine*. Fourth Estate, 2008.

du Sautoy, Marcus. *The Number Mysteries*. Fourth Estate, 2010.

Edelman, Gerald and Tononi, Giulio. *A Universe of Consciousness: How Matter Becomes Imagination*. Basic Books, 2000.

Ferreira, Pedro. *The State of the Universe. A Primer in Modern Cosmology*. Weidenfeld & Nicolson, 2006.

Ferreira, Pedro. *The Perfect Theory: A Century of Geniuses and the Battle over General Relativity*. Little, Brown, 2014.

Feynman, Richard. *The Feynman Lectures on Physics*. Addison-Wesley, 1964. Available at http://feynmanlectures.caltech.edu/

Gamow, George. *Mr Tompkins in Paperback*. Cambridge University Press, 1965.

Gleick, James. *Chaos: The Amazing Science of the Unpredictable*. Heinemann, 1988.

Goldstein, Rebecca. *36 Arguments for the Existence of God*. Atlantic Books, 2010.

Greene, Brian. *The Elegant Universe: Superstrings, Hidden Dimensions, and the Quest for the Ultimate Theory*. W.W. Norton, 1999.

Greene, Brian. *The Fabric of the Cosmos*. Knopf, 2004.

Greene, Brian. *The Hidden Reality: Parallel Universes and the Deep Laws of the Cosmos*. Knopf, 2011.

Guth, Alan. *The Inflationary Universe: The Quest for a New Theory of Cosmic Origins.* Addison-Wesley, 1997.

Hawking, Stephen. *A Brief History of Time: From the Big Bang to Black Holes.* Bantam, 1988.

Kaku, Michio. *Hyperspace: A Scientific Odyssey Through the 10th Dimension.* Oxford University Press, 1994.

Kapitaniak, M., Strzalko, J., Grabski J., and Kapitaniak, T., 'The three-dimensional dynamics of the die throw', *Chaos* 22(4), 2012.

Koch, Christof. *The Quest for Consciousness: A Neurobiological Approach.* Roberts & Company, 2004.

Koch, Christof. *Consciousness: Confessions of a Romantic Reductionist.* MIT Press, 2012.

Krauss, Lawrence. *A Universe from Nothing: Why There Is Something Rather Than Nothing.* Free Press, 2012.

Kurzweil, Ray. *The Singularity Is Near: When Humans Transcend Biology.* Viking, 2005.

Kurzweil, Ray. *How to Create a Mind: The Secrets of Human Thought Revealed.* Viking, 2012.

Lakatos, Imre. *Proofs and Refutations: The Logic of Mathematical Discovery.* Cambridge University Press, 1976.

Laskar, Jacques and Gastineau, Mickael. 'Existence of collisional trajectories of Mercury, Mars and Venus with the Earth', *Nature* 459, 817–819, 2009.

Levin, Janna. *How the Universe Got Its Spots: Diary of a Finite Time in a Finite Space.* Princeton University Press, 2002.

Lightman, Alan. *Einstein's Dreams.* First Warner Books, 1994.

Livio, Mario. *The Accelerating Universe: Infinite Expansion, the Cosmological Constant and the Beauty of the Cosmos.* John Wiley & Sons, 2000.

Maddox, John. *What Remains to be Discovered: Mapping the Secrets of the Universe, the Origins of Life and the Future of the Human Race.* Free Press, 1998.

May, Robert M. 'Simple mathematical models with very complicated dynamics', *Nature* 261, 459–467, 1976.

McCabe, Herbert. *God Still Matters.* Continuum Books, 2002.

Monk, Ray. *Ludwig Wittgenstein: The Duty of Genius.* Jonathan Cape, 1990.

Mulhall, Stephen. *Wittgenstein's Private Language: Grammar, Nonsense and Imagination in Philosophical Investigations,* SS243–315. Clarendon Press, 2006.

Mulhall, Stephen. *The Great Riddle: Wittgenstein and Nonsense, Theology and Philosophy.* Oxford University Press, 2015.

Nagel, Jennifer. *Knowledge: A Very Short Introduction.* Oxford University Press, 2014.

Poincaré, Henri. *Science and Method.* Thomas Nelson, 1914.

Polkinghorne, John. *Belief in God in an Age of Science.* Yale University Press, 1998.

Polkinghorne, John. *Quantum Theory: A Very Short Introduction.* Oxford University Press, 2002.

Polkinghorne, John. *Quantum Physics and Theology: An Unexpected Kinship.* SPCK, 2007.

Penrose, Roger. *The Emperor's New Mind: Concerning Computers, Minds, and the Laws of Physics.* Oxford University Press, 1989.

Penrose, Roger. *The Road to Reality: A Complete Guide to the Laws of the Universe.* Jonathan Cape, 2004.

Penrose, Roger. *Cycles of Time: An Extraordinary New View of the Universe.* Bodley Head, 2010.

Peterson, Ivars. *Newton's Clock: Chaos in the Solar System.* Freeman, 1993.

Ramachandran, V.S. *A Brief Tour of Human Consciousness: From Impostor Poodles to Purple Numbers.* Pi Press, 2004.

Randall, Lisa. *Knocking on Heaven's Door: How Physics and Scientific Thinking Illuminate the Universe and the Modern World.* Bodley Head, 2011.

Rees, Martin. *Just Six Numbers: The Deep Forces that Shape the Universe.* Weidenfeld & Nicolson, 1999.

Rees, Martin. *From Here to Infinity: Scientific Horizons.* Profile Books, 2011.

Saari, Donald and Xia, Zhihong. 'Off to infinity in finite time', *Notices of the American Mathematical Society*, Volume 42 Number 5, 538–546, 1995.

Sacks, Jonathan. *The Great Partnership: God, Science and the Search for Meaning.* Hodder & Stoughton, 2011.

Sample, Ian. *Massive: The Hunt for the God Particle.* Virgin Books, 2010.

Seung, Sebastian. *Connectome: How the Brain's Wiring Makes Us Who We Are.* Houghton Mifflin Harcourt, 2012.

Silk, Joseph. *The Infinite Cosmos: Questions from the Frontiers of Cosmology.* Oxford University Press, 2006.

Singh, Simon. *Fermat's Last Theorem.* Fourth Estate, 1997.

Singh, Simon. *Big Bang: The Most Important Scientific Discovery of All Time and Why You Need to Know About It.* Fourth Estate, 2004.

Smolin, Lee. *Time Reborn: From the Crisis of Physics to the Future of the Universe.* Allen Lane, 2013.

Steane, Andrew. *The Wonderful World of Relativity: A Precise Guide for the General Reader.* Oxford University Press, 2011.

Steane, Andrew. *Faithful to Science: The Role of Science in Religion.* Oxford University Press, 2014.

Stewart, Ian. *Does God Play Dice? The New Mathematics of Chaos.* Basil Blackwell, 1989.

Stoppard, Tom. *Arcadia.* Faber & Faber, 1993.

Sudbery, Anthony. *Quantum Mechanics and the Particles of Nature: An Outline for Mathematicians.* Cambridge University Press, 1986.

Taleb, Nassim. *The Black Swan: The Impact of the Highly Improbable.* Allen Lane, 2007.

Tegmark, Max. 'The Mathematical Universe', *Found.Phys.* 38: 101–150, 2008.

Tegmark, Max. *Our Mathematical Universe: My Quest for the Ultimate Nature of Reality.* Knopf, 2014.

Tononi, Giulio and Sporns, Olaf. 'Measuring information integration', *BMC Neuroscience* 4, 2003.

Tononi, Giulio 'Consciousness as Integrated Information: A Provisional Manifesto', *Biol. Bull.* vol. 215 no. 3: 216–242, 2008.

Tononi, Giulio *Phi. A Voyage from the Brain to the Soul.* Pantheon, 2012.

Watts, Fraser and Knight, Christopher (eds). *God and the Scientist: Exploring the Work of John Polkinghorne.* Ashgate Publishing Limited, 2012.

Weinberg, Steven. *Dreams of a Final Theory: The Search for the Fundamental Laws of Nature.* Hutchinson Radius, 1993.

Williamson, Timothy. *Knowledge and its Limits.* Oxford University Press, 2000.

Woit, Peter. *Not Even Wrong: The Failure of String Theory and the Continuing Challenges to Unify the Laws of Physics.* Jonathan Cape, 2006.

Yourgrau, Palle. *A World Without Time: The Forgotten Legacy of Gödel and Einstein.* Basic Books, 2005.

Zee, Anthony. *Quantum Field Theory in a Nutshell.* Princeton University Press, 2003.

The following website for the Stanford Encyclopaedia of Philosophy is full of great material: http://plato.stanford.edu/

INDEX